Evidence-Based Policing

Translating Research into Practice

Evidence-Based Policing

Translating Research into Practice

Cynthia Lum

and

Christopher S. Koper

OXFORD
UNIVERSITY PRESS

OXFORD
UNIVERSITY PRESS

Great Clarendon Street, Oxford, OX2 6DP,
United Kingdom

Oxford University Press is a department of the University of Oxford.
It furthers the University's objective of excellence in research, scholarship,
and education by publishing worldwide. Oxford is a registered trade mark of
Oxford University Press in the UK and in certain other countries

Published in the United States of America by Oxford University Press
198 Madison Avenue, New York, NY 10016, United States of America

British Library Cataloguing in Publication Data
Data available

ISBN 978-0-19-871994-6

Links to third party websites are provided by Oxford in good faith and
for information only. Oxford disclaims any responsibility for the materials
contained in any third party website referenced in this work.

Acknowledgments

This book is a culmination of the support, assistance, mentorship, and partnership of many people and organizations.

Lawrence Sherman, who early on trained both of us to care about policing and police research partnerships from an evidence-based perspective. He has understood—and provided great support for—our endeavors over the years, for which we are exceedingly thankful.

David Weisburd, whose work on place-based criminology made a substantial impact on our thinking about crime prevention at places, and for supporting our translational efforts in the Center for Evidence-Based Crime Policy.

Research colleagues who we have worked with on some of the studies discussed in this book. In particular, we are grateful to former research assistant and now colleague, Cody Telep, who continues to work with us on populating the Matrix, and who takes the torch forward on studies of police receptivity to research. Our extensive work in recent years with Julie Hibdon, Daniel Nagin, Bruce Taylor, James Willis, and Daniel Woods has also been incredibly valuable to the ideas we develop throughout the book.

Practitioner and academic colleagues without whom many of the studies and activities we discuss would not be possible, and with whom we have spent a great deal of time discussing ideas surrounding evidence-based policing. In particular, we thank Hassan Aden, Jim Bueermann, Jim Burch, Brian Cummings, Jeffery Egge, Nicholas Fyfe, John Kapinos, Stephen Mastrofski, Carl Maupin, Linda Merola, Renee Mitchell, Rebecca Neustadter, Peter Neyroud, Sandra Nutley, Renee (Tate) Richardson, Jamie Roush, Darrel Stephens, and Howard Veigas.

The police departments we have worked closely with, including officers, supervisors, analysts, and staff members who supported our work, especially in the police departments of Fairfax County, Richmond, Alexandria, and Leesburg (Virginia); Minneapolis (Minnesota); New York City (New York); Jacksonville (Florida); Sacramento (California); Redlands (California); Charlotte-Mecklenburg (North Carolina); and the Northern Virginia Criminal Justice Training Academy.

Research and editorial assistants over the years whose efforts has been invaluable to many of the projects in this book, including Breanne Cave, Julie Grieco, Stephen Happeny, Julie (Willis) Hibdon, Bill Johnson, Nancy Michel, Jordan Nichols, Ajima Olaghere, Amber Scherer, Megan Stolz, Cody Telep, Heather Vovak, and Xiaoyun Wu.

We are especially grateful for financial support from the Bureau of Justice Assistance and the National Institute of Justice of the U.S. Department of

Justice, the Laura and John Arnold Foundation, the International Association of Chiefs of Police, the Police Foundation, and the Department of Homeland Security to carry out many of the projects discussed in this book. In particular, support from the Bureau of Justice Assistance made the Matrix and the Matrix Demonstration Projects possible, and our exchanges with staff at the BJA have strengthened our efforts.

Figures reproduced in Chapters 3, 4, 8, 12, and 14 were originally published in the following articles: "The Evidence-Based Policing Matrix" (by Cynthia Lum, Christopher Koper, and Cody Telep, 2011, *Journal of Experimental Criminology* 7); "Just Enough Police Presence: Reducing Crime and Disorderly Behavior By Optimizing Patrol Time in Crime Hot Spots" (by Christopher S Koper, 1995, *Justice Quarterly* 12); "Receptivity to Research in Policing" (by Cynthia Lum, Cody W. Telep, Christopher S. Koper, and Julie Grieco, 2012, *Justice Research and Policy* 14); "Institutionalizing Place-Based Approaches: Opening a Case on a Gun Crime Hot Spot" (by Christopher S. Koper, Jeffery Egge, and Cynthia Lum, 2015, *Policing: A Journal of Policy and Practice* 9); and "Assessing the Evidence Base of a Police Service Patrol Portfolio" (by Howard Veigas and Cynthia Lum, 2013, *Policing: A Journal of Policy and Practice* 7). We would like to thank our co-authors on these papers and also Springer Verlag, Taylor and Francis Group, Sage Publication, and Oxford University Press for the relevant permissions to use these figures.

We thank all of you, and the countless others we have encountered in our travels and projects whose questions, debates, and insights made us think more carefully about evidence-based policing.

Contents

Part One Evidence-Based Policing—The Basics

Part Two Evidence-Based Approaches to Policing

Part Three   Implementing Evidence-Based Policing

Part Four Researchers and the Advancement of Evidence-Based Policing

List of Figures

List of Tables

Evidence-Based Policing—The Basics

WHAT IS EVIDENCE-BASED POLICING?

In recent years, the term "evidence based" has become increasingly common in the world of criminal justice policy and practice, especially policing. The idea of evidence-based policing—that law enforcement agencies should somehow use research knowledge to help guide strategic and tactical decisions—has become an anchoring concept for government funding for research and technical assistance in policing. Some municipalities, for example, are scaling back spending on a variety of local programs to reduce and prevent crime unless they can show evidence of effectiveness. The term can be heard in criminal justice undergraduate and graduate programs as well, with new courses on evidence-based crime policy and program evaluation being more regularly taught. Given the importance and pervasiveness of the evidence-based movement, understanding what it means, how it can be achieved, and its prospects and pitfalls for policing are essential information for both researchers and practitioners.

Sherman (1998) was likely the first to articulate the principles of an evidence-based approach to policing. In an address to the Police Foundation in 1998, he said that "police practices should be based on scientific evidence about what works best" (Sherman 1998, 2). In particular, Sherman focused on two dimensions of a research orientation in policing: (i) using the results of scientifically rigorous evaluations of law-enforcement tactics, strategies and policies to guide decisions; and (ii) generating and applying analytic knowledge from internal and external sources. Both, he argued, could improve feedback systems in police practice and facilitate learning and progress.

Since Sherman began the conversation in 1998, a variety of meanings has been attributed to evidence-based policing from advocates and skeptics alike. In this book, we use a broad and holistic definition: Evidence-based policing means that research, evaluation, analysis, and scientific processes should have "a seat at the table" in law enforcement decision making about tactics, strategies, and policies. Further, we define evidence-based policing as not just about the process or products of evaluating police practices, but also about the translation of that knowledge into digestible and useable forms and the institutionalization of that knowledge into practice and policing systems. Thus, evidence-based policing can involve many different types of activities, including:

- using rigorous evaluation methods to examine the effectiveness (of various outcomes) of a police training program, a patrol deployment approach, an investigative strategy, or an organizational policy;
- reflecting on and discussing research knowledge and analysis at managerial meetings or within operational units;
- training officers on what is known about effective police practices regarding crime control, internal management, police-community-citizen interactions and relationships, reducing disparity and bias, or dealing with disorder, traffic, and other order maintenance concerns;
- using crime analysis to guide the deployment of resources to crime hot spots or to target individuals or groups at high risk for violence;
- using generalizations from research knowledge to adjust current practices or create new ones for patrol, investigations, supervision, internal affairs, and police-community interactions;
- conducting rigorous surveys of community members (or specific groups within the community) to assess their satisfaction with police services and to determine how the delivery of those services might better conform to community concerns and priorities;
- using risk assessment instruments developed and validated by researchers to identify problematic situations—for example, domestic violence cases with a high potential for escalating into more serious future violence, or early warning systems to flag officers for problem behaviors;
- conducting surveys of officers to solicit their views on agency policies and strategies;
- using systematic social observations, ethnographies, or other systematic qualitative approaches to gain a detailed picture of police culture, practices or behaviors;
- examining how technology is used in the organization to improve the acquisition and deployment processes; and
- partnering with researchers and community members to carry out any of these activities.

Many police agencies use these and other evidence-based practices to varying degrees. However, the evidence-based policing philosophy stresses regular, institutionalized, and consistent use of research, analysis, and science to inform a broad range of activities. Of course, this is much easier said than done. What do we mean when we say that research and science should be incorporated into the activities of law enforcement? Which body of science or types of analysis should the police use? How much of law enforcement practice should be influenced by research knowledge or scientific practices? What systems within law enforcement should be informed by science? Who within a law enforcement agency needs research? Who should generate this research? How can we translate and incorporate research into existing policing systems? Why should science play a role in policing?

While it may seem reasonable in theory to incorporate the values, outcomes, or processes of science into policing, education, medicine, public health, social work, and other public sectors, achieving these goals in practice can be challenging. Law enforcement agencies, like other organizations, are complicated systems constrained and shaped by rules, values, incentives and procedures. They are steeped in tradition, organizational cultures/frameworks, and legal directives that have little to do with research knowledge or scientific processes. Relationships between the scientific community and law enforcement, and the views of officers of education, haven't always been positive in the history of policing. Adjusting the philosophy and culture of policing to embrace a more scientific approach may require fundamental changes in long-standing practices deeply embedded within the organization. It requires a willingness to change, and it takes time.

Take, for example, the idea of aligning patrol deployment with the research knowledge we now have about patrol shift lengths. Schedules may have to be adjusted from twelve-hour shifts to ten-hours shifts, since the latter have been shown to lead to less officer fatigue and better performance (Amendola, Weisburd, Hamilton et al. 2011). Such a change will undoubtedly jostle agency politics and could provoke police officer and union resistance. Changing shift hours will require a major adjustment in the days that individual officers work, and extra shifts may have to be added to ensure that enough officers are working at any given time. Changes in shifts will impact officers' secondary employment schedules and family arrangements, which may impact officer job satisfaction and willingness to engage in other innovations or practices. All of these factors challenge the implementation of an evidence-based approach to shift work.

The challenges do not stop at implementation. Evidence-based policing necessitates strong partnerships and increased communication and collaboration among researchers, analysts, and law enforcement officers. This requires determining where these partnerships fit into policing systems and how such partnerships will be supported. It also requires a cultural adjustment on the part of academics and researchers. As with the world of law enforcement, the world of science is constrained by rules, values, incentives, and procedures, and it is also steeped in stubborn traditional and organizational cultures that differ from those of law enforcement. At the most philosophical level, science is about generalizing from samples to populations. Policing's focus, in contrast, is almost entirely on individual situations and their specific aspects. While science should be dispassionate, policing—even under the rule of law—is filled with emotion, subjectivity, and discretion. Science values outcomes which are generated from the rigorous application of accepted methods. Policing values the correct and consistent application of standard operating procedures and legal rules, emphasizing the process more than the outcome. Furthermore, the performance metrics of the research world are not tied to one's contributions in partnering with those in public service, but rather in publishing in high-quality, scientific outlets.

Thus, the effective practice of evidence-based policing brings with it many complexities, challenges, and nuances that will be explored and discussed throughout this book. We warn the reader now—there are no shortcuts or easy approaches to successfully implementing evidence-based policing. Although some critics have tried to reduce evidence-based policing to simplistic definitions, such as equating it with randomized controlled experiments, "Compstat," or a sole focus on "what works to reduce crime," evidence-based policing requires much more detailed and critical thought and effort.

A Starting Point: The Standard Model of Policing

A useful place to begin to detail a more holistic definition of evidence-based policing is to describe the "standard" model of policing, sometimes referred to as the "traditional," "professional," or even "reactive" model. This model continues to be the dominant model in policing in the United States and the United Kingdom. Even though other models have been introduced (i.e., community-oriented policing, problem-oriented policing, intelligence-led policing, predictive policing), the standard model of policing is deeply engrained in today's policing culture and systems. Describing it helps us build a base from which to compare, contrast, and understand various reforms and innovation in policing, including evidence-based policing.

The standard model can best be seen and described by examining the daily activities of patrol officers. These activities exemplify the key features of the standard model and serve as a primary source from which other core characteristics of police organizations emerge. Patrol is also where almost all officers (up to the chief) receive their initial training, socialization, and professional development. Patrol officers are also the most visible group in policing and have the most interaction with citizens, offenders, and victims. Understanding what patrol officers and their supervisors do is therefore central to understanding the standard model of policing and its influence on police organizations.

A patrol officer's day usually begins with a roll call and sometimes an inspection of appearance. During roll call, announcements are made, including lookouts for wanted or suspicious individuals or vehicles, discussions of places or situations that need extra attention, internal announcements, and alerts about policy changes. Patrol officers are usually assigned to a beat, post, or sector—a geographic area known to the dispatcher who assigns them calls throughout the day through a computer-aided dispatch system. People call 999 or 911 (standard emergency response phone numbers in the United Kingdom and the United States, respectively) to report crimes, suspicious behavior, and other complaints and concerns unrelated to crime. Dispatchers then assign officers to respond to calls in or near their assigned areas. To handle each call, officers apply their training, rules of criminal procedures, different technologies available to them, standard operating procedures of their organization, the force and legitimacy of the law, their past experiences, their personal knowledge, and information obtained from the situation itself.

No matter what other special tasks the officer is assigned or decides to undertake during patrol, this reaction to citizen calls for service is the backbone of modern policing. A great deal of training is focused on actions that may be needed in this response, including the use of force, arrest, dispute resolution, connecting citizens to other resources (e.g., medical, ambulatory, fire, or social services), investigation, and evidence-processing. Two common characteristics of this reactive model of policing are responding quickly to calls for service (especially for more serious offenses) and applying discretion, proper legal rules, accepted procedures, and agency policies to resolve the situation. Discretion is an especially dominant aspect of patrol in the standard model; officers can choose to arrest or not (even if a crime has been committed), determine various courses of action, or decide to document the incident by taking a report. Detective work is an extension of this case-by-case response to a call for service, when greater attention to a particular case is warranted.

This process of responding to calls for service continues throughout the officers' shifts, but it is not everything that uniformed officers do. In places with low crime rates or smaller populations, only one or two calls for service may be received per day for any given officer. Even in the most populated and crime-ridden jurisdictions, calls for service are separated by sometimes brief and sometimes lengthy periods of time. This "non-committed time," as Kelling, Pate, Deickman et al. (1974) referred to it in the landmark Kansas City Preventive Patrol Experiment, is the period in between calls for service when an officer is not doing any business related to a particular call, processing evidence or making an arrest, or doing other necessary activities such as bathroom or meal breaks or conducting required tasks. Empirical estimates of non-committed time are surprisingly high; they range from 25% (Weisburd, Wooditch, Weisburd et al. 2015) to as much as 80% of an officer's day, with most estimates in the range of 40% to 80% (Famega 2005; Famega, Frank, and Mazerolle 2005).

In the standard model of policing, officers' behavior during non-committed time is marked by two characteristics that are also evident when the officers are answering calls: high levels of discretion and low levels of supervision. How officers use their non-committed time in addition to preventive patrol and administrative duties varies considerably from officer to officer and agency to agency. At a minimum, officers are expected to carry out preventive patrol in their areas of responsibility to create a sense of police "omnipresence" and deter crime in an officer's assigned beat. However, officers may also listen to their radios (or more recently, view their mobile computer terminals) to learn where their colleagues are assigned so they can back up fellow officers when necessary. Some officers may use non-committed time to proactively seek out offending, patrol in high-crime areas, talk to community members, stop suspicious people and vehicles, check in with local businesses, or develop problem-solving strategies. Some may focus on traffic enforcement, carry out follow-ups on citizen complaints, or conduct pedestrian stops to mitigate open-air drug dealing. During this non-committed time, officers also might write reports, meet with their supervisors, get gas for their vehicles, run personal or work-related errands, or wait for another call.

The choice, frequency, and types of activities that officers engage in during their non-committed time depends almost always on individual officer preference, and sometimes on specific directives by supervisors or on the cultural expectations of a particular shift or squad. There is also very little supervision of this discretionary activity. First-line supervisors generally take on a passive and reactive role in the standard model and are focused on checking reports, responding to officer misconduct or major crimes, and managing administrative duties of patrol. Although modern automatic vehicle locators may show where officers are during these times, they are mostly unsupervised by either the squad sergeant or the dispatcher.

Overall, the goals of both patrol and investigations under this model are to detect crime and disorder, bring offenders to justice, and settle other problems, disputes, and issues that might arise from individual calls for service. Follow-up criminal investigations in the standard model become a triage and extension of the initial response to a call for service. The standard model's reactive nature also leads to a heavier focus on applying and following correct procedures and policies, getting paperwork and reports processed to support these routines, and avoiding errors, accidents, and mistakes in carrying out these procedures. All of this results in a reactive, procedures-oriented, and case-by-case approach (see further descriptions by Kelling and Moore 1988; Weisburd and Eck 2004).

Because this approach to policing is so dominant, and because it is so engrained in uniformed patrol and in the mindset of almost every officer who shares that experience, characteristics of the standard model permeate and shape other systems within policing. These systems include academy and post-academy "field" or "in-service" training; incentives, promotions, and rewards; systems of management, supervision, and accountability; and leadership (Lum, Telep, Koper et al. 2012). The model's reactive, individual-case, procedures-oriented approach is not only reflected in these systems but is also fostered and nurtured by them. For example, training focuses on learning correct procedures, how to apply appropriate force (if necessary) to make an arrest, and how to investigate a situation. Even the physical training in academies is carried out from the perspective of arrest and use of force, and is seen as central to those roles (as opposed to, e.g., physical training to maintain the health, awareness, or acumen of the officer). Promotions and rewards are often based on experience with, knowledge of, and successful implementation of standard operating procedures. Most command and leadership is top down and militaristic, feeding off a reactive, rules-oriented organization in which responsibility for specific procedures is clear. This approach to policing creates first-line supervisors who are often passive and reactive, focused on checking reports for accuracy, reacting to officer problems and mistakes, or helping officers apply correct procedures. Although managerial schemes such as "Compstat" have pushed police to be more attuned to crime trends and analysis, one only needs to attend Compstat meetings to see the emphasis is often on individual cases and arrests.

Technological systems also reinforce the everyday aspects of the reactive, standard model (see Koper, Lum, Willis et al. 2015c; Manning 1992; 2008). The advents of computer-aided dispatch systems, patrol cars, and radios were seen as major advances in policing—to get officers to victims and citizens in need more quickly and with greater accountability. However, these technologies have reinforced a reactive approach to policing. Even the technologies that are viewed as "innovative" today, especially in the areas of forensics, surveillance, and detection, often focus on facilitating arrests or catching offenders.

Alternatives to the Standard Model

Because of its dominance, the standard model of policing is often viewed as the "basic" model of policing—that which is necessary at a minimum, or perhaps one that is so dominant it would be hard to imagine policing any other way. However, in the late 1970s and into the 1980s, policing practice and research began to discover limitations in the standard model. Fast response to 911 calls did not seem to help in apprehending suspects or even preventing crime (Sherman and Eck 2002; Spelman and Brown 1981). Random preventive patrols by officers, either in vehicles or on foot, to create an omnipresence also did not seem to deter crime (Kelling et al. 1974; Police Foundation 1981; Trojanowicz 1986). No link between reactive arrest and crime rates was found (see reviews by Nagin 1978; 1998; 2013; Sherman and Eck 2002). In the case of some offenders, such as juveniles or unemployed domestic abusers, arrest might even have increased offending (Klein 1986; Sherman, Schmidt, Rogan et al. 1991; Sherman, Schmidt, Rogan et al. 1992; Smith and Gartin 1989).

These limitations, as well as public protests about police activity in the 1960s and 1970s, led to the emergence of alternatives to the standard model. In reality, these alternatives were additions to, rather than a replacement of, the standard model. Take, for example, community-oriented policing. Community policing calls for the police to be responsive to citizens and value their input and partici- pation in prioritizing and directing police operations and resources (Mastrofski 1998; Mastrofski, Worden, and Snipes 1995; Skogan 2004; Skogan and Hartnett 1997; Skolnick 1999; Trojanowicz 1994; Trojanowicz and Bucqueroux 1997). While responding to 911 calls and arresting offenders may still be necessary, community policing, sometimes called "democratic policing," emphasizes that police must be accountable, transparent, open, responsive, reliable, and fair (Mastrofski 1999). During non-committed time, officers within a community- oriented policing model are expected to use that time to strengthen relation- ships with citizens through such activities as attending community meetings, conducting follow-up visits with victims or witnesses, or addressing quality-of- life problems.

Another alternative approach, which was later co-opted by community policing proponents, was problem-oriented policing (POP), first articulated by Goldstein (1979; 1990). The POP model questions the focus on responding to individual calls for service, arguing that individual calls in combination signal broader underlying problems. Problem-solving policing therefore calls for police not to respond to individual calls for service on a case-by-case basis, but to ana- lyze those calls to detect underlying problems and then address those problems proactively. Eck and Spelman (1987) explain this process through their "SARA" model—"scanning," "analysis," "response," and "assessment." Much of the "response" in POP is based on the premise that crime can be averted by chang- ing malleable features of the social or physical environment or people's routines that may contribute to crime opportunity (see discussions in Brantingham and Brantingham 1993; Clarke and Cornish 1985; Felson 1994; 1995). For example, these changes might include improving lighting, closing problem bars, increas- ing CCTV surveillance, or even adjusting the spatial and temporal patterns of police patrol to tackle hot spots (see Sherman and Weisburd 1995; Sherman, Gartin, and Buerger 1989a). They are also linked to what Mazerolle and Ransley (2005; 2006) describe as "third-party policing," in which police work with regu- latory authorities to address problem issues in the social and physical environ- ment (see also Buerger and Mazerolle 1998).

The POP model, like the community policing approach, has impacted polic- ing. Many officers are now familiar with the tenets of community policing and the SARA approach, and organizations like the federal Office of Community Oriented Policing Services[1] and the Center for Problem-Oriented Policing[2] have

---

[1] See http://www.cops.usdoj.gov/.
[2] See http://www.popcenter.org/.

supported these activities. The most recent Law Enforcement Management and Administrative Statistics (LEMAS) survey[3] conducted in the United States found that of the agencies surveyed, 71% mentioned community policing in their mission statement and 41% of agencies encouraged their officers to use problem solving.

However, in many agencies, these approaches have not permeated into everyday patrol. With community-oriented policing, some have argued that it became more rhetoric than reality (Greene and Pelfrey 1997; Mastrofski 2006; Rosenbaum 1994; Roth, Ryan, Gaffigan et al. 2000; Seagrave 1996). Police often delegate this approach to a specially assigned community service officer or unit rather than adopt it as a structural change (Mastrofski 2006). A similar situation is found with problem-oriented policing, perhaps because agencies believe it to be too involved, complex, or resource intensive for patrol officers to accomplish as part of their regular duties. In practice, problem solving tends to involve limited analysis, limited community partnership efforts, and heavy reliance on enforcement tactics—characteristics in total that some have called "shallow" problem solving (e.g., Braga and Bond 2008; Braga and Weisburd 2006; Cordner and Bielbel 2005; Eck 2006).

A more recent alternative to the standard model is intelligence-led policing. Ratcliffe (2008) states the concept was first conceived and operationalized in the United Kingdom (see Audit Commission 1993; HMIC 1997). He defines intelligence-led policing as efforts that focus on targeting serious offenders, triaging crime problems, making greater use of surveillance and informants and, most importantly, making intelligence central to decision making (see Ratcliffe 2008, 83–4). Ratcliffe argues that the meaning of intelligence-led policing has broadened over time, and he defines it as a managerial strategy that emphasizes information analysis, sharing, and use to develop strategies to address policing problems. Intelligence-led policing differs from the standard model in that it uses a managerial approach grounded in information and analysis, rather than call and case response. Management models such as Compstat[4] or predictive policing[5] arguably fall under the broader umbrella of intelligence-led policing, with their heavy emphasis on the use of crime analysis, computerized mapping, and data to manage police operations.

We discuss many aspects of these and other alternatives throughout this book. We raise them here to make three important points. First, the standard model of policing is not the only way police can do business. Indeed, the goal of the many alternatives is to reduce calls for service and reactive

---

[3] See http://www.bjs.gov/index.cfm?ty=dcdetail&iid=248.

[4] CompStat is a managerial approach that stresses data-driven problem identification and assessment, geographic resource allocation, problem solving, and greater accountability for managers (see Silverman 2006; Weisburd, Mastrofski, McNally et al. 2003b).

[5] Predictive policing is a model that focuses police resources proactively on places, people, and times predicted to be at high risk (see Bratton and Malinowski 2008; Perry, McInnis, Price et al. 2013).

arrests in the first place, thereby reducing the heavy reliance on the standard model. Following from this first point is the second: The standard model of policing may not be the "best" approach to policing. By saying "best," we encourage the reader to think about a variety of outcomes that might be sought in policing. These include crime prevention, improving citizens' trust and confidence in the police, detecting and catching offenders, protecting citizen rights, reducing disparity or mistreatment, improving clearance rates, strengthening collective police efficacy in the community, or even improving police officer job satisfaction and professional development. The standard model may not best achieve any of these goals; perhaps these alternatives perform better. As both the "Maryland Report" (see Sherman, Gottfredson, MacKenzie et al. 1997; Sherman, Farrington, Welsh et al. 2002) and the National Research Council (2004) report found in their extensive reviews of research about policing, there is now empirical evidence that the mainstays of the standard model are not strongly linked either to crime control outcomes or to improving citizens' trust and confidence. Finally, the third and most provocative point: Despite the emergence of these alternatives, none has been able to dethrone the standard model from its dominance in policing.

But if not the standard model, then which model is "best"—community policing, problem solving, intelligence-led policing, Compstat, predictive policing, etc.? And, if we can find a viable alternative, how do we implement it within a system of policing in which the standard model dominates? The problem with selecting any alternative is how to determine which is best to achieve preferred outcomes. Should we rely on expert opinion and beliefs about "best practices"? Should we go with an alternative that seems ideologically aligned with our governance (i.e., community policing) or one based on a logical and rational structure (i.e., problem-solving or data-driven approaches)? Further, is evidence-based policing just another alternative and what more does it add?

Evidence-Based Policing—Another Alternative?

The answer to whether evidence-based policing is another alternative to the police models discussed above is both "yes" and "no." Yes, evidence-based policing is an alternative to the standard model because it transcends the reactive, case-by-case, and procedures-oriented policing approach while inserting an alternative method of decision making—research, analysis, evaluation, science—into the daily activities, tactics, internal policies, and short- and long-term strategies of policing. At the same time, no, it is not an alternative to the standard model, or even other models. Evidence-based policing does not reject or stand in juxtaposition to any of these alternative approaches or even to the standard model of policing. Rather, it can encompass tactics, strategies, and perspectives of community policing, problem solving, intelligence-led policing, predictive policing, managerial innovations (e.g., Compstat), or even the standard model itself.

Evidence-based policing is an approach to law enforcement that suggests that if a particular policing model, action, strategy, tactic, or internal managerial approach will be used to achieve an outcome (whatever that outcome is), then those actions should be connected to the desired outcomes. The connection should not be based on guessing, anecdotal experience, or gut feelings, as these may be wrong. Rather, experience, anecdotes, and gut feelings need to be tested. Thus, determining the connection between action and outcome needs research, analysis, evaluation evidence, and empirical information. If, for example, we plan to use a community-oriented policing strategy such as community meetings to improve police–citizen relationships and reduce fear of crime, then we should follow through with this idea not because someone guesses it might lead to these effects but because we have reliable evidence that it does. Police ought to also know if community meetings might worsen police–citizen relationships or increase fear. If we think hiring more educated officers will reduce incidents of use of force or citizen complaints, then we should have some assurance this will happen before we limit ourselves to hiring only college-educated personnel. Yet another example: If we want police to adopt body-worn cameras, then we need to understand their intended and unintended effects on police organizations and the outcomes they seek.

As we emphasized in the opening of this chapter, we take the definition of evidence-based policing even further: Evidence-based policing doesn't just require the generation and use of research knowledge to guide decision making. It also includes the processes and efforts used to make that information digestible, to translate it into usable forms, and to incorporate and institutionalize it into regular systems of policing. This extension of evidence-based policing is, of course, the biggest challenge, which we hold for discussion until Chapter 3.

Foundations for evidence-based policing have already been laid. First, research evidence is challenging the standard model, as well as some aspects of its alternatives. We have already mentioned research that finds the mainstays of the standard model are not necessarily the best options to prevent crime, reduce fear, or improve police–citizen relationships; growing knowledge indicates that alternatives to the standard model can improve these aspects of police performance. We also now have a great deal of knowledge about the nature of crime as well as the nature of policing that leads us to believe there is room for improvement in policing. It is also important to point out that an evidence-based approach does not prohibit the adoption of new methods of policing for which there is little or no evidence. However, if we continue to spend money on such strategies and tactics, we have a responsibility to build alongside these innovations some evidentiary justification that they are achieving what their proponents claim. We also need to be willing to let tactics go if they are shown to be ineffective or harmful.

This idea of using objective scientific information and criteria to inform public policy more generally and police policy more specifically reflects a common value in modern democracies: There must be evaluative and objective accountability for governmental actions and spending (Chalmers 2003; National Research Council 2004; Sherman 2003a; 2003b; Sherman et al. 2002). More basically, as Dewey (1954) asserts, policy proposals are testable hypotheses, which should be subjected to study and flexible to adjustment and learning. The rigid use of perceived best practices, consensus-based decision making, traditions, and the stubborn reliance on experience, emotions, "hunches," and gut feelings, which have been dominant forces behind police decision making in the past, is challenged by an evidence-based approach. Not only have these approaches sometimes failed to connect actions with outcomes, but they also are susceptible to bias, nearsightedness, cronyism, or other negatives that can unintentionally harm citizens and officers.

This notion that evidence-based approaches are implied by the values and ethics of modern democratic governance—particularly of government accountability and reducing harm (Chalmers 2003)—is mirrored in many social arenas, but especially in public health and medicine. Many requirements (and laws) stipulate that medical treatments and remedies must be supported by believable and rigorous scientific testing and replication and that those treatments must provide the least amount of harm or negative side effects (or, at least, those side effects must be reported). Our demand for evidence-based treatment is so strong that doctors spend a significant proportion of their income insuring themselves against lawsuits if they commit malpractice. However, when the police carry out an intervention that does not work, or that increases crime or recidivism or worsens police–community relations, it is much less likely that they will be held similarly responsible. Former National Institute of Justice Director Jeremy Travis went so far as to assert in his keynote address at the Sentencing Project's 25th anniversary celebration in 2011 that "[w]e need a professional ethic that views failure to adopt those proven policies and practices as a form of justice malpractice." While this type of legal accountability is not likely to be soon adopted in criminal justice practice, the idea behind evidence-based policing emphasizes that law enforcement should, at least, be held accountable to the knowledge we already have about many aspects of policing. Police should be deploying patrol officers, specialized units, detectives, supervisors, and commanders in ways that can be shown to achieve whatever results are sought (i.e., crime or fear reduction; legitimate, fair, and respectful treatment; or responsiveness to community concerns).

Of course, this does not imply that we should foster patrol automatons that do not use discretion, experience, and "craft" to achieve their work. Simply telling officers where to go to patrol based on statistics about crime hot spots is not, and will not foster, evidence-based policing. At the same time, overvaluing experience, or believing that officer discretion, experience, and craft cannot be shaped or developed from research knowledge is also faulty thinking.

Decisions about what types of treatments or tactics to employ in any given situation should not only be influenced by experience, but also by knowledge of the law, standard operating procedures, and, in the case of evidence-based policing, research knowledge and analysis.

Do we mean to suggest that evidence-based policing means just to do everything that has been shown to work through a scientific study and drop everything else? Of course not. Does this mean that the experience, empathy, and care that officers show in making decisions about everyday situations do not matter anymore? Certainly not. Does it mean that officers should stop reacting to crime and making arrests? Most definitely not. However, an evidence-based approach does mean that we can no longer ignore research knowledge about aspects of policing or alternative decision-making processes that provide guidance on achieving the outcomes that police themselves wish to accomplish.

The Benefits and Challenges of Evidence-Based Policing

As the reader might conclude, the cliché "it's complicated" is an understatement with evidence-based policing. The notion that scientific information could be helpful to policing seems reasonable and attuned to democratic norms regarding government more generally. But how we achieve evidence-based policing and incorporate such a perspective into the everyday activities of policing is more challenging, requiring a great deal of effort beyond finding the supply of good-quality knowledge. These challenges frame much of the rest of the suggestions in this book on how to achieve evidence-based policing. But first, it is important to emphasize the benefits of evidence-based policing.

The first obvious benefit is easier to say in theory but more challenging to produce. If police agencies employ strategies and tactics that can reduce and prevent crime, increase case clearance, improve relationships with citizens, or improve internal management and accountability, then the chances that they will achieve these goals is higher than if they employ strategies not shown to yield such outputs. On the flip side of this same coin, evidence-based policing also provides a mechanism for identifying policies that may yield harmful effects or no effect at all. Doing so can reduce an organization's risk in increasing harm, having no impact on crime, agitating police–community relations, or spending money wastefully. And, using more objective judgments to select internal and external strategies is arguably more ethically justifiable and legitimate than other nonscientific methods such as best guessing or choosing approaches based on anecdotes or personal preferences. All of this can strengthen police accountability to themselves, city councils, state officials, and taxpayers. Hence, evidence-based policing may lead to greater transparency, legitimacy, and accountability in practice, which could improve police–citizen relations and trust.

Connecting decision making to outcomes also has specific benefits to alternative decision-making perspectives that have already been adopted in policing. Programs such as community-oriented policing, problem-solving strategies, or predictive policing could be strengthened through an evidence-based policing perspective. An evidence-based perspective allows for "outside review" of these seemingly positive strategies that provides a way to objectively assess their merits, and dig deeper into *which* community policing, problem-solving, or predictive policing tactics work best and when.

Basing decisions on scientific knowledge might even increase satisfaction in police work (an assertion itself that needs research). Satisfaction may be increased because outcomes are more clearly linked to inputs. Of course, achieving this will require officers to know that their inputs led to successful results and that they also are aware of why an input could be connected to a particular output. Officers' job satisfaction might also increase due to the adoption of activities that can successfully prevent and reduce crime while also reducing reactive and repetitive work (i.e., reacting to multiple and repeating 911 calls)—though officers will need to understand how strategies that might initially seem like "more work" create this benefit for them.

More broadly, evidence-based policing could also increase job satisfaction by providing creative ways to carry out the profession and by challenging the status quo. Indeed, Weiss and Bucuvalas (1980) found that challenging the status quo is one reason bureaucrats may be receptive to using research in their practices. A related point is that applying critical, analytic, and proactive thinking in police work is also more akin to transformational, as opposed to transactional, leadership and deployment styles. Transformational approaches create more satisfaction among both supervisors and subordinates because more creative and proactive thinking is involved (Bass 1985; McCardle 2011). In this manner, evidence-based policing could change the organizational and cultural forces that cause police agencies to follow a reactive, procedures-oriented bureaucratic model that inhibits growth and dynamic learning. If using certain strategies, tactics, and internal practices lead to more positive results, this may then lead to greater motivation and job satisfaction.

There are also benefits to academics as well that go beyond seeing their research used. If demand for science increases, then researchers will need to work harder to meet that demand and carry out research that is relevant to the field. As we are already seeing, more interest in science and research in policing can help strengthen the relationships and interactions between police and researchers and provide more opportunities for scholars to contribute to the public good. It creates opportunities for experienced scholars to learn new things and also to mentor newer academics in a practical approach to criminology.

Despite these benefits, there are many challenges in adopting and achieving evidence-based policing, precisely because—as we have noted—evidence-based policing is complicated. To achieve evidence-based policing, research knowledge needs to be translated into digestible forms. Even then, that information must be implemented, institutionalized, and held to account in the everyday practices, cultures, systems, activities, and habits of policing. In Chapter 3, we describe the *Evidence-Based Policing Matrix*, which tries to make high-quality research easier to access. However, ease of access may not be enough to prompt the use of that research. Laments continue about the proverbial "gap" between research and practice in policing (Bayley 1998; Lum 2009; Lum et al. 2012; Mastrofski 1999; National Research Council 2004; Sherman 2013; Weiss and Bucuvalas 1980; Weisburd 2008). Lessons learned in other fields suggest that closing this gap will be hard. Even in the field of medicine, where we might expect that practices are guided by the best scientific research, this problem persists (Chalmers 2003; Sherman 2003a). There is little empirical research in the field of "translational criminology" on how wide this gap is, or how to overcome it, an issue we discuss in Chapter 15.

We also know more generally how difficult it can be for any reform to change the status quo and the standard approach to policing. Putting aside questions of their evidentiary base, while elements of alternatives such as community policing, problem solving, and intelligence-led policing have crept into policing, they have done so through specialized units, ad hoc special programs, and specifically assigned officers. Rarely are they institutionalized into the everyday actions and deployments of an agency's two largest activities—patrol or investigations—which continue to operate in the standard model. More specifically, our experience with police agencies as well as actual analyses of how time is used by police (see Famega et al. 2005; Kelling et al. 1974; Mastrofski, Park, Reiss et al. 1998; Whitaker 1982; Weisburd et al. 2015; Wu and Lum 2016) indicates that very few have policies, practices, performance metrics, or standards related to what police should do in their non-committed and discretionary time. Yet much of the evidence related to police efforts to control and prevent crime, for example, point to the use of this time as being the most important in achieving results.

Reactivity and the aspects of the standard model are institutionalized in almost every fiber of the policing organization. This reactivity is pervasive in leadership as well, especially at the first-line supervisory level, where guiding and monitoring proactive activities would occur. Additionally, procedures-based decision making is standardized through general orders and standard operating procedures in the standard model. One would be hard pressed to find a police agency with a standard operational procedure that demanded the use of research in some aspect of decision making or spending in the organization. Many general orders are likely not built from research at all, but from the experience of leaders within the agency, or from model policies provided by other organizations.

Thus, the institutionalized barriers to evidence-based policing that the standard model imposes cannot be overstated. In particular, evidence-based decision making competes with—and often loses to—the believed merits of the most important influence on decision making in the standard model—experience.

Of course, experience is always important to any profession. But in policing, it can often be overvalued. In combination with high levels of discretion, this can work against officers being receptive to outside knowledge. We discuss this at length in Chapter 8, but the point we want to make here is that when experience becomes so over-valued in policing, it can impede learning or change. Additionally the over-valuation of experience comes into conflict with evidence-based policing when research reveals something that contradicts conventional wisdom. Related to this is a suspicion of research and even crime analysis, which are viewed as not arising from the policing experience. What may result is a resistance by officers to adjust their discretion based on this suspicious or threatening knowledge.

Aside from these challenges, there are many other concerns about evidence-based policing. Even if an agency is committed to becoming more evidence based, transforming abstract research findings into tangible law enforcement tactics, practices, and strategies is a difficult venture, just as is applying one's general education to a workplace task. An excellent example of this is directed patrol to crime concentrations or "hot spots" (see Chapter 4). We now have overwhelming evidence that when police redeploy according to crime concentrations, not pre-defined political boundaries, they can have significantly more impact on crime prevention (see Chapter 4). But to change to this approach, officers will need to get used to a whole different style of patrol, adjust in their minds the places they are responsible for, and possibly alter their shift schedules. Police unions may get involved (and have in certain jurisdictions), arguing that such a redeployment increases the potential risk to officers and, therefore, is not justified. In addition, a common argument by police chiefs is that moving an officer out of a no-crime neighborhood, albeit logical, will raise complaints by citizens who no longer see a police officer in their neighborhood (a claim itself with no supporting evidence). Moreover, if rewards and promotions are based on numbers of arrests and the ability to know criminal procedures and case processing, such rewards systems would have to be adjusted to include the prevention of crime and the ability to proactively problem solve in hot spots. This example illustrates that fundamental changes in multiple systems of policing, including training, promotions, supervision, management, leadership, and technology use, may have to be implemented to increase the chance for research receptivity. Implementing evidence-based approaches is not as simple as knowing where hot spots are located or telling officers to patrol them because it is the logical or evidence-based thing to do.

The challenges of evidence-based policing are not only within police organizations but also within academic and research organizations. Research knowledge is not often written in ways that make it straightforward or accessible for officers to receive or use in practice. Like officers, researchers are also subject to their own activities, habits, cultures, systems of promotion, reward, supervision, technologies and constraints. An academic may take on a project to help an agency evaluate a deployment practice, but establishing those relationships and doing more evaluations not only takes time, experience, and money but may not yield enough fruit in terms of publications for tenure or promotion. University researchers might have little incentive to conduct research in the field, especially younger scholars who are judged on the quantity of publications.

There may also be false expectations and beliefs about the role of researchers and research in policing, some of which has been propagated by academics themselves. Despite what some have argued (see Laycock 2012; Sparrow 2011), researchers in the evidence-based policing mode have rarely claimed that research or scientific processes can run all aspects of a police department's daily operations or resolve all law enforcement concerns, just as problem-oriented policing, community-oriented policing, intelligence-led policing, or the professional model cannot. Others claim that policing is too complex to be studied systematically. Some have also criticized the evidence-based movement in policing for focusing too narrowly on certain values such as crime control or fear of crime. While it is true that proponents of evidence-based policing have tended to concentrate more of their attention on crime control, there is certainly nothing about the philosophy of evidence-based policing that precludes its application to improving a wide variety of community outcomes (e.g., citizen satisfaction) and internal management processes (e.g., improving the quality of training and promotion processes)—indeed, quite the opposite. Nor is it true that evidence-based policing is just about running experiments, as many types of research can inform police practice. Nonetheless, such views (however unfair or inaccurate) may lead to a widening communication gap between researchers and practitioners.

At the same time, there are some practical difficulties in generating and using research in a law enforcement setting that need to be considered when trying to mesh science with policing. Assigning some people or places to receive an intervention while others do not for the purposes of an evaluation study might not be possible or allowed by agencies who are partnering with researchers to assess their programs. For example, with body-worn cameras, police chiefs may have to distribute cameras to all officers at the same time, not just to a random selection of officers, so that adequate evaluation can be accomplished. Or, patrol commanders might want to address the "hottest" hot spots of crime first, or perhaps those that are most amenable to a new tactic, thereby prioritizing resources to these areas and ultimately creating limitations on doing rigorous evaluations of those interventions. Researchers are often playing catch-up to interventions that have already been implemented by police agencies, and trying to find rigorous ways to examine the effects of those activities or interventions after-the-fact. Further, there are many other entities and environments involved in evidence-based policing, not just academics and law enforcement practitioners (Sanderson 2006; 2009). Citizens and community groups, public health agencies, social service workers, the court and corrections, schools, and other groups likely have a stake (and a say) in what the police do, complicating the implementation of evidence-based policing further.

All of these challenges are the focus of this book. This volume is intended to provide the reader with resources and examples of evidence-based policing as well as guidance on how to practice it. The book includes detailed discussions of definitions, research evidence, and scientific processes that could be applied to policing; supplies examples of evidence-based policing in practice; and provides tools to help implement and institutionalize evidence-based policing. As a way to illustrate the application of evidence-based policing, we will focus primarily on police efforts to deal with crime. We focus on this area because a great deal of work has already been developed on this topic and it reflects our expertise. However, we strongly emphasize to the reader that we use this area for illustrative purposes only, not to equate a particular area of research or research methodology with evidence-based policing.

In conclusion, while the notion of evidence-based policing may, in theory, seem reasonable, rational, and even democratic, translating and using research in police daily practice is much more complex and nuanced in reality. Evidence-based policing is a decision-making perspective, not a panacea. It is grounded in the idea that policies and practices should be supported by research evidence and analytics, not blindly determined by them. And, an evidence-based policing perspective means that at least research is not ignored and that it at least becomes a part of the conversation on what to do about reducing crime, increasing legitimacy, or addressing internal problems. For evidence-based policing to occur, the generation of research has to be matched with translation and implementation.

2

WHICH EVIDENCE FORMS THE BASE FOR EVIDENCE-BASED POLICING?

In Chapter 1, we described evidence-based policing as a perspective that promotes the use of research knowledge and processes in police decision making, whether for internal agency management or for preventing crime and improving citizen–police relationships. We don't have, and don't always need, research to guide every aspect of everyday police practice and management. But an evidence-based policing perspective means that, when feasible, research should at least be considered when making significant policy decisions. But which research evidence should constitute the basis for evidence-based policing? And how should that body of research be translated into useable forms? In this and Chapter 3, we focus on these issues.

Thinking About What Research to Use

Let's begin with the first question about which evidence should form the basis for evidence-based policing. Although police agencies can (and sometimes must) generate their own internal research knowledge, they can also draw upon the wider body of research already available to inform their practices. In policing, we are at an advantage; numerous studies over the past few decades speak to many aspects of police activities, interventions, policies, and management. At the outset, we emphasize what we said in Chapter 1—many types of research can inform police practice and therefore underpin evidence-based policing. Some research is intended to be descriptive and can help law enforcement understand different kinds of problems and develop strategies and services to address those problems. For example, surveys can tell us about citizen trust and confidence in the police and their satisfaction with police services. Descriptive analysis can show us the location of crime hot spots or the prevalence of police accidents and injuries. Some research provides rich detail about the nature of policing or police–citizen interactions using methods such as in-depth interviewing, systematic social observations, or ethnographies. Other studies track the delivery of police services and interventions, which then becomes vital information for research that evaluates the impact of those interventions on outcomes.

Two important points should be made about these various forms of research. The first is that they all can inform evidence-based policing. Contrary to assertions by some critics, evidence-based policing does not discriminate among types of research approach. The second point is that within each type of research approach, quality can vary. Surveys, ethnographies, outcome evaluations, and descriptive analyses can all be done well or poorly. Here is where evidence-based policing *does* discriminate; it promotes the use of the "best available" or the highest-quality evidence within each of these different designs. In other words, if you are going to use survey results to inform your interactions with citizens, then you want to use survey results that come from a well-crafted survey, in which a representative and randomly selected sample was drawn from the population or group of interest. You don't want to gauge the pulse of your community, for example, using survey results that come from a convenience sample of ten individuals who happen to attend a community meeting.

Most researchers would generally agree that not all research is created equal. If data collected on a topic were fabricated, poorly gathered, missing too many entries, inaccurate, or biased toward a certain result, then it would not be wise to use the results of research based on those data to make important policy decisions. Police officers already know this from their experience; if officers and detectives receive poor or misleading information from an informant, or if they gather it in a way that is illegal or violates the chain of evidence, this could result in their losing a suspect, making an illegal arrest, losing a case in court, or getting injured. Similarly, decisions made using poor-quality research could lead to millions of dollars wasted on ineffective interventions, programs, or managerial strategies; unnecessary degrading of police–civilian relations; greater harm to victims, bystanders, suspects, or officers; and other negative consequences. Bad research evidence that starts with bad data can be made worse if the research methods used to draw conclusions about that information are not scientifically sound. Some methods that are used to develop "best" practices are not systematic or scientific, such as consensus meetings of a select group of police leaders. While these approaches can be valuable in generating ideas, and while experience itself is valuable in understanding and implementing policing, this information on its own is not enough to achieve evidence-based policing.

So, what research should police use when trying to implement evidence-based policing? The short answer is that all types of research—surveys, descriptive studies, statistical modeling, experiments and quasi-experiments, systematic social observations, ethnographies, and in-depth interviews—can and should be used. However, when agencies use these research studies, or even when they apply now common policing techniques such as crime analysis or problem-oriented policing that are rooted in research, they need a general understanding of what constitutes good research within these approaches.

The Program Evaluation Framework

A basic understanding of research quality is thus essential in implementing evidence-based policing. However, it is not our aim in this book to review all research studies in policing and assess them based on methodological quality. That enormous undertaking was attempted by a National Academies of Sciences National Research Council panel in 2004. Nor are this chapter and book about research methods; evidence-based policing does not require police officers to be highly trained social scientists. Instead, in this chapter, we provide the reader with a sense of how to judge certain types of research studies that are central to evidence-based approaches. In particular, we use as an example one area that forms a major component of evidence-based policing—outcome evaluations of police efforts to prevent and control crime; As we discuss throughout this book, the research base on crime control strategies is well developed and holds many valuable lessons for policing. This particular research area also provides a useful heuristic for understanding the difference between good and bad quality research, and the value of research to policing more generally.

Before turning to the specifics of these studies, it is helpful first to introduce the framework of program evaluation and discuss different types of evaluation studies. Broadly, program evaluation refers to research that is designed to assess the effects of programs, policies, and interventions on the conditions they are intended to address. We use the term "program" here to refer to any kind of practice, intervention, or policy intended to achieve a desired outcome. Several types of research are relevant to evaluating programs. These include assessments of program needs and theory, studies of program implementation, evaluations of program outcomes, and studies of program cost-efficiency (Rossi, Lipsey, and Freeman 2004). In brief, program needs assessment involves studying the nature and magnitude of the problem that a program is intended to address, and assessing the need for a program and how it should be designed. Assessment of program theory involves examining expectations and assumptions about how a program should operate and how the program should affect the problem it is intended to address. The assessment of program implementation (also called process evaluation) involves examining the operations of a program to determine if it was implemented as planned. Outcome or impact assessment then focuses on whether and how a program actually affects the social conditions it is meant to address. Finally, cost-efficiency analyses (which have been rare to this point in policing research) examine whether the benefits of a program, estimated in monetary terms, outweigh its costs, and whether a program provides the most cost-efficient method of achieving a desired outcome relative to other alternatives.

All of these forms of program evaluation are relevant to evidence-based policing, and we return to these concepts at points throughout the book. In this chapter, however, we highlight outcome evaluation research, which often represents the "bottom line" in judging program effectiveness and determining what works to achieve desired results (Rossi et al. 2004). Police practitioners who wish to implement evidence-based practices in their agencies need, as a starting point, to have some understanding of what outcome evaluation research has shown to be effective in policing. This can also help them understand that not all evaluation research is created equal; the findings of some studies can be relied upon more than others, depending on the strength of research methods used.

However, understanding and using outcome evaluation research can be challenging. Outcome evaluation constitutes one of the most technically difficult areas of program evaluation, and not all forms of these evaluations are equally rigorous and convincing. Luckily, many outcome evaluations of policing practices have already been carried out, and agencies can use them in assessing their own policies and procedures. To help practitioners interpret and use this work, we briefly highlight the key characteristics of good evaluation studies here. Understanding these concepts can help police officials become better consumers and users of research, as well as better producers of their own evaluation evidence. After we discuss basic concepts in outcome evaluation, we then provide an overview in Chapter 3 of what we have learned to date from rigorous studies about the effectiveness of police practices. In Chapters 4 through 6, we discuss some of these findings more specifically.

Basics of outcome evaluation studies in policing

In evaluating the outcomes of police practices, it is helpful first to note that many policing studies focus on the delivery of police services and interventions. Such studies are vital to evaluating practices and thus form an important component of the research base for evidence-based policing. At the same time, we want to stress that documenting police activity and service delivery is not the same as showing that those activities have achieved desired outcomes. For instance, documenting that patrols and arrests increased in a particular area is not the same as showing that these interventions reduced crime or fear of crime. Similarly, successfully delivering drug abuse resistance education to children as required does not guarantee the program will reduce their future drug use.

In scientific outcome evaluation studies, one typically measures the change in an outcome of interest following the implementation of a program. (For the sake of discussion, we assume that the program was implemented as intended.) For instance, did crime decline in neighborhoods that received a new community policing program? Crime and other social outcomes (e.g., fear of crime, citizen satisfaction with police, police use of force, etc.) can change over time for many reasons, however, so we also try to isolate changes resulting from the program from changes caused by other factors.[1] This requires an assessment of what would have happened in the absence of the program, something that evaluators often refer to as a "counterfactual." This assessment is often, and most rigorously, performed by comparing a treatment group that receives a program (alternatively, we might refer to them as a "program," "intervention," or "target" group) to a control (or "comparison") group that does not receive the program. The treatment and control groups may consist of people, places, or other units (e.g., organizations) under study.

When using a research design with a treatment and control group, one can compare pre- to postprogram changes for the treatment group to changes that occurred in the control group during the same period. Or, if pre-program measures are not available, one can compare the level of change in the outcome measure(s) for the treatment and control groups after program implementation, provided there are good grounds for believing the groups were comparable on the outcome measure(s) prior to the program. The change (or outcome level) for the control group then serves as the counterfactual (or in other words, our best estimate) for what would have happened in the treatment group had it not received the program. In the example above, one could compare changes in crime in the neighborhoods that received the community policing program (the treatment group) to those in neighborhoods that did not receive the program (a control group). If crime declined in the neighborhoods that received the intervention but not in the neighborhoods that didn't, and if both groups of neighborhoods were comparable, then we might believe that the program reduced crime. However, if crime declined equally in both groups of neighborhoods, it would suggest that something other than the intervention caused crime to decline in both places.[2]

But what if crime goes down in the treatment group by 15% and falls in the control group by 13%? Can we conclude that the treatment was effective since crime dropped more in the treatment group than in the control?

---

[1] Note that the selection of outcome measures is a key consideration in program evaluation. Briefly, outcome measures used to evaluate a program must be observable, measurable indicators that are valid for the social conditions the program is intended to change, reliable (meaning they produce consistent results when used repeatedly to measure the same thing), and sufficiently sensitive to detect changes of the sort that the program is expected to create (Rossi et al. 2004).

[2] Other types of patterns might also suggest program effects. For instance, crime might rise in control areas but remain steady in treatment areas. Or, as we describe next, crime might decline in both sets of areas, but decline more substantially in the treatment areas.

These two percentages appear different, but statistically the difference may be due to chance. Next month, if we did the same test, crime might go down in the treatment group by 20% and in the control group by 22%! Analysts use statistical tests to determine whether differences in the treatment and control group outcomes are greater than what would be expected based on chance. If the probability of the observed differences occurring by chance are low (typically 5% or less, though sometimes a 10% cut-off is used), then the differences are considered to be "statistically significant" and indicative of a program effect.

But first, for comparisons to provide a valid indication of program impacts, the treatment and control groups must be equivalent on characteristics and experiences related to the outcome (Rossi et al. 2004). For example, if we were studying how a program affects criminal behavior among individuals, we would not want to compare a group of teenage boys who received the treatment to very elderly women who did not. Characteristics and experiences relevant to a person's criminal behavior might include things like age, gender, race/ethnicity, prior offending, substance abuse history, and changes in home environment; therefore, it would behoove us to compare two groups similar on these characteristics, one which received treatment, and one which did not. Similarly, in studying crime prevention interventions at places, we would want to compare places that are similar in terms of levels of crime, population density, demographic characteristics, land use, and other environmental characteristics. If we compare treatment and control groups that have different characteristics on how they respond to a particular intervention, our estimates of program effects may be biased.

Imagine, for instance, that one was evaluating a police program designed to reduce delinquency among high-risk or already delinquent youth. Further, assume that police could only admit a limited number of eligible youth into the program. Given discretion over program admittance, officers might pick youths they think are more likely to be responsive to the program and have a better chance of being diverted from future offending (like youths with less serious histories of delinquency or strong family support). In this scenario, it would not be surprising to find that youths admitted to the program had lower levels of postprogram delinquency than youths who were not selected. Can we conclude from this that the program "worked"? Perhaps. Maybe the program works for those youth especially amenable to the program—but maybe it does not work. The youths selected for the program may simply have had a lower chance of committing future delinquency before they entered the program.

Experimental and quasi-experimental research

Assessing program effects thus requires that we select treatment and control groups that have people or places that are equivalent on relevant characteristics and experiences, or that we find ways to account for their differences in statistical analyses. Analysts try to achieve this by using both randomized experiments and nonrandomized, quasi-experimental study designs.

Many argue that the best way to create equivalent treatment and control groups is by randomly assigning eligible units (people, places, etc.) to either the treatment or control condition (e.g., Cook 2003; Rossi et al. 2004; Weisburd 2003). Outcome evaluation studies based on randomization are referred to as randomized controlled experiments (RCEs) or randomized controlled trials (RCTs). When using random assignment, every eligible unit has an equal probability of being placed into the treatment group (also sometimes referred to as the experimental group). There are simple procedures that can be used to randomly assign units to treatment and control conditions, but one can also think of this as doing a coin flip to determine group assignment for each eligible unit. Statistically, this is the best way to produce treatment and control groups that are equivalent—on both characteristics that can be measured and those that cannot (including potentially important factors of which an analyst may be unaware). Although group differences may still sometimes result from chance (and can be more likely with small samples), randomization provides the best way of avoiding systematic biases in group assignment and producing equivalent groups. When conducting a randomized experiment, the analyst can then have greater confidence that postintervention differences between the treatment and control groups are due to program effects rather than other factors. Accordingly, scientists place great weight on experimental results when judging program efficacy.

However, randomized experiments are not always feasible or desired when conducting outcome evaluations. For example, sometimes police chiefs want to know if an existing practice is effective. Or, they would like to know whether a change in organizational policy leads to improved job satisfaction, but can't alter the policy for some and not others (e.g., increased pay). In these cases, researchers can use nonrandomized, quasi-experimental study designs to estimate program impacts. Many studies in policing have used these approaches to test the effect of an intervention or practice. There are many types of quasi-experimental designs, but we focus our discussion here on those that examine before-and-after changes in outcome measures for both treatment and comparison groups that were not formed by random assignment. With these designs, researchers can still compare people and places that receive a program or intervention to those that do not. However, they must use methods to minimize or statistically account for differences between the groups.

One broad group of quasi-experimental techniques involves selecting comparison group units that are matched to treatment group units on selected characteristics that are thought to be related to the outcome variable and the likelihood of program participation. If evaluating a neighborhood community policing program, for instance, researchers could select one or more comparison neighborhoods that are very similar to the neighborhood receiving community policing on characteristics such as population size, demographics, poverty levels, and crime rates. More complex matching techniques with large treatment and control groups can involve sophisticated statistical modeling to identify and select control units that are most similar to treatment units on a range of characteristics (i.e., propensity score matching).

Another group of quasi-experimental techniques involves measuring relevant characteristics of the treatment and control groups and incorporating these features into statistical models that attempt to sort out program effects from the influence of these other factors. With such models, analysts attempt to statistically control for characteristics and experiences that may differ across groups and be related to the outcome of interest. In evaluating a delinquency prevention program, for example, an analyst might compare outcomes for program youth and nonprogram youth in a statistical model that also includes (and hence controls for) measures of factors such as the youths' age, gender, prior offending, neighborhood, family characteristics, and school performance.[3]

Overall, the rigor of quasi-experimental study designs can vary considerably based on the range and thoroughness of variables selected for statistical controls or matching, the size of the treatment and control groups, and the statistical techniques used. Analysts can also strengthen these designs by measuring outcomes for the treatment and control groups at multiple time points before and after the intervention (i.e., time series designs) in order to better control for preprogram trends that may have differed between the groups and affected their postprogram patterns.[4] Further, while studies with quasi-experimental designs form an important component of the evidence base on evaluation in policing, it is important to keep in mind that these types of studies have a greater chance than randomized experiments of overstating or understating program effects. In criminal justice studies in particular, it seems that quasi-experimental studies are more likely to show positive and larger program effects than randomized studies (Weisburd, Lum, and Petrosino 2001). Whereas the accuracy

---

[3] In situations that involve program selection criteria that are explicit and known (e.g., imagine a program targeting high-risk offenders as determined by a cut-off point from a formulated risk score), this information can also be incorporated into a model of program effects (this is a particularly rigorous form of quasi-experimental design referred to as a regression-discontinuity design).

[4] Our discussion focuses on quasi-experimental designs that employ control groups. However, other quasi-experimental study designs can also be useful in different contexts if followed rigorously. For instance, some time series designs without control groups involve using pre-intervention trend data for the treatment group to project what the outcome measure would have been for the treatment group had the program not been conducted. This projection is then compared to the actual postprogram outcome data (this type of design is most typically used when studying an intervention that was conducted in one particular place, such as a neighborhood or city that does not have a particularly suitable matching place to use as a comparison). Some other quasi-experimental designs involve looking at multiple outcomes that are expected to be more or less affected by a program. If studying a police program to reduce drunk driving, for example, one might compare pre- and postprogram changes in alcohol-related auto accidents to those for auto accidents not involving alcohol, based on the expectation that the program would affect the former but not the latter (and thus the latter would form a comparison outcome series).

of quasi-experimental results is contingent on factors that can be measured and incorporated into the study design, randomized experiments implicitly control for unmeasurable as well as measurable differences between groups.

Judging, weighing, and using the evidence

While some might argue that randomized experiments provide higher-quality evidence, the goal of evidence-based policing is the *use* of research. Today, in 2016, limiting the evidence base to only randomized experiments would reduce the range and the type of research evidence police agencies can draw upon to make decisions. Despite the large quantity of evaluation research currently available, only a minority of studies have used randomized controlled trials (Lum and Mazerolle 2014; Lum and Yang 2005; Mazerolle, Lum, and Braga 2014; Sherman and Eck 2002).

Thus, the results of quasi-experimental studies can be valuable to evidence-based policing, particularly if they employ reasonably rigorous methods and yield consistent results. However, as discussed above, if we set our threshold too low and consider much lower-quality studies, which are less reliable or believable, our knowledge base might include unreliable information. There are many examples of criminal justice interventions that were deemed effective using scientifically weak assessments (or no assessment at all) but were later discovered to be ineffective or even harmful when they were more rigorously studied (e.g., DARE, boot camps, "scared straight" programs, some reactive arrests, and some community policing strategies).

Given all of this, researchers and the police have to find the right balance when weighing evidence from stronger and weaker study designs. Those engaged in evidence-based policing do not have to be social scientists, but they need to have some understanding of the ranges of quality in different types of research. And although we have only discussed these issues in detail with regard to outcome evaluation, we stress that these issues also pertain to other types of research. For example, survey research can also be of high or low quality. Randomly selecting households in an entire county to receive a survey versus having citizens at a community meeting fill out that same survey can lead to widely different results about what people think about a law enforcement tactic. Similarly, identifying "hot spots" of crime depends on the quality and type of data used. Ethnographic studies that involve extensive observation and interviewing of subjects can also be done well or poorly, leading to very different results.

Understanding that one experimental study or survey is not the definitive answer is also important. Even if a study uses randomization, there may be problems with other methodological aspects or with implementation of the program that cloud the findings. Or, one study might show an intervention didn't work to improve community trust, while ten other studies showed positive effects. More is not always better, but replication of research in different types of places or on various types of people (known as "external validity") is also an important factor that strengthens the evidence base of policing practice. These basic concepts are important for those engaged in evidence-based policing to understand when making decisions about which research they should use.

What We Know from Evaluation Research

At this point, law enforcement personnel may feel overwhelmed by this conversation about the values, nuances, and complexities of law enforcement-related research. How can we effectively judge research, sift through this information, use it, and generate more, if needed? Fortunately, many of these issues have already been tackled by the research community, who have not only collaborated with police practitioners to generate high-quality research knowledge, but have also sifted through, collated, and organized the large amount of research knowledge (especially program evaluation research) currently available. Within the field of evidence-based crime policy more generally, researchers have worked to make sense of the supply of research, examine the range of research methods used, and engage in discourse on the practical concerns of generalizing findings from the research. Our own work on the Evidence-Based Policing Matrix, discussed in Chapter 3, is in the spirit of these efforts. It attempts to keep up with this ever-expanding body of research knowledge and translate it into a usable form for police and analysts to view and use.

Many of these efforts have focused on collecting and collating the evaluation evidence on police strategies to prevent, reduce, or control crime, to reduce fear of crime and, to a lesser extent, to improve citizens' trust and confidence in the police. This does not in any way mean that the evidence base of policing is limited to these areas. However, the attention paid to these programs during the past several decades provides us with a fruitful source of knowledge to use in further study.

Three recent and influential collating efforts have been particularly important in strengthening the movement towards evidence-based policing.[5] The first was the 1997 University of Maryland report to Congress, conducted by Lawrence Sherman and colleagues, on "What Works, What Doesn't, and What's Promising" in crime prevention, sometimes referred to as "the Maryland Report" and later updated in a published book entitled, *Evidence-Based Crime Prevention,* edited by Sherman, Farrington, Welsh, and MacKenzie (2002; see specifically the chapter by Sherman and Eck for its review of policing research). At the time, the U.S. Attorney General was asked to provide the U.S. Congress

---

[5] Earlier reviews of police research included Clark and Hough's (1980) compilation of papers on police effectiveness, a series of reviews by Sherman (1983; 1986; 1990; 1992), and a special issue of *Crime and Justice: A Review of Research* (Tonry and Morris 1992).

with a review of the effectiveness of state and local crime prevention programs. Sherman and his colleagues reviewed more than 600 studies on a broad range of crime prevention programs focused on families, schools, communities, labor markets, places, police, sentencing, and corrections.

They also graded each study according to a "Scientific Methods Scale" to assess its methodological quality, similar to what we described above (see Sherman et al. 2002, 13–21). They judged programs as "working" if they were supported by at least two studies of higher methodological quality (i.e., experiments and rigorous quasi-experiments) and the preponderance of all remaining studies. They judged tactics as "promising" if they were supported by at least one rigorous study and the preponderance of less rigorous studies. Programs were categorized as "not working" if at least two methodologically rigorous studies showed ineffectiveness and a preponderance of evidence in other studies showed ineffectiveness. Sherman et al.'s contention was that more scientifically rigorous studies should be given more weight in guiding practice; consequently, these studies were emphasized in recommendations about "what works" in policing and other criminal justice areas.

That systematic review of research by Sherman and colleagues was a major momentum builder in the movement toward evidence-based crime policy.[6] Not only did the review point out that research could inform practice, but also that some research challenged current approaches and thinking in criminal justice. In policing, practices such as reactive arrest, increasing the number of police, and responding quickly to 911 calls for service were not as strongly supported by research findings as were policing strategies that proactively targeted resources on specific places and people at highest risk for criminality or victimization. Sherman and his colleagues also challenged conventional thinking about popular programs such as DARE and gun buyback programs, finding them ineffective.

The Maryland Report also was an important stepping stone for Sherman and others forming the international Campbell Collaboration in 2000.[7] With the support of philanthropist Jerry Lee, this collaboration advocated more rigorous evaluations of social interventions (see Farrington and Petrosino 2001) and worked to clarify research findings, gaps, and needs in evaluating these programs. Modeled after the Cochrane Collaboration for medical and public health interventions, the Campbell Collaboration sponsors in-depth and rigorous reviews of research (called "systematic reviews") on various types of social interventions, including those related to criminal justice. These reviews, which often include statistical analyses that combine results from multiple studies

---

[6] The movement towards evidence-based crime policy and evidence-based policing can be also be seen as part of a larger trend towards the use of evaluation research to improve the performance and accountability of social programs more generally (e.g., see Nutley, Walter, and Davies 2007; Rossi et al. 2004).

[7] See http://www.campbellcollaboration.org.

(referred to as meta-analyses), are intended to help researchers and policymakers draw conclusions from the totality of evaluation research on a specific topic. For example, if five studies examine the impact of pretextual car stops to reduce gun violence and each has different findings, what can we conclude from all five studies? In making these assessments, Campbell reviewers consider the methodological rigor of the studies and, where possible, statistically combine results across studies to estimate the average effect of the intervention under investigation. The Campbell Collaboration, like the Maryland Report, emphasizes the importance of collating, judging, and filtering the totality of research evidence in policing (and other areas) by methodological rigor and intervention type, so that high-quality research knowledge can be distilled to inform practice.

Drawing generalizations from these reviews and identifying key lessons and useful information for policymakers and practitioners are other significant contributions of Campbell systematic reviews. Each review has a one-page summary designed to provide practitioners and policymakers with a quick assessment of the totality of high-quality research about the intervention under consideration. The Campbell Collaboration also has a "users group" that focuses on how to get reviews out to the public, and a website to facilitate dissemination. As of this writing, at least a dozen reviews on police-related inventions have been completed on topics including, among others, hot spots policing strategies, community and problem-oriented policing, pulling levers-focused deterrence interventions, policing of disorder, use of procedural justice, methods of interviewing suspects, and responses to domestic violence. We reference many of these reviews in Chapters 4 through 6.

A third major effort to collate research in policing was the National Academy of Sciences National Research Council's (NRC) report on *Fairness and Effectiveness in Policing* (National Research Council 2004). For this report, the NRC's Committee to Review Research on Police Policy and Practices, chaired by Wesley Skogan and Kathleen Frydl, brought together a number of senior police scholars to assess the state of police research in a range of areas covering crime prevention effectiveness, as well as organizational and cultural dimensions of policing that can be used for evidence-based policing. For example, when assessing research on the "effectiveness of police activities in reducing crime, disorder and fear" (Chapter 6), the committee issued strong conclusions about specific policing strategies and also provided, as discussed shortly, a conceptual framework that highlights some dimensions of police strategies associated with effectiveness.

In total, these efforts have produced a number of recommendations and conclusions about police crime prevention strategies. Four key points noted by the NRC (2004, 246–7; also see Weisburd and Eck 2004), which have been echoed in other key reviews, include the following:

1. The standard model of policing that emphasizes random patrol, rapid response to calls for service, follow-up investigations by detectives, and

unfocused enforcement efforts has not been effective in reducing crime (also see Sherman 1997; Sherman and Eck 2002).

2. Some of the strategies falling under the umbrella of community policing have been effective in reducing crime, disorder, and/or fear of crime, while others have not (also see Bennett, Holloway and Farrington 2008; Gill, Weisburd, Telep et al. 2014; Sherman 1997; Sherman and Eck 2002).

3. Police strategies that are more focused and tailored to specific types of crimes, criminals, and places are more effective (also see Braga, Papachristos, and Hurcau 2012; Koper and Mayo-Wilson 2012; Mazerolle, Soule, and Rombouts 2007; Weisburd, Telep, Hinkle et al. 2010).

4. Problem-oriented policing—a strategy involving systematic analysis of crime and disorder problems and the development of tailored solutions (Goldstein 1979)—is effective (also see Weisburd et al. 2010).

These three efforts—the Maryland Report, the Campbell Collaboration (in regard to its policing reviews), and the NRC Report—showcase valuable lessons for evidence-based policing. First, researchers have been working to review and synthesize research so that important findings can be understood and used by law enforcement agencies to shape their policies and procedures. Second, as the research base continues to grow, researchers and police have to continue to find reliable ways of judging and sifting through research. And finally, we need ways to translate research into usable, easy-to-read, and digestible forms in order to achieve evidence-based policing.

Notwithstanding these advancements, gaps still exist in both our knowledge about police crime prevention efforts and how such knowledge can or should inform the implementation of effective strategies. Many police crime prevention strategies have yet to be evaluated rigorously. Ambiguities in the existing evidence also remain, in particular, the question of why some types of strategies tend to work better. And most important to practitioners, how can we move beyond lists of effective and ineffective strategies evaluated in isolation in order to draw generalizations about effective policing approaches and apply those generalizations across different jurisdictions, settings, policing units, and crime types? In other words, rather than simply saying that strategies *A* and *B* are effective and strategies *C* and *D* are not, can we develop broader generalizations, or principles, about effective approaches that police can use in selecting and developing strategies more generally?

As these questions suggest, and as we argued in Chapter 1, evidence-based policing is not only about identifying or even synthesizing research to inform practice; it is also about figuring out ways to translate that information and use it. This added dimension of evidence-based policing—translation—creates more complexity in answer to our question of "which evidence" should be used for the evidence base of policing. Following from this, we need to derive more strategic principles from existing police research that would help us translate the research reflected in these past reviews. In particular, we need more specific and wide-ranging generalizations from the literature that coincide with the organizational structure and vernacular of policing to make the utility of the evidence more obvious. Although existing research syntheses have facilitated the adoption of evidence-based policing to some extent by focusing on specific tactics and strategies, research has generally had no more than a modest impact on police practices (Bayley 1998). On the contrary, U.S. police agencies and their international counterparts are well known for not using evidence-based practices in everyday patrol and investigations.

Many of the causes for this are organizational, related to the stubborn and slow-changing nature of police culture, tradition, and practices (Bayley 1994; Mastrofski 1999; O'Neill, Marks and Singh 2007; Sherman 1984; 1998). Yet as Lum (2009) asserts, the next step in moving toward evidence-based policing is to build on existing evidence, systematic reviews, and research infrastructures to create translation tools for conveying that evidence to police practitioners. Translation tools highlighting general principles of police effectiveness that can be applied across a range of conditions and problems may be more useful to practitioners than lists of specific strategies that are effective or ineffective. For researchers, such translation tools may also illuminate useful generalizations about why particular prevention efforts are valuable and what areas of research are needed. Toward this end, we created the *Evidence-Based Policing Matrix,* which we discuss in Chapter 3.

3

TRANSLATING RESEARCH
The Evidence-Based Policing Matrix

In Chapter 2, we described the importance of using good-quality evidence to inform policy, using the specific example of outcome evaluations. We also introduced major efforts that have been undertaken to review the research evidence in policing that take into account the scientific rigor of studies. In this chapter, we explore likely the first online translation tool—the Evidence-Based Policing Matrix—that not only organizes outcome evaluation research in policing, but is designed to facilitate its translation into practice.[1] The Evidence-Based Policing Matrix, (hereafter, "the Matrix") visually maps out the field of evaluation research in policing related to crime prevention in a freely accessible, online, and annually updated tool. Not only does the Matrix enable the police to see the evidence base and draw generalizations from the research on police crime control efforts, but they can also access specific findings and ideas about strategies and tactics. In Part Three of this book, we then describe specific ways to use the Matrix to translate and institutionalize research into practice.

The Evidence-Based Policing Matrix

The Matrix[2] is a freely available, interactive, web-based tool that houses all police crime control intervention research of moderate-to-high methodological

---

[1] Since the development of the Matrix, others have developed other tools for synthesizing the research evidence, such as CrimeSolutions.gov by the Office of Justice Programs of the U.S. Department of Justice (see https://www.crimesolutions.gov/TopicDetails.aspx?ID=6), and the College of Policing (United Kingdom) Crime Reduction Toolkit (see http://whatworks.college. police.uk/toolkit/Pages/Toolkit.aspx).

[2] See http://cebcp.org/evidence-based-policing/the-matrix/.

quality. It is updated annually by the authors and their research team. Like other systematic reviews, the Matrix provides a forum where research evidence can be collected, judged, organized, and disseminated, so that law enforcement officials can draw generalizations from the literature to help inform their practices. Like a visual systematic review, the Matrix also encourages research use and translation through its interactive interface.

We initially developed the idea for the Matrix in 2007 while writing about the potential for criminologists to contribute to counterterrorism studies (Lum and Koper 2007; 2011). Since few evaluations of counterterrorism and homeland security programs are publicly available, and since it remains difficult to carry out evaluations in this arena, we considered ways in which existing evaluations of law enforcement and crime prevention could be applied to the thinking about counterterrorism. Inspired by Rosenberg and Knox's (2005) three-dimensional grid for conceptualizing childhood well-being and youth violence prevention, we created the visualization of a "Crime Prevention Matrix." Our idea was to organize high-quality existing research on crime prevention interventions (like those in policing) by "mapping" the interventions into a visualization based on their common characteristics (e.g., their targets and crime prevention mechanisms). We reasoned that doing this might reveal common characteristics of effective crime prevention interventions in ways that might not be apparent from prior research reviews. In turn, we argued that homeland security measures could then be evaluated based on whether they shared the characteristics of effective versus ineffective crime prevention interventions as revealed by this visualization.

In 2008, we applied this idea to the evaluation research on police and crime control—hence, the "Evidence-Based Policing Matrix" (see Lum 2008; 2009; Lum, Koper, and Telep 2011b). We created a three-dimensional matrix shown in Figure 3.1. The axes of the Matrix reflect the most common characteristics of crime prevention strategies and tactics in policing. We describe these in more detail below, but in brief, they include: the target of the intervention (*x*-axis), the level of focus or specificity of the prevention mechanisms (*y*-axis), and the extent to which an intervention can be considered reactive, proactive, or highly proactive (*z*-axis). The creation of these dimensions was done purposefully and empirically, using the most common dimensions identified from both policing research and practice.

Target of the intervention (*x*-axis)

One common dimension characterizing police crime control interventions is the type (or scope) of the intervention target, as shown with the *x*-axis of Figure 3.1. Targets of policing interventions often range from individuals to larger social aggregations of individuals and the smaller and larger spaces they occupy, up to the jurisdiction or nation/state level. These are the most common targets for which police agencies organize and also discuss their strategies,

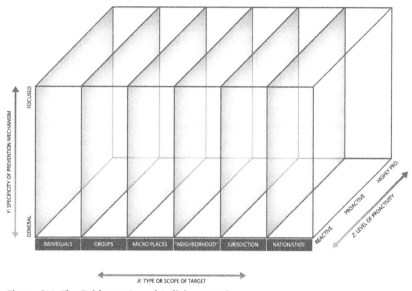

Figure 3.1 The Evidence-Based Policing Matrix

Reprinted with permission of Springer, from the *Journal of Experimental Criminology*, Volume 7, Issue 1, 2011, Cynthia Lum, Christopher Koper, and Cody Telep (Copyright © 2010, Springer Science+Business Media B.V.).

and also can be used to characterize all policing interventions that have been evaluated. For example, the "Individuals" portion or "slab" of the Matrix would include strategies or interventions intended to deter individuals generally from crime or strategies that target specific categories of persons, such as repeat offenders (see, e.g., Martin and Sherman 1986), potential juvenile drug users (see, e.g., Rosenbaum and Hanson 1998), or those who commit domestic/intimate partner violence (see, e.g., Sherman and Berk 1984). Strategies that focus on people offending in tandem, such as gangs or co-offenders, would be categorized into the "Groups" slab (e.g., pulling levers interventions to combat gang violence—see, e.g., Braga, Kennedy, Piehl et al. 2001). We discuss both individual and group-based strategies in Chapter 5.

Law enforcement agencies also use tactics and strategies that focus less on people and more on specific addresses, locations, places, and neighborhoods. Targeted places can be described by size, from smaller or "micro" places, to larger geographic units. Micro-place interventions target very specific geographic locations such as a block, street segment, specific address, or cluster of blocks (see Eck and Weisburd 1995; Weisburd 2002; Weisburd, Bernasco, and Bruinsma 2009). Interventions such as hot spots policing (see e.g. Sherman and Weisburd 1995), problem-oriented policing focused on drug markets (see, e.g., Weisburd and Green 1995), and the use of civil remedies at problem addresses (see, e.g., Mazerolle, Price, and Roehl 2000a) represent examples of micro-place-based interventions. Larger and more amorphous places can include neighborhoods, census tracts, communities, and police boundaries (beats, sectors, districts) within a jurisdiction. Strategies such as Neighborhood Watch (see, e.g., Bennett 1990), community policing, problem solving (e.g., see Skogan, Harnett, and Lovig 1995), and foot patrol (see, e.g., Trojanowicz 1986) are often implemented and evaluated in these types of areas. We discuss these types of strategies in Chapters 4 and 6.

While the vast majority of police agencies in the United States are confined by local government boundaries, policing interventions can also be city-, county-, or parish-wide, or even span regions and states. These geographically broader interventions are often much more general in nature. Examples might include police enforcement of local gun carrying laws (see, e.g., Villaveces, Cummings, Espetia et al. 2000) or jurisdiction-wide crackdowns on drunk driving. An even larger geographic aggregation is the nation/state, which is a politically distinct geopolitical area with laws and a criminal justice system that often determine sentencing and corrections of offenders. In policing, interventions carried out and evaluated at the national level might include regional task forces, multia-gency/multijurisdictional information-sharing agreements, or other efforts by federal (i.e., national) law enforcement and homeland security agencies to pro-tect the nation at large. We discuss these strategies in Chapter 6.

Specificity of the prevention mechanism (*y*-axis)

In addition to target type, tactics and strategies can also be described by the specificity, focus, or the extent to which their prevention mechanisms are tai-lored. This specificity can range from very general to highly focused, as indi-cated by the *y*-axis of Figure 3.1. Characterizing crime prevention tactics by their degree of specificity is common and has been discussed by a number of scholars (e.g., Erickson and Gibbs 1975; Sherman and Berk 1984; Stafford and Warr 1993; Weisburd and Eck 2004). Theoretically, this axis should be viewed as a continuum since many tactics share both general and specific deterrence goals (see Sherman 1990) and divisions can be murky. But for simplicity, we characterize studies as "general" or "focused," noting that the level of specificity of an intervention is an empirical matter.

For example, tactics that are more general in their prevention mechanisms include increasing patrol presence in a neighborhood (see, e.g., Kelling, Pate, Dieckman et al. 1974), zero tolerance arrest policies and crackdown approaches that are not specifically focused (see, e.g., Reiss 1985; Smith 2001), or DARE programs given to all seventh-grade students irrespective of their individual drug use (see, e.g., Rosenbaum, Flewelling, Bailey et al. 1994). These types of interventions are based on more general notions of deterrence and prevention, even if they are focused on particular people or places.

Crime prevention interventions become more focused or specific when they are applied to specific types of problems or involve more tailored prevention tactics. These interventions might involve the coordination of multiple agen-cies that handle different aspects of a particular problem and target specific mechanisms that produce crime. Using nuisance abatement laws to reduce drug dealing on a street block (see, e.g., Mazerolle et al. 2000a), employing the "pulling levers" approach, which involves a combination of specific deterrence and prevention interventions, to target violent gangs (see Braga et al. 2001; Braga, Pierce, McDevitt et al. 2008; McGarrell, Chermak, Wilson et al. 2006), or targeting identified risk factors for juvenile crime (see, e.g., Weisburd, Telep, Hinkle et al. 2010), are all examples of more tailored, specific interventions.

To clarify further, we defined specificity to mean the specificity of the intervention mechanism rather than the specificity of the target. For example, some hot spot policing interventions might be considered "general" in nature despite their focus on a specific place, especially if police are simply increasing patrol presence at hot spots and not carrying out a special operation or problem-solving scheme to reduce a certain type of crime.

Level of reactivity or proactivity of an intervention (z-axis)

Finally, policing interventions can also be described by how reactive or proactive they are, as shown in the z-axis of Figure 3.1. We categorize interventions along this dimension by examining both the timing with which a program is implemented relative to a criminal event and also the time horizon for the program's intended effects (e.g., long versus short term). Interventions that "strengthen the reaction" of the police and target the crime after or while it is occurring are in the reactive realm of this scale. Often these are considered "traditional" approaches to policing and include mainstays such as rapid response to calls for service, reactive arrests, and follow-up investigations. Examples include the use of mandatory arrests for domestic violence (see Sherman and Berk 1984), investigation of repeat offenders (see Martin and Sherman 1986), second responder programs for family abuse (Davis, Weisburd, and Taylor 2008), and even zero-tolerance arrest schemes (arrests for misdemeanor offenses) when such efforts are only reducing the discretion to arrest across a city. We also include random "preventive" beat patrol (whether in a vehicle or on foot) in this categorization (see Kelling et al. 1974), since assigning an officer to a beat has the intention of deterrence but is done primarily to ensure that all areas are covered for quick response to calls for service.

Proactive to highly proactive interventions are those that use some form of anticipation or analysis of previous incidents, situational factors, and/or environmental or personal characteristics to prevent crimes before they occur. Proactive strategies like crackdowns at high-crime areas, for instance, are intended to reduce crime hot spots and the likelihood of future crimes at those places (see, e.g., Lawton, Taylor, and Luongo 2005; Sherman and Weisburd 1995). However, proactive strategies, while future-thinking, are often immediate and short-lived. *Highly* proactive strategies, in contrast, focus on early risk factors and long-term prevention. Such programs include gang resistance education programs (see, e.g., Esbensen 2002), drug resistance programs (e.g., DARE), some problem-oriented policing interventions (see, e.g., Braga, Weisburd, Waring et al. 1999; Mazerolle et al. 2000a; Mazerolle, Ready, Terrill et al. 2000b), and after-school programs for juveniles. It is important to note that while the terms "highly" and "proactive" may seem more positive than "traditional" and "reactive," this does not mean that research shows the former approaches work better than the latter. Indeed, some highly proactive approaches have been found to be ineffective (like DARE). Additionally, we could define many proactive strategies as reacting to an existing problem. But we distinguish them in the Matrix because their goal is anticipating and preventing future crimes, often based on analysis of prior crime patterns.

Overall, given past literature and our studies, we believe these three dimensions of the Matrix represent the most common ways that interventions in policing (and crime prevention more generally) can be described. To then map the research evidence into the Matrix so that we can use it, we look at each intervention evaluated, and describe it along our three axes. For example, Figure 3.2 illustrates the mapping of three interventions. The dot in Figure 3.2 denoted by "A" indicates an intervention that focuses on individuals, is general (not focused) and highly proactive. This could be a drug abuse resistance education program (e.g., DARE), for example. The dot labeled "B" might be a tactic that focuses on a street corner (a micro place) and is proactive but general in nature—perhaps a general hot spot patrol tactic. The dot labeled "C," in contrast, might be an intervention that is implemented at the neighborhood level, but is proactive and highly focused. This could be a community-oriented or partnership-based approach such as Project Safe Neighborhoods, which tries to

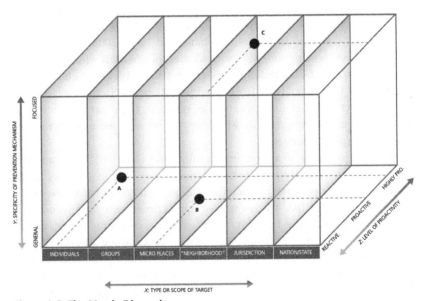

Figure 3.2 The Matrix Dimensions

reduce violent crime through these partnerships (see, e.g., Bynum, Grommon, and McCluskey 2014). Notice how each intervention is described by the inter-section of one of the three common dimensions of police crime control activity.

Now, imagine doing this for *all* the higher-quality studies of police crime control interventions. Mapping the interventions will reveal which specific intersecting dimensions appear to have clusters of effective interventions attracted to it. In this way, we can then understand more generally the char-acteristics of interventions that have a greater chance of working. We describe this process now.

Selecting Interventions for the Matrix

To populate the Matrix, the next step was to make decisions about which research would be included in the Matrix, and where each study would be placed. As discussed in Chapter 2, this question of "which evidence" ultimately raises questions about research methodology and whether studies using weaker designs should be excluded. We felt that only including randomized controlled experiments would be overly restrictive from the perspective of police officers who may use the Matrix, not to mention there are very good quasi-experimental and statistical analyses of interventions that provide confident results. At the same time, it was important to be careful not to include research that used weaker designs in which we are not confident about their results. Thus, given the amount of policing research available, we chose to populate our Matrix with: (i) studies of interventions that were primarily conducted or led by police and that focused on controlling crime and disorder; (ii) studies that contained measures of crime or disorder as outcomes; and (iii) studies of at least moderate-to-high methodological quality.

Regarding the first criterion, the Matrix does not include studies in which the police only provided consultation or played a relatively minor role in a program's execution (see, e.g., Rosenbaum, Lewis, and Grant 1986). Given that our goal was for this Matrix to be useful for law enforcement practitio-ners, we narrowed our scope of research to those studies in which police offi-cers played at least a moderate role. Of course, this does not mean that other research evidence—most importantly, on the nature of crime, offending, and victimization—should not be known to law enforcement. But given that practi-cally we could not cover all of this research, we made this choice.

Regarding our second criterion, we include studies in the Matrix that have some measure of crime or disorder as an outcome. For example, we do not include studies that measure fear of crime. Of course, we do not think fear of crime is unimportant. However, we chose to include only interventions that had some type of crime, disorder, or victimization measure in order to gener-ate a Matrix that could be most useful for police in reducing crime. We also did not wish to mix outcomes that could be contradictory. For example, some interventions may reduce people's fear of crime (such as a harsh crackdown on offenders or some community policing strategies), but they do not reduce crime. For purposes of this discussion, we maintain our focus on translation of crime control research.

Finally, we restrict the Matrix to studies that are at least moderately rigorous in terms of scientific methodology. Thus, while we include randomized controlled experiments in the Matrix, we also have higher-quality quasi-experiments as we described in Chapter 2. These quasi-experimental studies had to have a comparison group that was the same type of unit as the intervention group (e.g., a police beat if the target area is a police beat). Additionally, the study had to meet at least one of the following criteria: (i) the comparison group was well matched; (ii) there was some use of multivariate controls; or (iii) the study used time series analysis. We further classify studies in the Matrix as "very rigorous," "rigorous," or "moderately rigorous" based on the specifics of their designs. Very rigorous studies are randomized experiments, while those coded as rigorous generally correspond to quasi-experiments that have multiple treatment and comparison units that are well matched or balanced through statistical controls. Studies coded as moderately rigorous often involve comparisons of one treatment area and one comparison area or otherwise involve treatment and comparison groups that are not as well matched.[3]

Some might critique our inclusion of quasi-experimental research in the Matrix. Our decision to include studies of "moderate" methodological rigor reflects a practical mentality that bears on the discussion in Chapter 2 as to "which evidence" police should consider in their efforts to be more evidence based. The goal of the Matrix is to serve as a translation tool that enables police to use scientific evidence to guide practice. While compromising on rigor is certainly not a value of science, the general knowledge gleaned from moderately rigorous studies may be valuable to police in generating tactics of at least reasonable or "promising" effect. However, an important benefit of the Matrix is its ability to be completely transparent about the methodological rigor of each study, and thus it cautions practitioners about the believability of any single study.[4]

Mapping the Evidence Base into the Matrix

Once we decided on which evidence to include in our translation tool, it was time to code each study, map the evidence into the tool, and build the online

---

[3] Our methods scale is similar (although not exactly the same) to that used by Sherman et al. (1997; 2002) with our very rigorous, rigorous, and moderately rigorous categories corresponding roughly to their Scientific Methods Scores (SMS) of 5, 4, and 3, respectively.

[4] Researchers who want a fuller explanation of our methodological choices might consider reading Lum et al. (2011b).

content. Plotting all policing evaluation studies into the Matrix reveals clusters of studies at intersecting strategic dimensions. This helps us better understand: (i) the types of interventions that have been studied most extensively (and, conversely, the areas where evaluation research has been lacking); and (ii) the characteristics of interventions that have been the most and least successful in reducing crime. Police can also compare their current strategies to this map of the evidence base to quickly assess the promise of their strategies and identify research that is relevant to their approaches.

To map our selected studies, we coded them for the three dimensions or characteristics of the intervention as described above, the type of research design used, and outcomes measured and results. Each study is initially coded separately by two of the three senior members of the Matrix team (Lum, Koper, and Telep). If two reviewers do not code the study consistently, the remaining team member also codes the study, followed by group discussion to reach consensus.[5] This system of multiple reviewers is especially useful to ensure agreement on whether a study meets at least the "moderate" level of methodological rigor that we defined for the Matrix. At the outset of developing the Matrix in 2009, we conducted a major systematic review and search of all evaluations of police crime control interventions, examining library databases, prior research reviews, websites of professional and governmental organizations, and also reaching out to police evaluators so that unpublished or non-academic ("gray literature") materials would also be captured in our review. This intensive process is repeated each year to ensure the Matrix is up-to-date on all available research that has met our criteria. In 2009, we initially located ninety-seven published studies that met the methodological and substantive criteria for inclusion. By 2016, a total of 146 studies were in the Matrix.

Our coding of each study allows us to determine where in the Matrix to place the study. However, we also wanted a quick way to show the results of every study so that when looking at a cluster of entries in a particular area of the Matrix, one could quickly discern the findings of those studies. We thus symbolize the findings of each study using the following key:

- *Significant effects (black dot)*—indicates that the intervention led to a statistically significant effect in reducing crime or criminality.

o *Nonsignificant effect (white dot)*—indicates the intervention did not lead to any statistically significant effect. Although some might interpret this to mean that the intervention "did not work," Weisburd, Lum, and Yang (2003a) point out that such terminology is inaccurate. Statistical insignificance only states that for this particular study we cannot conclude that the null hypothesis of "no difference" is false.

---

[5] When reviewing studies that have been reviewed and rated for methodology by others (e.g., Sherman et al. 1997; 2002), we conduct our own new review of each study using this coding system.

- *Mixed effects (gray dot)*—indicates there were multiple primary outcomes in the study, at least one of which showed positive effects and one of which showed nonsignificant or backfire effects. Mixed effects might also include studies in which outcomes were only positive for a certain subgroup of targeted offenders or places. Although many studies have both significant and nonsignificant findings, we code a study as having mixed results only when the authors emphasized the mixed nature of the findings. Examples might include arrest for domestic violence deterring employed but not unemployed suspects (see Sherman, Schmidt, Rogan et al. 1992); restorative justice reducing recidivism for violent crime but not property crime (see Sherman, Strang, and Woods 2000); or crack house raids reducing crime but only for a twelve-day period (see Sherman and Rogan 1995).

▼ *Statistically significant backfire effect (upside-down triangle)*[6]—indicates the outcome of the study was statistically significant, but in the opposite direction of the hypothesis. This would be considered a "harmful" intervention (see Weisburd, Lum, and Petrosino 2001), where an intervention significantly increased offending in some individuals or crime in some areas.

Once this coding is completed, each evaluation is then added into the Matrix.[7] Figure 3.3 illustrates this effort, and readers can access the most updated Matrix at any given time.[8]

Mapping the studies in this way immediately allows the viewer to obtain five pieces of information about an intervention in a single visualization. The first four come from the single symbol itself: the intervention's target, specificity, proactivity, and the results of an evaluation of this intervention's effectiveness. However, the Matrix is interesting not simply because of its display of single studies or these four characteristics. The fifth piece of information results from the relative position of dots to each other, resulting in clusters of evaluated interventions at intersecting dimensions. Thus, one can see whether an intervention is surrounded primarily by black dots (other interventions showing effectiveness) or by white or gray dots (other interventions not necessarily showing effectiveness). The one item not shown is the methodological rigor of the study, but this can be easily seen by clicking on a study in the Matrix.

The online interface of the Matrix also facilitates viewing the quality of categories of interventions and also the specific nature of each intervention. For example, to examine the specific details of all of the studies in the "Individuals" portion or "slab" of the Matrix, users can click into the Individuals slab[9] and

---

[6] This symbol appears red in color on the website.

[7] This visual mapping of the Matrix is not meant to be precise; dots are spread out only to aid with visual presentation and are not statements about the relative proactivity or specificity of an intervention.

[8] At http://cebcp.org/evidence-based-policing/the-matrix/.

[9] See http://cebcp.org/evidence-based-policing/the-matrix/individuals/.

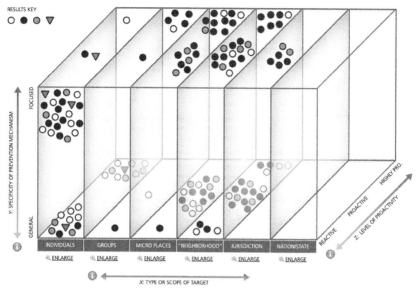

Figure 3.3 The Evidence-Based Policing Matrix with Studies Included
Updated annually at http://cebcp.org/evidence-based-policing/the-matrix/.

view all of the interventions that have been evaluated that focus on individuals (see Figure 3.4, which shows only a portion of the full screen of the Individuals slab of the Matrix). This allows law enforcement officials and other users to quickly understand the field of evidence focused on individuals, see the results according to methodological rigor and findings easily, and obtain short practitioner-focused summaries of these individual-based interventions (including their findings).

Further, a detailed and structured summary of each study (also developed through a rigorous process involving the Matrix team) can be accessed by either clicking on a dot in the overall Matrix illustration in Figure 3.3 or by selecting the authors of a study within a Matrix slab like Figure 3.4. Take, for example, a study by Mazerolle et al. (2000a) on the use of civil remedies to control drug problems in Oakland, California. The information provided for this study is included in Box 3.1[10] and includes details about the study reference, its location in the Matrix, the police practice or intervention examined, the method used in this evaluation, and the results of the study. Further, given that evidence-based policing is not simply about making a decision to deploy an intervention based on the findings of a single study, each study description has links (where applicable) to the broader literature on this issue, other similar studies in the Matrix and, at the bottom of the page, other reviews about this subject.

---

[10] See also http://cebcp.org/evidence-based-policing/the-matrix/micro-places/micro-places-mazerolle-price-et-al-2000/.

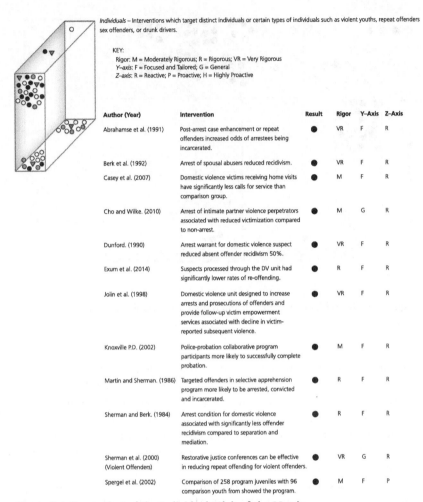

Individuals – Interventions which target distinct individuals or certain types of individuals such as violent youths, repeat offenders sex offenders, or drunk drivers.

KEY:
Rigor: M = Moderately Rigorous; R = Rigorous; VR = Very Rigorous
Y–axis: F = Focused and Tailored; G = General
Z–axis: R = Reactive; P = Proactive; H = Highly Proactive

Author (Year)	Intervention	Result	Rigor	Y–Axis	Z–Axis
Abrahamse et al. (1991)	Post-arrest case enhancement or repeat offenders increased odds of arrestees being incarcerated.	●	VR	F	R
Berk et al. (1992)	Arrest of spousal abusers reduced recidivism.	●	VR	F	R
Casey et al. (2007)	Domestic violence victims receiving home visits have significantly less calls for service than comparison group.	●	M	F	R
Cho and Wilke. (2010)	Arrest of intimate partner violence perpetrators associated with reduced victimization compared to non-arrest.	●	M	G	R
Dunford. (1990)	Arrest warrant for domestic violence suspect reduced absent offender recidivism 50%.	●	VR	F	R
Exum et al. (2014)	Suspects processed through the DV unit had significantly lower rates of re-offending.	●	R	F	R
Jolin et al. (1998)	Domestic violence unit designed to increase arrests and prosecutions of offenders and provide follow-up victim empowerment services associated with decline in victim-reported subsequent violence.	●	VR	F	R
Knoxville P.D. (2002)	Police-probation collaborative program participants more likely to successfully complete probation.	●	M	F	R
Martin and Sherman. (1986)	Targeted offenders in selective apprehension program more likely to be arrested, convicted and incarcerated.	●	R	F	R
Sherman and Berk. (1984)	Arrest condition for domestic violence associated with significantly less offender recidivism compared to separation and mediation.	●	R	F	R
Sherman et al. (2000) (Violent Offenders)	Restorative justice conferences can be effective in reducing repeat offending for violent offenders.	●	VR	G	R
Spergel et al. (2002)	Comparison of 258 program juveniles with 96 comparison youth from showed the program.	●	M	F	P

Figure 3.4 Screenshot of the Individuals Slab of the Matrix

What the Matrix Tells Us

The Matrix is meant to be a translation tool. By visually mapping research and also by creating freely accessible information about that research through the Matrix interface, officers can more easily access and understand the field of knowledge than by reading individual research articles or even systematic reviews. But more importantly, mapping the totality of the research reveals certain generalizations that might be useful for police in developing their own tactics for their jurisdictions.

Take, for instance, the cluster of studies located in the "Individuals" slab of the Matrix. These groupings show us that policing interventions that focus on individuals often result in mixed, nonsignificant, and sometimes backfiring results. The Matrix also makes it clear that many of these individual-based

Box 3.1 Information Provided in the Matrix for Each Study

Study reference

Mazerolle, Lorraine G., James F. Price, and Jan Roehl. 2000a. "Civil Remedies and Drug Control: A Randomized Field Trial in Oakland, CA." *Evaluation Review* 24: 212–41.

Location in the Matrix; Methodological rigor; outcome

Micro places, Focused, Highly Proactive; Very Rigorous; Effective.

What police practice or strategy was examined?

The Oakland Police Department created the Beat Health Unit, a "civil remedy" to reduce drug and disorder problems across the five beats in the city. Civil remedies seek to reduce signs of physical and social incivilities in the hope that cleaned-up places will break the cycle of neighborhood decline and decrease victimization, fear of crime, and alienation. The Beat Health officers worked in conjunction with municipal partners to open cases against specific places which had generated high levels of emergency calls, narcotics arrests or special requests from community members. Police would communicate landlords' rights and tenants' responsibilities, provide ideas for simple crime prevention measures, and gain the citizens' confidence that the police are supporting them in their efforts to clean up the problem location.

How was the intervention evaluated?

The study used a randomized experiment examining the impact of the intervention on calls for service in spatially distinct street blocks. One hundred study sites were randomly assigned to be experimental (receiving a Beat Health team of a police officer and a police service technician) or control (receiving "business-as-usual" patrol). All eligible problem sites referred to the Beat Health Unit over a two-month period were included in the study. Calls for service were examined during the twelve months prior to the start of the experiment and during the twelve-month period following the 5.5-month intervention period.

What were the key findings?

The average number of drug call incidents per treatment sites decreased 7%, while the control group experienced an average *increase* in drug calls for service of 54.7%. Within the treatment blocks, residential sites experienced greater decreases in drug call incidents than commercial sites (13.2% versus 45.2%, respectively). The control commercial properties fared even worse, with a 1,000% increase in the number of drug calls for service incidents from before the intervention period to after the intervention period (from 2.57 mean calls to 36.14 mean calls).

What were the implications for law enforcement?

The authors suggest that civil remedies could become an important intervention within the police problem-solver's toolbox, particularly if attention is paid to maintaining the crime control gains and implementing tactics to handle possible spatial displacement of crime problems.

Where can I find more information about this intervention, similar types of intervention or related studies (links)?

All studies in the matrix on micro places.
Using Civil Actions against Property to Control Crime Problems.
Information on nuisance abatement.
Street-Level Drug Law Enforcement: A Meta-Analytic Review.
Civil Remedies and Crime Prevention: An Introduction (POP Guide).

---

strategies are reactive—a quality that has been recognized by both police practitioners and researchers as being less effective in fighting crime. Further, the ones that are proactive do not seem to yield positive outcomes (DARE is one example). Although some studies in this slab point to beneficial results (particularly when interventions are more focused), this particular region of the Matrix generally suggests that targeting individuals may be less effective than focusing on other types of targets. This generalization is important given that many of the mainstays of police activity fall into these areas of the Matrix, including reactive arrests, responding quickly to 911 calls, case-by-case investigations, and offender targeting. In an empirical analysis of police activity, Veigas and Lum (2013) found that nearly half of documented interventions in the agency they examined (both regular and special) fell into the "Individuals" slab, and almost all, save a few, were reactive in nature. But the Matrix, and also previous reviews, indicate that realms of effective interventions do not target individuals in reactive or general manners.

To explore this further, Table 3.1 shows the breakdown of the 146 studies currently in the Matrix by dimension, outcome, and methodological rigor. Most evaluation studies in policing that focus on crime control and prevention evaluate interventions that target individuals (32.2%), neighborhoods (31.5%), or micro places (24.7%). Slightly more than half of the studies (56.8%) examined focused interventions, and almost three-quarters (72.6%) evaluated interventions that were at least moderately proactive. These patterns within the evaluation studies are not coincidental, but reflect the choices of researchers and innovative police practitioners who have advanced evaluation research in policing. They also do not reflect the reality of strategies deployed in policing, which we know are remarkably individual-based, reactive, and general in nature. Unfortunately, this means that we often have gaps in the evidence base about current and frequently used policing practices. An excellent example is police investigations, for which we have very little evaluation knowledge in terms of their crime control effects (see Braga, Flynn, Kelling et al. 2011).

Table 3.1 Characteristics of Matrix Studies (*n* = 146)

	n	%		*n*	%
x-axis (Target)			**Outcome**		
Individuals	47	32.2	Mixed results	27	18.5
Groups	10	6.8	Nonsignificant results	43	29.5
Micro places	36	24.7	Significant backfire	4	2.7
Neighborhoods	46	31.5	Significant success	72	49.3
Jurisdictions	7	4.8	Total	146	100.0
Total	146	100.0			
y-axis (Specificity)			**Methodological rigor**		
General	63	43.2	Moderately rigorous	76	52.1
Focused	83	56.8	Rigorous	19	13.0
Total	146	100.0	Randomized experiment	51	34.9
			Total	146	100.0
z-axis (Proactivity)					
Mostly reactive	40	27.4			
Proactive	66	45.2			
Highly proactive	40	27.4			
Total	146	100.0			

Table 3.1 also indicates that the majority of studies included in the Matrix are of moderate methodological rigor, while a little over one-third are randomized controlled experiments. Additionally, almost half of the studies in the Matrix show a significant positive result for the intervention evaluated. However, as we detailed in Chapter 2, studies with less rigorous research designs tend to show more positive results in policing studies; at the same time, their results may also be less convincing. In other words, the dominance of moderately rigorous and also successful studies in the Matrix deserves some attention so that statistically significant findings are not overemphasized.

The cross-tabulation in Table 3.2 shows the distribution of Matrix studies by method (moderately rigorous, rigorous, or very rigorous) and whether the study showed that an intervention led to a statistically significant successful outcome. A significant relationship emerges, indicating that as studies become more methodologically rigorous, they are *less* likely to show a clear significant success. This provides specific and updated support from the policing literature for Weisburd et al.'s (2001) finding that as studies increase in methodological rigor, they are less likely to find positive results.

This tendency becomes even more visually obvious when comparing mappings of the seventy-six moderately rigorous studies to mappings of the seventy rigorous and very rigorous quasi-experimental and experimental designs.

Table 3.2 Cross-Tabulation of Level of Rigor versus Study Results

	Level of Methodological Rigor		
Study Results	Moderately Rigorous	Rigorous	Very Rigorous
Significant success	49 (64.5%)	8 (42.1%)	15 (29.4%)
Any other result	27 (35.5%)	11 (57.9%)	36 (70.6%)

$\chi^2 = 15.465; p < .000.$

Table 3.3 Cross-Tabulations of Matrix Axes versus Study Results

	x-axis		y-axis		z-axis	
	Person-Based	Place-Based	General	Focused	Reactive	Proactive
Sig. Success	21	47	22	50	16	56
	(36.2%)	(57.3%)	(34.9%)	(60.2%)	(40.0%)	(52.8%)
Any Other Result	37	35	41	33	24	50
	(63.8%)	(42.7%)	(65.1%)	(39.8%)	(60.0%)	(47.2%)
ColumnTotal	58	82	63	83	40	106
	(100%)	(100%)	(100%)	(100%)	(100%)	(100%)
χ^2	$\chi^2 = 6.061\ (p = .017)$		$\chi^2 = 9.186\ (p = .003)$		$\chi^2 = 1.913\ (p = .115)$	

These are shown, respectively, as images (A) and (B) in Figure 3.5. Notice that the number of studies that showed statistically significant positive outcomes drops substantially (especially in the "Neighborhood" slab) when a stronger methodological cut-off point is employed. Also visually striking is that more interventions targeting individuals appear in Figure 3.5B. This indicates that we know with fairly definite certainty that individual-level, reactive strategies in policing do not necessarily produce clearly positive results.

But what might be said of intersecting dimensions and the likelihood that studies of a certain method, outcome, or type might fall into them? In Table 3.3, we present cross-tabulations examining the relationship between each of our three dimensions with study results. We have dichotomized each variable to better display the overall trends in our data. For the x-axis, we collapsed the individual and group categories into one "person-based" category and combined the micro place and neighborhood categories into one "place-based" category. (The seven jurisdiction-level studies were excluded from this analysis.) For results, we again examine whether a study resulted in a statistically significant success or not.

The cross-tabulation shows a significant difference in results between the two x-axis general categories represented in the Matrix—person- versus place-based. More than half (57.3%) of place-based studies showed significant crime and

A. Quasi–experiments of moderate quality

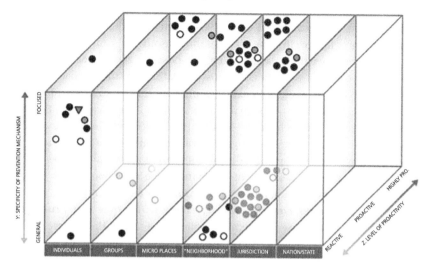

B. Studies using stronger quasi and also randomized experimentation

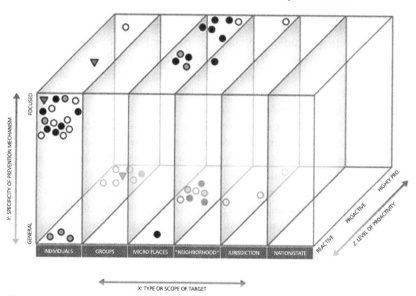

Figure 3.5 Comparisons of Matrix Studies Using Moderate and Strong Methods

disorder reductions in contrast to 36.2% of person-based interventions, a relative difference of 58% ($\chi^2 = 6.061$; $p = .017$). This reinforces quantitatively our finding that realms of effectiveness are generally found in the place-based slabs of the Matrix.[11] In examining the y-axis, focused interventions are 72% more

---

[11] Removing the neighborhood-based studies, which are generally weaker methodologically, would further strengthen the basis for this generalization.

likely to find a statistically significant effect than general interventions (60.2% to 34.9%), and this finding is statistically significant (χ^2 = 9.186; p = .003). This lends support to Weisburd and Eck's (2004) contention that focused interventions are more effective in reducing crime and disorder.

Finally, we combined the proactive and highly proactive z-axis categories to compare proactive to reactive studies. The cross-tabulation shows that proactive interventions are 32% more likely to reduce crime than reactive strategies (52.8% to 40.0%; χ^2 = 1.913; p = .115), though this difference is not statistically significant.[12]

We explore the research in the Matrix more specifically in Chapters 4, 5, and 6. However, three important generalizations emerge from the totality of the studies in the Matrix, as suggested by our analysis above, and it appears that police have a greater likelihood of achieving crime reduction success if they develop their crime-fighting interventions around these principles.

Generally, officers can be more effective when they are proactive, not reactive. In the past four decades, police have shifted their interest from being primarily reactive and enforcement-oriented to being more proactive and preventative. This primarily means anticipating crime, disorder, and other problems before they happen using tools such as crime analysis, community surveys, and other sources of information. Proactivity means addressing the cause of a pattern of crime, not just responding to a single crime. Being proactive is not only the stuff of specialized problem-solving units, but is also much needed in everyday patrol. This proactivity includes a wide gamut of activities intended mostly to prevent and deter crime and recidivism, but also to build citizen and community relationships that improve police service delivery and citizen trust and confidence in police. Such activities are now well-known innovations, such as problem solving, intelligence-led policing, directed or hot spots patrol, community policing, focused deterrence strategies, and even the use of procedural or restorative justice. Police should proactively make contact with serious repeat offenders and probationers to create a deterrent effect. And since officers' noncommitted time can account for between 25% and 80% of their shift (Famega 2005; Famega, Frank, and Mazerolle 2005; Weisburd, Wooditch, Weisburd et al. 2015), there is the potential for materially reducing crime if officers use their noncommitted time to increase their presence in the community and perform crime prevention activities.

Police can be very effective if they focus on places, not just on people. We discuss this issue at length in Chapter 4 but note here that crime tends to be highly concentrated in small areas and very specific locations (like particular

---

[12] In comparison to our earlier analysis of the first 97 studies placed into the Matrix (Lum et al. 2011b), this analysis finds notable drops in the success rates of both proactive and place-based interventions, from 69% to 57% for proactive interventions and from 62% to 53% for place-based interventions (though place-based interventions still have a clear statistical superiority to person-based interventions). These changes may be due in part to the higher share of randomized controlled trials (which are less likely to show positive results) in the current version of the Matrix.

addresses and street blocks) within a given jurisdiction (see, e.g., Sherman et al. 1989a; Weisburd, Bushway Lum et al. 2004), making crime more predictable by places than by persons (Eck and Spelman 1998; Weisburd 2008). Through their features and social characteristics, places play a key role in creating (or restricting) criminal opportunities, and problem locations can generate very high numbers of offenses over time. Hence, targeting criminal opportunities at a high-crime location can potentially affect the behavior of many offenders and would-be offenders connected to that place and likely have a much greater effect on crime (in most instances) than solving any one criminal case or arresting an individual offender. Consistent with this logic, police interventions focusing various patrol, enforcement, and problem-oriented prevention efforts on high-risk areas and micro locations generally have good success rates. Interventions targeting micro places appear to be particularly effective based on the highest-quality evidence.

Officers are more effective when they tailor their actions to identifiable problems. Effective interventions are often ones that are tailored to the specific problems and needs of people or places that are the subjects of intervention. Such measures often fall within the broad framework of problem-oriented policing. Problem solving can take many forms, perhaps the most famous being the problem-solving model SARA (scanning, analysis, response, assessment) developed by Eck and Spelman (1987) based on ideas from Herman Goldstein's book, *Problem-Oriented Policing*. The problem-oriented philosophy, which we will discuss at various points throughout the book, encourages police to address underlying conditions and problems that contribute to crime in a community and to consider both enforcement and preventive (i.e., nonenforcement) strategies, as appropriate. This approach also lends itself to the development of multifaceted strategies for use in collaborations with government entities and community stakeholders (e.g., residents, businesses, and community groups). In practice, however, the potential of a problem-solving approach is often not realized, as police strategies tend to be general and procedures or offender oriented rather than tailored and problem oriented.

In sum, the results derived from the Matrix demonstrate quantitatively the relevance of the clustering of studies in the Matrix we identified in Figure 3.3. Proactive, focused, place-based interventions, and also those that are more tailored, are more likely to reduce crime and disorder than strategies concentrating on individuals, or those that are reactive and/or general in nature. Of course, there are important qualifiers. Not all strategies that reflect these generalizations will be effective; some might even backfire. Some strategies that reduce crime might also cause a noxious reaction from communities or be implemented in ways that are unconstitutional. There may not be enough resources to implement interventions, or political forces may inhibit change. We will discuss all of these challenges in Part Three of this book. However, it is important to drive the point home that research *has* provided an important evidence base for police crime control efforts, as summarized here and discussed throughout the rest of this book.

Translating Research into Practice

Evidence-based policing involves generating the evidence, synthesizing it, and translating and using it. More generally, evidence-based policing encompasses a set of values that moderates the relationship between science and research on the one hand, and police practice on the other. Our goal in this first part of this book is to leave the reader with a stronger understanding and appreciation of the nuances of the research evidence behind evidence-based policing. In other words "being more evidence-based" as a police agency is not simply about learning from another agency that something worked, or even seeing positive effects of a program in one's own agency. It also isn't about learning about the results of a single study, no matter how important the author or rigorous the method, and then blindly implementing that intervention in one's own agency. Rather, being skilled at evidence-based policing requires an appreciation of both the strengths and weaknesses of science, the compromises that might have to be made to translate research, and the important efforts that others have made to synthesize and make sense of a large body of research. It also involves being able to identify research evidence and science that are not useful to policing, or where we still have gaps in our knowledge.

There are many critiques of the evidence as it currently stands, and of efforts like the Matrix to translate it. We organized the research in this way because of our interest in developing a translation tool that would make the field of police evaluation research meaningful to practitioners. Hence, we did not restrict ourselves to selecting only those studies that involved randomized controlled experiments, although we do include in our tool the ability to examine only those studies that use more highly rigorous evaluation methods. Some in both practice and scholarship could criticize this, arguing (and rightfully so) that we should not be as confident in moderately rigorous studies given the weak methods by which their conclusions were drawn. We also recognize criticisms of "vote counting" in research syntheses (e.g., Wilson 2001) and do not suggest that a count of studies in a particular area of the Matrix provides definitive conclusions about "what works" in policing. Rather, this approach allows us to develop some initial generalizations about the state of policing research and the types of strategies that appear most effective. Our online approach also provides practitioner-friendly, digestible, and short summaries of research with relevant links.

And of course, as we discussed in Chapter 1, crime control interventions are not the only things that police care about. Police are concerned with many other things, from their own legitimacy and relationship with the community and political leaders to resources, technology, and job satisfaction. All of these areas have been researched in some way or another, and the fact that we have chosen to devote our time to develop and sustain this Matrix does not mean that other research is less valuable. They all represent the "evidence base" of policing and we encourage others to develop similar tools for other bases of evidence.

At the same time, we believe the Matrix and its online presence is innovative. It presents the police crime prevention research in a way that is more accessible and translatable for both researchers and practitioners. Through this generalization, the results of our Matrix, as well as the tool itself, have numerous implications for research and practice that we will explore throughout the rest of the book. Most obviously, research evidence can be used to guide police agencies in their assessment, selection, or creation of crime prevention strategies. Evidence could also be used to redirect officers to different activities during their everyday patrol. We discuss these possibilities by examining the research in more detail in Chapters 4, 5, and 6. In Chapter 11, we also present a tool called *The Playbook*, which essentially converts research findings from the Matrix and beyond into easy-to-follow ideas and suggestions ("plays") that can be implemented by patrol officers. The Matrix could also be used for training, supervision, promotion, and leadership purposes. An agency that may wish to transition its first- and second-line supervisors toward a more evidence-based approach might incorporate the Matrix into its promotions process. These strategic and leadership uses of the Matrix are explored in Chapters 10 and 14.

In addition, the Matrix can provide guidance to practitioners, researchers, and funders of research as to what types of evaluations are still needed in policing. Organizing research enables us to see where researchers have amassed the most and the highest-quality evidence in terms of programmatic dimensions that are meaningful to practitioners. For example, the policing of gangs is a high-priority issue for police, yet very little strong evaluation research exists in the "Groups" slab of the Matrix to meet the demand for evaluated gang programs. Police technology is another example of a high-priority, less-researched area, an issue we discuss in Chapter 7. Additionally, organizational tools like the Matrix can also be used as a "common ground" for conversations between researchers, police practitioners, and funding agencies when collaborating to evaluate, study, and ultimately reduce crime.

Of course, the Matrix is far from being the cure-all to institutionalizing scientific research and evidence into police practice. But efforts like this may represent the "next step" in translating scientific evidence into practice and institutionalizing evidence-based policing that go beyond systematic reviews. Incorporating evidence into practice requires not only building upon the already existing infrastructure for evidence-based approaches, but also creating a stronger capacity in agencies to implement effective interventions and to maintain the practice of evidence-based policing. Practical changes must occur within police agencies for evidence-based policing to be used, including drastically increasing the number and skill sets of crime analysts and more freely interacting with academic and evaluation researchers. At the same time, researchers can perhaps facilitate these changes through scientific assessment and translation of the sort that we have presented here.

Evidence-Based Approaches to Policing

4

PLACE-BASED APPROACHES AND HOT SPOTS POLICING

As discussed in Part One, the promises and opportunities of evidence-based policing are also met with many challenges. Even if evidence-based policing seems reasonable or logical, implementing research findings into practice can be difficult for police agencies, or any other organization with long-standing histories, traditions, and cultures. Here in Part Two, we explore specific areas of evidence for various policing practices in detail, especially focusing on the "Individual," "Micro-place," and "Neighborhood" portions (or "slabs") of the Matrix. Many of these examples have been implemented in the course of evaluations conducted collaboratively by researchers and police agencies. Some have been developed and sustained by police departments irrespective of evaluation. All give us ideas about what is possible in both evaluating law enforcement activities and converting research into action.

In this chapter, we begin with examples of evidence-based crime control interventions that target places with high levels of crime, especially those that fall in the "Micro place" slab of the Matrix. Police and researchers have long recognized that crime is concentrated in particular neighborhoods and administrative areas within a locality, and law enforcement agencies have focused more of their attention on these areas. However, recent advancements in information technology, geographic information systems, and environmental and place-based criminology have enabled police and analysts to identify and focus more precisely on particular locations that generate the most crime. This has given rise to what is referred to as "hot spots" policing—i.e., policing focused on small and specific geographic locations where crime is concentrated.

As shown in Chapter 3, the totality of the research in the Matrix indicates that place-based interventions targeting crime hot spots have been successful in reducing crime. Indeed, hot spots policing has been one of the most

significant policing innovations of recent decades, and it is an area of policing research that has often been translated into practice (Lum and Fyfe 2015;
Wellford and Lum 2014). Police agencies now commonly use crime mapping
to identify hot spots (Burch 2012; Reaves 2010; Weisburd and Lum 2005), and
they cite hot spots policing as a leading approach to the reduction of violence and other crime problems (Police Executive Research Forum 2007; 2008).
There is also substantial consensus among researchers that hot spots policing is effective in reducing crime and disorder, particularly when police apply
problem-solving approaches to addressing problems at these locations (Braga
et al. 2012; Lum, Koper, and Telep 2011b; National Research Council 2004;
Sherman and Eck 2002; Taylor, Koper, and Woods 2011a; Telep and Weisburd
2012; Weisburd 2008; Weisburd, Groff, and Yang 2012).

At the same time, there are also significant limits to the use and institutionalization of hot spots policing research in practice. The promises and challenges
of translating hot spot research into policing practice are the subjects of this
chapter. We highlight the evidence on hot spots policing and discuss ways that
police can (and do) incorporate knowledge about hot spots policing into their
everyday operations. We particularly focus on the use of preventive patrol and
problem-solving to manage hot spots. In the process, we discuss some of the
limitations to hot spots policing as practiced and offer suggestions and illustrations for more effective use and institutionalization of micro-place policing
strategies.

Crime Hot Spots and the Foundations
of Place-Based Policing

In its most basic form, hot spots policing entails the allocation of police
resources to places where crime concentrates. The term itself is not connected
to any particular intervention that police might carry out at a hot spot. This is
an important point, as critics of evidence-based policing sometimes equate hot
spots policing with zero tolerance policing, the use of stop-question-and-frisk,
or crackdowns. While such enforcement-oriented tactics have been used at hot
spots, hot spots policing encompasses a much wider variety of police strategies
and tactics that might be implemented at crime concentrations, including many
that are not enforcement oriented. Further, as noted by Eck (2005), there is no
universally accepted definition of the term "hot spot." Analysts and researchers
have used a number of methods to identify locations of crime concentration
that vary considerably in size and crime risk. In practice, police may describe
hot spots as high-crime places ranging from a single address or street segment to
a group of adjacent streets and intersections, or even a neighborhood or patrol
beat. However, researchers and police have increasingly used the term to focus
on much more specific places such as particular addresses, intersections, street
blocks, and clusters of blocks that have the highest risk for crime.

The evidence-base for hot spots policing does not arise only from evaluation research on the effectiveness of hot spots deployment. More fundamentally, the evidence-base of hot spots policing is found in environmental and place-based criminology (see descriptions by Sherman, Gartin, and Buerger 1989a; Weisburd 2002). Numerous studies have found that the majority of crime is geographically concentrated at very small locations. Indeed, approximately half of serious crime consistently tends to occur at 5% or less of a jurisdiction's addresses, intersections, and street blocks (e.g., Pierce, Spaar, and Briggs 1988; Sherman et al. 1989a; Weisburd, Bushway, Lum et al. 2004). Crime may be even more concentrated in suburban and rural areas (Gill, Wooditch, and Weisburd 2016; Hibdon 2013). Indeed, this finding is so common that Weisburd (2015) has called this phenomenon the "law of crime concentration" (see also Spelman and Eck 1989; Weisburd 2008). Further, while police agencies might sometimes describe hot spots as larger locations such as police beats, reporting areas, or even entire neighborhoods, research has found that there is often a high level of block-to-block variability and clustering of crime even within high-crime areas and neighborhoods (Sherman et al. 1989a; Weisburd et al. 2012).

The concentration of crime at these very specific places also tends to be stable over time. In a study of crime in Seattle, Weisburd et al. (2004) found that about half of crime was generated by 4–5% of the city's street segments, and this concentration remained stable over a fourteen-year period. The most problematic locations also tended to be stable over time; indeed, a mere 1% of the city's street segments consistently produced roughly 80 to 100 crime incidents per year throughout the study period (Weisburd et al. 2004, 302). Additionally, the Seattle study showed that changes in crime at chronic hot spots could have a substantial impact on a jurisdiction's overall crime rates. A 24% drop in crime in Seattle during the study period was attributable to crime drops in just 14% of the city's street segments.

Environmental and place-based criminologists have also discovered that these locations, sometimes referred to as "micro" hot spots, are often nodes for business, leisure, and/or travel activities, and they commonly have features or facilities that create criminal opportunities and facilitate offending (Eck and Weisburd 1995). In the language of routine activities theory (Clarke and Felson 1993; Cohen and Felson 1979; Felson 1987; Sherman et al. 1989a), they are places that bring together motivated offenders, suitable targets, and an absence of capable guardians. Examples include locations with bars, convenience stores, parks, bus stops or depots, apartment buildings, parking lots, shopping centers, motels or hotels, adult businesses, and the like (e.g., Block and Block 1995; Braga, Weisburd, Waring et al. 1999, 551–2; Groff and Lockwood 2014; Koper, Egge, and Lum 2015a; Sherman, Gartin, and Buerger 1989a, 45; see also Eck and Weisburd 1995). In related perspectives on crime opportunity (e.g., crime pattern theory and rational choice theory), such locations are also referred to "crime facilitators," "crime attractors," or "risky facilities" (Brantingham and Brantingham 1991; Felson 1987; Sherman et al. 1989a). In addition, hot spot locations are often characterized by high levels of social disorganization as measured by low property values and high levels of social and physical disorder (e.g., places with high levels of loitering and abandoned buildings or vehicles) (Weisburd et al. 2012). Scholars also argue that micro hot spots are critical locations for crime prevention because street segments are key behavior settings for understanding human interactions. At the street block level, people are more familiar with one another and their routines, and behavioral norms and routines are more established (Taylor 1997; 1998; Weisburd et al. 2012; Wicker 1987).

This basic research on hot spots suggests that focusing attention on these locations has the potential to make police more effective and efficient in several ways. For one, it concentrates their attention on the places where crime is most likely to occur, increasing the chances that officers can detect and prevent crime. Moreover, focusing on high-crime places is likely to be more effective than just focusing on high-crime individuals, given that crime is more concentrated by place than among persons and that places don't move (Spelman and Eck 1989; Weisburd 2008). Targeting criminal opportunities at a high-crime location can potentially affect the behavior of many offenders and would-be offenders connected to that place. In turn, targeting hot spots can have a much greater effect on crime (in most instances) than solving any one criminal case or arresting an individual offender (Lum and Nagin 2016).

Furthermore, police can arguably establish a more visible presence and generate greater perceptions of their deterrence capabilities in the small space of a hot spot than over larger areas like a patrol beat or an entire jurisdiction (e.g., Nagin 2013; Sherman and Weisburd 1995). Focusing attention on these very specific locations can also help officers to identify tangible conditions that contribute to crime and disorder at these places and to develop both prevention and enforcement interventions tailored to the particulars of these places and their problems.

Numerous studies have demonstrated the effectiveness of police interventions focused on hot spots. Nearly 60% of micro place policing studies in the Matrix have shown significant success, and an additional 22% have shown at least partial indications of success. By the same token, a recent in-depth review by Braga et al. (2012) of nineteen experimental and quasi-experimental studies of enforcement-oriented hot spot interventions—including a variety of patrol, order maintenance, crackdown, and/or problem-solving activities—found that these efforts reduced at least some form(s) of crime or disorder in twenty of twenty-five tests (80%) across these studies.[1] Importantly, in most studies that addressed the issue, there were no obvious or consistent signs that crime was displaced to nearby areas. On the contrary, studies were more likely to find

---

[1] Our compilation of hot spots policing tests in the Evidence-Based Policing Matrix is more recent than that examined by Braga, Papachristos, and Hurcau (2012) and is based on somewhat different selection criteria. Nevertheless, the inferences from the two sources are similar.

evidence that crime reduction benefits are extended to areas outside the hot spot—i.e., a phenomenon referred to as a diffusion of crime control benefits (Clarke and Weisburd 1994; Weisburd, Wyckoff, Ready et al. 2006).

The research on spatial displacement and diffusion is of particular importance for translating hot spots research into practice. A long-standing argument in police practice and culture against proactively targeting crime concentrations is that crime will just be displaced, or moved elsewhere (Weisburd 2002). This persistent argument had (and still has, in some cases) long been used to discourage translating the knowledge about crime concentrations and effective hot spots policing into practice. Yet, in contrast, research and theory suggest that intervening at a hot spot will not simply move crime to another location; that any displacement that does occur is far from total displacement; and that hot spots policing will likely result instead in a diffusion of benefits as described above. This is because offenders operating at a targeted hot spot cannot easily move their criminal activities elsewhere unless they find other locations that offer similar criminal opportunities. Offenders also have to feel comfortable moving to these other locations (Weisburd et al. 2006). Opportunity theories and studies of offenders' travel patterns indicate that people are most likely to commit crimes close to where they live, close to where they have lived in the past, or in other places that fall within their normal activity spaces (e.g., locations near their jobs or near their family, friends, and associates) (e.g., see reviews in Ackerman and Rossmo 2015; Eck and Weisburd 1995; and Gabor and Gottheil 1984; also see Bernasco 2010; Weisburd et al. 2012). These are places where offenders are most likely to be familiar with available criminal opportunities and where they feel they are less likely to draw attention; moving to other unfamiliar locations involves greater effort and may increase their risks of detection and/or victimization (also see Weisburd et al. 2006).

Overall, it is fair to say that there now is a strong research base for hot spots policing that consists of both primary research about the geographic nature of crime and evaluation research about the effectiveness of law enforcement interventions targeting crime concentrations. But how can police translate this wealth of knowledge about hot spots into practice? More importantly, what types of strategies should police use when they approach hot spots that are amenable both to the citizens that live there and to the principals of good crime prevention?

Implementing Place-Based Policing

We remind our readers that evidence-based policing is not merely about knowing that crime concentrates, why it concentrates, or that concentrating police resources at hot spots can be effective. Evidence-based policing requires thinking about how such knowledge is used and translated into daily police practices and also understanding and dealing with the consequences of that implementation.

In practice, hot spots policing efforts often involve short-term patrol, enforcement, and investigative responses to recent crime spikes in targeted locations (Koper 2014). While these can be effective in reducing such flare-ups and managing hot spots (Santos and Boba-Santos 2015), we also know that more tailored and problem-solving approaches at hot spots can be more effective than general police presence at hot spots in achieving and sustaining effects (Braga et al. 2012; Taylor et al. 2011a; Weisburd, Telep, Hinkle et al. 2010).

Digging deeper into the evaluation research on hot spots policing provides some clues as to how to achieve effective hot spots policing. Studies have shown that a variety of police interventions at hot spots can produce short- or long-term reductions in crime and that these effects can range from modest to larger effects. These interventions include directed patrol, foot patrol, or fixed presence (e.g., DiTella and Schargrodsky 2004; Koper, Taylor, and Woods 2013b; Lawton, Taylor, and Luongo 2005; Ratcliffe, Taniguchi, Groff et al. 2011; Sherman and Weisburd 1995; Telep, Mitchell, and Weisburd 2014); order maintenance and drug enforcement crackdowns (Braga and Bond 2008; Braga et al. 1999; Sherman and Rogan 1995; Weisburd and Green 1995); operations focused on known repeat offenders at hot spots (Groff, Ratcliffe, Haberman et al. 2015); and problem-solving interventions that might entail situational crime prevention, nuisance abatement, clean-up activities, and various other prevention-oriented measures (e.g., Braga and Bond 2008; Braga et al. 1999; Eck and Wartell 1998; Mazerolle, Price, and Roehl 2000a; Sherman, Buerger, Gartin et al. 1989b; Taylor et al. 2011a).

Moving beyond these generalizations, it is harder to say what specific tactics works best for different types of hot spots as defined by crime problems and other features (see Braga et al. 2012). While police have had success with several approaches to hot spots, there have been few comparative assessments to determine which hot spots strategies are most effective, used individually or in combination (some exceptions are noted below). When surveyed, practitioners identify problem analysis and problem solving, targeting offenders, and directed patrol as the most common and effective strategies in general for hot spots. However, police officials also vary widely on how they define hot spots and what they think might be the most effective strategies for different types of hot spots (Koper 2014).

Despite these complexities, we can pull some guidelines from the existing research to guide practice. These guidelines reflect four key pillars that we recommend should form the foundation of an agency's hot spots policing strategy. These pillars are: (i) conducting geographic crime analysis emphasizing micro places and trends; (ii) regularly directing proactive patrol to hot spots (and doing so in ways that maximize a deterrence effect); (iii) using problem-oriented policing to develop long-term prevention strategies tailored to the specific problems of individual hot spots; and (iv) engaging with the community for both enhancing prevention and understanding their reactions to police activity in hot spots.

Geographic crime analysis of micro places and trends

Geographic crime analysis is a central element of hot spots policing, and is a prerequisite to any hot spots deployment approach. However, conducting hot spots policing in the most optimal ways will require police agencies to shift their analyses and operational emphasis to smaller geographic units of analysis. Social scientists commonly define hot spots in terms of micro places (i.e., specific addresses, intersections, street blocks, and clusters of street blocks), and many field studies showing effective deployment of hot spots policing have been based on such locations, as opportunities for crime are viewed to be highly connected to characteristics of places. In contrast, police have traditionally tended to focus their attention on larger areas such as patrol beats, neighborhoods, and other administratively defined areas (such as police districts or precincts). Although police practitioners are no doubt aware of the importance of micro places in generating crime, it is not clear whether they concentrate their efforts on these locations in a systematic or sufficient way. In a survey of large (primarily) U.S. agencies, only 19% exclusively defined hot spots in terms of micro places only, while roughly two-thirds defined neighborhoods as hot spots, about half identified patrol beats as hot spots, and almost one-quarter applied the term to areas larger than patrol beats or neighborhoods (Koper 2014).

In tandem with sharpening geographic analysis to micro hot spots, police must also seek to understand the social, environmental, physical, and routine activity characteristics of hot spots that contribute to attracting, generating, or facilitating crime opportunities at these places. We provide one tool to help with this analysis called "Case of Place" in Chapter 12. This type of analysis provides an important context to crime patterns, just as understanding motivation and context provide important clues to solving a crime.

As an example, for some years, the Minneapolis Police Department's (MPD) primary method of pinpointing hot spots has been to identify clusters of high-risk blocks using kernel density analysis (a common form of geospatial statistical analysis). MPD crime analysts draw boundaries around these clusters, creating "focus zones" that commanders use to guide operations. This facilitates the targeting of patrol and other operations on areas that are more precise than typical neighborhood or patrol beat boundaries. Although the size of these zones varies, a typical one might be roughly 0.25 square miles (one-half mile by one-half mile) or smaller and contain roughly 1,000 to 2,000 people.

More recently, MPD crime analysts have complemented this cluster approach with analysis of high crime street segments (e.g., Koper et al. 2015a). This has been helpful in understanding and addressing crime problems within focus zones, which are often driven by key street segments with features such as convenience stores, bus stops, and apartment complexes that draw people and create opportunities for crime and victimization. At the same time, studying the wider areas around these key street blocks can illuminate possible interconnections between actors (i.e., offenders, targets, and guardians), routine activities, social features, and crime problems across multiple high-risk segments within focus zones. In the words of Sergeant Jeff Egge, director of MPD's crime analysis unit, this type of iterative and multi-level approach enables the analyst to maintain a "steady hand on the tiller" that can yield a more comprehensive understanding of hot spots.

In addition to refocusing geographic analysis and deployment to smaller micro crime places, agencies may need to adjust their geographic analyses by giving more attention to long-term hot spot patterns. As research has found, hot spots are often stable over many years; yet police generally do not incorporate multi-year analyses into their tracking of hot spots (Koper 2014). Instead, police are most likely to identify and react to hot spots in a "whack-a-mole" fashion (Willis, Mastrofski, andWeisburd 2007) based on short-term crime patterns that may reflect emerging hot spots, spikes at chronic problem locations, or random events at otherwise low-intensity locations. Although these operations are necessary, a greater focus on long-term patterns and a commitment to dealing with chronic problems will make the police more effective in sustaining crime prevention effects over the long run.

Proactively directing patrol to hot spots

Our second pillar for translating hot spots research into practice is that agencies *regularly* direct proactive patrols to hot spots and do so in ways that maximize their deterrence effect. At the most basic level, this means deploying patrol officers and specialized units to patrol particular hot spots at particular "hot times." The potential benefits of focusing patrol on hot spots during patrol deployment were first demonstrated in the Minneapolis Hot Spots Experiment (Sherman and Weisburd 1995). The patrol intervention in this study, which consisted of officers patrolling the assigned hot spots for as much time as possible between calls for service, was characterized as "intensified but intermittent" police presence. This strategy reduced total calls to the police at the hot spots by 6–13% over the one-year study period. These results were driven largely by the intervention's impact on what the researchers categorized as "soft" crimes (e.g., disturbances, drunken behavior, break-in alarms, and vandalism). More serious crimes also declined, although not significantly.

Several additional studies since then have reaffirmed the crime prevention value of focusing vehicle or foot patrol on these locations (e.g., Lawton et al. 2005; Koper et al. 2013a; Ratcliffe et al. 2011; Rosenfeld, Deckard, and Blackburn 2014; Telep et al. 2014), particularly when this is done on a daily or frequent basis (Koper 2013). However, reorienting patrol to crime hot spots will require deployment adjustments for many police agencies, as patrol officers are usually assigned to a police beat or district and guided by responding to 911 calls rather than by directives to proactively address crime hot spots. Such a reorientation could involve simple changes within existing patrol deployment structures or major changes to deployment schemes.

An example of a simple change is to direct patrol officers to crime hot spots when they are not handling calls for service within their existing daily patrol deployments (as was done in the Minneapolis study). This approach to reorienting officers to hot spots may be least disruptive to existing patrol schedules and can serve as the cornerstone of an agency's place-based policing strategies. To implement this type of patrol strategy, agencies will have to produce crime analysis that identifies micro hot spots, and they will have to ensure that this information is accessible and conveyed to patrol officers (e.g., through their mobile computer units or through information passed out daily or weekly at roll calls). Shift supervisors also have to resist the urge of officers to tell them that they "already know where the hot spots are," as we now know that officer perceptions of hot spots can be inaccurate or incomplete (Ratcliffe and McCullagh 2001). Ideally, agencies should also develop systems to track and monitor officers' time and activities in hot spots, and managers should use this information to guide, monitor, and evaluate officer performance (e.g., see Aden and Koper 2011; Brown in progress).

Chronic hot spots should be priority locations for daily patrols, given that these are the most persistent problem places and contribute substantially to crime patterns. Police can address these locations with both visible patrol presence and more problem-solving approaches, which we discuss shortly. But as a general idea, a long-term commitment to targeting chronic hot spots can also include ongoing operational adjustments that address new locations (emerging and "pop-up" hot spots as discussed above) or even chronic hot spots that have experienced recent spikes or that appear to be at elevated risk for criminal activity. For example, studies have shown that street blocks that have experienced a burglary are at elevated risk for another burglary for approximately fourteen days following the initial event (see Bowers and Johnson 2005; Johnson and Bowers 2004; 2014; Johnson, Bernasco, Bowers et al. 2007). Similarly, some police agencies are now using "predictive policing" computer programs that attempt to provide more refined estimates of hot spot locations that are at higher risk of experiencing criminal events during very specific time frames (i.e., a particular week, day, and/or time) (Hunt, Saunders, and Hollywood 2014; Mohler, Short, Malinowski et al. 2015).[2] However, these studies have provided mixed evidence as to whether operations based on these predictions are an improvement over operations guided by standard geographical crime analysis (see also Kennedy, Caplan, and Piza 2015).

---

[2] These software programs have been developed by commercial businesses, so the basis for their risk predictions is not clear. Presumably, they are based on features of the locations combined with data about long-term patterns and recent crime and disorder incidents.

A more radical way of reorienting patrol deployment to hot spots is "flipping" patrol. Currently, patrol officers are deployed to reporting areas such as patrol beats, and their primary responsibility is answering calls for service as well as keeping a watchful eye on crime and disorder that may occur in that beat. In this more traditional patrol deployment, anything above and beyond responding to calls for service and investigating crimes is extra activity at the discretion of officers. A "flipped" patrol deployment would be one in which officers were dynamically assigned to crime hot spots rather than patrol beats ("dynamic" because such hot spots may change), and where responding to calls for service would not be the anchoring activity of officers. Indeed, the goal would be to reduce the amount of calls for service that officers have to respond to by using more proactive and targeted approaches in-between calls for service. Of course, officers still must answer calls when they do arise. But the emphasis would be on long-term crime reduction strategies designed to prevent crime calls from happening in the first place. This type of deployment change also means that new performance metrics would need to be developed, as well as ways for officers to communicate to the records management or computer-aided dispatch system the variety of activities they were doing.

Another way that agencies can adjust deployment towards hot spots is by supplementing daily patrol with activities conducted by specialized units. In practice, police often use mobile units of different types to respond to problems at hot spots with short-term patrol, enforcement, and investigative activities (Koper 2014). However, these units could also be used proactively to prevent flare-ups by rotating their operations periodically across different places (Sherman 1990) and carrying out problem-solving exercises in hot spots (we return to the latter issue below). Some research even suggests that brief operations in hot spots (e.g., two weeks) can have residual deterrent effects that reduce crime for several weeks after an operation has ended (Koper et al. 2013b).

Reorienting the daily deployment of patrol officers, whether using simple or more radical approaches, does not mean police should create hot spots or predictive policing automatons who just look at maps and go to them (a critique of hot spots policing sometimes used by police or researchers as a justification to stick to the status quo). Officers need to know *why* these places are hot and the various tools at their disposal to cool them. This may require more training, mentoring, guidance, and practice to enhance their understanding of the underlying opportunities and routines that lead to these hot spot conditions, so they can be best positioned as well as mentally motivated to carry out hot spots policing. This will require better academy and field training about understanding the nature of crime in one's beat, a topic we save for Chapter 10. However, we mention it here because police receive many hours of training on how to respond to specific calls for service, do investigations, make arrests, and process evidence. Yet, they are given almost no guidance at all about understanding why crime concentrates or how to address crime hot spots.

Calibrating patrol dosage to optimizing deterrence at hot spots

Increasing police visibility at hot spots through regular visits by patrol officers or specialized units will likely have significant deterrent effects on its own. However, in developing patrol strategies for hot spots, practitioners face several operational and practical considerations. Two key operational concerns are what patrol dosage levels to use at hot spots and what officers should do while at hot spots. Focusing first on the dosage issue, operational questions include how often officers should visit hot spots, how long they should stay per visit, and what overall dosage levels they should try to achieve per day or per week. At the extreme, police could establish fixed presence at hot spots around the clock or during all high-risk hours (e.g., DiTella and Schargrodsky 2004; Lawton et al. 2005). As a practical matter, however, this may be too resource intensive, as agencies will likely need to spread resources across numerous hot spots in a jurisdiction. Indeed, maintaining even two to three hours of patrol per day at hot spots, as done in the Minneapolis study, may not be feasible for some agencies and officers. Officers may also be resistant to such static assignments.

Fortunately, evidence suggests that police need not establish round-the-clock or otherwise intensive fixed presence at hot spots to reduce crime. In fact, there is some theory and research suggesting that such deployments may have diminishing crime control returns and even reduce crime prevention effectiveness if they become too predictable and routine or if officers lose focus (Koper 2013; Sherman 1990). Although existing research does not yet provide specific guidance on optimal patrol levels and schedules for hot spots,[3] there is growing evidence that short, periodic, and unpredictable patrol visits provide an efficient way of reducing crime at these places.

In an early study on optimizing patrol time in hot spots, Koper (1995) used data from the Minneapolis experiment to investigate if there might be an optimal length of time for police to stop in a hot spot during a patrol visit. Using data collected by trained observers who had been sent to the Minneapolis hot spots to record police presence and criminal and disorderly behaviors, Koper studied approximately 17,000 instances when police either drove through or stopped at a hot spot and examined whether any criminal or disorderly behaviors occurred up to thirty minutes after the police left the location,

The key finding of that study is represented in Figure 4.1. The horizontal axis in the figure represents the length of each police presence (the study focused on drive-bys and stops of up to twenty minutes in length), and the vertical axis represents the "residual deterrent" effect of the officer's presence, or how long crime was deterred *after* the officer left the hot spot. Higher numbers represent a greater residual deterrent effect (note that the numbers on the

---

[3] See Sherman, Williams, Ariel et al. 2014 for an in-depth discussion of theoretical concerns surrounding this issue.

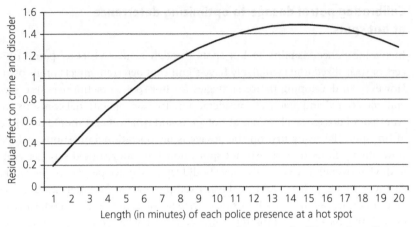

Figure 4.1 The Duration Response Curve (later known as the "Koper Curve")

Recreated with permission of Taylor and Francis Group, from *Justice Quarterly*, Volume 12, 1995, Christopher Koper (Copyright © 1995 Routledge).

vertical axis do not correspond to particular units of time). Figure 4.1 shows that in general, residual deterrent effects increased with each minute that officers remained at a hot spot, and staying for ten minutes created residual effects that were superior to those generated by driving through the location (i.e., they were significantly different in statistical testing). However, these residual deterrent effects leveled off and even declined somewhat if officers stayed at the hot spot for longer than fifteen minutes. This finding suggests that the residual deterrent effects of police stops at hot spots are maximized when the stops are roughly fourteen to fifteen minutes; staying longer brings diminishing returns to this deterrent effect.[4]

To provide some further sense of what this means, Figure 4.2 illustrates the likelihood of a criminal or disorderly behavior occurring within thirty minutes of police leaving a hot spot in Minneapolis. This probability is shown separately for drive-bys and stops of eleven to fifteen minutes. When police drove through a hot spot, there was a 16% chance of a criminal or disorderly behavior occurring at the location within the next thirty minutes. In contrast, this likelihood was reduced to 4% when police remained at the location for eleven to fifteen minutes. Hence, stopping at the location for eleven to fifteen minutes, as opposed to driving through, was associated with a 75% reduction in the likelihood of new criminal or disorderly behavior in the short-term aftermath of the police visit.

This finding, which has come to be known as the "Koper Curve," suggests that police can potentially maximize the effectiveness and efficiency of preventive patrol by making ten-to-fifteen-minute visits to micro hot spot locations on

---

[4] See Koper (1995) for further discussion of the details and theoretical issues surrounding this finding.

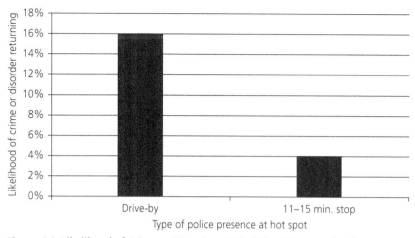

Figure 4.2 Likelihood of Crime or Disorder within Thirty Minutes of Police Presence

a periodic basis. Koper's study did not address how often officers should make these visits, but he suggested that officers make them on a random and unpredictable basis (so that offenders cannot anticipate them) and that they make the visits a part of their regular patrol routine.

A small but accumulating body of evidence from field experiments suggests that a hot spots approach utilizing the Koper Curve works without causing too much burden on patrol. An experimental study in Sacramento (CA), for example, tested the effects of making twelve-to-sixteen-minute patrol stops at hot spots every few hours during an entire shift (Telep et al. 2014). As in the Minneapolis study, the emphasis was on manipulating patrol dosage; what officers did at the hot spots was left to their discretion. Results showed the proactive patrol stops reduced total calls for service by 11% at the experimental locations and reduced serious crimes by 25%. In contrast, the control locations experienced increases in calls for service and crime during this same period. Another field experiment in St Louis (MO) found that making regular fifteen-minute patrol stops in gun crime hot spots significantly reduced gun crime in the targeted locations, though this effect was contingent on officers' self-initiated activities (Rosenfeld et al. 2014). In smaller jurisdictions, making just one fifteen-minute stop a day may be sufficient to reduce crime at hot spots (Hegarty, Williams, Stanton et al. 2014). Results from other studies, some of which are preliminary, indicate that variations of the Koper Curve strategy have been used successfully in Los Angeles (Mohler et al. 2015), Birmingham (United Kingdom) (Smallwood, Ariel, and Wain 2014), and the London subway system (Ariel and Sherman 2012).[5]

---

[5] Positive results with the Koper Curve strategy have also been reported in places like Seattle (Dermody 2013) and Alexandria, Virginia (Aden and Koper 2011), though these reports are not based on carefully controlled studies.

These studies do not prove that fifteen minutes is always the most optimal time for officers to spend in a hot spot, and we do not recommend rigid adherence to a fifteen-minute guideline that would preclude officers from spending longer amounts of time at hot spots when needed for problem-solving or community engagement activities (see below) or other reasons. However, what these studies do suggest is that short, periodic patrol visits to hot spots can be sufficient to reduce crime, even for hot spots in high-crime urban environments. Accordingly, police may be able to manage their hot spots effectively with modest dosages of patrol (and cost). As officers build this into their discretionary time, they might further calibrate the number and length of their visits, depending on the nature and severity of problems at the assigned hot spots. Also, officers should vary the daily timing of these visits so as not to be predictable.

Problem-solving at hot spots

What else should officers do at hot spots besides daily patrol? A possible answer is found in another important pillar for effective implementation of hot spots policing—problem solving. As discussed in Chapter 1, the model of problem-oriented policing (POP), first articulated by Herman Goldstein (1979; 1990), calls for police to transcend reactive incident-driven policing by studying and addressing underlying problems that contribute to crime and disorder in the community. Goldstein's notion was for police to take proactive, preventive action against the causes of continuing crime and disorder issues. Further, Goldstein argued that police responses to these problems should not be limited to traditional law enforcement actions but, rather, should also include the use of civil legislation and reliance on other municipal and community resources. Eck and Spelman (1987) later developed the well-known SARA model for implementing POP, which consists of four steps denoted by the acronym: *scanning* for problems; *analysis* of problems; development and implementation of *responses*; and follow-up *assessment* of results. POP thus represents a process of identifying problems and developing responses rather than any specific type(s) of response.

As noted, POP may be particularly effective in the context of hot spots policing insofar as focusing attention on these very specific locations can help officers to identify tangible conditions that contribute to crime and disorder at these places and to develop both enforcement and prevention measures tailored to the particulars of these places and their problems. In addition to targeted enforcement actions, reported problem-solving efforts at hot spots have often included measures such as situational crime prevention (see Clarke 1980; 1997), nuisance abatement, municipal/county code enforcement, securing or removing abandoned buildings, clean-up activities, and improvement of social services (e.g., Braga and Bond 2008; Braga et al. 1999; Eck 2002; Eck and Wartell 1998; Mazerolle et al. 2000a; Mazerolle, Ready, and Terrill 2000b; Taylor et al. 2011a; Sherman et al. 1989b; Weisburd et al. 2010). Police often implement such measures in cooperation with place managers (Eck 1994) and other stake-holders (such as business owners and managers, residents, and other government agencies) with interests in or responsibility for the area. Notably, Braga et al.'s (2012) assessment of rigorous hot spots studies found that interventions grounded in a problem-oriented policing framework tend to produce larger reductions in crime than those based solely on traditional patrol and enforcement measures.

One study that illustrates the benefits of structured problem solving relative to other enforcement-oriented approaches was conducted in Jacksonville, Florida, where police and researchers separately tested the effectiveness of POP and directed patrol at violent crime hot spots (Taylor et al. 2011a; also see Koper, Taylor, and Roush 2013a). Hot spots in this study were randomly assigned to problem-solving, directed-saturation patrol, or routine (i.e., "control") operations for a ninety-day experiment. Problem-solving activities at the first group of locations were conducted by teams of supervisors, officers, and crime analysts who received training in the principles of problem-oriented and intelligence-led policing. The officers and analysts attempted to identify and address the underlying factors driving crime in these locations, working closely with community partners where possible. Officers working the problem-solving locations implemented a wide array of interventions of the sort noted above, with a particular emphasis on prevention-oriented measures.

Results indicated that the problem-oriented policing intervention produced stronger and more lasting effects on violent crime than did the directed saturation patrols.[6] The Jacksonville study, along with many others, thus underscores the importance of complementing day-to-day patrol at hot spots with problem-solving and situational crime prevention efforts,[7] whether conducted by special units or regular patrol officers, to potentially achieve larger and more lasting reductions in crime. We should also emphasize the importance of considering prevention measures as well as enforcement actions in problem-solving interventions. One criticism of POP efforts in practice is that they often fall short of the POP ideal in that they involve limited analysis, limited community partnership efforts, limited organizational support (e.g., officers not having

---

[6] Further analysis (not included in the initial study) suggested that the greatest effects in the POP locations stemmed from situational crime prevention measures (also see note 7), use of nuisance abatement and code enforcement, and targeted investigations (also see our discussion of offender-based approaches to hot spots in Chapter 5).

[7] Situational crime prevention (SCP), developed by Ronald Clarke (1980; 1983; 1997). SCP can include a wide variety of measures to block criminal opportunities and increase risks for offenders. Examples include improving lighting, strengthening access control to buildings and homes, putting up barriers to redirect traffic, and improving visibility at a location (e.g., removing shrubbery or other items that block visibility around or into a building). There is much evidence that SCP can be effective in reducing crime at places, whether implemented by police or others (Eck 2002). For additional discussion of the utility of applying situational crime prevention measures to hot spots, also see Braga and Bond (2008) and Telep and Weisburd (2015).

enough time or other support to problem solve well), and heavy reliance on enforcement tactics—what some have called "shallow" problem solving (e.g., Braga and Bond 2008; Braga and Weisburd 2006; Cordner and Bielbel 2005; Eck 2006; for examples of unsuccessful POP efforts at hot spots, also see Groff et al. 2015; Sherman et al. 1989b). Placing more emphasis on in-depth problem analysis and prevention may help police to produce more lasting reductions in crime at hot spots. This could also improve their relationships with community residents and stakeholders, as prevention measures are more likely to be implemented in cooperation with other community actors, and reduce reliance on heavy enforcement tactics that have greater potential to produce friction with community members and erode police–community relations.

In Chapter 12, we introduce an approach called the "Case of Place" strategy that we have developed to help police agencies institutionalize investigation and problem solving at hot spots. The Case of Place idea emphasizes problem places as targets for criminal investigation while also providing a structured way of using police data and other available government and community information to analyze crime problems at a hot spot, identify their causes, and develop responses emphasizing enforcement and prevention.

Community engagement and hot spots

The final pillar we suggest is that police anchor their hot spots approaches in engagement with the residents and community at crime hot spots. This is a much less researched area in the hot spots policing evaluation literature, but we believe that agencies can improve their place-based approaches by incorporating community-oriented principles.

We discuss community policing in more depth in Chapter 6 but note here that it has been described as both a philosophy of policing and an organizational strategy (Greene 2000; National Research Council 2004) in which police embrace a larger vision of their function that involves working with community groups and citizens in co-producing safety, crime prevention, and solutions to local concerns. In practice, community policing efforts include a wide array of tactics to increase communication, interaction, and collaboration between police and citizens: For example, foot patrol, neighborhood watch, community meetings or newsletters, efforts to reduce social and physical disorder, conflict resolution, and various types of problem-solving efforts.[8] Community policing has also encompassed efforts to build collective efficacy and empowerment in communities (see Sampson 2011) and often involves police working with an array of citizen and government organizations to reduce crime and improve the quality of life in communities.

---

[8] Although community policing has recently encompassed ideas of problem solving, it is distinct from problem solving, which may or may not involve community members or resources (Gill, Weisburd, Telep et al. 2014; Scott 2000).

Most research evaluating community policing has examined its effects in larger geographic units, such as police beats or neighborhoods, given that the target of these interventions is often inclusive of a larger social and geographic location (see Chapter 6). As applied to hot spots policing, we suggest that, beyond providing visibility and enforcement, officers might also use regular patrol visits to hot spots as an opportunity to enhance their agency's community policing strategy, but in more targeted ways. This might include making community contacts and learning more about the actors, features, dynamics, and problems of the locations. Officers will sometimes need to emphasize field interviews, traffic stops, and other forms of order maintenance enforcement at these locations, and they should learn about and make contact with known offenders who operate in and around the locations (we say more about the issue of focusing on high-risk people in hot spots in Chapter 5). At the same time, officers should also emphasize making positive contacts with residents and business people who can serve as additional guardians of the location by helping to enhance informal social controls, providing valuable information, and assisting with problem-solving projects. Developing good relations with community members may also bolster officers' abilities to persuade others to change problem behaviors and conditions when needed. In all of these ways, getting to know hot spots better through regular presence and interaction should facilitate officers' long-term efforts to develop stronger behavioral controls and problem-solving strategies for the locations.

At a minimum, officers can exercise community policing by being transparent with residents about the crime prevention and enforcement activities they are carrying out in those communities, and solicit feedback about their efforts. Some evidence indicates that a community approach at hot spots can yield meaningful fruit for police legitimacy. For instance, in a Kansas City, Missouri crackdown on gun crime, officers knocked and talked with almost 800 residents in a targeted hot spot area, providing information to residents about the upcoming crackdown as well as tips and information about crime prevention. (Sherman, Shaw, and Rogan 1995)[9] Before and after surveys of the intervention found that citizens were less fearful and more positive about their neighborhood than respondents in a control area that did not receive a crackdown. Informing and also surveying residents about police operations in hot spots can thus improve police legitimacy with residents and provide a feedback mechanism for citizens to monitor police efforts.

The importance of including community policing components into a hot spots approach cannot be overstated. Recall that the displacement hypothesis—that crime would just move around the corner—was a major excuse

---

[9] The hot spot in this study was larger than the types of micro hot spots that we have featured in this chapter, but the study serves to illustrate our broader point about using community policing approaches to complement aggressive enforcement in high-crime locations.

against implementing hot spots policing for many years (Weisburd 2002). More recently, the "displacement excuse" has been replaced by yet another unsubstantiated argument—that hot spots policing leads to disparities in policing because it concentrates police enforcement efforts on communities of color or the disadvantaged. Not only is this unsubstantiated, but research indicates that there is a great deal of street-by-street (and even house-by-house) variability in crime within socially disadvantaged and concentrated minority areas that can help police to focus their efforts and thereby minimize collateral damage to relations with the community more broadly. Further, surveys like the ones conducted in the Kansas City project mentioned above indicate that minority residents are very much concerned about crime in their areas. But they are also concerned with *how* the police decide to deal with crime. Adopting an approach that increases transparency, feedback, and engagement with the community on police strategies and tactics at crime hot spots can make the difference between hot spots policing that worsens community-police relations and hot spots policing that improves them. As Lum and Nagin (2016) argue, a bedrock of policing is not just crime prevention—it is also paying attention to community reaction to those efforts.

Conclusion

Targeting high-crime places is one of the most effective approaches that the police can use to prevent crime and increase their legitimacy. However, *how* they carry out place-based policing matters, not only to accurate targeting of the problem, but also to citizen reaction to their efforts. Simply going to crime hot spots and carrying out enforcement measures may not be enough to create a long-term effect and may result in community backlash. We suggest more accurate identification of crime hot spots through micro-geographic analysis of crime and disorder, and a stronger emphasis on analyzing the environmental, social, geographic, situational, and routine activities context of crime concentrations. Once these spots are identified, agencies have to develop and alter their patrol deployment to proactively patrol these places, and do so in ways that are unpredictable and use resources most efficiently. Problem-solving and community-oriented approaches at crime hot spots can further enhance the long-term effectiveness of police actions and help strengthen police–citizen relationships. Finally, reorienting place-based policing to these fundamentals can help institutionalize it as a regular, systematic feature of everyday patrol and investigative operations rather than, as often practiced, a set of ad hoc or temporary activities that are often limited to specialized units.

5

INDIVIDUAL-FOCUSED STRATEGIES

In this chapter, we examine the evidence-base of common police approaches that are focused on individuals. As we discussed in Part One, the emphasis on individuals, as opposed to places, for instance, has been the hallmark of the standard model of policing. The focus on individuals emerges from responding to calls for service, investigating crimes, and the fact that the law and standard operating procedures heavily anchor these activities. In turn, a great deal of academy and in-service training focuses on understanding how to respond to individual calls and crime reports. It is fair to say that, even with all of the innovations in proactive, community-oriented, and place-based strategies, police activity continues to be dominated by individual-focused strategies, in particular, offender-focused approaches.

At the same time, our Matrix indicates that offender-based approaches have not been as successful overall as place-based policing strategies in preventing crime or reducing recidivism. In part, this is because offender-based strategies often use arrest as their primary strategy. While arrest is a central feature of the standard model of policing, it is arguably an insufficient response to address many of the complex individual and social problems that contribute to crime (e.g., mental health problems, the impulsivity of juveniles, criminal opportunity structures in the environment, and social problems like poverty and family disruption). Of course, police have to arrest and bring offenders to justice; this is a necessary response to serious offending. And, there are times when prevention approaches do not work with some offenders. But an evidence-based approach to policing requires police to expand and balance their toolkits with measures that can prevent crime before needing to arrest. Indeed, Dan Nagin, the leading expert on criminal deterrence, views arrest as a failure of deterrence and prevention (Nagin 2013). Many police practitioners themselves have observed that they cannot arrest their way out of crime.

In this chapter, we take a closer look at the evidence-base of offender and individual-based approaches in policing that appears in the Matrix. We begin with a discussion of reactive arrests and rapid response to calls for service, which are both essentially offender-focused strategies that are embedded in the standard model of policing. We then broaden our discussion to other general offender-based approaches that stress prevention or alternative ways of reacting to individual offenders. We highlight the conditions under which these approaches seem to be effective when they are sufficiently targeted on high-risk individuals and groups and/or combined with strategies focused on high-risk places. In addition to being targeted, successful offender-based strategies are often multi-faceted strategies that combine elements of prevention and deterrence. We conclude with some suggestions about how police might best implement or refine individual-based approaches in effective ways.

Arrest as an Offender-Focused Intervention

Other than issuing tickets, citations, and warnings, physically arresting offenders is one of the most common ways that police intervene with offenders and try to assist victims. For decades, police have defined their role and function by arrest (Bittner 1970; Reiss 1971), and officers, detectives, and their supervisors and commanders view arrest as a "success" for the department and community. Even the development of rapid response to 911 calls with the advent of cars, radios, and the computer-aided dispatch system was meant to decrease the time in which an officer could reach a victim and improve the likelihood of catching the offender at the crime scene. It is fair to say that the use of arrest has become the primary offender-based strategy used by police, and this is evident in training, standard operating procedures, and rewards and incentives systems (Reiss 1984). One only needs to attend a Compstat meeting or a roll call; the apprehension of offenders is often a focus of these meetings.

At the same time, police can exercise a good deal of discretion in deciding whether to arrest offenders (Reiss 1984), depending on the type of crime in question and other situational factors. As a matter of policy, the police can also shift their focus to specific classes and categories of offenders they wish to arrest, and they can decide not to arrest (or cite) individuals whom they know have broken the law. Thus, in addition to using arrest to bring offenders to justice for specific crimes, police also use arrest as a prevention tool.

In this preventive mode, the deterrent effects of using arrest come from a variety of mechanisms. For example, arrest may reduce the offending of those arrested, convicted, and sentenced through incapacitation and/or by deterring their future offending because they don't want to experience arrests again for various reasons. This is referred to as specific deterrence (i.e., the deterrent effect that a sanction has on the person receiving the sanction). Arrests may also reduce the offending of other, non-arrested people by increasing their perceived certainty that offending will result in detection and arrest—a process referred to as general deterrence (i.e., the effect that sanctioning one person has on others in the community). While both these effects may seem logical, arrests may or may not have these desired effects under different circumstances, or they may even cause increases in crime in some contexts. For example, some arrested offenders may increase their subsequent offending, perhaps due to feelings of anger or defiance, interactions they have with other arrested offenders, or because of other social consequences of arrest (like greater difficulty finding future employment). Arrests might also sometimes increase crime in the community more generally—if, for instance, their overuse creates anger in the community (thus undermining police legitimacy or authority), or if they destabilize illegal markets (like drug markets) in ways that create greater conflict among the actors in those markets.

All of these considerations add complexity to our discussion of the effectiveness of arrest as a police strategy and broaden the questions we ask. For example, is the use and threat of arrest effective when reacting to serious crimes? How about when police decide to use arrest on certain types of offenders (e.g., domestic violence, drug users, people who illegally carry weapons)—does that reduce their recidivism and/or deter offending by others more generally? Can we effectively use arrest as a prevention strategy (e.g., by arresting individuals for minor crimes to prevent more serious crimes)? An evidence-based approach requires us to look carefully at different uses of arrests and if, when, and where those uses are effective.

Reactive investigation-and-arrest for serious offenses

Responding to and investigating serious crimes, and then apprehending offenders are, of course, central and necessary functions of the police, as we describe above. But from an evidence-based policing perspective, there are two key questions to consider about this common policing approach. First, does research evidence give us clues as to whether police can improve their success rate in detecting and apprehending serious offenders? Second, if the police can find and arrest more offenders who commit crime (thus improving the clearance rates of crime), can that reduce crime, and by how much, through processes of incapacitation, specific deterrence, and general deterrence?

Concerning the first question, police do a number of things to increase their detection and apprehension of serious criminals. For one, rapid response to calls for service is designed to help with detection and apprehension of offenders, as it is believed to improve the odds of apprehending offenders fleeing crime scenes. Although there has never been a field experiment (or quasi-experiment) testing the effects of rapid response, several descriptive studies of crime reporting have shown that there are typically delays of several minutes or much longer in the reporting of crime to police by citizens. Thus, speeding up response does not necessarily increase the chance of arresting the offender (Kansas City Police 1977; Pate, Ferrara, Bowers et al. 1976; Spelman and Brown 1981). Perhaps this has changed with the advent of cellphones, which make it easier to call the police more quickly, or the use of "next generation" 911 systems that allow for text calls and real-time video.[1] However, for many crimes, delays in calling may be due to delays in discovering a crime has occurred or in the reporting of crime by victims. As a result, making reasonably feasible improvements in response times would be unlikely to have much impact on criminal apprehension (Sherman and Eck 2002).[2]

Another way that police try to improve their ability to investigate and arrest offenders for crimes that have already occurred is by improving their ability to apprehend offenders through good investigative practices. Research suggests there are several ways in which police might improve their likelihood of apprehending offenders and getting successful prosecutions in serious cases. Landmark studies have focused on using "solvability" factors (i.e., factors that predict the likelihood of successfully identifying a suspect in a case) to screen and prioritize cases for investigation (Chaiken, Greenwood, and Petersilia 1976; Eck 1979; 1983; Greenwood and Petersilia 1975). Some have found that solvability may be more related to resources, patrol officer actions, or how quickly investigators get to the scene of a homicide (Chaiken 1975; Wellford and Cronin 1999). Others have examined how case outcomes can be improved through better investigative techniques, including more accurate eyewitness identification procedures (e.g., Klobuchar, Steblay, and Caliguiri 2006; Mecklenburg 2006; Wells, Small, Penrod et al. 1998); the use of data systems (Danziger and Kraemer 1985; Eck 1983); collection of DNA evidence for property offenses (Roman, Reid, Reid et al. 2008; Wilson, Weisburd, and McClure 2011); the use of new surveillance technologies like license plate readers (Taylor, Koper, and Woods 2012); better techniques for suspect interrogation (Meissner, Relich, Bhatt et al. 2012); and working with prosecutors to build stronger evidentiary cases against serious offenders (Abrahamse, Ebener, Greenwood et al. 1991).[3]

Despite many of these research findings, Horvath, Meesig, and Hyeock Lee's (2001) survey of a nationally representative sample of agencies suggests that

---

[1] At the time of writing, new computer-aided dispatch systems known as "next generation" systems have been developed, including new standards related to these systems (see http://www.911.gov/911-issues/standards.html). These systems allow callers to text their emergency to call centers, or take pictures and videos to send to emergency responders.

[2] In addition, studies show that people reporting non-emergency issues are equally satisfied if police take their reports in a manner that does not require a rapid response (like a delayed patrol response or taking the report by phone) (McEwen, Connors, and Cohen 1986).

[3] Some of this evidence comes from field experiments, while much of it comes from other forms of research. Hence, some of these interventions have been tested for their effects on apprehension, and others have not. We do not review these studies in detail, as our emphasis is on research that relates police strategies to crime reduction rather than research on ways to improve investigations and prosecutions.

investigative practices had not changed much over time, at least as of the early 2000s. More generally, clearance rates for serious crimes (i.e., the rate at which these investigations are closed through arrest or other special circumstances, like the death of an offender) have been remarkably stable over the past several decades (Braga, Flynn, Kelling et al. 2011; Lum, Wellford, Scott et al. 2016d; Vovak 2016). This despite substantial fluctuations in the rates of serious crimes, not to mention advancements in police data systems and forensics technologies that could have been expected to improve clearance rates. The lack of use of solvability factors or other evidence-based approaches in investigations may be a reason for this.

Further, even if police can improve their ability to detect and apprehend offenders and clear investigative cases, this may not reduce crime, irrespective of its benefits in serving justice or maintaining public confidence. We do not review studies of clearance rates and crime rates here as this has been done extensively elsewhere and raises complex statistical issues about these studies that are beyond the scope of this discussion (see Durlauf and Nagin 2011; Nagin 1998; 2013). But suffice it to say these studies have failed to provide clear or consistent evidence that reactive arrest and higher clearance rates reduce crime. This finding is likely due in part to the difficulty of separating out the effects that clearance rates have on crime from those that crime can have on the clearance rate (i.e., higher crime rates might produce greater workloads for police, making it more difficult to solve cases) (e.g., see Nagin 2013; Nagin, Solow, and Lum 2015; Vovak 2016).[4] Given the research, an evidence-based approach presses the police to re-think their emphasis on reactive arrests and how they might balance arrest with other approaches.

Discretionary arrests for youth and domestic violence offenders

In addition to investigate-and-arrest approaches, the police can also use their discretion to arrest or not to arrest. As a matter of policy, this means that organizations can make strategic decisions to increase or decrease the use of arrest for certain categories of offenders and to use certain types of arrests, notably those for minor offenses, as a strategy for crime control. Here, we address discretionary arrests for youth and domestic violence offenders, and in the next section, minor arrests for purposes of crime control.

With respect to juveniles, there is some evidence that arrest causes juvenile offenders, particularly those who are inexperienced, to increase their perception of the risk of apprehension, which can deter them (Nagin 2013; Smith and Gartin 1989). However, other evidence suggests that more formal arrest

---

[4] Studies of clearance rates and crime rates are not included in the Evidence-Based Policing Matrix because they have been based on correlational research designs that do not meet the standards of scientific rigor that we established for the Matrix.

processing of juvenile offenders, especially those who have committed minor offenses, increases their offending (Klein 1986). A related point is that numerous studies of juvenile court processing suggest on balance that prosecuting juveniles for minor and property offenses is harmful to their future offending (Petrosino, Turpin-Petrosino, and Guckenburg 2010). The implication for police is that it may be better to handle minor juvenile offenders in less formal ways (i.e., diversion) whenever possible, perhaps in cooperation with parents, guardians, schools, and/or social service agencies.[5] At the same time, police agencies should be cautious about how they use diversion. Research indicates that suspects who are from non-white minority groups are more likely to be arrested than white suspects (see a review of this literature by Kochel, Wilson, and Mastrofski 2011). Additionally, Lum (2011) discovered that police tend to handle incidents less formally in places that have higher concentrations of wealthy white residents compared to places with higher concentrations of poorer black residents. Given this evidence, while diversion and discretion with juvenile arrests can be positive, *how* agencies use diversion fairly also matters.

There have also been numerous experiments and quasi-experiments testing the effects of arrest discretion on misdemeanor domestic violence offenders. The first of these studies was conducted in Minneapolis, Minnesota in the early 1980s (Sherman and Berk 1984). In that study, the Minneapolis police, working in collaboration with researchers, randomly assigned misdemeanor domestic violence cases to one of three conditions: arrest, "advice" (which sometimes included informal mediation), or separation (i.e., an order to the suspect to leave the premises for eight hours). A six-month follow-up study using both arrest records and victim interviews suggested that arrested offenders were the least likely to commit new assaults against their partners.

The Minneapolis study, as well as political pressure by women's groups, sparked a series of additional domestic violence studies, as well as many new laws and policies mandating arrest in domestic violence cases that are in place today. However, subsequent studies failed to consistently replicate the Minneapolis findings; some found that arrest deterred future assaults, while others found that it increased recidivism or had no effect. Moreover, several studies found that arrest affected different types of offenders in different ways. A common pattern is that arrest seems to deter employed offenders but have a backfire effect on unemployed offenders, increasing their recidivism (Berk, Campbell, Klap et al. 1992; Pate and Hamilton 1992; Sherman, Schmidt, Rogan et al. 1991; Sherman, Schmidt, Rogan et al. 1992). Long-term follow-up studies have also suggested that arrest increases the likelihood of death for both offenders and victims measured over the course of multiple decades (Sherman

---

[5] The decisions of prosecutors and juvenile court authorities will also dictate how arrested youth are handled.

and Harris 2013; 2015). The causal mechanisms explaining this association are not clear.

Enacting policies to arrest employed domestic violent offenders while not arresting those who are unemployed would raise obvious legal and ethical problems for police, not to mention that law and policy already limit police discretion about arresting domestic violence offenders in many jurisdictions. Nonetheless, this evidence base for domestic violence is useful to police policies, even within a mandatory arrest environment. These studies flag when the risk of recidivism and retaliation might be higher. Law enforcement agencies can act on the totality of evidence by prioritizing domestic violence cases that have risk factors identified in the research for follow-up visits, more intensive investigation, and case preparation (e.g., see Exum, Hartman, Friday et al. 2014), and/or other interventions with social services (though we are not aware of any studies that have explicitly tested such approaches with unemployed offenders). We revisit this issue later in considering other types of individual-focused responses to domestic violence beyond arrest.

Using minor arrests as a general tool for community crime control

Although arresting serious offenders is a central police function, most arrests made by the police are for minor crimes and disorderly behaviors. In 2014, for instance, police in the United States made roughly 11.2 million arrests.[6] About 4.5% of these arrests were for what U.S. agencies classify as "Part I" violent crimes (i.e., murder, rape, robbery, and aggravated assault), and 14% were for Part I property crimes (i.e., burglary, larceny-theft, motor vehicle theft, and arson). The remaining arrests—accounting for more than 80%—were for minor offenses (typically misdemeanors and ordinance violations) classified as "Part II" offenses. The most common Part II arrests were for drug violations, simple assaults, and driving under the influence. Many others involved a variety of minor and public order offenses such as disorderly conduct, drunkenness, vandalism, loitering, drinking in public, fare evasion (e.g., on subways), littering, blocking traffic, minor drug use, graffiti, and other minor property offenses, just to name some.

Police can manipulate their use of arrest as an intervention more readily when addressing less serious crimes. Officers in the field have more discretion about using arrest when handling these sorts of incidents, and police agencies can influence the level of these arrests through policy decisions. In the United States, there was a clear shift towards more aggressive use of minor arrests during the 1990s, in large part as a way of controlling more serious offending. Indeed, the use of misdemeanor arrests increased dramatically in the 1990s,

---

[6] See Federal Bureau of Investigation's Uniform Crime Reports data at https://ucr.fbi.gov/crime-in-the-u.s/2014/crime-in-the-u.s.-2014/tables/table-29.

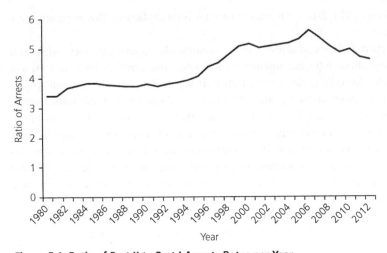

Figure 5.1 Ratio of Part II to Part I Arrests Rates per Year
Calculated from public data retried from the Federal Bureau of Investigations Uniform Crime Reports (https://ucr.fbi.gov/).

only to start declining in the late 2000s. Figure 5.1 shows the relative increase of misdemeanor or Part II arrests compared to arrests for more serious (Part I) offenses in the Uniform Crime Reports.

Several factors likely contributed to this trend. These factors include the war on drugs, the "broken windows" theory of policing (Wilson and Kelling 1982) discussed below, a growing emphasis on arresting misdemeanor domestic violence offenders, and greater attention to other problems like gun violence and illegal gun carrying. A critical policy question, of course, is whether a greater emphasis on making arrests for these types of offenses will reduce crime. And even if so, do they create other problems, such as community backlash, that offset the crime reduction benefits?

The idea of using arrests for misdemeanor offenses to control crime grew in part from an idea known as the "broken windows" theory of policing (Wilson and Kelling 1982), which became influential during the 1980s and 1990s. This idea states that social and physical disorder can erode informal social control in a community when left unchecked, thus giving rise to more serious forms of offending. This emphasis on controlling minor crime and disorderly behavior was also fueled by research showing that areas with high levels of serious crime are often characterized by high levels of disorder (e.g., Skogan 1990). This research indicates that social disorder has substantial effects on citizen fear because citizens witness and experience it more often than serious crime (Lewis and Maxfield 1980; Lewis and Salem 1986; Skogan 1990).

We note up front that Kelling and others have argued that policing disorder can involve community and problem-solving strategies and not just making large numbers of arrests (see Kelling and Coles 1996; White, Fradella, and Coldren 2015). Indeed, their original theory did not explicitly support massive misdemeanor arrests. Additionally, we also note that while serious crime

84

and disorder often occur in the same places, there are mixed findings and academic debates about whether disorder causes more serious crime (see Harcourt 2001; Sampson and Raudenbush 1999; Yang 2010). However, because of the centrality of arrest in policing culture and function, the use of misdemeanor arrests to combat crime is the form of "broken windows" policing that has been most widely adopted and has been the subject of much controversy (Lum and Nagin 2017).

Sometimes called "zero tolerance," this style of policing is characterized by higher levels of arrest for minor offenses. Because of the increase of arrest-based interaction with offenders, this style of policing also became enmeshed with other activities, including aggressive use of traffic and pedestrian stops to find people carrying drugs, contraband, and weapons, and to deter would-be offenders more generally. These practices in both the United States and the United Kingdom increased the use of stop-and-question (also known as "field interviews"), as well as stop-question-and-frisk (SQF) activities. Practitioners and proponents of this style of policing believe that more aggressive, vigilant forms of policing increase offenders' perceptions of the risk of apprehension by police, thereby controlling crime and disorder. Additionally, by increasing their contacts with troublesome and suspicious people, it is also believed that police can increase their odds of detecting more dangerous offenders such as those carrying weapons or those wanted for more serious crimes (see reporting by Goldstein 2014, on New York City Police Commissioner William Bratton's views about "broken windows" policing).

What is the research evidence on this type of policing? A recent review of twenty-eight experimental and quasi-experimental studies suggests that policing disorder can be an effective way to reduce both serious and minor offending (Braga, Welsh, and Schnell 2015). However, the results also revealed an important distinction: disorder-focused strategies are primarily effective when they are used as part of a community problem-solving approach to address social and physical disorder at particular places like micro hot spots. Such approaches use disorder enforcement in a more targeted way based on analysis of problem locations, and are more likely to involve other types of prevention efforts to reduce crime. In contrast, policing approaches that emphasize aggressive enforcement targeting individual disorderly behaviors—like widespread zero-tolerance crackdowns in large areas—tend not to have significant effects on average. (Readers should note that many of these studies are included in the Evidence-Based Policing Matrix under placed-based strategies in the "Micro place" or "Neighborhood" sections. We discuss them here under offender-focused strategies to illustrate a broader point about the limits of generalized arrest-based strategies that emphasize action against individual offenders.)

A good example of the former approach comes from a disorder reduction strategy that Lowell, Massachusetts implemented at micro hot spots as part of an experiment (Braga and Bond 2008; also see Chapter 4). Police implemented disorder reduction strategies using a problem-solving framework at the targeted hot spots that involved a mix of situational crime prevention measures, social service activities, and order maintenance enforcement. Overall, the program reduced calls for service at the hot spots by 20% and produced even larger reductions in serious crimes like robbery, assaults, and burglary. Additional analyses showed that misdemeanor arrests contributed modestly to the reductions in crime, but the greatest effects stemmed from the situational crime prevention measures. In other words, disorder enforcement helped to reduce crime when used in this geographically targeted way, but it was also used as part of a more holistic, multi-faceted strategy that went beyond the use of arrest.

A related point is that more targeted use of disorder enforcement may raise offenders' perceptions of sanction risk in the places where it is most needed (i.e., hot spots that provide the easiest opportunities and targets for victimization) while minimizing police use of arrest more generally (Nagin et al. 2015). The latter consideration is not insignificant when considering some of the other costs involved in the widespread use of misdemeanor arrests for crime prevention. As discussed by Lum and Nagin (2016), these costs include time that officers spend off the street processing minor arrests (an estimated two to four hours per arrest), increases in jail populations and costs (which have roughly tripled since 1980), and negative consequences for offenders (which include financial costs as well as other potentially adverse long-term effects on things like their ability to obtain employment). As recent experience has shown, overly aggressive enforcement approaches can also fray police–community relationships, particularly if not executed professionally and with community input, and increase the likelihood of use of force incidents that spark public outcry (e.g., see the President's Task Force on 21st Century Policing 2015).

Other Individual-Based Strategies

Besides arrest or the threat of arrest, police use other strategies to reduce offending by individuals. Some emphasize prevention, while others are alternative approaches to arrest for particular types of offenders. While many of these strategies have not been evaluated rigorously, there is a reasonably good evidence base for some.

Early risk prevention

Police commonly use a number of individual-focused prevention programs, particularly for youth (e.g., police athletic leagues, police volunteer programs, and programs providing different types of education and training). Two that have been evaluated rigorously include Drug Abuse Resistance Education (DARE) and Gang Resistance Education Training (GREAT), both of which are implemented in schools.

Police taking part in the DARE program visit schools (often elementary and middle schools) to educate youth about the dangers of drug use and provide training to help them resist social pressures to use drugs. There have been several rigorous studies testing the effects of this program on subsequent drug use among youth attending the program (the studies have often examined tobacco and alcohol use as well as the use of more serious drugs). Unfortunately, the evaluations have almost uniformly found no benefits from the program (for more recent studies, see Perry, Komro, Veblen-Mortenson et al. 2003; Rosenbaum and Hanson 1998; Sloboda, Stephens, Stephens et al. 2009). Some studies have even shown backfire effects; Sloboda et al. (2009), for example, found that DARE can worsen alcohol and cigarette use among youth who are non-users at the start of the program. Nonetheless, the program is politically popular and continues to be widely used throughout the United States and abroad (Sherman 2013). Although police may find it difficult to abandon this politically popular program, there may be better ways to focus these efforts on youth who are at higher risk or already showing signs of drug problems (Sloboda et al. 2009).

Another youth prevention program used by police is the Gang Resistance Education and Training program (GREAT), initially developed in Phoenix and now administered by the U.S. Department of Justice. GREAT is also delivered in a school setting, typically for middle school youth. The program is intended to help youth acquire knowledge and skills that will prevent them from becoming involved in delinquency, violence, and gangs. An evaluation of the program carried out with students in thirty-one schools found that it reduced the likelihood of participants joining gangs and had positive effects on several attitudinal, behavioral, and skill-related outcomes (e.g., more positive attitudes towards the police and less involvement with delinquent peers) (Esbensen, Peterson, Taylor et al. 2012). It is not clear that the program reduces violence among participants, but the other positive findings suggest that it may have value as a part of an agency's gang prevention and suppression efforts. We say more about these efforts below.

More recently, some police officers and agencies have become involved in mentorship programs, some in tandem with other school-related programs (see McGuire and Caliman 2016). According to a recent systematic review (Tolan, Henry, Schoeny et al. 2013), mentorship programs have shown positive results with regard to certain outcomes and are especially effective when mentors are professionally motivated to contribute to such programs. McGuire and Caliman (2016) argue that this evidence, as well as the fact that police often have a great deal of contact with delinquent youth, suggests that police could impact delinquency by participating in mentorship programs. Such programs would be considered more targeted programs (discussed later), but we mention them here because these might be one way that police can transition from more general school-based approaches like DARE or GREAT that may not be as effective to more targeted programs that focus on high-risk youth.

Restorative justice conferences

Another individual-oriented approach that police have tried with juvenile and adult offenders is participation in restorative justice conferences. Restorative justice conferences are grounded in theories of re-integrative shaming (Braithwaite 1989) as well as community justice (Braithwaite 1999) and provide an alternative to a more retributive justice system. Parties involved in a crime, including the suspect and victim and their supporters or family members, community members, and the police or other moderators, work together in restorative conferences to determine how the harm caused by a crime might be repaired for the victim and the community, as well as how the offender can be reintegrated back into the community. Restorative justice conferences can take on many forms, and the police may not necessarily be involved. As described by Sherman, Strang, and Woods (2000), the conference discussion produces an outcome that the offender is expected to fulfill, often involving apologizing to the victim and providing financial restitution and/or personal or community service work.

Restorative justice is more commonly practiced in Australia and New Zealand but is also used for juveniles in some states in the United States (for an example of the latter, see McCold and Wachtel 1998). Several tests of the strategy have been conducted, mostly in the United Kingdom and Australia, with a variety of violent and property offenders including both juveniles and adults. In the Matrix, we only include those studies that involved the police as major actors. In general, this approach seems to increase offender and victim satisfaction with the justice process, but the police-involved restorative justice programs tend to have non-significant or inconsistent effects on offending across studies.[7]

Enhanced responses to domestic violence

Over the years, police and other social service providers have developed augmented approaches for handling domestic violence in addition to arrest, in which the police are more involved in cases even after an arrest occurs to prevent future violence. One common strategy involves follow-up visits by police, often conducted with other social service providers that provide counseling and other assistance. These approaches have also shown mixed results with regard to reducing offender recidivism. A review of studies testing these types of follow-up visits concluded that they do not reduce repeat victimizations but may increase victims' calls to police (Davis, Weisburd, and Taylor 2008). Perhaps these findings suggest that second responder approaches have varying impacts on different types of offenders, as do arrests.[8]

---

[7] Sherman, Strang, Barnes et al. (2015) are more optimistic about these findings for specific types of offenders.

[8] The mixed findings might also reflect differences in the type, quality, or implementation of program elements across sites, particularly as they pertain to the social service aspects of these interventions.

Another approach is to establish specialized units for handling domestic violence cases (see Jolin, Feyerherm, Fountain et al. 1998). A study of one such unit in Charlotte-Mecklenburg found that it reduced re-offending by 50% over an eighteen-to-thirty-month follow-up period (Exum et al. 2014). As reported, this unit addressed domestic violence cases through intensive investigation (e.g., conducting detailed follow-up interviews, identifying and correcting missing information in patrol reports, preparing case materials for the district attorney, etc.) and victim assistance (e.g., filing restraining orders) for selected cases. Such units may facilitate better risk assessment and tailoring of multi-faceted interventions to the particular circumstances of individual cases.

The use of risk assessment instruments to identify cases that pose a high risk of serious future violence may be particularly helpful (Campbell, Webster, and Glass 2009; Roehl, O'Sullivan, Webster et al. 2005; also see, e.g., https://www.dangerassessment.org/). A recent test conducted in seven Oklahoma jurisdictions suggests that using risk assessment instruments to identify domestic violence victims at high risk for serious subsequent violence and putting those victims in direct contact with social service providers prompts victims to engage in more protective strategies and reduces the frequency and severity of future violence they experience (Messing, Campbell, and Wilson 2015b; Messing, Campbell, Webster et al. 2015a). Further work is needed to improve the predictive accuracy of these instruments.

The more positive indications from studies of special domestic violence units and police use of risk assessment instruments for domestic violence seem to underscore two generalizations about effective police interventions, which is that they tend to be focused on high-risk targets and tailored to the specifics of particular problems and cases. In the next section, we turn to targeted offender-based approaches that are more firmly grounded in these concepts.

Targeted Offender-Based Approaches

Crime is concentrated among offenders much as it is among places. For example, studies of arrest records and offender interviews indicate that the worst 10% of offenders commit a little more than half of all crimes (Blumstein, Cohen, Roth et al. 1986). Further, the risk of being involved in crime as an offender or victim are higher among certain readily identifiable groups including gang members, probationers, parolees, and others with prior criminal histories or involvement in delinquent/criminal lifestyles. These individuals and groups thus provide important strategic targets for police crime reduction strategies. Indeed, this is a central aspect of the intelligence-led policing philosophy (Ratcliffe 2008), which emphasizes the use of intelligence information and risk assessment to guide police operations.

Some police agencies employ repeat offender programs that involve proactive investigation of known high-rate offenders and/or post-arrest efforts to enhance evidentiary cases against such offenders. These programs have shown success in securing arrests and convictions of repeat offenders (Abrahamse et al. 1991; Martin and Sherman 1986), but the impacts of such initiatives on crime rates have not been studied. Nevertheless, there is evidence that targeted offender approaches focused on certain high-risk groups can reduce crime. These strategies have focused in particular on probationers, parolees, gangs, and high-risk persons in hot spot locations.

Probationers and parolees

Police efforts to enhance monitoring of probationers and parolees in cooperation with probation and parole agencies (e.g., through home visits, searches, and provision of other services) can be an important evidence-based approach to reducing crime. Probationers and parolees are at higher risk for offending and victimization, including that for very serious crimes. For example, studies have shown that people with criminal records are at elevated risk for involvement in homicide and shootings generally (e.g., Cook, Ludwig, and Braga 2005; Scocas, Harris, Huenke et al. 1997). Probationers and parolees in particular account for a substantial share of offenders and victims in such cases (e.g., Kennedy, Piehl, and Braga 1996; Tierney, McClanahan, and Hangley 2001). Further, probationers and parolees are already under the supervision of the criminal justice system, which gives police and authorities a greater ability to control their behavior. General police initiatives focused on supervising probationers and parolees have shown some promise in reducing crime (e.g. Worrall and Gaines 2006), though the evidence has not been entirely consistent (Giblin 2002; Rose and Hamilton 1970; also see Williams-Taylor 2009).

Some research suggests that efforts to deter these populations from future crime can be enhanced through the better use of risk assessment and multi-faceted services. One successful example is a program developed by the Knoxville (Tennessee) Police Department and the Tennessee Board of Probation and Parole to help parolees reintegrate successfully into the community (Knoxville Police Department 2002). Based on an analysis of parole revocation data, the agencies determined which parolees were at highest risk to re-offend and identified risk factors for recidivism, which included chemical dependency, unstable family relationships, mental health issues, educational and vocational deficiencies, and unsuitable housing. The agencies then used this assessment to develop team supervision and treatment plans tailored to the needs of individual parolees. An analysis of the program's effects found that it reduced re-incarceration by 44% (45% of those in the program were re-incarcerated within two years of their release from prison in comparison to 89% in a historical comparison group).

Advances in risk assessment are also helping police, probation, and parole authorities to more precisely identify and supervise probationers and parolees who are at the greatest risk of being involved in serious violence like homicide.

A program in Maryland, for example, uses sophisticated statistical predictions developed by researchers to identify the roughly 2 of every 100 probationers and parolees who are at the greatest risk of committing homicide or being a homicide victim (Mahoney 2012).[9] As part of this program, police work closely with probation and parole agents. Agents are assigned to police intelligence units to ensure that information on violent incidents involving probationers and parolees is immediately conveyed to supervising agents, and police work in close collaboration with probation and parole agents to monitor offender behavior and obtain and execute warrants in a timely fashion. An evaluation of the program is reportedly underway.

Another example of police collaborating with other agencies to address a high-risk population is a gang intervention program implemented in Mesa, Arizona (Spergel, Wa, and Sosa 2002). We mention the program here because most of the subjects were juvenile or young adult gang members who were on probation for non-violent offenses. The intervention involved a case-management approach in which a team of gang police, probation officers, case managers, and outreach workers monitored and provided social services to the program subjects. These services and activities included individual and family counseling, group discussions, referrals to a variety of community agencies, and surveillance, supervision, monitoring, and (when appropriate) arrest. An evaluation of the program showed that program youth had arrest levels 18% lower than those of a comparison group over a four-year period. Further, the neighborhoods where the program was implemented experienced a 10% reduction in selected juvenile-type crimes compared to other neighborhoods that did not receive the program.

More generally, police are increasingly collaborating with other criminal and juvenile justice agencies to improve supervision and services for probationers and parolees as part of broader crime prevention initiatives like the "pulling levers" strategy discussed below (e.g., Braga, Kennedy, Waring et al. 2001; Papachristos, Meares, and Fagan 2007; also see Koper, Woods, and Isom 2016). While this often makes it difficult to distinguish the unique effects of the probationer–parolee initiatives from those of other program elements, evidence from some studies suggests that controlling these populations can play a central role in reducing serious crimes such as gun violence (Papachristos et al. 2007).

Gangs and other groups at high-risk for violence

Gang members provide another target for offender-focused strategies, as they contribute significantly to crime and violence. Numerous studies show that gang members are more likely to engage in serious violence, possess and carry weapons, and sell drugs (e.g., Bjerregaard and Lizotte 1995; Decker, McGarrell,

---

[9] For further discussion of the types of statistical techniques used to generate these risk assessments, see Berk, Sherman, Barnes et al. (2009).

Perez et al. 2007; Esbensen and Huizinga 1993; Kennedy et al. 1996; Sheley and Wright 1993; Thornberry et al. 2003). Gangs are also heavily implicated in lethal violence; Egley and Ritz (2006) estimated at one point that roughly one-quarter of homicides that occur in cities of 100,000 or more people were classified as gang related. This figure can rise to half or more of homicides in cities such as Los Angeles, Chicago, Stockton (CA), and Lowell (MA) (Braga, Pierce, McDevitt et al. 2008; Decker et al. 2007; Egley and Ritz 2006). The disproportionate involvement of gangs in homicide was also illustrated by a study in Boston showing that gang members accounted for only 1% of the city's youth but were involved in 60% of the city's youth homicide cases (Kennedy et al. 1996).

Responses to gangs by police and other criminal justice and social service practitioners include various suppression, social intervention, organizational, and community mobilization strategies (Decker 2008; Decker et al. 2007; Howell 2000).[10] Suppression strategies appear to be the most common police response to gangs (Decker et al. 2007, 4). These commonly involve various patrol and enforcement efforts—saturation and/or directed patrol, truancy and curfew enforcement, enhanced enforcement of laws and ordinances against minor crime and disorderly behavior, and targeted investigations—in areas with gang presence. (Note these types of intervention appear in the both place-based and group sections of the Evidence-Based Policing Matrix.) Some studies have reported success with these approaches (Bynum and Varano 2003; Fritsch, Caeti, and Taylor 1999 [specifically curfews]), while others have shown no effects or less clear results (Cahill, Coggeshall, Hayeslip et al. 2008; Decker and Curry 2003; Fritsch et al. 1999 [specifically saturation patrols]). Even when effective, suppression interventions can be resource intensive and may not produce lasting effects (also see Howell 2000, 3–4).

Experts typically recommend a more balanced approach to gangs that supplements suppression with other social service and prevention efforts (Klein and Maxson 2006; Spergel and Curry 1993). Thus, there have been many efforts, often with federal sponsorship, that combine the efforts of criminal justice, social service, and community groups in a more comprehensive, multi-faceted way (e.g., see Decker 2003; 2008; Decker et al. 2007). Integrating these efforts can sometimes prove difficult (e.g., Decker and Curry 2003), and there have not been many rigorous evaluations of such programs. However, the Mesa gang intervention program discussed above (under "Interventions with probationers and parolees") provides some affirmative evidence for the utility of multi-faceted gang interventions that blend prevention and suppression (Spergel et al. 2002).

---

[10] As of 2013, 83% of large police departments in the United States (those with 100 or more officers) had special units or designated personnel to address gangs, as did 20% of small police departments (Reaves 2015).

Another well-known and fruitful approach to dealing with violence by gangs and other at-risk groups is the "pulling levers" or "focused deterrence" strategy that was developed in Boston during the 1990s to reduce gang and youth violence (Braga et al. 2001; Kennedy et al. 2001). In broad terms, this strategy concentrates law enforcement, prosecution, and social service resources on high-risk groups, typically through face-to-face contacts known as "notification meetings." The Boston project involved a collaborative, problem-solving effort among police, prosecutors, probation and parole officers, juvenile justice officials, schools, federal law enforcement, social service workers, academic researchers, and local clergy. First, a project analysis was completed, which attributed much of Boston's youth homicide problem to gangs (loosely defined). Then, working group members warned gang members through notification meetings, other direct individual contacts, and indirect channels (e.g., gang outreach workers and flyers) that continued violence would be met with severe sanctions. These sanctions included targeted multi-agency crackdowns and referrals for federal prosecution (which often provides for harsher sanctions than are available at the state level). In this way, practitioners sought to use a deterrence-based approach that was focused on a high-risk group and raised offenders' perceptions of risk through direct communications that clarified the consequences of offending and broke down offenders' sense of anonymity from authorities. When necessary, working group members followed through on these threats, which resulted in high-profile arrests, convictions, and harsh sentences. At the same time, the project made various social services available to gang members to help them avoid violence (e.g., assistance with drug treatment or employment services).[11] An evaluation of the program found that it reduced youth homicides in Boston by 63%, while also reducing gun assaults and calls to police for shots fired (Braga et al. 2001). Subsequent analysis verified that shootings declined specifically among gangs that were directly targeted by the program (Braga, Hureau, and Papachristos 2014).

This approach has been used successfully to target high-risk groups (e.g., gangs, probationers, and parolees) citywide or in high-risk areas in several cities. Although questions remain about the specific effects of the various components of the strategy, quasi-experimental evaluations (most of which are in the Matrix) have shown that the overall strategy has reduced gun crime, homicide, and/or other violent offenses, sometimes substantially. These effects have been seen in places like Indianapolis (Chermak and McGarrell 2004; McGarrell, Chernak, Wilson et al. 2006), Lowell, MA (Braga, Pierce, McDevitt et al. 2008), Stockton, CA (Braga 2008), Chicago (Papachristos et al. 2007), Cincinnati (Engel, Tillyer, and Corsaro 2011), Los Angeles (Tita, Riley, Ridgeway et al. 2005), and even Glasgow, Scotland (Graham 2016). (See Braga and Weisburd 2012, for a more

---

[11] The Boston approach is also commonly known as "pulling levers" in reference to the fact that authorities pull all available levers, so to speak, in gaining compliance by targeted groups.

thorough review and meta-analysis of "pulling levers" studies.) This approach also provided an important impetus for the development of similar federal programs, including the Strategic Approaches to Community Safety Initiative (SACSI), Project Safe Neighborhoods (PSN), and the Comprehensive Anti-Gang Initiative (CAGI). Rigorous evaluations of the latter two programs, which include many of the pulling levers components, indicate that they have helped to reduce violence in many communities throughout the nation (McGarrell, Corsaro, Hipple et al. 2010; McGarrell, Corsaro, Melde et al. 2012; McGarrell, Corsaro, Melde et al. 2013). More recently, the approach has also been used to attack drug markets (Corsaro, Hunt, Hipple et al. 2012).

The pulling levers strategy has been a particularly important development in law enforcement approaches to reducing violence. The success of this program also underscores an important generalization about evidence-based policing approaches. That is well-targeted programs implemented in a problem-solving framework can facilitate the development of tailored, multi-faceted solutions. However, the use of this approach can be challenging for police in that it requires extensive multi-agency collaboration. In particular, the cooperation of U.S. Attorneys who can threaten harsh penalties for repeat violent and gun offenders is arguably a particularly important element of the strategy.[12] Strategies like pulling levers and other comprehensive gang-related approaches require the dedication of special units that can focus on gang problems and coordinate with other agencies and officers in the field.

High-risk persons in hot spot locations

Together the studies on targeted offender-based strategies and hot spots policing (see Chapter 4) imply that strategies targeting high-risk people may be especially effective when focused in high-risk places. Indeed, many of the successful interventions in the place-based sections of the Matrix have involved combined approaches that target high-risk people and places (e.g., Azrael et al. 2013; Bynum and Varano 2003; Corsaro et al. 2012; Groff, Ratcliffe, Haberman et al. 2015; Nunn, Quinet, Rowe et al. 2006; Papachristos et al. 2007; Uchida and Swatt 2013). Some studies suggest that targeted offender approaches are more effective when combined with an emphasis on hot spots (Uchida and Swatt 2013). Focusing on key individuals who regularly offend in high-crime places fits well with the philosophies of problem-oriented policing and intelligence-led policing, and it provides a way for police to use their resources in ways that can potentially maximize both efficiency and effectiveness. At the same time, these targeted approaches can minimize the need for police to use more

---

[12] Although police in large U.S. cities frequently participate in multi-agency efforts (including PSN) to reduce gun violence and put a great emphasis on prosecution of gun offenders by U.S. Attorneys, most do not actually engage in notification meetings (Koper, Woods, and Kubu 2013c), perhaps due to the effort and coordination necessary to run these meetings.

widespread aggressive tactics (like zero-tolerance crackdowns) that have greater potential to strain police–community relations.

These initiatives may be particularly effective when they are informed by good intelligence about offenders. An example of this comes from Philadelphia, where police implemented an intelligence-led offender-based strategy within targeted violent crime hot spots (Groff et al. 2015). Their approach involved a focus on repeat violent offenders who either lived in or were suspected of being involved in violent crimes in the target areas, which averaged 0.044 square miles in size with three miles of streets. Offenders were targeted for the intervention if they had a history of violent offenses and criminal intelligence suggested they were involved in a criminal lifestyle. Working with an intelligence analyst, dedicated teams of officers drawn from the districts' tactical operations squads identified and maintained a list of individuals thought to be causing problems in the hot spots. The offender-focused team members (who were freed from answering calls for service) relied heavily on surveillance, aggressive patrol, and partnerships with beat officers. The special unit and area patrol officers also made frequent contact with the targeted offenders; contacts ranged from making small talk with known offenders to serving arrest warrants for recently committed offenses. The initiative was conducted over a twelve–twenty-four-month period, and reduced violent crimes overall by 42% in the target areas and violent felonies by 50%.

Offender-focused initiatives in hot spots can also extend beyond enforcement to incorporate other interventions with the offenders and locations. For instance, attempts to reduce serious crime in drug market hot spots by incapacitating key operators in the drug trade have yielded mixed results (McCabe 2009; Nunn et al. 2006; Roman, Cahill, Coggeshall et al. 2005). However, these efforts might be enhanced through the application of pulling levers approaches that channel multi-agency resources to promote both deterrence and rehabilitation among drug market actors (e.g., see Corsaro et al. 2012). Or, they might work better if combined with interventions that address other features and problems of drug crime hot spots (see Mazerolle, Soole, and Rombouts 2007 on the effectiveness of geographically focused problem-solving efforts to address drug problems).

Another more general form of targeting high-risk people in high-risk areas involves the application of stop-question-and-frisk (SQF), particularly on those suspected of carrying weapons. SQF has been employed more extensively by police as a crime prevention tactic in recent decades. Although it is often coupled with zero-tolerance disorder reduction strategies and drug enforcement, it has arguably been most valuable as a tool for reducing gun violence (see discussion in Lum and Nagin 2017).[13] The effects of SQF on crime have been examined and debated

---

[13] SQF was the source of the landmark 1968 Supreme Court decision *Terry v. Ohio* that laid out the constitutional standard required for its use—police officers had to have a "reasonable

in numerous studies, most of which are correlational in design and thus not included in the Matrix. For example, an analysis by the New York State Office of the Attorney General (2013) concluded that a large majority of SQFs do not result in arrest. However, proponents argue that SQFs serve a preventive function, helping to generally deter crime. The evidence for this claim is mixed. An early analysis by Smith and Purtell (2007, 2008) found the use of SQF may reduce robbery, murder, burglary, and auto theft citywide, but not assault, rape, or grand larceny. Rosenfeld and Fornango (2014) critiqued Smith and Purtell's studies, arguing that upon closer examination and with more specified modeling, they could not find significant effects of SQF on robbery or burglary. However, others have found evidence of a deterrent effect of SQF (see Weisburd, Telep, and Lawton 2014; Weisburd, Wooditch, Weisburd et al. 2016; Wooditch and Weisburd 2016).

But of course, law enforcement agencies in democracies are not only concerned with crime control, but also with citizen reactions to their tactics and whether tactics are lawful. Stop-question-and-frisk is a controversial tactic that is believed to have contributed to friction between police and minority communities and been implemented in ways that are discriminatory. Evidence supporting the crime control effects of SQF must therefore be balanced against evidence of the unconstitutional or discriminatory use of such tactics (Lum and Nagin 2017). And research can also provide us with important hints about how law enforcement agencies can restrict the use of SQF in ways that citizens can accept. For example, if used lawfully and in a more targeted way as a tool to reduce gun crime in hot spots, SQF may be effective (Cohen and Ludwig 2003; McGarrell, Chermak, Weiss et al. 2001; Rosenfeld, Deckard, and Blackburn 2014; Sherman et al. 1995; also see a review of gun-focused patrols by Koper and Mayo-Wilson 2006; 2012). Using SQF in this more focused manner may also help police to secure community support for this strategy. This was done, for example, through meetings with community leaders and door-to-door contacts in studies of gun patrols in Indianapolis and Kansas City, Missouri (McGarrell et al. 2001; Sherman et al. 1995) while limiting its use and potential collateral damage to police–community relations. Further, training officers in how to conduct SQFs in a manner consistent with the law and with principles of procedural justice (Tyler 1988; 1990) may further minimize negative collateral effects from this tactic if it improves the likelihood that the subjects of SQF at least feel that they have been treated fairly and respectfully (see Mazerolle, Bennett, Manning et al. 2013).

Conclusion

Regardless of whether evidence indicates that more arrests and case clearances reduce crime, arresting serious offenders is important in bringing justice to

---

suspicion" that the person or persons being stopped had committed a crime or were about to do so *and* that the individual was armed.

victims and maintaining a community's trust and confidence in the police. Arrest may also contribute to crime reduction through incapacitation and deterrence, although deterrence can also be achieved by threatening to arrest or by increasing the perceived risk of being arrested, even if an arrest is not made. At the same time, we also know that the use of arrest as a crime control strategy doesn't necessarily yield crime prevention and reduction benefits. Thus, while arrest continues to be an important function of the police, it is not the only solution, nor even the most important. This is why being knowledgeable about the evidence on individual or offender-focused strategies in policing is paramount. Understanding when these strategies work, as well as their limitations, can strengthen an agency's community safety strategy.

In particular, police interventions focusing enforcement and prevention on high-risk groups such as gangs, probationers, parolees, and known repeat offenders show promise in reducing crime, particularly when focused on actors in high-crime locations. Offender-focused approaches also seem to be more effective when they are multi-faceted and based on good risk assessment and intelligence. Examples include the pulling levers strategy that concentrates multi-agency enforcement and prevention efforts on groups at high risk for violence; joint agency programs to supervise and treat high-risk probationers and parolees; dedicated units to monitor and apprehend known repeat offenders in hot spots; and domestic violence units that can develop more in-depth investigations and interventions into high-risk domestic violence cases.

To implement such approaches, patrol officers and special units in the field need to be aware of and monitor problem actors in their areas of responsibility. Making regular contact with these individuals and groups may help to reduce their offending by letting them know they are known and under watch. Police agencies will also need more systematic efforts to both identify high-risk people, groups, and networks through crime analysis and intelligence and disseminate this information to officers in the field, with operational guidance on what to do with that information. As we emphasized in Chapter 4 and as we will drive home in Chapter 13, this requires that agencies invest in high-quality crime analysts who can assist with this task. Tracking problem individuals and groups linked to hot spots might also become a regular part of tracking and diagnosing problems at those locations (see our discussion of the "Case of Place" concept in Chapter 12). Crime analysis and research staff in policing agencies, perhaps working in collaboration with outside researchers, should also continue their efforts to develop, refine, and test risk assessment instruments that can be used to inform targeted offender strategies. Such efforts should pay attention to innovations in analytic approaches as well, such as network analysis to better understand gangs and co-offending. Finally, police benefit when they partner with other organizations (notably, prosecutors, probation and parole authorities, juvenile justice officials, and social service providers) to develop coordinated and tailored approaches to managing high-risk people through enforcement and prevention services.

Finally, to implement evidence-based policing requires the police to see offender and place-based approaches in tandem and to take on a balanced approach with an expanded toolkit to deal with crime. An expanded toolkit not only includes more proactive approaches, but also incorporates a more refined understanding of possible consequences (especially negative consequences) to proactive offender-based approaches to control crime.

6

NEIGHBORHOOD AND JURISDICTION INTERVENTIONS

While Chapter 4 examined the evidence and practice of micro place-based and hot spots policing, and Chapter 5 focused on strategies related to individuals, this chapter highlights the evidence and practice of "neighborhood-" and "jurisdiction-" level interventions. Law enforcement agencies still typically organize many of their operations around geographic spaces that are larger than the types of micro places we discussed in Chapter 4. Studies of interventions in these larger areas provide valuable lessons about the nature and challenges of the evidence in evidence-based policing, as well as the need for flexibility in implementing evidence-based tactics and strategies.

Neighborhoods and Larger Geographic Areas in Policing

Police agencies typically divide their jurisdictions into large geographic divisions, districts, zones, or areas, each of which often has its own chain of command. This decentralization enables police agencies to be responsive to the particular conditions and needs of different parts of the jurisdiction, and allocation of resources is often organized by these areas. These large administrative areas are typically divided into further subunits, such as sectors, down to the smallest subareas, which are referred to as patrol beats, posts, or reporting areas. In many agencies, the police beat or patrol area represents the primary geographic assignment given to patrol officers in the field and is usually much larger than the micro places we described in Chapter 4. Police commonly define their beats and other administrative areas based on natural geographic divisions and boundaries, population density, political and neighborhood boundaries, distance and travel times (usually by vehicle), and differences in workload (i.e., calls for service and crime) throughout the jurisdiction.

Similarly, community groups are also organized by geographic units that extend beyond street blocks or corners. They may encompass larger communities, political boundaries, or cultural enclaves where people live and which may have historical significance. Law enforcement leaders and officers may attend community meetings in these neighborhoods and interact with organizations and leaders within these places. Citizen requests may come from these organizations and leaders, which also makes police agencies more attuned to them.

Police strategies are often devised, implemented, and evaluated within these administrative and community boundaries. These efforts represent another form of place-based policing, and their evaluations can be found in the "Neighborhood" portion/slab of our Matrix.[1] These studies of police strategies focus on administrative areas such as police beats, neighborhoods, districts, and the like. We refer to this research loosely as neighborhood studies, although the areas in question do not always correspond to a particular neighborhood as might be defined by residents.

Additionally, we also discuss jurisdiction-level studies that appear in the Matrix.[2] Although the jurisdiction-level designation suggests no particular focus, our discussion below shows that successful jurisdiction-wide interventions often involve focusing on high-risk geographic locations and groups throughout an agency's territory of responsibility.

Interventions in the "Neighborhood" and "Jurisdiction" sections of the Matrix tend to be successful. More than half (55%) of the forty-seven interventions in the "Neighborhood" section are classified as successful, and 70% have shown at least mixed indications of success (based on the composition of the Matrix as of this writing). Although few in number (seven), evaluations of jurisdiction-level interventions have also produced a high success rate (five of seven, or 71%), and all have shown at least some indications of benefits. However, an important caveat is that the neighborhood- and jurisdiction-level studies have used less rigorous methodologies, which could bias them towards finding favorable results (Weisburd, Lum, and Petrosino 2001; also see Chapter 2). Many of these evaluations were quasi-experimental and typically involved only one or small numbers of areas in the treatment and control conditions. This means that successful findings may be due to the intervention, but they could also be explained by other factors, such as the amenability of the location to the

---

[1] The "Neighborhood" slab of the Matrix can be accessed at http://cebcp.org/evidence-based-policing/the-matrix/neighborhood/.

[2] The "Jurisdiction" slab of the Matrix can be accessed at http://cebcp.org/evidence-based-policing/the-matrix/jurisdiction/.

intervention. In contrast, the scientific rigor of the evidence is considerably stronger for micro place and individual-based interventions, which have often been studied using randomized experiments.

There are understandable reasons for the lower level of methodological quality in neighborhood and jurisdiction studies. Notably, it is much less feasible to develop randomized experiments with large samples when conducting area-level studies. The larger the geographic unit of analysis, the fewer overall units there will be to compare within a jurisdiction. It may also be difficult in some cases for police to mount area-level interventions across large numbers of areas for purposes of rigorous testing. However, despite their weaker scientific base, these studies give us valuable insight into proactive, prevention-oriented innovations and activities that the police are undertaking. Further, the police value neighborhood-based approaches, and communities and police often anchor their interactions at the neighborhood or even jurisdiction level. Evidence-based policing has to be flexible to these realities. Only focusing on micro approaches because of their stronger evidence base may miss out on opportunities to evaluate, improve, and further develop tactics and strategies that are often used by law enforcement to engage with communities.

In the next sections, we review the evidence base for neighborhood- and jurisdiction-level interventions, highlighting what we know about their effectiveness and discussing the lessons they hold for evidence-based policing. In our discussion below, we group neighborhood- and jurisdiction-level strategies into two groups: community policing strategies, which have featured prominently in area-level policing studies, and other types of strategies.

Community Policing

Community policing became a very prominent law enforcement philosophy in the last two decades of the twentieth century, and it has been the subject of numerous evaluation studies. We discussed the definition of community policing briefly in Chapter 4 and reiterate here that it generally involves police agencies, including and involving community groups and citizens in co-producing safety, crime prevention, and solutions to local concerns. More specifically, Skogan (2006) describes three core and densely interrelated elements of community policing: (i) citizen involvement in identifying and addressing public safety concerns; (ii) the decentralization of decision-making to develop responses to locally defined problems; and (iii) problem-solving.

Community policing is often hard to implement and to evaluate because it is a philosophy rather than a specific set of programs (Mastrofski 2006; Mastrofski, Willis, and Kochel 2007). Moreover, what is defined as community policing also varies over time and across police agencies (Eck and Rosenbaum 1994; Greene and Mastrofski 1998). Early research on community policing focused on tactics such as foot patrol, neighborhood watch, and community meetings or newsletters that emphasized greater communication and interaction between police and citizens. However, the advent of problem-oriented policing (see Goldstein 1979; 1990) and advocacy efforts by the Office of Community Oriented Policing Services of the U.S. Department of Justice expanded the definition to include problem-solving efforts, particularly those done in collaboration with other elements of the community (i.e., citizens' groups, business, and other government agencies) (see discussion by Gill, Weisburd, Telep et al. 2014). Thus, in practice, community policing efforts have often included tactics such as foot patrol, neighborhood watch, community meetings or newsletters, efforts to reduce social and physical disorder, conflict resolution, and various types of problem-solving efforts. Community policing has also encompassed efforts to build collective efficacy and empowerment in communities (see Sampson 2011) and often involves police working with an array of citizen and government organizations to reduce crime and improve the quality of life in communities.[3]

By its nature, community policing is a proactive, crime prevention approach to policing. As the National Research Council report on *Fairness and Effectiveness in Policing* asserted, "community policing may be seen as reaction to the standard models of policing.... While the standard model of policing has relied primarily on the resources of the police and its traditional law enforcement powers, community policing suggests a reliance on a more community-based crime control that draws not only on the resources of the police but also on the resources of the public." (National Research Council 2004, 233). As a proactive crime prevention approach, community policing tries to address and mitigate community problems (crime or otherwise), and in turn, build social resilience, collective efficacy, and empowerment to strengthen the infrastructure for the co-production of safety and crime prevention. These ideas draw from a variety of program theories about the crime prevention mechanisms at work in community policing. For example, with neighborhood watch or police–citizen patrols, increased guardianship may create a deterrent effect. Guardianship may also be the result of building collective efficacy in neighborhoods so that citizens feel empowered to apply informal social controls to risky behavior, suspicious incidents, or unsupervised youth. Skogan discussed community policing as playing an important role in reducing fear, which can lower the chances of citizen withdrawal and isolation, two factors that when left unchecked may lead to further crime and disorder (see Skogan 1986; 1990).

---

[3] More recently, the community policing idea has expanded to encompass notions of procedural justice and police legitimacy (see Tyler 1990; see also reviews by Mazerolle, Bennett, Manning et al. 2013 and Nagin and Telep forthcoming), as well as the improvement of police accountability through citizen review boards, body-worn cameras, and improved complaint processes. These efforts by the police have not been evaluated for their crime prevention effects and therefore do not appear in the Matrix, nor do we discuss them here. However, see Nagin and Telep (forthcoming) for an extensive review of these studies and their results.

Others suggest that community-oriented policing may facilitate problem-oriented policing, which offers tailored approaches to specific concerns (see, e.g., Goldstein 1990; Scott 2000), a process which has been found to be effective in crime prevention (Weisburd, Telep, Hinkle et al. 2010). Here, the community plays a role in identifying and explaining problems, as well as suggesting responses to them. Because of community policing's emphasis on both neighborhood-level processes of social control and police relationships with the community as a whole, these interventions have most commonly been implemented and evaluated in neighborhoods or administrative areas that approximate meaningful neighborhoods (though as we discussed in Chapter 4, these notions also have relevance to the control of crime problems at micro places).

Before examining community policing studies in the Matrix, three prior reviews of the crime control impacts of community policing are worth mentioning. In the first comprehensive review of community policing evaluations, Sherman and Eck (2002) reviewed twenty-three studies of community policing strategies including neighborhood watch, community meetings, door-to-door contacts, police storefronts (substations in the community), increasing information flow to citizens, and legitimacy policing. They concluded that some community policing efforts were promising, such as those that increased community participation in priority setting or door-to-door visits by the police. However, other efforts that had no clear crime risk-factor focus did not seem to have strong research support.

Similarly, the narrative review of community policing studies by the National Research Council (2004) referred to above concluded that broad-based community policing programs generally do not reduce crime but do seem to improve other important outcomes such as citizen views of the police (see also Weisburd and Eck 2004). Any observed crime prevention impacts are more directly associated with specific strategies—such as distinct problem-oriented policing initiatives—implemented within community policing programs.

Most recently, a Campbell Collaboration systematic review, sponsored by the United Kingdom's National Policing Improvement Agency, examined a variety of crime, disorder, and other community outcomes from twenty-five community policing studies (Gill et al. 2014). This review, which was based on a statistical meta-analysis that combined data across studies to estimate average effect sizes, concluded that community policing programs generate positive effects on citizen satisfaction, perceptions of disorder, and police legitimacy, but are generally limited in their ability to reduce crime, or even fear of crime.

Thus, reviews of studies of community policing across more than two decades seem to have consistently produced similar results. Community policing efforts produce numerous benefits that may indirectly contribute to crime prevention through greater community satisfaction or by facilitating problem solving, collaboration, and cooperation with the police. However, the direct impact of community policing on crime prevention and control remains dubious.

Similar patterns can be seen in our Matrix. It should be noted that in the Matrix we use a slightly more restrictive selection criteria than have other community policing reviews.[4] Nevertheless, there are roughly twenty studies in the neighborhood section of the Matrix that could qualify as community policing studies under a broad conceptualization of the term. Some of these interventions include: organizing residents and increasing community involvement to set priorities and determine responses to specific problems (Connell, Miggans and McGloin 2008; Giacomazzi 1995; Lindsay and McGillis 1986; Mazerolle, Adams, Budz et al. 2003; Tuffin, Morris, and Poole 2006); general increases in contacts with citizens, including door-to-door contacts, business checks, newsletters, and/or storefronts (Mazerolle et al. 2003; Pate, Lavrakas, Wycoff et al. 1985a; Pate, Skogan, Wycoff et al. 1985b; Wyckoff, Pate, Skogan et al. 1985); neighborhood watch (Bennett 1990) and other police efforts to organize community block groups (Pate, McPherson, and Silloway 1987); and community policing approaches that combine many of these strategies (Skogan, Harnett, and Lovig 1995). Other studies that might be characterized as community policing highlight foot patrol (Police Foundation 1981; Trojanowicz 1986); enforcement and clean-up initiatives targeting disorder, often in combination with other measures like foot patrol, community contacts, and projects to address physical deterioration (Pate et al. 1985a; 1985b); community programs to improve property marking through door-to-door visits (Laycock 1991); and multi-agency initiatives emphasizing a range of enforcement and prevention measures (Koper, Hoffmaster, Luna et al. 2010; also see Koper, Woods, and Isom 2016).

In general, the results of these studies have been mixed, with some programs showing significant effects on crime and others not. However, one pattern that can be discerned from these studies is that community policing programs seem to produce better results when they place a strong and systematic emphasis on police–community contacts and addressing neighborhood problems in collaboration with community members. A good example of this is the Chicago Alternative Policing program (CAPS) evaluated by Skogan and colleagues (1995). The CAPS program reorganized policing around small geographical areas in which officers assigned to beat teams (who were also free from responding to 911 calls) identified and dealt with a broad range of neighborhood problems in partnership with neighborhood residents and community organizations. These officers met with members of the community on a regular basis at beat meetings and developed plans for tackling neighborhood problems. A prioritizing

[4] For example, the Matrix does not include evaluations that use time series studies without comparison groups, or studies that compare an intervention location with larger, noncomparable units, such as the rest of the jurisdiction (see, e.g., Esbensen 1987, which is included in the Gill et al. (2014) review, but not in the Matrix). The Matrix also includes only those studies that show at least some police involvement (so community activities to prevent crime that do not involve the police are not included).

system was also developed for coordinating the delivery of municipal services to support these local problem-solving efforts. An early evaluation of CAPS suggested that it reduced robberies and burglaries and had other positive effects on citizens' perceptions of their neighborhoods and the police. (In a similar vein, see, e.g., Connell, Miggans, and McGloin 2008; Mazerolle et al. 2003; Pate et al. 1985b; Tuffin et al. 2006.)

Nonetheless, it remains challenging to reach definitive conclusions about the crime prevention effects of community policing. To begin with, studies of community policing suffer from design weaknesses due to a number of causes. Agencies often implement interventions before an evaluation plan can be properly designed, and evaluation is likely a low priority in implementing many community-oriented policing strategies. Also, community policing encompasses a variety of activities, which are sometimes vague, philosophical, or indirectly linked with actions. Interventions can also include multiple and unevenly resourced components, which means that identifying, measuring, and tracking the mechanisms of prevention that contributed to an effect is difficult.

Further complicating evaluations of community policing is the size of the unit of analysis. Hot spots studies indicate that police can create deterrent effects when matching crime prevention resources to the precise geographic locations that need them. Community policing, on the other hand, tends to be implemented in larger areas and neighborhoods that have places with and without crime. This might dilute the dosage of intervention at the micro places most needing it. At the same time, substantial effects in targeted hot spots might be harder to measure at the community level. Neighborhood- and area-level studies also tend to have weaker research designs, usually based on comparing one or a small number of treatment areas selected for the intervention to one or a small number of non-randomly selected comparison neighborhoods. Hence, even those community policing studies satisfying the methodological requirements of the Matrix are still mostly modest in methodological rigor.

Notwithstanding these issues, it is again worth emphasizing that community policing strategies have important benefits with regard to improving citizens' views of police and their communities (Gill et al. 2014). Community input and reaction is an important outcome that democratic police should seek irrespective of reducing neighborhood-level crime rates (Lum and Nagin 2017). Further, community policing approaches can also be helpful in addressing crime problems at micro places, as discussed in Chapter 4. For these reasons, community policing approaches are worthwhile for police even if their crime reduction benefits are limited. Further, community policing approaches may help police to develop the community trust and cooperation needed to carry out other crime prevention strategies, particularly ones that necessitate more aggressive enforcement to tackle serious crime problems like gun carrying and gun violence (e.g., McGarrell, Chermak, Weiss et al. 2001; Sherman, Shaw, and Rogan 1995).

Other Area-Level Strategies

In addition to community policing strategies, police carry out a variety of other neighborhood- and jurisdiction-level activities. Those strategies that have been evaluated and that appear in the Matrix have tested a variety of approaches ranging from general patrol to strategies targeting specific problems like gun violence, drugs, disorder, and driving under the influence. A few generalizations emerge from these evaluations that are relevant to agencies trying to develop a more evidence-based approach to neighborhood-based strategies and tactics.

One pattern found in the research in the Matrix is that successful neighborhood interventions often use analysis and intelligence to target high-risk locations, individuals, and/or groups within those neighborhoods. An example is Operation LASER (Los Angeles' Strategic Extraction and Restoration), a program designed to reduce crime in selected reporting districts of Los Angeles (Uchida and Swatt 2013).[5] The program involved both an offender-based component that provided intelligence on chronic offenders to officers (for use in investigations and proactive activities) and a chronic location component that involved directed patrol and use of CCTV at hot spot locations. The intervention reduced crime by 7% per month in places that received both interventions (though districts that received only the chronic offender intervention did not have significant reductions). Other examples of targeted interventions within neighborhoods and larger areas include:

– directed patrols to reduce gun carrying and gun crime focused on particular places and people within beats or larger areas in cities including Pittsburgh, Indianapolis, and Kansas City, Missouri (Cohen and Ludwig 2003; McGarrell et al. 2001; Sherman et al. 1995);
– a district-level homicide reduction initiative in Milwaukee that involved (among other components) police efforts to better manage high-risk places, such as violent taverns and nuisance properties, and high-risk offenders on probation or parole in the community (Azrael, Braga, and O'Brien 2013);
– an intervention to reduce shootings in Los Angeles by blocking streets leading to shooting hot spots within neighborhoods having high levels of gang violence (Lasley 1998);
– a beat-level initiative in Houston that focused patrols and other activities in hot spots (Caeti 1999); and
– interventions to reduce violence in numerous cities through federal programs like Project Safe Neighborhoods and the Comprehensive Anti-Gang Initiative that focus a variety of enforcement, prosecution, and preventive interventions on high-risk groups and places (McGarrell, Corsaro, Hipple et al. 2010; McGarrell, Corsaro, Melde et al. 2012; Papachristos, Meares, and Fagan 2007).

---

[5] See also http://www.smartpolicinginitiative.com/tta/spotlight/los-angeles-ca-site-spotlight.

By the same token, several of the pulling levers and focused deterrence studies discussed in Chapter 5 (and mostly included in the "Groups" slab of the Matrix) have documented jurisdiction-level impacts resulting from interventions with high-risk groups, notably violent gangs. Finally, it is also worth reiterating that many successful community policing programs involve addressing problems within neighborhood areas (e.g., Skogan et al. 1995). In practice, this may often necessitate interventions with very specific micro places and people in a neighborhood, though these may typically go undocumented.

Another characteristic of successful neighborhood- and jurisdiction-level interventions is that they target particular problems with strategies tailored to those problems. For instance, several studies in the Matrix highlight strategies that were developed to tackle gun crime and other serious violence. In these studies, police have often worked with partner agencies using a data-driven, problem-solving framework. They have also employed a wide range of patrol, enforcement, prosecution, and/or prevention efforts targeted on high-risk places and groups as well as other problems and conditions believed to contribute to violence (e.g., Azrael et al. 2013; Bynum, Grommon, and McCluskey 2014; Florence, Shepherd, Brennan et al. 2011; Koper et al. 2010; Lasley 1998; McGarrell et al. 2001; 2010; 2012; Papachristos et al. 2007; Sherman et al. 1995; Tita, Riley, Ridgeway et al. 2003; Uchida and Swatt 2013; White, Fyfe, Campbell et al. 2003; Villaveces, Cummings, Espetia et al. 2000). Other illustrations include a multi-jurisdictional initiative to reduce auto theft by targeting investigative operations on stolen vehicle dump sites identified through spatial and temporal analysis of vehicle thefts and recoveries (Krimmel and Mele 1998) as well as a multi-agency strategy to reduce drunk driving at a university using DUI checkpoints, media coverage, and a student-designed social marketing campaign at the university (Clapp, Johnson, Voas et al. 2005).

A final point we emphasize is that many successful neighborhood- and jurisdiction-level interventions outside the community policing realm have also been multi-faceted efforts in which police worked with other partner agencies and sometimes community groups, often within a broad problem-solving framework. Once again, programs to reduce gun violence and other serious violence serve as leading examples. The pulling levers, focused deterrence, and Project Safe Neighborhoods projects which have been referenced several times have commonly involved numerous criminal justice, social service, and community groups working in collaboration to coordinate and target their efforts. In Milwaukee, for instance, police took part in a homicide review commission that brought together criminal justice, social service, and public health agencies to improve responses to homicide and shooting incidents and to develop prevention strategies based on analysis of homicide data (Azrael et al. 2013). The strategy was credited with reductions in homicide in the districts where it was implemented. Similarly, as part of an information-sharing program between hospitals and police in Cardiff, Wales (United Kingdom), police used hospital emergency room data to continuously adjust police patrols (with respect to time and place), target problematic licensed premises, and inform deployment of CCTVs; the program reduced violence according to both hospital and police data (Florence et al. 2011). An illustration of another sort comes from British Columbia, where police formed multi-agency units with community services, fire services, and electricity providers to provide a coordinated approach to investigating marijuana growing operations and running publicity campaigns to solicit public assistance (Malm and Tita 2006). Jurisdictions that adopted the approach experienced reductions in marijuana growing while other jurisdictions experienced increases.

Conclusion

Police agencies inevitably will develop tactics and strategies that they implement at the neighborhood level or throughout a jurisdiction. Many of these strategies have evaluations which present promising findings on their outcomes. At the same time, this evidence is only moderately convincing; often studies of neighborhood- and jurisdiction-level approaches are conducted with weaker designs, giving us less confidence in their results. The reasons for this are many, ranging from the difficulties of evaluating multifaceted and geographically broad interventions to the fact that many interventions are evaluated after the fact.

Despite these challenges in the evidence, the research can provide agencies with some guidance. Successful neighborhood strategies are those that try to focus on high-risk places and people within the larger geographic area, are targeted and tailored to address specific problems, and involve stakeholders who can help successfully implement the intervention. In earlier chapters, we argued that police should anchor their crime prevention efforts around micro hot spots, specific problems, and high-risk groups of offenders. However, we do not see this as being inconsistent with strategies that give attention to larger areas like neighborhoods. In practice, police can use these approaches in tandem. The most optimal crime prevention approaches may prove to be ones that integrate a focus on micro places and high-risk groups within the broader social context of larger neighborhoods and areas (e.g., see our discussion in Chapter 4 of reorienting beat patrols around micro hot spots); indeed, several studies in the neighborhood and jurisdiction sections of the Matrix support the utility of such integrated approaches. Managing hot spots and high-risk groups thereby helps police with managing crime within the broader community.

On a related note, we caution readers about using the Matrix to compare the success rates of interventions focusing on micro places and larger areas as a way of assessing the relative merits of these approaches. The neighborhood- and jurisdiction-level studies in the Matrix were done with less rigorous research designs on average, which can bias them towards finding more favorable results (Weisburd et al. 2001). However, future evaluation research might give more attention to the comparative benefits of focusing activities on places of differ-ent size, addressing a number of questions raised by Koper (2014). For example, are police more likely to reduce crime when they emphasize micro places? Do they tend to prevent larger numbers of crimes or perform more efficiently as measured by metrics like crimes prevented per officer-hour expended?[6] Also, are police more or less likely to receive effective cooperation from community partners or to encounter community resistance when their efforts are targeted on micro places? A related issue is the need for research demonstrating that interventions targeting micro hot spots can produce crime reductions discern-ible over larger areas like neighborhoods and patrol beats (as they should in theory if they are not displacing crime to other locations). Additional research should also demonstrate how police can incorporate policing of micro hot spots into everyday operations, including routine patrol (Koper 1995; Sherman and Weisburd 1995; Telep, Mitchell, and Weisburd 2014) and even detective work (Koper, Egge, and Lum 2015a; Lum, Telep, Koper et al. 2012, 86), that are often organized around larger areas.

Attention to the broader community context around micro hot spots may also improve law enforcement's understanding of the problems that need to be addressed at those locations. The occurrence of crime at micro hot spots can often be linked to social features and happenings of nearby places, and particular crime problems at micro places can extend across multiple street segments (Weisburd, Groff, and Yang 2012). Studies of offenders' travel patterns also suggest that many crimes committed at high-risk blocks are likely to have been committed by offenders who currently live or previously lived nearby, if not on the blocks (e.g., see reviews in Eck and Weisburd 1995 and Gabor and Gottheil 1984; also see Bernasco 2010; Weisburd et al. 2012). Understanding these broader neighborhood patterns can thus prove important in understanding the dynamics of micro hot spots and developing interventions to reduce crime at those locations. Attending to the areas sur-rounding hot spots might also help police to detect and prevent geographic displacement by forcing offenders to travel farther to commit offenses (Bowers et al. 2011, 33).

Finally, engaging with neighborhood and community groups may help police to develop community capacity and support that is helpful in identifying and addressing more specific problem places, groups, and conditions within neigh-borhoods (e.g., Skogan et al. 1995). Nurturing police–community relationships and collaboration at the neighborhood level may thus facilitate police efforts to control high-risk places and groups within those neighborhoods. As we empha-sized in Chapter 1, it is important to understand that an evidence-based polic-ing approach does not require an either–or scenario with research. Studies on

---

[6] See, e.g., Bowers, Johnson, Guerette et al. (2011) who examined crime displacement and the diffusion of crime control benefits associated with geographically focused interventions target-ing areas of different sizes, finding similar results across different types of area.

neighborhood crime prevention, micro-crime places, and individuals are just pieces of a larger framework of incorporating research into an agency's overall strategic plan. Neighborhood-based research is not only useful in its own right, but can also inform the implementation of offender-focused and micro place approaches.

7

TECHNOLOGY

Evidence-Based Policing Playing Catch-Up

In the second part of our book, we have provided numerous examples of evidence-based policing, expanding upon the evaluation research underpinning these efforts. These efforts have focused on interventions for micro places, communities, individuals, and groups. Thus, at least with regard to crime prevention, police have a relatively robust base of knowledge and examples to begin building and modifying strategies to reduce crime. More generally, we know that when police target high-risk places, people, and situations, and when they use proactive, tailored, and problem-oriented approaches, they can increase their chances of being effective. Of course, how they convert and use this research in practice, and how they carry out these activities matters. We will explore these issues in great depth in Part Three of this book.

However, we end Part Two of this book with a discussion of one area of policing that we know much less about but that is believed to be central to carrying out effective crime prevention strategies—technology. Unlike the research evidence for the various crime prevention strategies of Chapters 4, 5, and 6, the evidence for the impact of technology on the police and outcomes that the police care about is weaker. For example, while television may lead us to believe that technology is often used to successfully solve crimes, we actually know little about whether technologies help the police with solving or preventing crime. We also do not know how technology impacts citizen–police interactions and relationships or citizen satisfaction, trust, and confidence in the police. The realm of policing technology, therefore, provides a good example of an area in which police are playing catch-up with regard to evidence-based policing. In this chapter, we discuss the potential impacts of technology on policing, what we know about its actual impacts, and what more we need to understand to implement technology in evidence-based ways. Drawing heavily upon our own work on police technology, we highlight four technologies to make our point: information technologies, crime analysis, license plate readers, and body worn cameras.[1]

Technology and Its Impact on Policing

Technological advancements have shaped policing in many important ways over the years. One needs only consider that the primary police strategy for much of the twentieth century—motorized preventive patrol and rapid response to calls for service—was developed in response to the invention and use of the automobile, two-way radio communications, and computer-aided dispatch systems in policing. In recent decades, there have been many significant developments with respect to information technologies, analytic systems, video surveillance systems, license plate readers, DNA testing, body-worn cameras, and other technologies that have had far-reaching effects on police agencies. Technology acquisition and deployment decisions are high-priority topics for police (e.g., Koper, Taylor, and Kubu 2009), and law enforcement agencies at all levels of governments are spending vast sums of money on technology in the hopes of improving agency efficiency and effectiveness.

The current emphasis on police technology reflects a belief among both police and citizens in technology's potential to enhance policing. For example, technology is believed to strengthen crime control by improving the ability of police to identify and monitor offenders (particularly repeat, high-rate offenders); facilitating the identification of places and conditions that contribute disproportionately to crime; speeding the detection of and response to crimes; enhancing evidence collection; improving police deployment and strategies; creating organizational efficiencies that put more officers in the field and for longer periods of time; enhancing communication between police and citizens; increasing perceptions of the certainty of punishment; and strengthening the ability of law enforcement to deal with technologically sophisticated forms of crime (e.g., identity theft and cybercrime) and terrorism. Technological advancements in automobiles, protective gear, weapons, and surveillance capabilities can reduce injuries and deaths to officers, suspects, and bystanders. Pressing operational needs exist in numerous areas to which technology is central, including crime analysis and information-led policing, information technology and database integration, and managing dispatch and calls for service

---

[1] This chapter draws upon many of our past efforts in the area of technology, including Koper, Taylor, and Woods (2013b); Koper, Lum, and Willis (2014); Koper, Lum, and Hibdon (2015b), Koper, Lum, Willis et al. (2015c); Lum, Merola, Willis (Hibdon) et al. 2010; Lum, Willis (Hibdon), Cave et al. 2011c; Lum, Koper, and Willis (2016b); and Lum, Koper, Merola et al. 2015.

(Koper et al. 2009). And to the extent that technology improves police effectiveness, strengthens communication between police and citizens, reduces negative outcomes from police actions, and increases police accountability, it may also have the added, indirect benefit of enhancing police legitimacy among citizens.

But these are only best guesses and hopes for technology. Because of the scarcity of evaluation research on technology, we do not know whether such outcomes are actually achieved. Much of the research we do have focuses on technology's efficiencies and outputs, rather than its connection to outcomes. Some research has indicated that while recent technological advances have undoubtedly enhanced policing (e.g., see Ioimo and Aronson 2004; Danziger and Kraemer 1985; Roman, Reid, Reid et al. 2008; Roth, Ryan, Gaffigan et al. 2000), it is not clear that they have made police more effective (Byrne and Marx 2011; Chan 2001; Garicano and Heaton 2010; Harris 2007; Koper, Lum, Willis et al. 2015c; Lum 2010). Technology thus presents a paradox; it may operate correctly and speed up various policing activities, but it may not actually lead to outcomes sought by the police or the community.

Take, for example, forensics and surveillance technologies. It is fair to say that forensics technologies have significantly improved and become more available over the past thirty years; these changes include improvements in DNA and fingerprint collection and analysis, as well as the development of mobile devices to make the collection of forensic evidence easier and faster. Surveillance technologies have also improved, with greater use of closed circuit televisions (CCTVs), license plate readers (LPRs), and even technology that can detect gunshots. Police data systems that can be used to identify and locate suspects have also become more extensive and integrated. Yet, despite these improved detection capabilities, national averages of clearance rates for property and violent crimes have remained stubbornly low and stable for the past thirty years, and in the case of homicide, are *declining* (Braga, Flynn, Kelling et al. 2011; Lum, Wellford, Scott et al. 2016d; Vovak 2016). Although there are likely many complex factors that influence clearance trends, it does not appear that advancements in police technology strongly correspond to obvious improvements in police performance.

Technology can also produce unintended consequences in police agencies. For instance, while manual report writing is tedious, agencies transitioning from paper reports to records management systems and automated report writing often go through significant growing pains. Officers have to adapt to new systems that may have added reporting requirements and require the use of the internet or wireless technology that is slow or unreliable. All of this may reduce expected gains in efficiency and have other unintended and undesirable consequences (see our discussion of information technology below). Another example of unintended consequences can be found in the adoption of computer-aided dispatch, or "999"/"911", systems. These systems were developed to improve officer response to calls for service not only to improve customer service and connectivity with citizens, but also to increase the possibility of apprehending

113

offenders. However, the notion that 911/999 systems improve offender appre-hension has been undermined by studies showing that response times have little effect on arrests due to delays in the reporting of crime (Sherman and Eck 2002; also see Chapter 5). Further, the burden of answering 911 calls, roughly half or more of which are not urgent (Mazerolle, Rogan, Frank et al. 2002, 98), leaves police with less time to engage in proactive or problem-oriented policing, which we now know from research can prevent and reduce crime. As we have argued elsewhere (see Lum 2010), 911 systems may have thereby reinforced a reactive, incident-based approach that marks the standard model of policing, which may have even hindered other innovations (e.g., see Sparrow, Moore, and Kennedy 1990).

In practice, the impact of technology on police effectiveness may be lim-ited or distorted by several factors. These include engineering problems (i.e., whether the technologies work), difficulty in implementing and using a tech-nology, legal or administrative limits on a technology's use, lack of fit between a technology and the tasks for which it is used, interdependencies between different technologies (within and across agencies), ancillary costs associated with using a technology (e.g., costs related to training, technical assistance, and maintenance), and the failure of technologies to provide certain expected benefits like time savings or increased productivity. Studies have varied in terms of findings on these issues (see, e.g., Chan 2003; Chan, Brereton, Legosz et al. 2001; Colvin 2001; Frank, Brandl, and Watkins 1997; Ioimo and Aronson 2004; Koper, Moore, and Roth 2002; Koper and Roth 2000; Kraemer and Danziger 1984; Manning 2008; Nunn 1994; Nunn and Quintet 2002; Roth et al. 2000; Zaworski 2004). In particular, organizational and cultural factors within an organization may mediate, in either positive or negative ways, the potential of technology to improve police effectiveness and legitimacy.

For instance, from a crime prevention perspective, new information sys-tems and analytic technologies like crime analysis can help police to more precisely identify the people, places, and problems that contribute most to crime. Yet these advances may have less impact if police managers fail to focus adequate resources on crime hot spots or if the results of crime analysis are not adequately disseminated (or accepted) throughout the agency, particularly among patrol officers and first-line supervisors. Consequently, the effects of these and other technologies may often depend on organizational culture and other organizational changes, such as the adoption of new management sys-tems, the implementation of analytic processes, and changes in deployment. In order to achieve the many improvements to existing police operations that might be sought with new technology, changes may thus be needed in an agency's organizational culture, practices, and infrastructures (e.g., Chan 2003; Chan et al. 2001; Garicano and Heaton 2010; Harris 2007; Koper et al. 2015c; Zaworski 2004).

The idea that organizational aspects can shape technology's outcomes is not unique to policing. Technology scholars Orlikowski and Gash (1994) theorize that "technological frames" mediate the impact of technology on outcomes in organizations more generally. Such frames reflect officer's expectations, knowledge, experiences, values, objectives, and roles within an organization, as well as the organization's history of technology use. In turn, these frames can shape technology uses and products in an organization and, therefore, the outcomes associated with those technologies (see also Boudreau and Robey 2005; Orlikowski 1992; Robey, Boudreau, and Rose 2000). Technological frames can also vary across members and units of a police service. Such "incongruence" (Orlikowski and Gash 1994, 180) can result in conflicts about the development, use, and meaning of technologies in a police organization, as well as different outcomes of technology (see Rocheleau 1993, for further discussion). For example, a police chief may view a new information system as increasing efficiency and accountability. However, patrol officers and detectives may see the same innovation as threatening their discretion or autonomy, or making their daily work more difficult and time-consuming (e.g., see Chan et al. 2001; Harris 2007; Manning 1992).

Frames are important to our discussion of evidence-based policing and technology. Manning (2008) argues that the dominant frame in policing is a reactive nature of policing, characterized and fostered by an incident-based, response-oriented, and procedures-dominated approach. Manning and others (see Harris 2007; Lum 2010; Sanders and Henderson 2013; Sanders, Weston, and Schott 2015) suggest that the technological and organizational frames that are nurtured by this reactive model filter technology adoption. This filtering process influences the way technology is used and the outcomes achieved with technology. In other words, adopting new technologies such as information and records management systems, body-worn cameras, license plate readers, analytic tools, or forensics technologies might produce benefits in administrative efficiency, accuracy and timeliness of crime data, response to calls, and detection capabilities. Yet these changes may not be sufficient to produce substantial improvements in police outcome effectiveness (crime prevention and control, improved relationships with citizens, stronger internal affairs and management, etc.) absent congruent technological frames and practices that promote technology use in these strategic ways.

Similarly, police leaders, scholars, and reformers may see technology as a means to facilitate innovations (e.g., problem solving; community policing; "hot spots" policing; third-party policing; evidence-based policing) that can reduce crime or improve citizen trust, rather than just as a means to react to crime or increase arrests and detections. However, these expectations might be overly optimistic if these objectives are not incorporated into daily policing tasks and expectations that ultimately can create the technological frames of officers, detectives, or supervisors. Hence, technology will not be used in evidence-based ways if an agency's approach to policing more generally does not involve evidence-based policing.

Examining the Evidence Base for Selected Technologies

The mediating effects of organizational frames and culture on technology's impacts provide a strong justification for improving the evidence base on technology application in policing. Not only do we need to identify how organizational frames and other factors shape technological outcomes, but we also need more evaluation research to discern what those outcomes are and whether they are aligned with broader policing goals. Four examples illustrate our point—information technologies, crime analysis (as a technology), license plate readers, and body-worn cameras.

Information technologies

Information technology (IT) is arguably the technology category with the most potential to impact activities related to evidence-based policing, as it has become well developed and affects almost all aspects of police work and management. IT within police agencies includes a wide array of databases and data systems (and their supporting hardware and software) for storing, managing, retrieving, sharing, and analyzing information both within and across agencies. Common components include records management systems (RMS) that capture criminal incident records, computer-aided dispatch systems that record and assign calls for service, and various other databases that may contain information and/or intelligence on persons, groups, personnel, and other matters. IT systems can also include those fostered by data collection over the internet (such as tiplines or other social media sites), as well as mobile computers and data terminals that give officers wireless access to information in the field and that allow them to file reports remotely.

By improving the ability of police to collect, manage, and analyze data, IT has enhanced the administrative efficiency of police organizations, improved their apprehension capabilities, and given them the ability to more precisely and proactively target the people, places, and problems that contribute most to crime and disorder in their communities (e.g., see Groff and McEwen 2008). Many police researchers have recognized the centrality of IT to police work and organizational change more generally (e.g., Boudreau and Robey 2005; Chan 2001; 2003; Ericson and Haggerty 1997; Harris 2007; Manning 1992; Mastrofski and Willis 2010). Accordingly, IT has been studied more extensively than other forms of police technology. Yet, this evidence base has produced complex and often contradictory findings on IT's impacts.

For example, in a national study of U.S. police agencies over the period of 1987–2003, Garicano and Heaton (2010) found that increases in the use of IT by police were not associated with improvements in case clearance rates or crime rates. Brown (2015) reported similar findings in a national study focusing on more recent changes (2003–2007) in police IT capabilities and clearance rates. However, Garicano and Heaton also found evidence that IT is linked to improved performance (i.e., higher clearance rates and/or lower crime rates) when complemented with other organizational changes, including greater use of specialized units, higher educational and training requirements for staff, and managerial practices indicative of Compstat. Other studies of IT in policing have also produced a somewhat clouded picture; while officers generally have positive attitudes towards IT improvements (though exceptions are noted below), the effects of IT have been mixed with respect to improving productivity, case clearances, proactive policing, community policing, problem solving, and other outcomes (e.g., Agrawal, Rao, and Sanders 2003; Brown 2001; Brown and Brudney 2003; Chan et al. 2001; Colvin 2001; Danziger and Kraemer 1985; Groff and McEwen 2008; Ioimo and Aronson 2003; 2004; Koper et al. 2015b, 2015c; Nunn 1994; Nunn and Quinet 2002; Palys, Boyanowsky, and Dutton 1984; Rocheleau 1993; Zaworski 2004).

In general, these studies highlight a number of factors that can offset the potential benefits of IT for officers. For example, officers may be hampered by technical difficulties and the complexities of using IT systems, particularly when the systems are new. Further, the adoption of new IT systems often leads to more extensive reporting requirements for officers. These factors may negate expected time savings, lessen (or fail to improve) time for interacting with citizens and engaging in proactive work, and create frustration and dissatisfaction for officers. Surveys and interviews in police agencies illustrate that negative implementation experiences and functionality problems with new technology have important ramifications for the acceptance, uses, and impacts of that technology and can produce negative effects on officers' attitudes and performance (i.e., job satisfaction and productivity) that last for long periods (Koper et al. 2015c; also see Koper, Lum, and Willis 2014). IT may have other unintended consequences that also have negative implications for organizational functioning and performance (e.g., see Chan et al. 2001; Koper et al. 2015c). Examples include reducing time that supervisors spend mentoring officers; worsening perceptions of inequality for line-level staff, particularly patrol officers who may feel heavily burdened and scrutinized by the reporting demands and monitoring that often come with new information and surveillance technologies; and encouraging an overemphasis on technical skills and computer literacy at the expense of skills in dealing with people in the community (on the latter point, see Palys et al. 1984).

Perhaps more importantly, police may also fail to use IT in the most strategically optimal ways for reducing crime. Although research shows that police are most effective in reducing crime when they focus their efforts on high-risk places and groups and use problem-solving strategies tailored to specific issues, police may not regularly employ technology towards these ends in practice. This is because perceptions and uses of technology are highly dependent on the norms and culture of an agency and how officers view their function (i.e., technological "frames," as discussed above). And because officers continue to frame policing in terms of reactive response to calls for service, reactive arrest to crimes, and adherence to standard operating procedures, they use and are influenced by technology to achieve these goals. In our own research with officers from four agencies, we found that patrol officers were much more likely to use IT to guide and assist them with traditional enforcement-oriented and reactive activities than for more strategic, proactive tasks (Koper et al. 2015c; also see Koper et al. 2014; Koper et al. 2015b; Lum et al. 2016b).

In addition, we found through these studies that officers judged technology against the value (or technological frame) of efficiency, not necessarily outcome effectiveness . Officers often verbalized these outputs as gaining information "faster" or with "greater ease" when they discussed IT, and they emphasized how technology helped them to accomplish tasks quickly. When these efficiency gains were not achieved, technology was seen more negatively, sometimes leading officers to avoid using it. This mindset affects not only discretionary uses of technology (which in turn impacts outcomes) but also definitions and expectations about outcomes themselves. For example, the term "effectiveness" was most often defined by officers (and used interchangeably) to mean "efficiency," or the ability to respond to crime and to quickly identify suspects, victims, witnesses, and other aspects of crimes to resolve cases. Less often did officers define effectiveness in terms of their ability to achieve specific outcomes of interest to the police department, such as preventing crime or improving relationships with citizens or community groups.

These tendencies are also extended to managers, as we found that supervisors were less likely to use IT to form crime prevention strategies with their subordinates and more likely to use it to check reports and assess performance measures of officers and squads. Supervisors typically provided little in the way of consistent training or direction to officers on ways to optimize technology use in their daily work and deployment habits. Our observations suggest that while technology has fostered strategic innovation and accountability at higher managerial levels in policing (e.g., through Compstat-type management processes), the innovative use of technology as a tool by middle- and lower-level supervisors to manage the performance of line-level officers is still neither institutionalized or clearly understood in many agencies.

All of this suggests that police may not fully capitalize on the aspects of technology that enable them to do things that could optimize their effectiveness.[2] Hence, while basic application of IT might have marginal effects in improving police efficiency, detection capabilities in the field, and officer safety in responding to calls, these improvements may not alone be enough to enhance police performance as measured by crime reduction or even case clearances. This is where we need to strengthen the evidence base in this area.

---

[2] This tendency is likely reinforced by the limitations of police IT systems, in terms of available data and functionality, for facilitating problem-solving tasks (e.g., Brown 2001; Brown and Brudney 2003; Nunn and Quinet 2002).

Crime analysis

The development and application of analytic technology in policing (i.e., crime analysis) also has a high potential for enhancing police effectiveness and has been strongly linked to that of IT. Despite the mixed findings of prior technology research, innovations like hot spots policing and Compstat have been linked to advances in IT. Strategic use of IT capabilities by police is thus likely central to realizing IT's full potential. One strategic use with demonstrated promise for improving the effectiveness of police is IT's application to crime analysis. As described by Taylor and Boba (2011, 6), "crime analysis involves the use of large amounts of data and modern technology—along with a set of systematic methods and techniques that identify patterns and relationships between crime data and other relevant information sources—to assist police in criminal apprehension, crime and disorder reduction, crime prevention, and evaluation." Common duties for crime analysts involve assisting detectives, mapping crime, identifying crime patterns, conducting network analysis, and compiling data for uniform crime reporting and managerial meetings (Taylor and Boba 2011).

The development and adoption of crime analysis have been significant trends in policing over the past few decades, as the use of crime analysis has become very common in law enforcement agencies (Burch 2012; Reaves 2010; Taylor and Boba 2011). Crime analysis is believed to hold great potential for improving the effectiveness of police, as we discuss in more depth in Chapter 13. While it has perhaps been linked most prominently to hot spots policing and Compstat, crime analysis is also used heavily for investigative work and can be a valuable component of problem-oriented policing (see Taylor et al. 2011a).

However, with the exception of its role in supporting hot spots policing (see, e.g., Kennedy, Caplan, and Piza 2015), we are not aware of much evidence demonstrating a clear link between the use of crime analysis and lower rates of crime (Lum 2013; Santos 2014). Although this may reflect a lack of study (e.g., we have seen no before-and-after assessments evaluating the impact of establishing crime analysis units on crime reduction), it is also likely that, as with other technological and analytical innovations, the potential impact of crime analysis is also limited by organizational factors. While agencies are obviously constrained by the sophistication of their crime analysis capabilities (see O'Shea and Nicholls 2003), other obstacles can also impede effectiveness, such as a police culture that doesn't value analytical work, the reactive nature of policing, and a disregard for crime analysis that is done largely by civilians (Lum 2013; Taylor and Boba 2011). In practice, officers may not use products like maps and may find them of little value in their work (Cope 2004; Cordner and Biebel 2005; Koper et al. 2015c; Paulson 2004). Indeed, crime analysis is largely produced for police managers. Additionally, while managers tend to be the heaviest users of crime analysis, they often focus largely on criminal apprehension and short-term tactical planning rather than long-term strategic planning (Harris 2007; O'Shea and Nicholls 2003; Taylor and Boba 2011).

In our technology fieldwork referenced above, we examined crime analysis in tandem with IT, and our conclusions about its uses and impacts were much the same as those for IT. Although officers were sometimes asked to conduct directed patrol in particular areas based on crime analysis (particularly in one agency that had a very advanced crime analysis unit and a strong managerial commitment to its use), they often did not take their own initiative in using crime analysis for self-directed proactive work and problem solving. Nor did they necessarily understand the value of crime analysis for facilitating such work. Even detectives, who often worked closely with crime analysts, most heavily used and valued crime analysis for tracking leads for cases they were investigating reactively. The use of crime analysis by detectives to anticipate future events using pattern analysis or for other types of proactive decision making that might help to prevent crime was rare. Again, these tendencies varied notably across agencies, but they were apparent among many officers and detectives even in an agency that placed a heavy managerial emphasis on crime analysis and data-driven policing.

These technological frames of officers thereby mediate the relationship between the adoption, implementation, and use of crime analysis and outcomes sought. Our work and that of others suggest that crime analysis can be leveraged to greater effect if police can learn to use this technology more systematically throughout their organizations to identify crime patterns, respond to crime problems, guide proactive patrol, and facilitate other innovations that are connected to evidence-based policing. We hold this discussion for deeper analysis in Chapter 13.

License plate readers (LPRs)

One technology that has been rapidly adopted by law enforcement to achieve crime control outcomes is license plate reader (LPR) technology. The story of LPR with regard to evidence-based policing is also one of the rapid adoption of technology in a low-information environment in which little outcome research was available at the time of adoption—but adoption moved forward nonetheless. LPRs are both a sensory and information technology which can be placed on mobile patrol units or in fixed locations to detect stolen automobiles, help with investigations, assist in finding missing people, or for general crime prevention purposes. Using a high-speed camera and database system, LPRs scan and read the alpha-numeric characters of license plates within view of the camera and then automatically (and instantaneously) compare the scanned plates against existing databases of license plates that are of interest to law enforcement. Plates "of interest" might include those associated with vehicles that have been recently stolen, are of interest to a police investigation, or linked to registered owners that have open warrants or are being sought by the police. When a match is made, a signal alerts the officer to proceed with further confirmation, investigation, and action. Hundreds of vehicle plates can be scanned in minutes by LPR technology, thereby automating a process that, in the past, was conducted by officers manually, tag-by-tag, and with much discretion. LPR is also an information technology, as these systems can collect and store large amounts of data (plates, dates, times, and locations of vehicles) for future records management, analysis, and dataset linking for investigation and crime prevention. Given these characteristics, LPR has the unique potential to improve police effectiveness by enhancing patrol, investigative, and other security operations.

Although limited by the data it accesses and by the frequency and way that it is used (Lum, Merola, Willis et al. 2010; Lum et al. 2011c), LPR technology is seemingly a force-multiplier to many crime prevention and homeland security efforts. Because of its intuitive appeal and fast automation of what was once a slow process, police have expressed high interest in this technology. About a quarter of U.S. police agencies were using LPRs as of 2009 (Roberts and Casanova 2012), and more than one-third of agencies with 100 or more officers were using them by 2010 (Lum et al. 2010; also see Koper et al. 2009). In our most recent national survey of LPR use in the United States (Lum, Koper, Willis et al. 2016c) the proportion of agencies with 100 or more officers using LPR had almost doubled to 59%. This diffusion of LPR technology has not only occurred rapidly but has also changed in nature very quickly. In 2010, most agencies with LPRs had no more than four devices (today, they have eight on average), primarily using them to detect stolen vehicles and tags in patrol. Today, new and expanded uses have transformed the vision that law enforcement has for LPRs from detecting auto theft to use in investigations and proactive patrol.

Like other technologies (see the discussion of body-worn cameras below), this rapid and changing adoption of LPR has also taken place despite the technology's high cost ($20,000–$25,000 per unit) and without much research on its crime control and prevention impact and cost-effectiveness. Prior studies of LPR conducted in the United Kingdom and North America have focused largely on the accuracy and efficiency of the devices in scanning license plates and on their utility for increasing the number of arrests, recoveries of stolen vehicles, and seizure of other contraband (Cohen, Plecas, and McCormack 2007; Maryland State Highway Authority 2005; Ohio State Highway Patrol 2005; PA Consulting Group 2003, 2006; Patch 2005; Taylor, Koper, and Woods 2011b; Taylor, Koper, and Woods 2012).[3]

However, there is very limited evidence on whether LPR use actually reduces auto theft or other crimes and what types of LPR uses best achieve those ends. Studies of LPR use and its effects on crime have tested small-scale deployment

---

[3] These sources also provide information on some of the technical limitations of LPR with regard to issues like misreads, false alarms, and difficulties with reading particular types of license plates or reading plates under particular types of conditions.

of LPRs with patrol units. One study that spanned two suburban jurisdictions in Virginia found that thirty-minute LPR patrols conducted once every few days (on average) in randomly selected crime hot spots for a period of two to three months did not reduce auto-related or other forms of crime in the targeted locations (Lum et al. 2010; Lum et al. 2011c). Although the experimental dosage was relatively low and the LPR databases were limited to information on stolen vehicles, Lum et al. argued that these conditions reflected the current state of LPR use, providing a realistic understanding of outcome effectiveness. The other study testing LPR was a randomized experiment in Mesa, Arizona (Koper, Taylor, and Woods 2013b; Taylor et al. 2011b; 2012). In that study, a small auto theft squad conducted short operations to detect stolen and other vehicles of interest at high-risk road segments that were identified as likely travel routes for auto thieves based on analysis of auto theft and recovery locations (see Lu 2003) and the input of detectives. As expected, the officers were much more likely to detect and recover stolen vehicles and apprehend auto thieves when using the LPR devices, though the numbers of hits and arrests were small. Further analyses revealed that the patrols produced short-term reductions in crime at the hot spots in both the LPR and non-LPR modes (Koper et al. 2013b), but the study could not definitively isolate the effects of the LPRs from the deterrent effects of the extra patrols more generally, due in part to the low number of LPR arrests (and to the fact that the LPR cameras were mounted on the cars even when not in use, thus potentially creating deterrent effects).

While informative, both the Mesa and Virginia studies were limited by the short duration or low dosage of the interventions, the small numbers of LPRs available, and the limited data fed into the LPR devices (the data consisted largely or entirely of manually downloaded information on stolen vehicles and license plates). Updated studies are thus needed to examine large-scale LPR deployments and LPR operations conducted with access to more extensive data systems.[4]

LPR has also raised questions about citizen privacy that have also not been fully evaluated. In their study of LPR use in Virginia, Lum et al. (2010) surveyed community residents in one of the study jurisdictions and found that while there was strong support for LPR use in general, this support can vary depending on the types of LPR applications under consideration (see also Merola, Lum, Cave et al. 2014). For example, using the devices to detect stolen automobiles or criminal behavior received much more community support than using them to detect parking violations. Additionally, the survey revealed that members of the public do not regard all uses as equivalent, but rather make significant distinctions in their concerns based upon the way in which systems are deployed. Several factors corresponded with decreased support for the technology, including using LPR in ways unrelated to vehicle crimes or prolonged

---

[4] The authors are currently carrying out such evaluations of the use of LPR for patrol and investigations, the results of which will be available by the end of 2017.

storage. Merola and Lum (2013) also found that support for an agency's use of technology depended on how much legitimacy and trust a person affords to the police. Those with more trust tend to support the use of LPRs more than those with less.

Improving apprehensions and deterrence with LPRs will also depend on many other operational decisions about how and where to deploy them. Police currently deploy more than half of their LPRs on patrol vehicles, and deploy most of the remainder in fixed locations (Lum et al. 2016c). However, the relative pros and cons of mobile versus fixed LPR deployments have yet to be studied. Decisions about where to deploy LPRs are especially critical from an evidence-based perspective, especially given our discussion about place-based policing in Chapter 4. Our sense is that many agencies deploy their LPRs with no particular strategy. LPR technology is often treated as a resource that has to be divided equally among administrative units (e.g., districts or divisions) within the agency, rather than allocated based on needs assessment. Assignment of LPRs to officers might similarly be made with no particular strategy, nor any guidance for the officers. Further, it seems that most agencies using LPRs do not collect performance measures associated with LPR use (Lum et al. 2016c). All of this is consistent with the technological frames (discussed above) that arise from a reactive and procedures-oriented mindset towards policing.

In contrast, a more strategic, evidence-based approach to using LPRs is to deploy them to crime hot spots and other locations (like highly traveled roads) where the risk of detecting stolen vehicles and other vehicles of interest will be higher (e.g., see the Mesa and Virginia studies discussed above). Agencies might also conduct their own pilot tests to determine optimal places and methods for LPR deployment based on sound analysis. For example, police in Surrey, British Columbia (Canada) conducted pilot tests with LPRs by assessing the number, rate, and types of LPR hits they could obtain on various roadways in the jurisdiction at different times of day (Cohen et al. 2007). This established baseline data for the agency that could guide LPR deployment and be used to evaluate trends over time. Another example comes from the Ohio State Highway Patrol (2005), which tested three modes of LPR deployment: fixed use at tollbooths on a major turnpike; mobile deployment on marked police cars on the same turnpike; and mobile deployment on an unmarked police vehicle in a high-crime area. They compared these modes of deployment with respect to technical performance (number and accuracy of reads), hits (including an assessment of the validity of those hits), arrests, and stolen vehicle recoveries (results were most promising for the mobile deployment in the high-crime area).

In sum, LPR technology has been rapidly embraced by police because it fits well into the domineering technical frame of efficiency and rapid reaction to crimes. However, a much stronger evidence-base for LPRs needs to be generated about their crime control, legitimacy, and privacy impacts so to better inform law enforcement leaders who acquire them. In the case of this and many other technologies, adoption came before outcome evaluation and relied almost exclusively on technical tests of the technology. An evidence-based approach to LPRs requires not only increasing this knowledge of this technology, but also using it to maximize the potential for LPRs to increase both criminal apprehension and deterrence while minimizing negative impacts on the community. In-depth program evaluation of LPRs can assist with this goal.

Body-worn cameras (BWCs)

Body-worn cameras (BWCs) provide another very contemporary example of the intersection between technology and evidence-based policing. As of this writing, recently publicized and controversial use-of-force events in Ferguson (Missouri), New York City, South Carolina, Baltimore, and elsewhere have led law enforcement agencies, citizens, civil rights groups, and city councils to push for the rapid adoption of BWC technology. The U.S. Department of Justice has dedicated $20 million to fund the purchase of and technical assistance for BWCs in the United States. Proponents of BWCs believe that these devices will deter problem conduct in police–citizen contacts (on the part of both police and citizens) and provide better evidence on police–citizen encounters that will foster public transparency and accountability in the handling of cases that do result in citizen complaints and/or use of police force. If achieved, these benefits could increase citizens' trust and confidence in the police.

As with LPRs, this rapid adoption of BWCs has occurred within a low evidence-based environment; researchers are only beginning to develop knowledge about the effects, both intentional and unintentional, of this technology. But in contrast to developments surrounding LPRs, there has been a rapid push in generating research evidence on BWCs, primarily spearheaded by the Laura and John Arnold Foundation, as well as the National Institute of Justice. In a recent study led by the authors (Lum, Koper, Merola et al. 2015), we examined both the existing and ongoing BWC research to identify existing gaps in the knowledge necessary to build the evidence base of this rapidly diffusing technology.

At the time of our review, we found over a dozen completed empirical studies of BWCs and thirty ongoing research projects, many of which were randomized controlled experiments and high-quality quasi-experimental studies.[5] This level of evidence generation for a law enforcement technology is unprecedented in the history of police technology adoption. In many ways, it reflects greater recognition of the importance of the evidence-based policing paradigm than with other technologies like crime analysis or LPR. The evidence building for BWCs also illustrates that evidence-based policing is not merely about crime control research, as some of its critics have inaccurately portrayed. Our survey of existing and ongoing research on BWCs highlighted issues that are

---

[5] To view all of these studies in this report, go to http://cebcp.org/wp-content/technology/BodyWornCameraResearch.pdf.

receiving significant research attention as well as knowledge gaps in need of more attention.

We found that the most common research that has been or is being conducted explores questions related to the impact of BWCs on the quality of officer–citizen interactions (including, e.g., the nature of the interaction/communication, displays of procedural justice and professionalism, and misconduct or corruption), as often measured by complaints and/or surveys. Also highly researched is the related issue of the impact of BWCs on officer use of force during these interactions. Other relatively common research topics include officer attitudes about cameras, the impact of BWCs on citizen satisfaction with police encounters, the broader impacts of BWCs on community attitudes and perceptions of the police and their legitimacy, the effects of BWCs on officer discretion (especially to arrest or cite individuals), and the impact of BWCs on suspect compliance to commands (and relatedly, assaults on officers). While findings are not definitive, they illustrate the complexity of questions that research needs to address given the rapid adoption of this technology.

For example, early results suggest that BWCs may reduce complaints against the police (see Ariel, Farrar, and Sutherland 2015; Farrar and Ariel 2013; Goodall 2007; Katz, Choate, Ready et al. 2014) or result in quicker resolution of complaints (see Katz et al. 2014; ODS Consulting 2011). However, whether or not that signals increased accountability, improved citizen satisfaction, and/or improved police or citizen behavior is still uncertain. There are signs that BWCs also reduce use of force by police, but with caveats. For instance, Ariel et al. (2015) find that BWCs reduce the use of force incidents, but Katz et al. (2015) find that arrest activity increases for officers wearing BWCs (Owens, Mann, and McKenna 2014, also seem to find similar impacts on individuals being charged). Interestingly, Ready and Young (2015) find that officers wearing cameras, while less likely to perform stop-and-frisks or make arrests, are more likely to give citations. In a recent review of ten experiments in the United States and the United Kingdom, Ariel, Sutherland, Henstock et al. (2016) found that BWCs may only reduce use of force if officers do not have much discretion on when to turn cameras on and off. These initial findings suggest that BWCs can at least discourage negative behaviors by officers; however, deeper research will be needed to determine if BWCs prompt more fundamental changes in officers' attitudes and behaviors the more police use this technology for training, supervision, accountability systems, and self-learning (e.g., see Koen 2016).

Some questions at the time of writing remain unanswered. For instance, will BWCs change discretionary officer behaviors by affecting officers' propensity to engage in proactive activities, issue citations, or make arrests? To the extent that officers frame BWCs as a tool for monitoring them, it might conceivably make them less likely to engage in proactive contacts out of fear that their actions will result in greater scrutiny, particularly if encounters go badly. This same concern might also prompt them to take a more legalistic approach in situations where they have discretion over issuing citations or making arrests (thus resulting in more minor citations and arrests). Substantial changes in officer behavior could then have ramifications, both good and bad, for police crime control efforts as well as police–citizen interactions and relationships. Studies are underway on this issue, but it is an area that arguably needs further research emphasis (Lum et al. 2015).

There is then the question of how BWCs affect citizens' views and behaviors. The decline in citizen complaints found in BWC studies to date is encouraging, but it may not mean that citizens are more satisfied with police contacts in general. Citizens' views of police more generally may also not change if the adoption of BWCs doesn't seem to bring changes in police accountability and actions. BWCs could also have unintended effects on citizens' actions. For example, might fear of being recorded on a police BWC discourage some people from contacting the police or cooperating with police as victims, witnesses, or informants? Also, might police adoption of BWCs worsen citizens' perceptions of the police due to privacy concerns? Some of these issues are currently under study, while others need attention.

Other significant research gaps also remain. While much of the existing and ongoing research focuses on officer behavior, this research tends to focus on police professionalism, use of force, and misconduct. However, BWC adoption has also been spurred on by more critical and hard-to-measure concerns, including whether BWCs can reduce implicit or explicit bias among police and differential police treatment based on race, sex, age, ethnicity, or other extralegal characteristics. Additional questions of misconduct or professionalism concern the potential impact of BWCs on officer compliance with Fourth Amendment standards (and analogous legal standards outside the United States) during stop-question-and-frisk—another area not yet examined. In a similar vein, while ongoing research is examining officer attitudes about BWCs, other measures of these attitudes, such as job satisfaction and retention, have not been investigated. Finally, several organizational issues warrant attention, including whether BWCs can: facilitate the investigation of critical incidents such as officer-involved shootings; improve training and affect policy changes; or impact the accountability, supervision, management, and disciplinary systems of an organization, including those related to internal investigations.

Thus, like LPRs, BWCs were adopted with relatively little understanding of their effects. In a period of only a few years, tens of millions of dollars (and perhaps more) have been spent on their acquisition. Of course, law enforcement cannot always wait for research before making a policy or technology decision. In the current environment, police agencies felt they needed to do something to improve their legitimacy with citizens as well as to protect themselves against unjustified complaints. And in fairness, unlike LPRs, the push to create an evidence base for this technology is stronger, due to a greater level of commitment and funding for research on BWCs by both the U.S. Department of Justice and private funders such as the Laura and John Arnold Foundation. Nonetheless, BWCs provide another example of how police can sometimes move quickly to adopt an innovation despite a lack of knowledge about the consequences of that innovation. This stands in contrast to experience with other innovations, such as problem-solving, community-oriented, hot spots, or targeted policing. The uptake on these innovations has been much slower even though we have lots of research knowledge to guide these practices. Politics, a belief that an innovation is "common sense" or straightforward, and the ease with which an innovation fits into policing's tasks, function, and existing technological frames all contribute to this state of affairs.

Integrating Technology and Evidence-Based Policing

We recognize that technology adoption is sometimes viewed outside of the realm of evidence-based policing; in some cases, adoption of technology is a reflection of modernizing the police force, increasing job satisfaction, and just making certain processes easier. But to *optimize* the use of technology requires viewing technology from an evidence-based perspective. Agencies may already have acquired LPRs and BWCs and want to know how to use them in ways that lead to outcomes that they seek, including not angering the communities in which they operate. Technologies such as crime analysis or information technologies have already been well-integrated into many police agencies, but thinking about how they are currently used and what organizational factors shape those uses is essential when agencies consider how to optimize technology use. Research knowledge on police strategies and tactics, technological frames, and outcome research on technology are all important parts of the evidence base for technology that can contribute to optimizing its use.

Based on our fieldwork in this area with James Willis as discussed in Koper et al. (2014; 2015c), we suggest several recommendations for agencies to optimize their adoption and use of technology within an evidence-based policing framework. For starters, there are a number of ways that police can potentially smooth the process of technological change and increase receptivity to new technology. For one, police managers should allow for a broad base of participation in the technology implementation process by various personnel who will be affected by the technology. This process should provide ample opportunities for pilot testing early versions of a technology for both technical assessment and outcome effectiveness, and soliciting input that can be incorporated into its final design. This process can be helpful in identifying and correcting technical problems with a technology and for determining its most effective applications. Staff at various levels should also have opportunities to offer insights on how technologies like IT, crime analysis, LPRs, and BWCs might be best integrated into assessments of performance. Allowing those who are being assessed to participate rather than simply imposing new requirements upon them will likely increase levels of understanding and acceptance of the technology being used in this way (Mastrofski and Wadman 1991).

Proper levels of training are also essential, especially for the most difficult technological changes. For example, learning how to use an IT system properly, in terms of both input and use of output, requires extensive training, follow-up, and consistent adjustment. Moreover, once basic training is done, agencies should prepare a systematic and continuous approach to follow-up, in-service training, reinforcement, ongoing technical support, and adaptation to new lessons. This should include dissemination of information about effective practices, success stories, and tips for easier or faster use of technology (such techniques are often discovered by individuals but not shared widely or systematically).

However, to reap the full potential benefits of technology in an evidence-based framework, police must also arguably address traditional and long-standing philosophical and cultural norms about the role of law enforcement. For example, research indicates that from a policy and practice perspective, adjusting organizational factors and frames may be just as useful as adjusting the use of the technologies themselves. Technological adoption is not only a long and continuous process of its own, but one that is highly connected to many other aspects of policing, including daily routines and deployments, job satisfaction, interaction with the community, internal relationships, and crime control outcomes. Thus, managing technological change in policing is challenging and closely connected to managing other organizational reforms (such as improving professionalism, reducing misconduct, and adopting community, problem solving, or evidence-based policing). Accordingly, strategizing about technology application is essential and should involve careful consideration of the specific ways in which new and existing technologies can be deployed and used at all levels of the organization to meet goals for improving efficiency, effectiveness, and agency management. Research evidence can provide knowledge to assist agencies with this task.

Most fundamentally, training about proactive and evidence-based strategies— and how technology can be used in support of those strategies—is needed. As we have discussed throughout this book, police are most effective in reducing crime when their strategies are proactive, focused (both on high-risk places and groups), and oriented towards problem solving and prevention. In our experience, however, officers often seem to have a limited understanding of how technology might help them in these regards, and their agencies typically lack reward systems to encourage innovative responses to crime. As discussed earlier, officers generally focus on using technology in support of answering calls and other traditional enforcement and surveillance activities. Given that an agency is trying to reduce, prevent, and control crime (rather than just react and respond to it), training regarding technology or other tools needs to incorporate how technology might be used more comprehensively for these goals. How, for example, can officers use their agency's information systems and crime analysis to guide their patrol activities between calls for service, identify and address problems at hot spot locations, and monitor high-risk people in their areas of responsibility? At the same time, how can managers use these technologies to encourage such work by their subordinates?

Training on the use of technology for evidence-based practices should also extend to the enhancement of police legitimacy in the community; for example, to include the application of procedural justice (e.g., Mazerolle, Bennett, Manning et al. 2013). Officers working with video and audio recorders in their car or on their person might benefit from training on how these technologies can reduce the chances of conflict in citizen encounters and maximize citizens' sense that they have been treated respectfully and fairly. Training might also emphasize issues such as how officers can use their technologies (such as information systems) to be more helpful to citizens in their encounters and how they might explain the purpose and uses of surveillance technologies (like LPR) that may arouse privacy concerns.

Finally, there is a need for both police and researchers to make a greater commitment to a strong research and development agenda regarding technology. This is currently lacking, as police often adopt new forms of technology like LPRs and BWCs before their impacts and effectiveness have been demonstrated and understood. Practitioners should review existing research about the uses, consequences, and effectiveness of technologies and also consider conducting their own pilot testing and evaluation of these technologies before making substantial investments in them (e.g., Cohen et al. 2007; Ohio State Highway Patrol 2005).

A related point is that police managers should do more to systematically track the ways that new technologies are used and the outcomes of those uses. This is particularly applicable to technologies like LPRs which, based on the authors' familiarity with several agencies, are typically deployed with no systematic tracking of how they are being used and with what results. Earlier, we noted some of the ways that police could better track LPR use and results. One could envision similar forms of tracking and evaluation for other technologies like in-car and body cameras and new forensics technologies, to name a few. This would help police to evaluate the benefits of new technologies relative to their costs—an important consideration given the costs of many new technologies and the general fiscal pressures faced by police agencies—and inform their assessments of which technologies are most beneficial.

Researchers can assist practitioners in these endeavors by collaborating on evaluation studies that carefully assess the theories behind technology adoption (i.e., how and why a particular technology is expected to improve police effectiveness), the ways in which technology is used in police agencies, the variety of organizational and community impacts that technology may produce (both intended and unintended), and the cost efficiency of technology. Additionally, research is needed to clarify what organizational strategies—with respect to training, implementation, management, and evaluation—are most effective for achieving desired outcomes with technology and avoiding potentially negative unintended consequences. In all of these ways, greater attention to technology implementation and evaluation can help police agencies optimize technology decisions and fully realize the potential benefits of technology for policing within an evidence-based framework.

Implementing Evidence-Based Policing

PART THREE

Implementing Evidence-Based
Policing

8

RECEPTIVITY AND THE DEMAND FOR EVIDENCE-BASED POLICING

In Parts One and Two we have shown that there is already a large body of research on many different aspects and outcomes of policing that have been generated by researchers and practitioners working together. There have also been attempts to synthesize this research using systematic reviews, National Academies of Science panels, and also web-based reference tools such as the Matrix and Crimesolutions.gov. At the same time, we surmise that the use of knowledge from research remains low, ad hoc, and not a regular part of policing. This assertion is strengthened by the continued dominance of the standard model in policing and the focus on crime reaction. However, as we continually emphasize, evidence-based policing involves more than generating research knowledge, or even police leaders paying attention to research and analysis. Recall our definition of evidence-based policing from Chapter 1:

> Evidence-based policing means that research, evaluation, analysis, and scientific processes should have "a seat at the table" in law enforcement decision making about tactics, strategies, and policies. Further, evidence-based policing is not just about the process or products of evaluating police practices, but also about the translation of that knowledge into digestible and useable forms that can be institutionalized into practice and policing systems.

Evidence-based policing involves a range of actions and processes to institutionalize the use of research in practice. But this is much easier said than done. Organizational, cultural, and technical barriers in both law enforcement and academic/research organizations can work against institutionalization and research use. There are also language, experience, and expectation gaps between researchers and practitioners that challenge research translation and use. This gap is certainly not new or unique to policing. As Weiss and Bucuvalas (1980) pointed out in their seminal work, *Social Science Research and Decision Making*, numerous commissions and inquiries by the National Research Council (NRC) and the National Science Foundation found that the "potential of social science research for informing the processes of government … has not been realized" (Weiss and Bucuvalas 1980, 9; see also Hirschkorn and Geelan 2008). In policing research, concern over the gap between research and practice also has been a recurring lament. Bayley (1998) bluntly stated that "research may not have made as significant, or at least as coherent, an impression on policing as scholars like to think…. Nor has research led to widespread operational changes even when it has been accepted as true" (4–5).

There are three aspects of evidence-based policing that can help explain this state of affairs and that also present the greatest challenges to, and opportunities for, evidence-based policing: translation, receptivity, and institutionalization. We have already discussed translation in our discussion of the Matrix and in Part Two, and will continue to do so throughout this section. We also will focus on the institutionalization of research in Chapters 9–14. But in this chapter, we focus on the receptivity to and "demand" for research by law enforcement practitioners. If law enforcement agencies and their agents don't see value in research or a need for using research, research processes, partnerships, and the like, then evidence-based policing is just impractical theory. Of course, we don't believe this, but understanding why some officers and supervisors may be more receptive than others, as well as understanding the demand for research more generally among police agencies, is an important conceptual framework for evidence-based policing.[1]

Receptivity to Research

Receptivity can come in many forms in evidence-based policing. Generally, we define it as the willingness of police practitioners (civilian or sworn personnel) to not only be aware of and understand research and research processes, but also to be open to the value of research and demand it. Nutley, Walter, and Davies (2007, 47–51) point out that receptivity is a common theme in models of research use. In particular, they reference Knott and Wildavsky (1980; see also Landry, Amara, and Lamari 2001) who discuss receptivity as "reception," "cognition," and "reference" to research as well as Glasziou and Haynes (2005), who define receptivity as awareness and acceptance of research findings

---

[1] Portions of this chapter were adapted with *Gratis Reuse* permission from SAGE, from Cynthia Lum, Cody Telep, Christopher Koper, and Julie Grieco, "Receptivity to Research in Policing," *Justice, Research and Policy* 14 (2012): 61–95. (Copyright © 2012, © SAGE Publications).

as applicable and "doable." Nutley et al. conceptualize receptivity to research not as the start to research use, but as a continuum throughout evidence-based practice that includes awareness, knowledge, and understanding of research as well as changes in attitudes, perceptions, and ideas about research. These concepts, they argue, are directly connected into "instrumental uses" of research knowledge involving policy and practice changes.

In policing, without good reception or a demand for research knowledge by police practitioners, it may little matter how much high-quality research is generated or synthesized and translated for use. And, it would be naïve to believe that sheer volume of research, compelling findings, or the synthesis and translation of research alone have such power to facilitate change. At the same time, receptivity can also be fostered and created within policing from these activities. For example, one hypothesis is that when agency actors partner with researchers to generate new research findings through field evaluations, this may improve receptivity to research in the future. Another hypothesis is that external pressures by funding agencies, city councils, the media, or citizens can increase police agency receptivity to research. Translation of research into digestible forms, such as the Matrix, Crimesolutions.gov, or systematic reviews, could also facilitate receptivity if it makes compelling findings more visible or influential. Moreover, our discussion of research institutionalization throughout Part Three of this book is predicated on the idea that subconscious receptivity to research can be generated by gradually incorporating knowledge into everyday activities of the police, without necessarily referencing changes in tactics and strategies as research oriented or "evidence-based."

At the same time, if police officers do not see the value of products from research or analysis, if first-line supervisors view such tactics as overly academic or not implementable, if commanders see such information or those who generate it as a threat to their own authority, or if chiefs and sheriffs try to force implementation without a plan to improve receptivity among their officers, evidence-based policing (or any other reform, for that matter) will hit formidable barriers within organizational systems and cultures. In a creative article comparing criminal justice to baseball, Cullen, Myer, and Latessa (2009) point to the vice-like strength of "insider knowledge" and experience as powerful organizational forces that often and successfully counter scientific knowledge. In baseball, this is manifested in scouts making decisions about which ball players to recruit based on gut feelings, individual observations, and their personal experiences. Insider knowledge has a history and mythology all its own, and is embedded in not only the mindset of ballplayers and managers, but the infrastructure in which the players operate, from the rules of the game to the traditions of scouting, line-up decisions, and the like. Similarly, Cullen and colleagues argue that the field of corrections is also "often based on 'common sense,' custom, and imitation—rather than on scientific evidence." (205).

Such commitment and reverence to insider knowledge is a natural barrier to being receptive to any outside knowledge, let alone research. In policing, insider knowledge and officer experience is highly valued, and often romanticized and mythologized by movies and television, and also sometimes by those who discuss the "craft" of policing. The overvaluation of experience is understandable. Most importantly, experience *is* necessary in any field, as it reflects the repetitive and reflective practice of a profession that provides individuals with the ability to be efficient and skillful in their work. Further, there is a great deal of person-to-person interaction in law enforcement, and the unit of interest is individual cases, victims, and suspects that seemingly have unique stories and experiences. At the individual police officer level, such individual exchanges can be memorable, and stories of heroism, fear, and comedy are replayed in officer exchanges with each other and their family and friends. The daily actions, exchanges, perspectives, beliefs, approaches, and displays of expertise that shape the craft of policing seem to emerge from these experiences, and police officers judge themselves and each other on whether they are good at this craft. And, of course, we don't have research to guide every aspect of police activity, making collective experience an important source of guidance for some police actions (and potentially the source of tactics that can be tested through research).

But like baseball, the craft and experience of policing are neither magical nor immutable. Experience is the by-product of the daily tasks of policing, the organizational structures and rules that support and create expectations and responses for those tasks, and the routine and repetitive exchanges that officers have with people. Thus, the craft can change when there are changes in the daily tasks of policing and the organizational structures that support them. For example, the craft that emerges from the standard model (and what officers might define as "good policing") emphasizes making arrests, detecting offending, reacting to calls, and following procedures. The craft in a problem-oriented approach, in contrast, would center on the ability to identify and respond to problems, the use of crime analysis, and measures of crime prevention. In other words, craft is the by-product of how police view, define, structure, and approach their jobs. Change the experience and what creates the experience, and you change the craft and what is considered "good policing."

The million-dollar question for evidence-based policing is how does research, which seems to be almost completely outsider knowledge, become insider knowledge, thereby shaping the craft of policing? While police chiefs and certainly elected sheriffs may feel compelled and responsible to listen to outsider knowledge from citizens or city councils, they likely feel little to no responsibility in listening to a researcher. In order for police actors to include research or insider knowledge to influence their decision making, they have to believe that:

– scientific information is legitimate and factual;
– scientific processes are useful to police strategies, tactics, or administration;
– researchers are "experts" who can offer valid information;
– research partnerships are worth the time, effort, and money to police organizations;

- the outcomes from research are believable and won't hurt the police; and
- law enforcement officers require, need, or can at least benefit from some outsider knowledge.

Receptivity is central to achieving these goals.

What Do We Know About Receptivity?

As will be discussed in Chapter 15, we will need a great deal more research on what approaches work best to increase receptivity to research in practice. However, we do have some empirical clues, mostly from other fields. In evaluation science, Carol Weiss's research is particularly groundbreaking (see Weiss 1988; 1998). For example, Weiss and Bucuvalas (1980), building on early work by Caplan, Morrison, and Stambaugh (1975), found in their interviews of mental health practitioners that they were generally supportive of social science research and knowledgeable about it. These practitioners also saw research as useful if it was relevant to their work, was plausible and feasible given their experience, provided explicit guidance, and was objective and of high quality.

Weiss and Bucuvalas also discovered that the use of, and receptivity to, research were further conditioned by an individual's personal beliefs and perceptions of the organization. For example, their subjects were more receptive to research, even if it critiqued their organization, as long as it meshed well with their personal beliefs and values. Research that challenged the status quo of the organization was actually viewed as valuable by decision makers. At the same time, the subjects felt that actual use of research as a change agent was uncommon, a finding also discovered by Edmond, Megivern, Williams et al. (2006) in studying social workers.

In the medical profession, Lacey (1994) and Wangensteen and colleagues (2011) found that many nurses, like the mental health workers in Weiss and Bucuvalas' sample, had positive attitudes toward research and in implementing research findings. Wangensteen and colleagues (2011) found that certain personal characteristics made nurses more positive toward research use, including those having critical thinking traits[2] and those who had recently graduated from school (on the latter point, also see Aarons' 2004 discussion of mental health providers). However, also like Weiss and Bucuvalas' respondents, the *use* of research findings in practice was low; only 24% of respondents defined themselves as users of research, despite their support for research.

The infrequent use of research in practice was also found by Chagnon, Pouliot, Malo et al. (2010), in their study of child protective service employees.

---

[2] Wangensteen, Johansson, Bjorkstrom et al. (2011), using the California Critical Thinking Disposition Inventory (CCTDI) subscales, defined critical thinking as truth seeking, open-mindedness, analyticity, systematicity, critical thinking, self-confidence, inquisitiveness, and maturity (Wangensteen et al. 2011, 2,438).

In their sample of both administrators and practitioners only 18% remarked that they frequently used research in their practice, with especially low use among practitioners. They found eight individual and organizational elements that could predict research application. These were collaboration in research knowledge development; perceived usefulness of research knowledge; perceived efforts by researchers to disseminate research knowledge; personal efforts to acquire research knowledge; favorable attitudes toward relations with researchers; the medium of communication used to obtain research knowledge; organizational context; and perceived cost of knowledge utilization.

These findings from the mental health and medical professions may not generalize to policing. In these professions, research may play a more accepted role than in policing, and there are also educational requirements that involve understanding the science for these fields. In policing, the law, not science, is the guiding principle. The little empirical research that we do have about receptivity to research in policing gives us some clues about the nature of policing and receptivity to research. One example is a case study by Birkeland, Murphy-Graham, and Weiss (2005), who examined why evaluation findings of DARE (Drug Awareness Resistance Education—see Chapter 5) are often ignored by schools. Of the eight schools they studied, six continued to implement DARE, despite negative evaluation results. The reasons that were given illuminate some of the difficulties of implementing evidence-based policing. Some schools and police officials felt that the evaluations were measuring unrealistic program goals. Others felt that the evaluations overlooked the program's ability to build relationships between police, students, and their families. Lastly, police and school officials felt that their own personal experiences with DARE outweighed any scientific evidence against it.

On the other hand, Palmer (2011) found complexities and contradictions similar to those found by Weiss and Bucuvalas (1980). Building on the Lum and Telep receptivity survey described below, Palmer surveyed all officers of inspector[3] and chief inspector[4] rank in the Greater Manchester Police Department in the United Kingdom about their receptivity toward conducting experimental evaluations and also in using research. Although his response rate to the survey was low, those who responded said that they relied highly on professional experience rather than research to guide decision making. However, officers did not reject the idea that research knowledge and evaluations should have some influence in policing. A majority of chief inspectors and inspectors surveyed read research from the Home Office (67%) or the National Policing Improvement Agency of the United Kingdom (NPIA) (54%), two sources of information similar to the Office of Justice Programs and the COPS Office of

---

[3] The rank of inspector is equivalent to a second-level supervisor in the United States, such as a Lieutenant.

[4] The rank of chief inspector is equivalent to a command level supervisor in the United States, such as a Major.

the U.S. Department of Justice. While the lower-ranking (but still supervisory) inspectors were less likely to read research from these sources, close to half still did (44% read Home Office reports and 48% NPIA reports). Those officers who were more likely to say that the police had sufficient knowledge without acknowledging research were also those who had the least exposure to scientific research. In other words, the more an officer knew about research, the less he or she believed the police organization had enough information on its own about crime and what to do about it.

Measuring Police Receptivity to Research

Overall, the empirical research on the "sociology of knowledge application" (Weiss and Bucuvalas 1980, 23) and receptivity is scant in policing. As part of our efforts to better understand police receptivity to research and evidence-based policing, we developed a "receptivity survey" with Cody Telep to gauge officer attitudes towards research and their understanding and use of it (see Lum et al. 2012). This survey is the first systematic attempt in policing to gauge receptivity.[5] The survey was created as part of our Matrix Demonstration Projects, which will be discussed extensively in the next chapters. The goal of creating the survey was to provide police agencies pursuing evidence-based policing with a way to measure and track receptivity in their agencies.

The survey instrument focuses on themes related to receptivity to evidence-based policing approaches. Questions include whether officers have heard of the term "evidence-based policing," and, if so, how they define the concept. The survey also gauges officers' exposure to research materials, their views regarding crime analysis and criminologists working within the agency, and how often they make use of materials from crime analysis. The survey also includes a series of questions on officers' views toward innovation, new ideas, working with outsiders (e.g., researchers), and education in policing.

Below, we present some findings from one of the first agencies we surveyed— the Sacramento California, Police Department (SPD)—which graciously agreed to partner with us on this project under the assistance of Sgt. Renee Mitchell, an advocate of evidence-based policing. Of the 700 sworn officers in the department, 523 officers answered the survey. The SPD's willingness to partner with us gave us what we believe is the first major insight into receptivity to research at the officer level. Telep also continued implementing this survey in other agencies (see Telep and Lum 2014; Telep and Winegar 2015) with some variations but similar findings.

---

[5] This can be accessed at http://cebcp.org/wp-content/evidence-based-policing/matrix-demonstration-project/ReceptivitySurvey.pdf.

Knowledge of evidence-based policing and research resources

One way to begin to gauge officer receptivity to evidence-based policing is in understanding whether officers know about it and are exposed to research knowledge in some form. In our survey, only one-quarter of respondents had heard of evidence-based policing, and we suspect this finding would be similar in many other agencies. Indeed, Telep and Lum (2014) found that only 28% of officers had heard of the term in Richmond, Virginia, a similarly sized agency. Interestingly, Telep and Lum found that nearly half (48%) were familiar with the term in a much smaller agency (Roanoke, Virginia) that has a chief who is an advocate of evidence-based policing. As we discuss in Chapter 14, leadership in evidence-based policing is an important factor in normalizing it into organizational culture and practice.

Additionally, we also gauged officers' general exposure to police research as a source of outsider knowledge by asking officers what journals or magazines they had read in the past six months, including both academic (e.g., *Criminology*) and professional (e.g., *The Police Chief*) publications. As Table 8.1 shows, three-quarters of the Sacramento respondents had not read any of the seven well-known publications listed in the survey, including very popular leadership magazines from non-research organizations (*The Police Chief, FBI Law Enforcement Bulletin*). Similar patterns were also found by Telep and Lum (2014) for Richmond and Roanoke, where 60% and 63%, respectively, had not read any of the listed publications. Clearly, gains in receptivity to research will not occur by hoping that practitioners are reading the materials that researchers spend most of their time writing. And, like Palmer's (2011) sample, this type of written information reaches the upper echelons of police staff more so than the rank and file.

Table 8.1 Officers' Responses to the Question, "In the Last Six Months, from Which of the Following Journals or Magazines Have You Read an Article or Feature?" (Multiple Choices Allowed)

	n	%
None of the above	402	76.9
Other	73	14.0
FBI Law Enforcement Bulletin	32	6.1
The Police Chief	18	3.4
Criminology and Public Policy	5	1.0
The Criminologist	4	0.8
Criminology	4	0.8
Justice Quarterly	4	0.8
Police Quarterly	4	0.8

Table 8.2 Officers' Responses to the Question, "In the Last Six Months, Have You Read any Formal or Written Information Provided by the Following Organizations Specifically about the Effectiveness of Particular Tactics or Strategies?" (Multiple Selections Allowed)

Source	n	%
Your own police agency	241	46.1
None of the above	236	45.1
Other	38	7.3
COPS Office	22	4.2
International Association of Chiefs of Police (IACP)	20	3.8
A university	13	2.5
Police Foundation	10	1.9
National Institute of Justice	9	1.7
Police Executive Research Forum (PERF)	9	1.7
BJA	8	1.5
Bureau of Justice Statistics	5	1.0
Office of Justice Programs	3	0.6
A library database	1	0.2

On the contrary, when we asked officers whether they had read any information about the effectiveness of particular tactics or strategies and if so, from where, officers were much more likely to cite formal or informal information provided by their own agency (46%, see Table 8.2) or to report that they had not received information on any of the choices we provided. Less than 5% of officers had been exposed to information from two major organizations in policing—the Office of Community Oriented Policing Services (U.S. Department of Justice) or the International Association of Chiefs of Police.

This is a crucial finding for understanding receptivity in policing, and underscores the importance of insider knowledge. The reason why receptivity is low in policing could be partly due to the simple fact that officers rely on their organizations to give them information, and that information does not include knowledge from research. This suggests that researchers will have a much better chance of increasing receptivity to research and ultimately to evidence-based policing if they work with insiders in a police agency and leverage internal mechanisms of dissemination and action. These can include formal mechanisms such as providing knowledge during academy and in-service training, roll call read-outs, memos and emails to officers, and discussions at managerial meetings. However, dissemination can also occur informally, for example, through well-respected thought leaders in the agency. These might be first-line supervisors who mentor and discuss information with their squads, or others who can rally commanders around innovations. The benefits to using insider mechanisms is that these systems also are attached to other systems (such as performance reviews or promotions) that can encourage, reward, and reinforce attention to disseminated knowledge. We discuss ideas for these types of dissemination in Chapters 14 and 15.

It is also important to consider the form of information disseminated, which emphasizes our point that receptivity is not isolated from translation. While it may not be realistic to think a sizable number of officers will regularly read academic journals, they may be more likely to read summary information from relevant studies or listen to quick soundbites provided by their supervisors or through videos. The reason why we provide a clear and short summary of each study in the Evidence-Based Policing Matrix, for example, is to facilitate the receptivity of this translated knowledge. Disseminating easy-to-digest forms of information within existing internal communication systems may be a good formula for improving receptivity, although officers will still likely require encouragement to use such information from within their agencies, which we will discuss in the next chapters.

Receptivity toward researchers and analysts

The receptivity to outsider knowledge also depends on its legitimacy with officers. Even if you can find internal mechanisms of information dissemination, receptivity will likely still be low if officers don't view information as useful or the source of that information as legitimate. These perceptions of research, researchers, and analysts likely vary among police agencies and are tempered by the agencies' and officers' experiences with researchers and their own educational experiences. To gauge this dimension of receptivity, we asked officers a series of questions about how they felt toward researchers inside and external to their agency. Overall, responses reflected some optimism and some pessimism toward researchers. Sacramento officers were more likely than not to feel analysts and researchers were integral to day-to-day work (25.0% versus 16.4%), for example. At the same time, officers seemed to have lukewarm feelings about the usefulness of products generated by crime analysts and researchers, as Table 8.3 indicates. The majority felt crime analysts seem to generate a lot of statistics that are "useful mostly to high command." Later, Telep and Lum (2014) found that how often officers use materials from crime analysts can vary across agencies. Specifically, 38%, 59%, and 81% of respondents in Sacramento, Richmond, and Roanoke, respectively, said that they used crime analysis "sometimes" or "often." The reasons for higher use in Richmond and Roanoke could be because crime analysis is more institutionalized and historically supported in these agencies.

Similar to what Palmer found in Greater Manchester, officers in Sacramento generally valued experience (insider knowledge) over scientific knowledge and expert opinion (outsider knowledge). More than four-fifths (83.4%) of respondents felt their own experience, rather than "expert opinion," was key to

Table 8.3 Officers' Responses to the Question, "Which Best Describes Your View about Crime Analysts, Statisticians, or Other Researchers Who Work in a Police Department?" (*n* = 490)

Response	n	%
They seem to generate a lot of statistics that are useful mostly to high command.	203	38.8
They are/should be an integral part of day-to-day field operations.	131	25.0
They don't seem to be a very integral part of the daily work of officers and supervisors.	86	16.4
They are a very specialized unit who work on very specific problems.	37	7.1
They are usually called upon on an ad hoc, when-needed basis.	27	5.2
I do not know if these individuals exist in my agency.	6	1.1

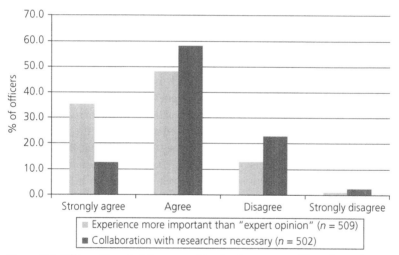

Figure 8.1 Officers' Level of Agreement to the Statements, "Experience is More Important than 'Expert Opinion' in Determining 'What Works' in Policing" and "Collaboration with Researchers is Necessary for a Police Agency to Improve Its Ability to Reduce Crime"

determining the most effective strategies to use (Figure 8.1). At the same time, it did not appear that the majority of police agents were opposed to researchers. For example, when we asked whether officers would be willing to take the initiative to approach an outside researcher for help with evaluating a policing tactic, a sizeable but still minority of officers (31%) said they would be unwilling. Additionally, 71% of officers either agreed or strongly agreed that collaboration with researchers is necessary for a police agency to improve its ability to reduce crime, also shown in Figure 8.1. Telep and Lum (2014) found similar results in Richmond and Roanoke.

These findings suggest an important lesson for researchers working with police agencies in building receptivity to research: don't ignore experience! Not only do officers have valuable insights that will improve research projects and partnerships, but they will also likely be more willing to cooperate with researchers who recognize and appreciate the value of officer knowledge and experience (see Weiss, Murphy-Graham, Petrosino et al. 2008 for an example of the problems that can result from not appreciating the professional judgment of practitioners). Indeed, we have spent a great deal of time just working with police agencies, without any research returns, because of the value we have found in learning about policing through understanding officer and supervisor experience. Even though the first author has firsthand policing experience, that understanding is not the same as objectively and more carefully learning about the variety of experiences and perspectives of police personnel as an outsider. At the same time, it is also important for both practitioners and researchers to acknowledge that sometimes experience can be overvalued, and that experience is malleable and subject to adjustment.

Knowledge of research findings on effective practices

An important aspect of receptivity to research is not just general receptivity as described above, but also knowledge, awareness, and acceptance of specific information that exists regarding policing practices. To further gauge officer knowledge of existing policing research, we asked officers about the effectiveness of a variety of police strategies that have been evaluated. We felt this would be more useful than asking officers more directly: "Do you use research?" Research use may be subconscious, and activities the police engage in may indeed be supported and guided by research, even if inconspicuous. In our receptivity survey, we thus asked officers to rate a series of common police tactics as "very effective," "effective," "somewhat effective," or "not effective." They could also choose, "I have not heard of this tactic." We asked about fourteen different tactics but highlight just a few key results here.

In Table 8.4, we present the results of all three agencies from Telep and Lum (2014) to show the variety of beliefs that exist about various policing practices, comparing Sacramento's findings with the later findings gathered from Richmond and Roanoke County. The survey results show that traditional beliefs about the standard model of policing, in particular the effectiveness of random (undirected) preventive patrol as well as rapid response to 911 calls, still persist (although less so with random patrols in Roanoke County).

When we asked about specific interventions for which we have evidence, there is much more variation. For example, when asked about hot spots policing, which is strongly supported by research, only 20% of Sacramento officers responded that the tactic is effective or very effective, compared to 67% in Richmond and 81% in Roanoke County. Notably, about 30% of respondents

Table 8.4 SPD, RPD, and RCPD Views on the Effectiveness of Various Strategies for Reducing Crime and Disorder

Strategy	% Very Effective	% Effective	% Somewhat Effective	% Not Effective
Sacramento Police Department (SPD)				
Problem-oriented policing ($n = 505$)	33.9	54.9	9.7	1.4
DARE ($n = 504$)	2	13.9	53	29.4
Community policing ($n = 506$)	24.3	53	21.5	1.2
Hot spots policing ($n = 490$)	3.5	16.9	41.2	29.8
Random preventive patrol ($n = 502$)	8.8	33.3	40	8.2
Rapid response to 911 calls ($n = 507$)	22.1	42.2	27.4	6.7
Richmond Police Department (RPD)				
Problem-oriented policing ($n = 322$)	18.9	46.3	26.7	3.4
DARE ($n = 322$)	5.6	20.2	47.5	23.6
Community policing ($n = 322$)	23.9	36.6	29.2	9.3
Hot spots policing ($n = 323$)	23.8	43	23.8	34.3
Random preventive patrol ($n = 323$)	13.3	31	37.5	6.8
Rapid response to 911 calls ($n = 324$)	25	34.3	31.2	4.9
Roanoke County Police Department (RCPD)				
Problem-oriented policing ($n = 83$)	24.1	45.8	13.3	3.6
DARE ($n = 84$)	7.1	25	39.3	28.6
Community policing ($n = 84$)	25	47.6	22.6	3.6
Hot spots policing ($n = 84$)	28.6	52.4	14.3	2.4
Random preventive patrol ($n = 84$)	8.3	18.1	50	15.5
Rapid response to 911 calls ($n = 84$)	25	36.9	23.8	10.7

This table was adapted with *Gratis Reuse* permission from Figure 3 of Cody Telep and Cynthia Lum, "The Receptivity of Officers to Empirical Research and Evidence-Based Policing: An Examination of Survey Data from Three Agencies," *Police Quarterly* 17(4) (2014): 359–85. (Copyright © 2014, © SAGE Publications).

in Sacramento felt that hot spots policing was not effective, a finding also discovered in Richmond (34% felt it was ineffective). This finding is especially interesting in Sacramento, as it had just undertaken a highly publicized experimental evaluation on hot spots patrols, which showed that they significantly reduced crime (Telep, Mitchell, and Weisburd 2014)!

A question for translational criminologists (see Chapter 15) is why there is sometimes a disconnect between officers' beliefs and research evidence. Part of the reason could be a general lack of awareness of research findings. However, resistance to research might sometimes arise from the context in which the research is done or presented. The negative reaction to hot spots policing in Sacramento may have been specific to their experiences with the hot spots experiment (which was just being completed at the time of the survey).

Anecdotal accounts of that experiment (see Mitchell 2011; 2014) indicated that some officers resisted or resented changes in their routines and discretionary behaviors, despite the documented major reductions in crime that resulted from the experiment. The experiment also was not completely supported by all leaders in the agency for various reasons. Additionally, officers' perceptions about whether they think an intervention is "effective" may be heavily clouded by whether they like the intervention or not, which may explain the results in Sacramento. This is an extremely important lesson about the impact that organizational factors and context can have on the acceptance of research evidence, even when that research is conducted completely by insiders.

The findings in Table 8.4 provide us with other hints at possible reasons for variations in perceptions of the effectiveness of particular strategies. Take, for instance, problem-oriented and community-oriented policing. In Sacramento, these two strategies had much more approval from officers, which is positive in that problem-oriented policing is supported by research evidence. (As an aside, this is also interesting because much of problem solving involves a hot spots approach and there is a great deal of overlap in these two approaches, as described by Braga, Papachristos, and Hurcau 2012). This could reflect more familiarity with problem solving among officers or it may reflect that the number of officers expected to do hot spots policing for the experiment likely far exceeded those doing problem solving. Future research in this area might gauge to what extent officers are expected to carry out different strategies and whether levels of involvement negatively impact their beliefs about those strategies. For example, in the Richmond Police Department, which anecdotally has a long history of implementing problem solving and community oriented policing at the officer level, a slightly lower proportion of officers (although still a majority) saw them as effective or very effective (65% and 60%, respectively).

Willingness to engage in research

In our receptivity surveys, we also asked officers questions to gauge their innovativeness and openness to trying new tactics, including carrying out evaluations of tactics, even if it meant stopping their existing activities. Nearly all officers (94.1%) were willing to try new tactics and ideas, and close to two-thirds (64.6%) felt that SPD used a mix of innovative and more traditional tactics (although, 22.4% of officers viewed the department's tactics as primarily traditional). Similar levels of willingness were also found in Richmond and Roanoke (Telep and Lum 2014). However, *how* these new ideas are presented to officers may matter in terms of their receptivity. In Sacramento, 75% of officers agreed or strongly agreed that when a new idea is presented by top commanders, it is usually a fad and that things will eventually return to normal. This nuance may reflect a cultural resistance to command (Bayley 1994) rather than a true resistance toward doing something new or different.

High-quality research evaluation often requires experimentation and may involve the police stopping their existing tactics or starting up new ones for some people or places and not others. In the Sacramento sample, 47.0% were somewhat willing and 27.2% were quite willing to do this, with a smaller percentage (8.8%) being very willing to stop a tactic to see if a problem gets worse. Compared to their British counterparts in Palmer's study, officers in Sacramento were more willing to stop a tactic for purposes of evaluation, even though they had less knowledge of and exposure to research. We also asked officers whether they would be willing to implement a small, place-based, randomized experiment by randomly selecting twenty areas where a problem occurs and using a coin flip to randomly assign ten to a treatment group that receives the tactic and ten to a control group that does not. Just over one-quarter of officers (27.5%) responded that they were unwilling to do this, while just over one-third (35.0%) were somewhat willing. About 36.0% of officers were either quite willing or very willing to try this method to evaluate a tactic (see Figure 8.2). And, like Palmer's officers, when SPD officers were asked whether they were willing to implement what is typically called a before/after design for evaluating a tactic, more than 62.0% of officers were quite willing or very willing to do so. The greater willingness to use this less rigorous evaluation tactic is clearly obvious in Figure 8.2. It might be expected that officers are more open to evaluations that are less disruptive to daily operations, even though the lower internal validity of such designs make the results less believable than those from a randomized trial.

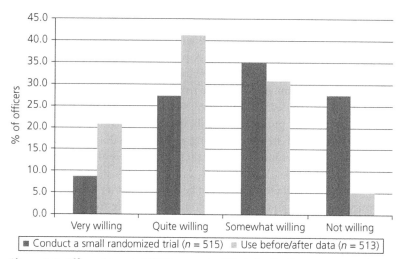

Figure 8.2 Officers' Level of Willingness to "Find the Top Twenty Areas Where This Problem Exists and Toss a Coin to Assign Ten Areas to Have the Tactic and Ten Areas Not to Receive the Tactic and Compare" and to "Use Data Before the Police Implemented the Tactic and Compare It to Data from After the Tactic was Up and Running" in Order to Test Whether a Particular Tactic the Police are Currently Using was Effective

Receptivity, Translation, and Institutionalization

The findings from previous studies, as well as our survey of Sacramento officers and Lum and Telep's additional surveys of officers in Richmond and Roanoke, tell us as researchers that we will have to try harder and be more creative if we want practitioners to pay attention to our efforts. Granted, the burden is not only on researchers but also on police leaders, concerned citizens, and government leaders. However, what receptivity studies tell us is that science cannot stand on its own. Even if findings are robust, receptivity of research (and ultimately evidence-based policing) relies on the mechanisms by which that information is delivered, the beliefs that officers have about research, researchers, and analysts, and how science impacts day-to-day operations (and beliefs about those operations). If officers in other agencies are like those we surveyed, they may rarely seek outside sources of information, and primarily rely on knowledge dissemination from within their own agency. Further, officers continue to believe in the efficacy of longstanding traditional approaches to policing, even though many of these tactics have not been shown to be too effective (see National Research Council 2004). In some agencies, they may be less informed about research on the effectiveness of practices than we might think.

Additionally, the deliverers of the research—crime analysts and researchers inside or external to an agency—are still viewed cautiously and sometimes with suspicion. While it may be clear to some that crime analysis is incredibly important to policing, and while the SARA problem-oriented policing model directly requires analysis and assessment for problem solving, officers question the role of researchers, analysts, and experts in their daily work (also see Koper, Lum, Willis et al. 2015c). Rather, experience is placed on a much higher pedestal than analytic or scientific knowledge. Yet, at the same time, officers show a willingness to try new things, to take the risks that evaluation might pose, and to at least work with outsiders. Others (Weiss and Bucuvalas 1980) have found similar nuances in other professional fields; decision makers are willing to challenge the status quo with new ideas as long as those ideas don't go against their personal beliefs or daily routines, which presents an interesting organizational paradox.

This organizational paradox should not be seen as a barrier to evidence-based crime policy but rather an opportunity to harness a force that could improve receptivity to research. Police researchers and police officers (and not just top commanders) need to work together to make research more digestible and ready for the consumer—law enforcement officers. Agencies that value research, evaluation, and analysis have to build these ideas into the officer's everyday experience. At a minimum, the few empirical findings in this area suggest that we have to rethink how scientists and their practitioner partners not only generate research but package both research processes and outputs for organizations and their employees. Research and researchers may be better received in police agencies if familiar and internal mechanisms of information dissemination are used to present their findings. Further, it appears officers do not reject new ideas up front, but they may be highly suspicious if they look like fads and if they come from the high command or outside experts. Officer input should thus be sought in developing and testing interventions.

As we emphasized at the beginning of this chapter, receptivity does not necessarily have to be a prerequisite for evidence-based policing. While it can make incorporating research into practice easier, it can also be an output of evidence-based policing, fostered by efforts to translate research and to institutionalize its use. The purpose of the Matrix, for example, is not only to translate research into digestible forms, but also to reduce barriers to the receptivity and use of research. However, the link between receptivity and translation is not just found in efforts by researchers to systematically review or make sense of the literature. Translation requires a commitment by all involved to information exchange and communication between researchers and practitioners. Increasing receptivity of research knowledge, processes, and partnerships also requires officers, supervisors, commanders, and other leaders to be aware of knowledge, accept it as factual, legitimate, and valuable, understand it, incorporate it into practice, and then foster a culture in which to do these things is considered normal. This means that translators within the police agency play important roles in improving receptivity of research. For example, police leaders can help translate research and increase receptivity by the way they present research knowledge and expect its use in their agencies. They are often the key in converting outsider knowledge into insider knowledge, and disseminating it through insider-knowledge channels (as implicated in Table 8.2 above). On the other hand, commanders or first-line supervisors who tell their subordinates that they just have to do evidence-based practices because that is what the sheriff or chief wants them to do, work against translation efforts.

As with translation of research, similar links can be described between receptivity and institutionalization of research into practice, which is discussed in detail in the next chapters. Receptivity doesn't need to take the form of officers reading, accepting, and then using research findings. Receptivity can also occur when officers accept evidence-based practices as normal and acculturate those practices into their everyday work. Sorry fellow academics, officers might not cite to your work, nor even know who created the innovation they are implementing! As we discussed in Part Two and as we will discuss at great length in the next chapters, ultimately receptivity to research evidence is not about acknowledgment of the research itself, but about the acceptance of evidence-based practices as the norm. This in turn requires that research-based practices be worked into policing systems and applied in ways that are feasible, give clear guidance to officers, and reinforce the use of these practices through systems of training, supervision, and rewards. Only then will the use of research and evidence-based practices become part of the normal routine and craft of good policing.

9

INSTITUTIONALIZING RESEARCH INTO PRACTICE

An Introduction

In addition to generating high-quality research knowledge, translating it into practice, and building receptivity to research, evidence-based policing also includes the institutionalization of research into the everyday practices of police officers. Institutionalization means that knowledge from research and research processes becomes a normal part of police operations—so much so that officers view operations informed by research knowledge as "business as usual." Institutionalization of research knowledge also means that expectations, rewards, promotions, supervision, accountability, training, deployment, and disciplinary systems can be and are adjusted to incorporate not only the law, standard procedures, and police experience (which they already do), but also knowledge from research, as well as scientific processes and methods.

Adjusting systems with research knowledge, as opposed to only exposing practitioners to research knowledge, has been described by other experts on evidence-based policy as "knowledge integration" (Best, Hiatt, and Norman 2008) or "embedded research models" (Nutley, Walter, and Davies 2007). In particular, the embedded research model developed by Nutley and colleagues suggests that research use is achieved when it is embedded into the systems of practice through standards, policies, procedures, and tools, or where funding or other resource or accountability mechanisms are used to coerce the use of research.

However, Nutley et al. (2007) also describe two other models of research use—the *research-based practitioner model* and the *organizational excellence model*. The research-based practitioner model is one in which practitioners learn about and keep abreast of research and apply it to their daily practice in instrumental ways. For instance, an agency might teach its staff about research findings (and their applications) through training programs, and it might find other ways to keep staff abreast of recent research findings (e.g., through agency news-letters or bulletins). The organizational excellence model, on the other hand, relies on leadership and management as well as organizational relationships with research partners to facilitate and encourage research receptivity and use. Under this model, for example, a police agency might use collaboration with researchers to regularly or periodically test new ideas and make adjustments to practices.

In our definition of evidence-based policing and research use, we intermix concepts of receptivity, translation, and institutionalization, all which cannot be divorced from efforts to change systems. In this regard, we agree with Nutley et al. (2007) that there are multiple models of research use (as well as hybrid approaches), none of which are necessarily superior or independent of others, although some might be more relevant than others for different organizations or stages in the process of adopting evidence-based policing. Thus, in the next chapters, we discuss and give examples of institutionalizing research into sys-tems of policing, but weave into our discussion efforts to promote receptivity, translation, and knowledge of research.

The idea of institutionalizing the use of research into policing systems and practice is a key factor in sustaining evidence-based policing. Take, for example, the community-oriented and problem-oriented policing reform movements. Community policing and problem-oriented policing were likely viewed and developed as broader philosophies for policing, ones that should occupy the minds of every police officer and supervisor during his or her daily activities. Unfortunately, community and problem-oriented policing have not panned out in these ways because they were not institutionalized into the everyday sys-tems of policing. Agencies often have small, specialized units dedicated to com-munity policing or problem solving. In many agencies, many patrol officers continue to operate within the standard model. While police leaders may view these specialized units as markers of progress, relegating innovations to special-ized units or other peripheral components of the organization (like research and planning) signals to officers these approaches are not "real" policing, or part of the craft of policing.

The same problem plagues evidence-based policing. The belief that research knowledge and practices derived from them hold some esoteric place in polic-ing is a problem caused by researchers and practitioners alike. Researchers often come into agencies with specific research projects in mind (Grieco, Vovak, and Lum 2014; Rojek, Martin, and Alpert 2014), or given their own professional norms, want to be recognized for their work and innovations, and want to carry out work that can be published in an academic journal. They may have little contact with first-line supervisors or rank-and-file officers and detectives, who may disdainfully see researchers as connected with the chief's agenda. Some research projects end in negative feelings between researchers and practitioners because of different goals they have for the outcome of the research. Similarly, sheriffs, chiefs, and commissioners, who often change frequently in agencies, want to build their own legacies and develop special programs to achieve goals. The adversarial nature between lower ranks and upper ranks in policing that Bayley (1994) describes is alive and well in policing, which then leads to grumbling complaints and "just do it because the chief says to do it" attitudes. All of these situations complicate efforts to incorporate research knowledge into everyday police practices.

But how is institutionalization achieved? How can research evidence be used to shape tactics and strategies the police employ every day? How can we incorporate crime prevention principles into the daily habits and craft of the patrol officer or detective? In what ways and under what conditions do research findings and other scientific processes (such as crime analysis and evaluation) make their way into the standard operating procedures of a police agency? And what types of infrastructure and policing systems facilitate or impede these processes?

The Matrix Demonstration Projects

In the next chapters, we show some examples to help agencies and their research partners tackle these tough questions. After developing the Matrix, we wanted to move forward with our police agency partners to develop a set of ideas and examples that police agencies could use to institutionalize research into practice. Thus, the Matrix Demonstration Projects were born.[1] The Matrix Demonstration Projects (herein, MDP) are named after the Evidence-Based Policing Matrix because they embody the spirit of finding innovative ways of translating and institutionalizing research into everyday use by law enforcement.

A few of these demonstrations highlight training about evidence-based policing and research evidence, consistent with Nutley et al.'s (2007) research-based practitioner model. Training is the most obvious and straightforward approach to institutionalizing research into police practice. But unfortunately, unless training efforts are sustained and then followed up with accountability mechanisms to that training, police will likely revert back to traditional models of operation. Commanders can teach officers about new knowledge at roll calls, but if officers return to their squads and their first-line supervisors scoff at that knowledge or ignore it, then training will not by itself institutionalize research into practice.

Thus, many of the demonstrations in the Matrix Demonstration Projects are more subtle examples of how to adjust existing practices in the major systems of policing. These can include systems of professional development, deployment,

---

[1] See http://cebcp.org/evidence-based-policing/the-matrix/matrix-demonstration-project/.

accountability and supervision, management and leadership, and planning, research, and crime analytic systems. In this introductory chapter we briefly describe these systems. We then provide deeper examples in Chapters 10 through 14.

Professional development systems

Systems of professional development include the training that an officer first receives before being sworn or authorized as a police officer. This usually occurs in a police training academy, but in some cases, is provided by college-level courses or private training. Other forms of professional development include "in-service" training, informal and formal on-the-job training, and leadership training. All of these formal, informal, internal, or external professional training systems provide opportunities to institutionalize research into practice. At the most basic level, incorporating research into professional development means teaching officers about effective patrol deployment practices or how to effectively engage with citizens. But institutionalizing research into professional development also includes using opportunities of field training, in-service training, and supervisory and leadership development. In Chapter 10, we provide some examples of research knowledge that might be incorporated into various levels of training.

Deployment systems

Adjusting the three largest deployment systems in policing—patrol, investigations, and specialized units—is a major task. This is especially the case with patrol, which makes up the bulk of policing activity and interactions with citizens. At least in the United States (although this will vary with non-U.S. agencies), patrol is also the deployment system that every single officer, including the chief executive, has experienced; patrol culture is thus deeply ingrained in the officer mindset and plays a significant role in fostering the organizational frames for officers we discussed in Chapter 7. These deployment systems are also difficult to adjust because they involve many subsystems that are deeply institutionalized into daily police work, including shift and unit scheduling, geographic assignment of officers, division of labor, and efforts to deal with crime.

Much of the discussion in Part Two of this book focused on examples of research use in patrol deployment, in particular at crime hot spots and as focused on high-risk repeat offenders and other particular problems. But how can lessons from research be incorporated into the daily practice of police officers? One idea we have developed to provide guidance to officers is a tool called *The Evidence-Based Policing Playbook* detailed in Chapter 11. This converts large amounts of research into "plays" (or tactical directives) without getting into the research that underwrites the play. These plays directly address particular problems and provide quick ideas for officers to use during their non-committed time.

In Chapter 12, we also present a unique idea for making investigations more evidence based and prevention oriented– the "Case of Place" approach. The Case of Place idea involves creating detective or other investigative units that shift the focus of investigation (and associated resources) from the traditional "person" or "suspect" to the unconventional "place." This innovation is grounded in research about effective crime control approaches and also provides a way to institutionalize that knowledge into investigations.

Accountability, supervision, management, and leadership systems

Accountability, supervision, and management systems include many aspects of policing, but we focus primarily on systems of supervision, promotions and rewards, strategic meetings like "Compstat," and other leadership activities related to strategic planning and partnerships with the research community. In Chapter 14, we provide some examples and ideas for incorporating research knowledge into performance reviews, promotions and rewards, and supervisor interactions with officers. We also discuss leadership systems, as well as agency infrastructure that supports interactions and collaborations with researcher partners.

Planning, research, and crime analytic systems

Planning, research, and crime analytic systems are also integral to evidence-based policing, as they represent efforts to apply analysis and research evidence into police operations. But as with other technologies and deployments, *how* these units are used matters. In Chapter 13, we discuss whether and how crime analysis units in particular are "evidence based" and consider ways they can be utilized that better reflect and support evidence-based policing.

How to Approach the Next Chapters

The systems above are only some areas in policing that might provide opportunities for research integration. When reading the next chapters, it is important to keep in mind a few important points. First, many other organizational systems and sub-systems might also be transformed to make policing more evidence based. Police agency personnel should think of other systems that touch and influence police behavior on a daily basis and consider them as possible opportunities to rethink practices using what we know from research, or even research processes. These can include systems related to hiring and retention, officer wellness, communication systems with the public, and even systems like roll calls, officer communication systems with dispatchers, systems related to fleet management, and others.

Second, as we have emphasized throughout this book, not all systems can be impacted by research on crime control, which we use here as our primary heuristic. Research in other fields such as management and business, education, and even health (e.g., when discussing officer well-being) can all be relevant in adjusting systems with research knowledge. For instance, if negative reinforcement systems have been shown in management research to reduce job satisfaction and retention and worsen problems like absenteeism, then perhaps the use of these systems in policing should be reconsidered. To provide another example, if educational research provides effective ways to improve adult education and knowledge retention, then perhaps these practices should be incorporated into police academies to make them more effective in disseminating knowledge. Our research on technology in Chapter 7 is a case in point; much of that research is not evaluation research on crime control but is important to consider when adopting new technology (and employing practices to adopt new technology).

Third, institutionalization may be subtle. The focus should be on practice and practitioners, not necessarily on ensuring that those practitioners know that a particular strategy or practice comes from research. Further, the institutionalization of research evidence can also be facilitated by many other secondary practices. For example, some research indicates that more educated officers are more open to innovations and reforms discovered in research (see Lum, Telep, Koper et al. 2012; Telep and Lum 2014). At the same time, simply hiring more officers who have higher levels of education may prove fruitless if organizational structures and cultures of reactivity and resistance to reform and research knowledge are stronger than the abstract benefits that a previous education might provide.

Fourth, perhaps one of the most important changes that might improve police receptivity to research and analysis is changing the community's and municipal government's expectations about what the police should and can achieve with regard to crime prevention or police–citizen relationships. Law enforcement executives and leaders could educate, engage, and debate with their city councils and the public about why police are undertaking certain approaches to crime and what types of interventions work (or do not work). As an example, chiefs and city council members may need to communicate about evidence-based policies in policing as a way to both reduce crime and efficiently spend public dollars. Discourse with the public may help the police understand implementation challenges, limits, or opportunities for implementing evidence-based practices, while at the same time conveying information about effective practices. Some communities may benefit from better knowledge about why they might not require the extra police patrols needed by other communities. The point is that the police are not fated to a single and unchanging public understanding and opinion about them. The argument that evidence-based policing cannot survive because of "politics" implies such a fate and assumes that local public officials are incapable of educating their public or reshaping expectations.

Finally, we note that while this part of the book provides several ideas about ways to institutionalize evidence-based policing, these ideas also need rigorous testing (as do many other ideas for the institutionalization of evidence-based practices—e.g., see Nutley et al. 2007). Some approaches to institutionalizing research into daily practice may work better than others and may work best under different conditions and situations. We hope the ideas offered in this section will encourage both innovation and testing, as we discuss in Chapter 15.

10

INCORPORATING EVIDENCE-BASED POLICING THROUGH PROFESSIONAL DEVELOPMENT

A direct route for institutionalizing research into police practice is through systems of professional development. These systems provide opportunities for personnel to learn and acquire skills and knowledge to carry out their mandate, and they occur at many different points in an officer's career. Training usually begins in the police academy before an officer is sworn in, but can later include "in-service" training. In-service training involves existing officers, detectives, supervisors, and commanders returning to the police academy or to another location to learn new skills, refresh existing ones, or to gain specialized knowledge. Systems of professional development can also be informal and on-the-job, such as mentorship and guidance by supervisors or the command staff, lessons from, and observations of, fellow officers or detectives, or through after-action discussions. Professional development may also be externally obtained, when officers pursue higher education or attend professional conferences. All of these formal, informal, internal, or external learning opportunities are a part of law enforcement's professional development system, and these systems can look different across agencies.

However, whether research evidence, evidence-based policing, or research and analytic processes are part of these professional development opportunities is empirically unknown. In theory, evidence-based policing could be incorporated into these systems in different ways. For example, officers could be trained on the research findings themselves. Or, they could be trained on specific tactics, strategies, or practices that are informed by research without learning about the research itself. Depending on who is receiving training, evidence-based approaches to professional development could also focus on where to find research knowledge, how to judge it, and how to use translation tools like the Matrix; how to operationalize and implement evidence-based strategies as well as processes and systems that support evidence-based policing more generally; or how to overcome barriers to research use. Training could also sharpen skills that may support or facilitate receptivity to evidence-based policing, such as critical and analytic thinking, problem solving, or even empathy (e.g., see discussion in Grieco 2016). Some training might focus on how to partner with researchers and analysts (as well as use their products), or how to carry out evidence-generating activities (such as program evaluation or crime analysis).

Further, different types of training to institutionalize evidence-based policing may be relevant at various levels of professional development. For example, evidence can be infused into initial academy training for new recruits as well as the initial "field training" an officer receives. This early training might be informational (i.e., what is the evidence) and practical (i.e., how to implement tactics that are evidence based). However, for existing officers and for supervisors and commanders, different types of training may be needed. In Figure 10.1, we provide one multi-level model of training toward evidence-based policing using a common educational approach known as "scaffolding." Scaffolding is an approach to learning and curriculum development in which current lessons are built on previous skills in a progression that strengthens understanding at each stage.

We note that our model in Figure 10.1 is stylistic; police departments are likely not this coordinated with regard to training and professional development. However, we use this model to anchor our examples in this chapter about the types of learning that may be needed at different stages of officers' careers to institutionalize evidence-based policing.

Academy Training

Police academy training for new (or existing) officers is likely one system of professional development in which the police adopt new skills or reforms. We say "likely" because despite the seemingly important role that basic training plays in professional development, we know very little about its actual impact. The connection between training in the classroom and how that training turns into police behavior and discretion is difficult to study and link in causal ways. To provide some contemporary examples, we don't know if implicit bias training reduces disparate outcomes between whites and non-whites in traffic stops by officers. We have little evidence on whether procedural justice training causes officers to behave in more procedurally just ways, and we are still uncertain

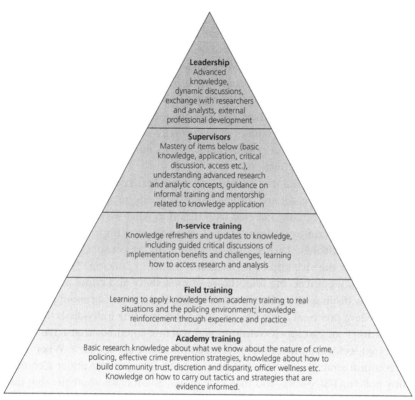

Figure 10.1 Types of Knowledge Acquisition for Evidence-Based Policing at Different Stages of Professional Development

of whether procedural justice leads to greater compliance with the law (for a discussion of this, see Nagin and Telep, forthcoming). We don't know if de-escalation training can reduce excessive use of force, increase officer safety, or reduce injuries to civilians. And, relevant to the subjects discussed in this book, we don't know whether training on effective crime prevention strategies and tactics actually affects officer behavior and discretion.

At the same time, research by Chan, Devery, and Doran (2003) indicates that academies are where police officers first learn about and assimilate an understanding of police operations as well as police culture. What is taught, and how those subjects are taught, can influence a new officer's views about the organization and their role as an officer in society. In the academy, officers can acquire perceptions of themselves and citizens, supervisors and their accountability, and the nature of crime, victimization, and offending.

Academy training most often includes learning the law and the agency's rules and standard operating procedures with regard to handling calls for service, submitting evidence, using force, making arrests, and investigating crimes. For example, one can see the variety of subjects that are covered in a basic training course for police officers at the California Commission on Peace Officer Standards and Training (POST).[1] These include recognizing and investigating different types of crimes, disorders, and emergency situations, patrol techniques, first aid, and the like. During academy training, new officers may also learn about common problems they will encounter in patrol and may even be advised by academy instructors about how they think citizens view the police. These lessons, regardless of their accuracy, are not lost on recruits. Grieco (2016) has found that that new trainees can experience a significant change in some of their perceptions about policing and citizens during the academy, in both positive and negative directions.

In our visits with training academies for the Matrix Demonstration Project and in examining academy curricula and surveying recruits, we hypothesize that very little is actually covered with regard to what we know from research about effective crime prevention tactics or strategies to improve trust and confidence with citizens. Rather, training (like many aspects of policing) continues to reflect the vice grip of the standard model in policing. Thus, while the research may point to the importance of proactivity and crime prevention to effectively dealing with crime, academies emphasize learning about procedures and the law, processes related to detaining and arresting individuals (including use of force and weapons training), and reacting to crimes that have already occurred (evidence-processing, investigations, crime scenes, etc.). When crime prevention strategies are covered, they may be incorporated under a community policing framework, and they may or may not include strategies that have been shown to reduce crime effectively or improve police–citizen relationships.

This failure to incorporate research knowledge into academy training is likely not due to an outright resistance by police academies to new knowledge and information. On the contrary, many of the academy leaders we have interacted with want to try and incorporate new knowledge into their training academies. But they also feel constrained by what they believe are strict requirements by their state law enforcement commissions to cover a certain number of hours of training for various topics. They also mention the lack of attention and resources that are given to training academies by law enforcement agencies that use them. Additionally, academy staff sometimes feel that what they teach is either forgotten or unlearned when the officer enters field training and patrol.

Some of these complaints may be true, but at least with regard to academy time, there may be more discretion and flexibility to incorporate new items into academy curricula than commonly believed. For example, the regular basic course for law enforcement officers of the California Commission on Peace Officer Standards and Training—dated 2012 at the time of this writing—has as one of its required "learning domains" a set of objectives entitled "*LD 03 Policing and the Community.*"[2] While this is one learning domain of forty-three,

---

[1] See https://post.ca.gov/regular-basic-course-training-specifications.aspx.

[2] See https://www.post.ca.gov/Data/Sites/1/post_docs/training/trainingspecs/LD03.doc.

it is filled with great potential for infusing research evidence on both effective crime prevention and community relations. Some of the learning objectives are descriptive, such as "Define community policing," "Discuss community policing philosophy," "Identify the essential components of community policing" (in which they include problem solving), or "Identify peace officer responsibilities in the community." This last one is interesting, as it focuses on describing various responsibilities, including "maintaining order; enforcing the law; preventing crime; delivering service; educating and learning from the community; and working with the community to solve problems." Most of these have been researched, and some efforts are more effective than others (either in reducing crime or in increasing community satisfaction). A more nuanced discussion of this learning objective could focus on that knowledge.

We note that this may not be how this learning domain is actually taught. But if a California police academy wanted to incorporate research knowledge discussed in this book into their curricula, this required learning domain may be where they could do so (among others). As a further illustration, one of the learning objectives from *LD 03* is to "Differentiate between proactive and reactive policing." Here, while the basic difference between the two is important to understand, an evidence-based approach might emphasize the differential effectiveness of proactive and reactive approaches as shown in scientific research. Further, it might also illuminate the relationship between the two modes, noting, in particular, the impact that proactivity can have on reducing the need to be reactive (i.e., responding to calls for service). It would also be important to examine available research on the consequences of certain types of proactivity (such as stop-question-and-frisk) that may work against good community relationships. Knowing the different kinds of proactive policing, which are effective in both reducing crime and maintaining citizen trust and confidence, and how to implement proactivity, are perhaps more essential learning objectives from an evidence-based perspective than only learning the difference between proactive and reactive policing.

These more nuanced and evidence-based discussions require a great deal of knowledge by academy staff about the research evidence and how that knowledge can be used. Thus, using training to institutionalize evidence-based policing means that academies must know about and keep up with that knowledge (and therefore hire more officers and civilians who have this knowledge). Additionally, critical thinking skills and the ability to recognize and think about nuances in knowledge are also core competencies for an officer attuned to evidence-based policing to acquire. Therefore, academy instructors also must possess these skills.

To make this point, consider as an example another learning objective in the POST's *LD 03* called "Discuss the broken windows theory." Recall in Chapter 5 we discussed that between the 1990s and the 2010s, more knowledge had been discovered about "broken windows" policing strategies that have challenged our thinking about this approach. The seminal article by Wilson and Kelling

(1982) first tied the police function of maintaining order and reducing public nuisances to the prevention of serious crime. However, over time, police
adopted a "broken windows approach" in a variety of ways. Many agencies,
including during the early days of its use in New York City, interpreted the
theory to mean using large amounts of misdemeanor arrests to "clean up the
streets." In places with high levels of violent and gun crime, broken windows
misdemeanor arrests naturally coincided with another tactic—stop-question-
and-frisk, or Terry Stops (referencing the U.S. Supreme Court case *Terry v. Ohio*,
which allowed for stop-and-search for weapons).

We rehash the story of broken windows to point out that knowledge in
policing is complex, nuanced, and often evolving. Today, broken windows
approaches are now being questioned and challenged by citizens, researchers, and police agencies. Further, as we discussed at various points in Part Two,
research on disorder-based policing has concluded that the strongest crime
prevention effects are generated by community and problem-solving interventions designed to change social and physical disorder conditions at particular
places, and that aggressive order maintenance strategies that target individual
disorderly behaviors do not generate significant crime reductions (e.g., see
Braga, Welsh, and Schnell 2015). At the same time, although stop-question-
and-frisk might be unpopular, other research indicates that it can be effective
when used as it was intended—to discover gun carrying and reduce violence
in gun-crime hot spots (e.g., see Koper and Mayo-Wilson 2006; 2012). Leaders
of academies that are evidence based must pay attention to this evolving and
growing research knowledge and find ways to adjust their curricula dynamically. In other words, just teaching officers about "what is broken windows"
could actually lead to tactical interpretations that aren't effective or that worsen
police–citizen relationships.

But many academies do not have the capacity to keep up with the vast amount
of criminological research out there, or even with translating it into teachable
strategies and tactics. Thus, free tools like the Matrix or Crimesolutions.gov
are valuable resources that already synthesize and update research findings for
academy instructors. Further, academies are primarily staffed internally, by
other sworn officers. However, institutionalizing evidence-based policing into
this early stage of officer training requires agencies to consider hiring outsiders
or even "pracademics" (see Huey and Mitchell 2016)—those with both police
and research knowledge and experience to strengthen an agency's professional
development strategy. At the same time, bringing into academies specialized
trainers on topics like evidence-based policing for each academy class can be
costly and unsustainable.

One solution that can be developed in partnership with researchers is creating available online learning modules so that new information can be shared
in a cost-effective way. For example, after exploring and interviewing staff from
numerous police academies in Maryland and Virginia, we discovered a need for
a basic module that describes what evidence-based policing is, provides a quick

review of the evidence and how it might be applied, and discusses challenges to implementing evidence-based policing. This module would also have to fit into academy curricula and include performance assessments. Thus, we created a free basic introductory module on evidence-based policing, consisting of four short lessons of less than fifteen minutes each. We also include a study guide with learning objectives, a common need for academy instructors and students alike. Finally, we provide access to a short quiz. This module can be found at the Matrix Demonstration Projects site under "Academy Curriculum."[3] Using this module could be a very cost-effective way to train officers about evidence-based policing while fitting that training into a one-hour time slot in academy or in-service curricula.

Another free example we created in the MDP focuses on training related to building trust and confidence in police agencies.[4] At the time of writing, recent events in Ferguson, Missouri, New York, and Baltimore have led law enforcement agencies to rethink how they can build and maintain trust, confidence, and satisfaction with the communities that they serve, especially communities of color. Our discussions with various academies indicated that staff needed more than just traditional diversity training or community policing modules to address these difficult issues with new officers. Through a collaborative team involving the director and staff members from the Northern Virginia Criminal Justice Training Academy in Virginia, we developed this free module to supplement existing training in police academies on this subject. The module is divided into three areas for various levels of professional development. The first focuses on awareness of the complex and difficult conversations about policing and race. Short videos from various perspectives attempt to create empathy, openness, and receptivity to the subject matter. Research evidence on the gap between perceptions of the police by citizens of different races is also presented. In the second module on education and training, we provide lessons from researchers on implicit bias (i.e., unconscious biases that officers may have against certain groups), procedural justice, and intercultural communication, three issues and actions thought to help mitigate and address conflict between police and people. In the third module, we present information for leaders, with resources and tools to consider for rethinking their approach to these tough issues. For each module, we also provide a step-by-step guide that can be easily followed, with discussion questions to facilitate learning.[5]

---

[3] See http://cebcp.org/evidence-based-policing/the-matrix/matrix-demonstration-project/academy-curriculum/.

[4] See http://cebcp.org/evidence-based-policing/building-trust/.

[5] Although much of our focus in this book has been on evidence-based policing as it pertains to crime control, this discussion provides an additional illustration of how evidence-based policing can be applied to other aspects of policing. Further, the trust and confidence training module could be used in conjunction with training on evidence-based crime prevention to prompt further consideration and discussion among officers about some of the nuances involved in balancing crime control with these other aspects of policing.

These are only two examples of modules that could be created through police–researcher partnerships to deliver cost-effective training for officers that facilitates evidence-based policing. Other examples are webinars given by the Bureau of Justice Assistance's Smart Policing Initiative[6] and resources from the Center for Problem Oriented Policing.[7] Such resources may not necessarily be given to students, but rather to staff members who then transmit knowledge and attitudes to new trainees. The bottom line is that academies are not as constrained by their existing curricula and requirements as they might believe. Partnering with researchers and using existing and free resources like the modules shown here can help bring research to the training table to overcome challenges of cost and sustainability.

Field Training

Academy training is only the start of building a learning infrastructure for evidence-based policing. Once recruits leave the academy, they enter field training, which plays a major role in an officer's early socialization. Field training is the probationary period after academy training during which new officers are usually paired with more experienced officers to learn the everyday skills of policing, to be eased into the daily tasks of patrol, and to be regularly supervised and assessed. Field training is where officers experience, observe, and apply knowledge and skills that they acquired in the academy to practical tasks. It also is the environment in which their initial impressions about what might be viewed as "good policing" are formed. Depending on the agency and field training officers' tendencies, field training is where proactive habits might be developed, and where positive attitudes toward problem solving and assessment can be inculcated. Alternatively, field training can also be the place where bad habits are reinforced, and reform and innovation are ignored.

The realities of field training vary across police agencies. Some may pair new officers with other officers who may be willing to be a mentor or field trainer, and other agencies may provide incentives (e.g., extra pay) for experienced officers to serve in this role. Some agencies build structure around their field training, providing specialized training to field training officers and requiring both trainees and their field trainers to fill out performance evaluations frequently. Other agencies have very little structure for field training. In some agencies, the "best" officers (however defined) have a tradition of being field trainers, while in other agencies it is an assignment dreaded and avoided by officers.

With the help of the Alexandria, Virginia, Police Department (APD), we took a closer look at field training activities and how research might be incorporated into this specific professional development system. APD is a progressive agency

---

[6] See http://www.smartpolicinginitiative.com/.
[7] See http://www.popcenter.org/.

whose chief and command staff were interested in rethinking field training and partnered with us to develop this demonstration. At the time of our collaboration, APD could be described as having a structured approach to field training. New officers were given a workbook which included a number of objectives and skills that they had to meet and perform in the presence of a field training officer, who would grade the new officer on his or her performance of the objective. The workbook (and therefore field training) covered a wide variety of activities believed to be the most common tasks in which patrol officers engage. This included lessons on accident investigations, arresting adults and juveniles, dealing with alarms, assisting other agencies, developing case jackets for basic investigations, carrying out criminal investigations, dealing with destruction of property, domestic violence, driving under the influence, and carrying out traffic stops.

As we described in Chapter 9, successful implementation of evidence-based policing involves embedding research ideas into everyday practices so that they are normalized into policing. Thus, working with field training supervisors in the APD, we took the existing APD field training workbook and, rather than replace existing requirements, focused on creating scaffolding adjustments that would incorporate more evidence-based approaches into existing requirements. These included adjusting the performance metrics by which officers are judged; changing some of the tasks carried out by trainees or developing new ones that were evidence informed; and modifying overall goals, objectives, written lessons, and standard operating procedures that trainees must read during their field training.

Adjusting performance metrics is a vital part of institutionalizing evidence-based practices and a topic we will return to in Chapter 14. Unless performance metrics of officers, supervisors, and leaders are aligned with the knowledge they are receiving or reforms or innovations they are asked to deliver, then there is little incentive or accountability for change. Performance evaluations for field trainees, therefore, presented opportunities for APD field trainers to provide feedback, mentorship, and practical education to trainees. Thus, adjustments to the performance grading sheet that field training officers complete may be one way to infuse evidence-based policing into the thinking and practices of both field training officers and new trainees.

Table 10.1 shows some of the performance metrics found in APD's workbook, which are likely similar to those used in many other police agencies. The first column shows the action being measured (e.g., motor vehicle operation, orientation, geography, etc.). The second "Original Description" column depicts how the performance of this activity is currently measured in the workbook. For example, for the action of "motor vehicle operation," performance is measured by evaluating a "recruit officer's competence to operate police motor vehicle during general and emergency situations." One might consider this as the most basic competency that a trainee must show in practice, given what he or she learned about motor vehicle operation in the academy. The third column reflects what we

Table 10.1 Ideas for Adjusting Performance Metrics in Field Training

Performance Measure	(A) Original Description	(B) Evidence-Based Adjustments to Performance Measure
Motor Vehicle Operation	Evaluate recruit officer's competence to operate police motor vehicle during general and emergency situations.	Evaluate the officer's knowledge on information regarding police pursuits or vehicle accidents—specifically, what research has shown about reducing officer and civilian fatalities. Evaluate the officer's competence on the strategic use of the vehicle for crime prevention (e.g., doing prominent surveillance or slow roaming in a hot spot). Evaluate the officer's competence on knowing how to use a mix of vehicle and foot patrol to enhance citizen interaction (teaching the officer not to overly rely on remaining in the vehicle).
Orientation and Geography	Evaluate recruit officer's competence to expeditiously respond to locations while operating a police motor vehicle during general patrol and emergency situations.	Assess recruit's knowledge about where crime tends to concentrate and how to access computerized crime maps from crime analysis or the RMS. Assess recruits on their knowledge of why crime occurs at certain places, including what environmental, physical, and social factors attract crime to those locations.
Written Communication	Evaluate recruit officer's competence to select and utilize appropriate departmental forms and prepare reports that accurately represent the situation in a timely, comprehensive, and logically organized manner.	Officers may be assessed on filling out other types of forms that facilitate proactive approaches to policing. These might be those related to Case of Places (see Chapter 12), crime prevention through environmental design (CPTED) assessments or problem-solving analyses using the SARA model. Officers could be evaluated on the use of specialized forms related to reducing nuisances or other problems (e.g., trespass or drunk-in-public enforcement orders) that further facilitate problem solving, proactive, place-based or tailored approaches. Agencies might also want to add a performance measure that evaluates an officer's ability to identify and access other sources of written information that might assist them in their duties (e.g., crime analysis, crime prevention or research information).

Table 10.1 Continued

Performance Measure	(A) Original Description	(B) Evidence-Based Adjustments to Performance Measure
Field Performance	Evaluate recruit officer's ability to recognize, analyze, and take action upon law enforcement-related activities and situations.	Evaluate recruit officer's ability not only to respond to calls for service, but to proactively reduce crime opportunities before they turn into crimes. Officers might be assessed on their ability to: conduct targeted, proactive patrol activities; identify problems and seek innovative and proactive solutions; utilize crime analysis, information technologies, and other resources; and connect separate crime incidents to each other.
Telecommunication Skills	Evaluate recruit officer's ability to effectively utilize law enforcement communications equipment (radio, telephone, computer) and follow established protocols.	Evaluate an officer's ability to learn and be comfortable with other forms of technologies—RMS, CAD, crime analysis, LPR, etc., with assessment focusing on how the officer utilizes these sources of information to enhance proactive and reactive operations (e.g., using information systems to review prior problems at a location when responding to calls or when conducting proactive activities).
Criminal Law and Ordinances	Evaluate recruit officer's knowledge of and ability to utilize substantive and procedural criminal law in field situations.	Evaluate recruit officer's knowledge of and ability to utilize knowledge about crime control, prevention, and fair policing that is found in various free resources. This may include information on crime prevention as well as information on topics like officer stress, use of force, officer safety, biased policing, community relations, problem solving, leadership, etc. Given that the vast majority of an officer's shift is spent in situations for which the law does not provide clear guidance, other information is needed.
Department Policies and Procedures	Evaluate recruit officer's ability to demonstrate knowledge of the department's policies, procedures, standard operating procedures (SOPs), and acceptable past practices and apply them.	The department's policies, procedures, SOPs and acceptable practices can include new information about how police can act to be more fair, legitimate and effective as described above. This is also a good opportunity for the recruit to learn and be assessed on current innovations in the department that may be well known

(*Continued*)

Table 10.1 Continued

Performance Measure	(A) Original Description	(B) Evidence-Based Adjustments to Performance Measure
		at the managerial level but less well known at the patrol level. This may be a good opportunity for the recruit to understand how patrol operations are viewed at the strategic, command level.
Traffic Enforcement	Evaluate recruit officer's ability to perform traffic enforcement and accident investigations.	Recruit officers may be evaluated on how traffic enforcement is used proactively to reduce crime. Officers may also be assessed on their ability to do basic hot spot, traffic, or problem analyses related to traffic—where are the accidents/speeding/DUIs occurring, and why? This is also a good opportunity to infuse research knowledge about potential disparities in traffic stops, procedural justice, and how to reduce bias in traffic enforcement.
Relationships	Evaluate recruit officer's interaction with individuals in the community and persons within the department.	Officers might be assessed on knowledge about why respectful interactions are essential to police legitimacy and crime control effectiveness. Officers might be required to read further information about issues related to police legitimacy, biased policing, community policing, and perceptions of police by minority communities. Officers might also be assessed on the relationships they establish for proactive and preventive policing approaches (e.g., establishing relationships with an apartment or business manager related to problems at a particular location, or neighborhood and community groups in the area). This might also include knowing problem actors in the officer's patrol area (probationers, parolees, gang members, gun offenders, and other known repeat offenders).

think an additional or adjusted competency might look like that touches research knowledge. Note that we do not suggest replacing the basic competency. Instead, we use scaffolding to build in additional competencies that might enhance the development of an officer's critical thinking, problem solving, prevention, or crime control skills. (Note also that many of the ideas for adjusting performance metrics and field training activities in Tables 10.1 and 10.2 correspond to aspects of policing other than crime prevention.)

An example of how a performance metric might be adjusted in field training can be seen in the "Orientation and Geography" measure. For many agencies, new officers are judged in field training on their ability to know where they are, where other officers are, their beat and precinct boundaries, and the street layout. The purpose of having this performance measure in a standard model of policing philosophy is that officers need to know how to get to emergency calls quickly and efficiently, and knowing their beat boundaries is essential to their deployment. But given what we know about effective patrol, an evidence-based adjustment of this performance metric might not only include these items, but also where crime patterns tend to concentrate, and why. Orientation of geography might include a new officer's understanding of the environmental, physical, and social factors of his or her beat that might lead to crime concentrating in those places and an understanding of the routine activities at those locations. Such an adjustment reflects not only solid evidence about the nature of crime at places, but also orients the officer to the importance of crime prevention at these locations, which evidence suggests is much more effective than randomly patrolling one's beat.

Another example is in the measure called "Field Performance." Here, field training officers traditionally would evaluate new officers' efforts in responding to calls for service or taking action in the field when they see suspicious situations or events that need a law enforcement response. To build on these skills from an evidence-based perspective, officers might also be assessed on what they decide to do in their non-committed time to prevent crime or proactively reduce crime opportunities. Here, officers could be judged on lessons that they learned in the academy with regard to proactive patrol, identifying problems and developing solutions to them, or utilizing crime analysis and information technologies to help them prevent crime. (Of course, this assumes and requires that academies are teaching this information.)

Yet another category of field training performance metrics that could be adjusted to reflect evidence-based practice is the "Department Policies and Procedures" category. As shown in Table 10.1, the core competency in this area requires officers in field training to "demonstrate knowledge of the department's policies, procedures, standard operating procedures (SOPs) and acceptable past practices and apply them." Imagine, however, if department policies, procedures, SOPs, and acceptable past practices also included innovations and reforms that reflected the evidence. For instance, imagine that the "standard" procedure was to patrol places proactively with problem-solving methods in

Table 10.2 Ideas for Adjusting Activities in Field Training

Activity	(A) Ways Officers in Field Training Must Show Competency	(B) Additions or Adjustments to These Requirements that Incorporate Knowledge and Skills that Reflect Research Evidence
Accident Investigation	Incorporates operational procedures for traffic crash investigations and traffic enforcement.	Learn how crime analysis can identify problem intersections and roadways; conduct problem-solving (SARA) or environmental (CPTED) analysis of hot spots of traffic or pedestrian accidents.
Adult Arrests	Incorporates operational and legal procedures for arrests, prisoner transport, public intoxication, and writs/warrant service.	Add information to and research findings on how officer treatment of suspect during an arrest may be connected to the arrestee's later recidivism. Or could assess officers on ability to address repeat offending and use arrests strategically for focused deterrence initiatives like Ceasefire or pulling levers. Positive performance might be measured by the *reduction* in arrests, if met with a reduction in crimes and calls for service, or by the diversion of an individual from being arrested (e.g., some juveniles who might benefit more from diversion than arrest).
Alarms and Building Searches	Operational procedures for vehicle/foot patrol, checking the premises, reporting requirements, and clearing alarm calls.	For repetitive alarm problems, workbooks might incorporate additional guidance on basic problem-solving skills to reduce repeat alarm calls.
Assisting Other Agencies	Procedures in assisting other agencies during vehicle pursuit, metro transit issues, or incident commands. Includes, but is not limited to working with child protective services, social services, and juvenile intake.	Lessons could also include exercises in dealing with crime problems that straddle borders (i.e., beats, sector, jurisdiction borders), and working with non-police entities to reduce problems at places. Officers might be assessed on their ability to connect problems from one system (e.g., subways) with crime problems outside of that system (e.g., burglary in residential areas nearby).

Table 10.2 Continued

Activity	(A) Ways Officers in Field Training Must Show Competency	(B) Additions or Adjustments to These Requirements that Incorporate Knowledge and Skills that Reflect Research Evidence
Beat Checks or Random Patrol	Operational procedures for formal and informal beat checks, as well as proper response to beat checks. Officers should review mobile databases daily and complete checks as many times as possible throughout the shift.	Learning about where hot spots are located from crime analysts. Could transition from beat checks to hot spots policing and proactive problem-solving approaches in between calls for service. May apply Koper Curve principle of fifteen-minute stops at hot spots between calls. Include lessons about the concentration of crime, where it concentrates, and how to effectively conduct hot spot policing in between calls for service. Officers would also learn that even in high-crime places, 40–80% of time is not spent in a call for service or on an arrest.
Criminal Investigation	Operational procedures to investigate a crime, as well as responsibilities for crime scene control. Specific procedures for the investigation of burglary, robbery, and white collar offenses.	Officers may balance lessons about criminal investigation of an *individual* with criminal investigation of a *place* or problem. Officers might attempt a mini case of place activity. See Case of Places demonstration at http://cebcp.org/evidence-based-policing/the-matrix/matrix-demonstration-project/case-of-places/. Also learn about solvability factors and procedures which lead to successful investigations.
Destruction of Property	Incorporates department procedures for field reporting as well as criminal investigations related to destruction of property. Also consists of items to include in written report.	Crimes that happen frequently, especially when related to property, may present good opportunities for problem-solving exercises (e.g., using a CPTED or SARA exercise to address the root of this problem). Learn about links between physical and social disorder and crime, and order maintenance/quality-of-life policing.

(Continued)

Table 10.2 Continued

Activity	(A) Ways Officers in Field Training Must Show Competency	(B) Additions or Adjustments to These Requirements that Incorporate Knowledge and Skills that Reflect Research Evidence
Domestic Violence	Departmental procedures include waiting for possible back-up to arrive, determining what happened, determining if probable cause exists and making an arrest if it does, and providing victim services to the remaining parties.	Add to the SOPs more information that reflects research on the effectiveness of arrest and other responses to domestic violence. For example, research has indicated that how an officer treats an offender or victim may reduce victimization and recidivism. Checklists may also prove useful here in supporting domestic violence cases. May also explore the connection between firearms availability and domestic homicides.
Drug and Vice Offenses	Responsibilities include the detection, arrest, and prosecution of individuals engaged in the illegal use and sale of controlled substances, illegal gambling, prostitution, pornography, and alcohol violations.	More information about what we know works/doesn't work in policing drugs, alcohol, etc., including POP guides or quick reviews of the research (e.g., Mazerolle's review on what works in street level drug enforcement). Officers might also try smaller-scale activities that reflect principles from Drug Market initiatives (see http://www.dmimsu.com/). Work with analysts, detectives and specialized units to identify drug corners and actors associated with those corners.
DUI Enforcement	Departmental procedures for identifying DUI offenders, approaching accidents or traffic stops, administering sobriety tests, and impounding vehicles.	Could use this as an opportunity for a SARA/POP exercise, especially if the jurisdiction has problem areas of DUI. Officers might identify underlying causes of DUI, map hot spots, and work on more targeted proactive enforcement activities. Officers may also be assessed on their knowledge about different approaches to proactive enforcement activities.

Table 10.2 Continued

Activity	(A) Ways Officers in Field Training Must Show Competency	(B) Additions or Adjustments to These Requirements that Incorporate Knowledge and Skills that Reflect Research Evidence
Juvenile Procedures	Operational procedures for juveniles taken into custody, as well as procedures for status offenses and serious habitual offender comprehensive action program.	Traditional approaches emphasize proper procedures for juvenile arrest. Other skills that could be learned that reflect research might be juvenile diversion, reducing the potential for juvenile problems before they occur, learning when curfews work, and working with place-managers to provide more guardianship of hang-outs. Further information about juvenile justice, recidivism, and victimization might be provided for officers to understand this type of offending better.
Missing Persons	Departmental procedures outlining the incident report to be completed for missing persons.	Here agencies might consider new research awareness about missing persons, as developed by the Scottish Institute for Policing Research. Officers might be required to simply review this material (see http://www.geographiesofmissingpeople.org.uk/).
Motor Vehicle Code	Incorporates department procedures for traffic offenses; including felony offenses, misdemeanor offenses, driver's license suspension or revocation, registration, reckless driving, signs and signals, lane usage, right-of-way, equipment, accidents, miscellaneous offenses, and speeding.	Could incorporate one-pagers concerning what we know about different types of strategies that use traffic stops to reduce crime, or even information educating officers about the problem of racial profiling in traffic enforcement. Officers might show competency in not only applying the motor vehicle code, but also competency in where they choose to carry out traffic enforcement and the service they provide during traffic stops. Officers might also learn other

(Continued)

Table 10.2 Continued

Activity	(A) Ways Officers in Field Training Must Show Competency	(B) Additions or Adjustments to These Requirements that Incorporate Knowledge and Skills that Reflect Research Evidence
		technologies to assist with traffic enforcement and also reduce potential bias, including LPR or speed cameras. Finally, officers might learn about procedural justice and fairness in conducting traffic stops, and how racial disparities might result from traffic stops.
Problem identification	[Not included in this recruit officer training manual.]	Interestingly, problem identification (either proactively, or from existing calls for service) is not a competency included in field training guides and workbooks in many agencies. Problem identification is a more proactive approach to dealing with crime, and its exclusion reflects a common focus on reactive, individual approaches.
Vehicle Impounds	Incorporates department procedures for parking enforcement, impound procedures, Lojack tracking, and combating auto-theft.	Instructional material regarding using license plate recognition, auto and auto theft, as well as a possible POP guide. Include information or tips about the detection of stolen vehicles and prevention of vehicle theft. Could also include learning about hot spots of auto theft and recovery, types of automobiles most often stolen, and ways of detecting stolen autos.

between calls for service. This would require that department policies and procedures include knowledge from research or be adjusted themselves. But again, this would be another example of using an existing performance measure in field training to institutionalize evidence into practice.

In addition to adjusting performance metrics, we also worked with APD to develop ideas on how actual activities and tasks of trainees might be adjusted to align better with research knowledge in policing. As we discussed in Figure 10.1, field training is where new officers have the opportunity to practice and solidify what they learned in the academy. However, if activities only reflect the standard model of policing, then we can't expect officers to learn and get used to activities that reflect evidence-based approaches. APD's field training workbook includes activities for new officers, which we recreate in Table 10.2. Again, the first column lists the activity, while the second column shows the existing requirements for officers to show competence with that activity. In the third column, we present an addition or adjustment to this activity, developed with APD field training officers.

For example, the activity of "Beat Checks or Random Patrol" includes officers engaging in activities such as conducting formal and informal beat checks, as well as proper response to beat checks. Officers should review mobile databases daily and complete checks as many times as possible throughout the shift. An evidence-based add-on might include officers becoming proficient in learning about where hot spots are located and interacting with maps produced by crime analysts. This could also include applying proactive problem-solving approaches at specific places within a beat that require frequent beat checks. Officers might learn how to apply the Koper Curve principle of fifteen-minute stops at hot spots to learn about dosage and style of patrol to increase crime prevention effects.

For "Destruction of Property," new officers are required, as shown in Table 10.2, to incorporate "department procedures for field reporting as well as criminal investigations related to destruction of property" and to know what to include in reporting this crime. New or modified activities that reflect an evidence-based approach might include officers applying problem-solving approaches to property damage, including identifying where and why these crimes reoccur, what environmental factors contribute to them (officers may be asked to complete a CPTED assessment), and exploring effective ways that these crimes might be mitigated by examining ideas from the Matrix or Crimesolutions.gov.

Finally, infusing evidence-based policing into field training requires modifying the overall goals, objectives, written lessons, and standard operating procedures that trainees must read during their field training. While new officers may read this material in the academy, they may also read it during field training. This provides an opportunity to modify that material to include knowledge from research, including language that reflects evidence-based policing, including proactivity, problem solving, procedural justice, and intelligence-driven approaches. Or, additional information could be provided at this stage, such as one-page summaries of knowledge about particular types of incidents or police interventions (domestic violence, drug market interventions, field and traffic stops, etc.). These can be one-pagers from Matrix studies[8] or other short reads

---

[8] E.g., see Figure 2.5, or another example at http://cebcp.org/evidence-based-policing/the-matrix/micro-places/micro-places-braga-and-bond-2008/.

on various topics. For example, see the free one-pagers that we have developed on various issues such as place-based policing, crime analysis, evidence-based policing, translational criminology, policing strategies, systematic reviews, and counterterrorism and homeland security.[9] In summary, field training provides a wealth of opportunities for incorporating research knowledge through the application and practice of strategies, tactics, and activities that reflect research evidence. A good way to begin is to find ways to infuse this information into existing field training structures such as activities and performance metrics that expose both new officers and field trainers to this information. However, adjusting both academy and field training efforts to be more aligned with research knowledge requires more attention, resources, and training provided to academies and their staff as well.

In-Service, Supervisor, and Leadership Training

In-service, supervisory, and leadership training are also part of the professional development of officers and provide further opportunities to institutionalize evidence-based policing. In-service training is provided to officers outside of their academy or field training probationary periods. It can be required of all officers and involve refresher courses or new training, or it can be specialized, available to officers that qualify, apply, or are chosen to receive such training. Often, in-service training is provided within the insider knowledge framework, either within police academies or at a regional level. In-service officers, as well as the content and tone of in-service training, differ from that of new recruits. Having garnered experience in the field, officers may be more cynical about reform and innovations, and have less incentive to be receptive to or implement new ideas. Further, if officers have never been exposed to evidence-based training that new recruits may be receiving , they may not only need this new training but also may be highly suspicious of it. Thus, at the in-service level, officers may not only need knowledge refreshers and updates to knowledge but also may need more critical and guided discussion of the implementation benefits and challenges of evidence-informed strategies and tactics (see Figure 10.1).

Some of this critical and guided discussion can be prompted by using new information that officers may not have received in the academy. For example, this might include information about research on effective crime prevention and how to access and use translation tools like the Matrix. Free video materials geared toward in-service officers are also available for agencies to use. We have video-recorded examples of this type of training that can be freely accessed from one of our workshops on evidence-based policing.[10] For example, we

---

[9] At http://cebcp.org/one-pagers/.

[10] At http://cebcp.org/evidence-based-policing/evidence-based-policing-workshop/. See also https://www.youtube.com/playlist?list=PL4E509820FD3010E9&feature=plcp or at http://cebcp.org/ebpsupervisor-training/.

include training on the Matrix, hot spot policing, conducting evaluations in agencies, and targeting crime reduction areas. We also record short lectures, such as our Congressional briefings, which provide a video of less than ten minutes to prompt discussion on a given subject.[11] Using these and other free videos and webinars by other organizations (e.g., the Bureau of Justice Assistance, U.S. Department of Justice) can be a cost-effective way for in-service training to incorporate research knowledge.

Additionally, because evidence-based policing is also focused on the importance of research and analysis, both supervisors and in-service officers need to understand the role that crime analysis plays in evidence-based policing (see Chapter 13), as well as how supervisors can take advantage of analytic information. For this purpose, we have created, in collaboration with crime analyst Jamie Roush (formerly of the Jacksonville, Florida, Sheriff's Office), free training for supervisors and commanders on the importance and use of crime analysis.[12] Like the evidence-based policing basic training modules, this training consists of a series of four fifteen-minute modules on how to use crime analysis in evidence-based ways.

In-service training can also include practical exercises that reinforce knowledge gained. Many in-service training sessions take place in the classroom, without any follow-up when officers return to their regular duty. However, other learning approaches may provide good examples of how to reinforce classroom learning in practice for existing officers. For example, some professional master's programs in criminal justice that are offered by universities require officers who are enrolled in these programs to carry out practicums in their own agencies, which may include trying out problem-oriented policing or CPTED exercises, conducting their own evaluations and research projects, or figuring out ways to implement findings from research. Practicums can also be used for in-service in agencies as well.

The practicum approach to professional development may be especially useful to first-line supervisors, especially using a working group environment. First-line supervisors are essential in implementing reforms, changes, and adjustments to police policy and practice. Yet this rank is often not provided the necessary tools, resources, and information to facilitate those adjustments. In-class training or policy directives may be inadequate to implement evidence-based approaches successfully. A working group approach with practicums may help to achieve this.

As an example, we worked with all first-line supervisors in a local agency in Virginia over the course of a year to train them on evidence-based practices and refresh their knowledge base. This approach used a working group model consisting of a local research partner (the authors) meeting with first-line supervisors (in this case sergeants) once a month to discuss contemporary deployment

---

[11] See http://cebcp.org/outreach-symposia-and-briefings/.
[12] These modules can also be accessed at http://cebcp.org/evidence-based-policing/the-matrix/matrix-demonstration-project/supervisors/.

and supervisory issues, such as crime prevention, race and policing, community relationships, internal accountability, or officer wellness. Sometimes, the topic of the day was determined by the sergeants, with guidance from the research partner. Sergeants were given a short article or feature to read prior to the meetings that prompted discussions about the issue. We would then provide guided discussions, tangible resources, or ideas about how supervisors might assess or implement evidence-based approaches.

The working group allowed for practicums to be used. For example, one lesson during this training was focused on taking advantage of non-committed time for police proactivity and crime prevention efforts. To increase supervisors' awareness of this time, we first provided supervisors with a short feature to read about proactivity during non-committed time. We then asked supervisors to go back to their patrol squads and try to determine how much non-committed time that officers had in their squads and how they were using this time. This sample lesson can be viewed in Box 10.1 below. This practicum allowed supervisors to gain experience in understanding their squad's non-committed time, and to examine more carefully what officers were doing when not answering calls for service. This type of awareness may be an important first step to making supervisors and their officers more receptive to using non-committed time for proactive crime prevention activities.

The challenge for police departments and their academies is how to incorporate this information into their systems of in-service or supervisory training. Videos can be shown and viewed, but learning materials may need to be created, including study guides and exams. Further, it matters who delivers the materials. If instructors or supervisors preface videos with statements like "The chief made me make you watch this" or "Look, you just have to do this to get your certification," this can render the material ineffective.

Conclusion

Training constitutes one important mechanism for institutionalizing evidence-based policing. Evidence-based policing agencies actively incorporate research knowledge like that found in Chapters 3, 4, 5, and 6, into training academies, field training, and in-service training. As we have described in this chapter, training on this knowledge doesn't have to take the form of academy recruits reading research articles. However, the patrol tactics and strategies that are taught to new officers starting in the academy should reflect research knowledge about what reduces crime and improves police-citizen relations. Officers in agencies that try to be evidence based should at the minimum be taught the basic generalizations that we know from research (i.e., the utility of proactive, place-based, and problem-oriented tailored approaches as discussed in Chapter 3). Similarly, the lessons that officers learn to garner trust and confidence from citizens should specifically incorporate the knowledge on procedural justice, implicit bias, community policing, and the like. Advanced agencies will also

Box 10.1 Supervisors Working Group Assignment on Non-Committed Time

This assignment is given to supervisors one week prior to a working group meeting, coupled with the article "Changing the Culture of Uncommitted Patrol Time: A Work in Progress" by Jim Dermody in Translational Criminology Spring 2013: 8–9 (http://cebcp.org/wp-content/TCmagazine/TC4-Spring2013)

A. For those who supervise patrol units

This week, think about each person in your squad and jot down what types of activities they tend to do during the time they are *not* answering calls for service. These would be just activities related to their crime control and community-oriented functions (no need to talk about breaks/admin/etc.). Does each individual have a particular "style" and how would you describe it? Does your unit as a whole have certain tendencies with regard to its deployment style? How much total non-committed time does your squad typically have in a week (% of total time)?

B. For those who supervise uniformed/plain clothes units/specialized units who do not answer calls for service

This week, think about each person in your squad and jot down what types of activities they tend to engage in, either individually or with assigned partners. Be specific. Does each person/pair have a particular "style" and how would you describe it? Then: does your unit as a whole have certain tendencies with regard to its deployment style? What types of tactics and strategies does your unit tend to use most often and why do you use that particular tactic?

C. For those who supervise investigative or other types of unit

This week, document what your unit tends to do on a daily basis given its particular charge. So, for example, is the primary function of your unit to investigate offenses that come to the unit from patrol? Do you feel like your unit could do other things that might impact the crime problem to which you are assigned other than its current approach? What might those things be?

D. Questions for the working group meeting

1. What did the sergeants discover?
2. What should be the role of the sergeant in influencing these tendencies?
3. How can first-line supervisors shape the discretionary tendencies of officers towards specific objectives (e.g., crime reduction, improved citizen–police relations)?
4. If non-committed time is not being used, what are some tangible ideas that the researcher can provide and how can those research-based ideas be translated into actions?

use community reaction data about specific tactics and strategies in academies in dynamic learning modules so that officers understand community sentiment in more systematic ways, as opposed to individual trainers giving their personal opinions on what they think the community thinks about the police (see more on this in Lum and Nagin 2017). In an evidence-based policing agency, evidence-based concepts are incorporated into the activities and performance metrics of field training to get officers in the habit of engaging in practices that are informed by research and analysis. Training for detectives might include solvability factors that are supported by research or training for using investigations for proactive prevention (e.g., using the "Case of Place" approach discussed in Chapter 12).

Supervisory and leadership training in an evidence-based agency focuses on presenting new knowledge as well as facilitating critical discussion about the challenges and benefits of implementing evidence-informed practices. Trainers, supervisors, and commanders in an agency that values evidence-based policing would have a working knowledge of important research findings (and sources) related to both crime prevention tactics and internal management. Agencies practicing evidence-based policing also use managerial meetings (such as Compstat) as dynamic learning and training environments, where new research findings are shown, discussed, and debated. These are also environments where personnel can practice using research strategically, as we will discuss in Chapter 14.

11

THE PLAYBOOK

Evidence for Everyday Patrol

If agencies want to incorporate and institutionalize the use of research knowledge into practice, then awareness of and receptivity to research findings, professional development, and knowledge generation may not be sufficient. As we discussed in our example of field training in Chapter 10, institutionalizing the use of research knowledge in practice requires the practice of evidence-based policing, with officers incorporating that practice into their daily habits and decision making. This means developing tactics that can fit into everyday police operations and that reflect research evidence. But how is this accomplished?

One opportunity to incorporate evidence-based practices into patrol operations is to take advantage of the non-committed time we discussed in Chapter 1. Research indicates two important facts about this time. First, even in high-crime areas, police actually have a significant proportion of their time free in between calls for service. But second, and perhaps more importantly, how officers use this time can not only reduce the frequency of calls that they handle in the first place, thereby preventing crime, but also shape their relationships with people with whom they interact.

To effectively use non-committed time to achieve these goals, officers and other uniformed patrol units need clear directives and training on what to do during these non-committed times. A supervisor might tell an officer to "go patrol crime hot spots," but officers need to know where hot spot are, what types of hot spots they are, and be trained on the best ways to deal with different kinds of problems at hot spots. We know from research covered in Part Two of this book that *how* police patrol these hot spots can matter in terms of the deterrent effect they create as well as the unintended consequences that might ensue, including community backlash against certain types of strategies the police might employ in hot spots.

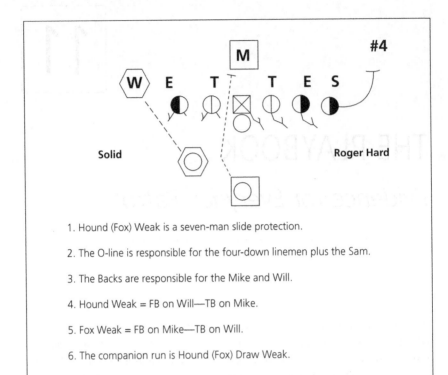

1. Hound (Fox) Weak is a seven-man slide protection.

2. The O-line is responsible for the four-down linemen plus the Sam.

3. The Backs are responsible for the Mike and Will.

4. Hound Weak = FB on Will—TB on Mike.

5. Fox Weak = FB on Mike—TB on Will.

6. The companion run is Hound (Fox) Draw Weak.

Figure 11.1 "Hound Weak" Football Play from an Arizona Cardinals Playbook

This figure is shown from the publicly available Arizona Cardinals' Playbook as provided by ESPN.com at www.espn.com/photo/2007/0828/cardinals_playbook.pdf.

To provide better, more specific, and evidence-informed guidance for patrol officers and specialized units, we think playbooks might be useful translation and institutionalization tools. In sports like football, playbooks hold the various formations and actions that players can take on the field (and even in practice) to achieve a goal. Unlike rulebooks (which may be equivalent to a law enforcement agency's standard operating procedures or even the law governing criminal procedures), playbooks are focused on specific deployments, actions, and outcomes (within the parameters of the rules of football), developed from specialized knowledge. Playbooks may be one decision-making tool in which research knowledge might be infused. Take, for example, this play shown in Figure 11.1, called the "Hound Weak" from an old Arizona Cardinals (a National Football League team in the United States) playbook, as obtained by *ESPN*[1] and also written about in *Business Insider* (see Nachman 2011). Notice how this play is shown with a diagram, followed by specific instructions on

---

[1] This play and its illustration is publicly available on ESPN.com at http://www.espn.com/photo/2007/0828/cardinals_playbook.pdf.

how to execute the play. As other plays discuss by Nachman (2011) show, play-books can also have very simple basic directives, such as how to stand in ready position, to very complex plays, where specific movements are carefully crafted to achieve a specific goal.

It is unknown whether or not some football plays are evidence based with reference to their relative effectiveness to other plays or to securing their objectives (a topic of another book perhaps!). But our point is that playbooks provide players with key information about the implementation of specific actions. Good players study, memorize, understand the playbook, and take the plays seriously, implementing them in games. They are not theoretical or abstract lessons remembered from training camp classroom settings. Nor do these plays have citations to the coaches or players that invented the plays. But playbooks are seen as essential tools in football.

In the same vein, evidence-based policing might be facilitated by playbooks. Standard operating procedures manuals (SOPs) rarely describe specific crime prevention strategies and tactics that officers can take in between their calls for service (and how to implement them). SOPs might talk about general patrol strategies or investigative approaches. But the nature of policing in the standard model has yet to incorporate knowledge about what patrol officers can do in their non-committed time to prevent and reduce crime. Patrol officers could use operational playbooks with clearly spelled out directives so that they can implement them to achieve outcomes.

Toward this end, we created a free resource for the Matrix Demonstration Project called the Evidence-Based Policing Playbook.[2] The Playbook contains evidence-based and operational ideas for law enforcement officers to use and adapt during their everyday patrol to reduce, prevent, and deter crime. Much of this knowledge comes from the Matrix, but some of it also comes from evidence about the nature of crime as well as police operations. Plays were also created in collaboration with a number of police agencies and officers, to ensure feasibility. At the beginning of the Playbook, we encourage officers and agencies to determine what are the crime problems and conditions that are relevant to their jurisdictions and to add other plays that may be relevant or useful. Plays also have to be modified as the evidence builds; what we think works today may need to be tweaked with new knowledge tomorrow (recall our example of broken windows policing). Agencies should consider incorporating crime analysts into the process of creating plays, as they can assist in identifying crime patterns, trends, and research knowledge. Another source of knowledge about possible crime conditions can come from members of the community or in discussion with other officers who have knowledge of specific places. Officers can capitalize on their own knowledge of and experience in their area, and

---

[2] This can be accessed at http://cebcp.org/evidence-based-policing/the-matrix/matrix-demonstration-project/playbook/.

spend time observing their area, noting and recording activities in those places that might contribute to crime. Finally, they can employ existing systematic approaches to identifying crime conditions and possible solutions. We give three examples inside of the Playbook—Case of Places, CPTED, and using the SARA problem-solving model.

In this chapter, we walk through some plays in the Playbook, using them as an example of how research knowledge can be translated into practical applications. The plays are organized into two types—"crime prevention plays" and "trust and confidence plays." Crime prevention plays use research knowledge from the Matrix and criminology to inform activities that patrol officers might undertake to effectively reduce and prevent particular conditions and problems. Trust and confidence plays are ideas from research to improve citizen interactions and satisfaction with the police.

We also include a section in the Playbook called "refreshers." These are brief and basic pieces of information that are referred to in other plays. For example, we refer to the *Refresher on Stop-and-Frisk* when we discuss hot spots plays. Plays using problem-solving or environmental crime prevention reference refreshers that discuss what SARA or CPTED means. Finally, the Playbook also includes *Other Ideas and Resources*, which provide officers and supervisors with places where they can get further information to develop other plays.

Crime Prevention Plays

The crime prevention plays in the Playbook begin with the *General Play*, as shown in Box 11.1. The *General Play* was created from the three general principles of effective crime prevention from the research evidence collected in the Matrix described in Chapter 3. While most of the plays in the Playbook are designed for specific conditions and problems, the *General Play* is meant to be used as general deployment guidance as well as a fallback play for patrol officers who want to work within the overall tendency of effective practices. Notice that specific research findings and citations that we discuss in depth in Chapter 3, 4, 5, and 6 are not provided within this play. As academics, we know that credit should be given to the countless criminologists who have contributed to creating the *General Play*. However, citations, footnotes, or other references to research in a playbook would appear overly academic and possibly reduce receptivity of this information, not to mention the large reference section at the end of an operations playbook that would be larger than the playbook itself!

Various plays follow the *General Play*, in alphabetical order, each presented by the play name and a short description of the condition that the play addresses. Take, for example, the *Burglary Prevention Play*, shown in Box 11.2. The condition being addressed is "an increase in residential burglaries in an area; the occurrence of a burglary in a block or high rise." Underneath the condition is

Box 11.1 The General Play

1. Target your efforts in specific places where crime concentrates (a specific address, alleyway, intersection, block, or cluster of blocks). Crime is extremely concentrated: approximately 50% of a city's crime occurs in less than 5% of its addresses and street blocks. In suburban and rural areas, this concentration may be even greater.
2. Proactive strategies are much more effective than reactive ones. General response to 911 calls, random patrols, and arrest after the fact are less effective in preventing crime. Proactive tactics use past information to anticipate hot spots and hot times of crime, repeat offenders and victims, and high-risk situations to direct activities.
3. Effective proactivity requires problem solving and developing tailored strategies. You are more likely to be effective if you tailor your strategy to a particular problem/condition. For ideas on how to develop problem-solving strategies, see the *Refreshers on The SARA Problem-Solving Model* and *CPTED*, as well as the *Case of Places Play*.[3]
4. Remember that citizens' reactions matter. The most proactive, place-based, and problem-solving plays will not be effective if they lead to negative community or citizen reaction or if they are unlawful or unconstitutional. Anticipating reactions and working with communities is needed for many plays. See the section on *Trust and Confidence Plays* as well as the *Refresher on Stop-and-Frisk*.

a simple statement, "Research indicates that once a home or apartment unit is burglarized, homes and units next door and/or very nearby have a heightened risk of burglary." This is an important concept for burglary prevention and comes from extensive spatial analysis by Kate Bowers, Shane Johnson, and others on near-repeats for burglary (see Bowers and Johnson 2005; Johnson and Bowers 2004; 2014; Johnson, Bernasco, Bowers et al. 2007). Including this piece of research evidence not only provides some on-the-spot opportunities for training about the evidence, but also justifies the next item in this play (warning nearby neighbors of their potential risk).

This play also mentions two ideas from research—situational crime prevention (SCP) and crime prevention through environmental design (CPTED). While some officers may be aware of SCP or CPTED, others might not, and so we provide refreshers on these topics in the Playbook. These are shown in Boxes 11.3 and 11.4. Ron Clarke, Derrick Cornish, Marcus Felson, and others' research efforts are reflected in these refreshers. We also provide a link to the Center for Problem-Oriented Policing's CPTED resource, which can also give

---

[3] This refers to a brief summary of our "Case of Places" idea as detailed in Chapter 12.

Box 11.2 The Burglary Prevention Play

CONDITION: An increase in residential burglaries in an area; the occurrence of a burglary in a block or high rise.

1. Research indicates that once a home or apartment unit is burglarized, homes and units next door and/or very nearby have a heightened risk of burglary, particularly over the next two weeks.
2. After a burglary, warn neighbors immediately of their heightened risk and suggest methods to target harden their homes, including locking windows and basement/back doors; engaging their alarm systems regularly, and encouraging more guardianship of their neighbors. See the *Refresher on Situational Crime Prevention*.
3. Work with place managers and·residents of buildings to determine the underlying mechanism that may be contributing to burglaries. Is a roof door unsecured? Are residents leaving their doors unlocked (e.g., college dorms), or are windows left open? Removing material below fire escapes or windows can reduce the ability of offenders to access fire escapes from the ground.
4. Work with place managers and residents for longer-term solutions, including the use of CCTV if available.
5. Have the agency CPTED unit conduct an environmental analysis of the area to determine what opportunities are contributing to crime. If a CPTED unit is not available, use the *Refresher on CPTED*.
6. Research indicates burglars often commit crimes within one mile of their own residence or activity space. Knowing, monitoring, and making contact with burglary probationers and parolees nearby may help prevent future crimes.

---

the officer more information if s/he wishes to learn more about these ideas. This play also mentions "place managers" and working with building residents to target harden against burglaries. This reflects criminological research by Paul and Patricia Brantingham, John Eck, Marcus Felson, and Tamara Madensen. But again, the play provides simple lessons and directives without citing the large amount of research underwriting the play.

Another play is named *Directed Koper Patrols* (Box 11.5). Although the authors would suggest there are many ways for officers to be deployed at crime hot spots, one basic approach is to provide visible presence. However, how long should officers stay at crime hot spots? As we already discussed in Chapter 4, Koper (1995) found that officers could maximize the residual deterrent effect of their directed patrol by staying in crime hot spots for twelve to fifteen minutes. Staying longer did not seem to provide additional deterrence benefits after officers left. Rather than explain the study and science behind this finding in the Playbook, the play is instead presented as a simple directive that can be used when officers have a bit of time in between their calls for service. The play also

---

Box 11.3 The Refresher on CPTED

This material is summarized from the Center for Problem-Oriented Policing's CPTED resource, located at http://www.popcenter.org/tools/cpted/.

CPTED or "Crime Prevention through Environmental Design" focuses on examining features of the environment and determining the opportunities they create for crime. Examples of these features are: bus stops where individuals congregate; trees and shrubbery that block visibility; lack of lighting; traffic direction or lack of signaling; abandoned buildings; alleyways or cuts in between buildings; empty lots hidden from the street, etc.

CPTED focuses on reducing the opportunity for offending and crime by adjusting these environmental features. For example, this might include cutting down shrubbery to increase visibility, adding lighting to a dark alley, boarding up abandoned homes used for drug distribution or prostitution, or improving traffic conditions by adding signage, signals, speed bumps, etc.

The strategies and goals of CPTED are varied. Adjustments can be implemented to:

- control or make access more difficult;
- deter offenders by increasing risk of apprehension;
- increase visibility;
- increase or encourage guardianship;
- regulate or adjust behaviors and routines;
- reduce the rewards for crime.

A related approach is *Situational Crime Prevention*, also provided below as a refresher.

---

provides a reference to a one-pager on the Koper Curve principle for officers who might be interested in learning more about the Koper Curve.

Because this play is directly connected to the idea of "hot spots," we also reference a *Refresher on Hot Spots Policing* for officers who may not be familiar with this concept (see Box 11.6).

Notice that the *Directed Koper Patrol Play* also provides "two important notes" when conducting traffic and pedestrian stops in high violent crime locations. These include referencing the *Refresher on Stop-and-Frisk* as well as a play in the trust and confidence section. The reference to the *Stop-and-Frisk* refresher is a vital part of this play. Stop-and-frisk has become an increasingly controversial strategy used by police officers in both the United States and the United Kingdom. The controversy behind stop-and-frisk is primarily the result of the unconstitutional overuse of stop-and-frisk to search for drugs and apprehend drug offenders, as well as the disrespectful and discriminatory ways in which some officers had been implementing stop-and-frisk, especially in communities of color. At the same time, stop-and-frisk can be used lawfully, done respectfully, and be impactful in reducing gun carrying. Here, a "refresher" is provided

Box 11.4 Refresher on Situational Crime Prevention

Ronald Clarke defined situational crime prevention as "comprising measures directed at highly specific forms of crime that involve the management, design, or manipulation of the immediate environment in as systematic and permanent a way as possible so as to reduce the opportunities for crime and increase its risks as perceived by a wide range of offenders." (In R. V. Clarke. 1983. "Situational Crime Prevention: Its Theoretical Basis and Practical Scope." In *Crime and Justice: An Annual Review of Research, vol. 4*, eds Michael Tonry and Norval Morris, 225. Chicago, IL: University of Chicago Press.)

In 2003 he and Derek Cornish produced the following chart, providing examples for twenty-five techniques for situational crime prevention in "Opportunities, Precipitators and Criminal Decisions: A Reply to Wortley's Critique of Situational Crime Prevention." *Crime Prevention Studies* 16: 41–96.

The chart is reprinted here for your use. The twenty-five techniques are organized into five categories of measures, intended to (i) increase effort; (ii) increase risks; (iii) reduce rewards; (iv) reduce provocations; and (v) remove excuses. These suggestions, while not all directly applicable to police work, may help officers to think about actions they can take on their own or in cooperation with other government and community partners to reduce opportunities for crime.

Increase the Effort	Increase the Risks	Reduce the Rewards	Reduce Provocations	Remove Excuses
1. Target harden: Steering column locks and immobilisers; anti-robbery screens; tamper-proof packaging	*6. Extend guardianship:* Take routine precautions: go out in group at night, carry phone; "Cocoon" neighborhood watch	*11. Conceal targets:* Off-street parking; gender-neutral phone directories; unmarked bullion trucks	*16. Reduce frustrations and stress:* Efficient queues and polite service; expanded seating; soothing music/muted lights	*21. Set rules:* Rental agreements; harassment codes; hotel registration
2. Control access to facilities: Entry phones; electronic card access; baggage screening	*7. Assist natural surveillance:* Improve street lighting; employ defensible space design; support whistleblowers	*12. Remove targets:* Removable car radios; women's refuges; pre-paid cards for pay phones	*17. Avoid disputes:* Separate enclosures for rival soccer fans; reduce crowding in pubs; fixed cab fares	*22. Post instructions:* "No Parking"; "Private Property"; "Extinguish camp fires"
3. Screen exits: –Ticket needed for exit; –export documents; –electronic merchandise tags	*8. Reduce anonymity:* –Taxi driver IDs; –"How's my driving?" decals; –school uniforms	*13. Identify property:* –Property marking; –vehicle licensing and parts marking; –cattle branding	*18. Reduce emotional arousal:* –Controls on violent pornography; –enforce good behavior on soccer field; –prohibit racial slurs	*23. Alert conscience:* –Roadside speed display boards; –signatures for customs declarations; –"Shoplifting is stealing"

Increase the Effort	Increase the Risks	Reduce the Rewards	Reduce Provocations	Remove Excuses
4. Deflect offenders: Street closures; separate bathrooms for women; disperse pubs	9. Utilize place managers: CCTV for double-deck buses; two clerks for convenience stores; reward vigilance	14. Disrupt markets: Monitor pawn shops; controls on classified ads; license street vendors	19. Neutralize peer pressure: "Idiots drink and drive"; "It's OK to say No"; disperse troublemakers at school	24. Assist compliance: Easy library checkout; public lavatories; litter bins
5. Control tools/weapons: "Smart" guns; disable stolen cell phones; restrict spray paint sales to juveniles	10. Strengthen formal surveillance: Red light cameras; burglar alarms; security guards	15. Deny benefits: Ink merchandise tags; graffiti cleaning; speed humps	20. Discourage imitation: Rapid repair of vandalism; V-chips in TVs; censor details of modus operandi	25. Control drugs and alcohol: Breathalyzers in pubs; server intervention; alcohol-free events

Box 11.5 Directed Koper Patrols Play

CONDITION: This is a basic, go-to play if you only have short periods of time in between calls for service. The Koper Principle* states that officers do not have to stay at hot spots of crime for long periods of time to create a deterrent effect after they leave.

1. Select a few (two to five) crime concentrations in specific places (problem blocks, intersections, and alleys) to focus on during your shift using crime maps and analysis, or if not available, determining addresses that have high levels of calls for service.
2. When not answering calls for service, go to these locations on a random basis, and patrol (including foot patrol) for ten to fifteen minutes. Repeat periodically and unpredictably. If problems are inside a store or business, walk inside of that location in addition to outside patrol.
3. At violent crime locations, consider conducting traffic and pedestrian stops. Two important notes:

   (a) When conducting traffic and pedestrian stops and engaging in stop-question-and-frisk, legality and professionalism are imperative. Please review the *Refresher on Stop-and-Frisk* for more information.
   (b) How officers treat individuals whom they stop matters. Courtesy, professionalism, restraint, and empathy, as well as cautiousness and alertness should always guide officer behavior. For more advice, see the *Improving Exchanges with Citizens Play*.

* See http://cebcp.org/wp-content/onepagers/KoperHotSpots.pdf.

Box 11.6 Refresher on Hot Spots Policing

We know that crime is incredibly concentrated: research studies in multiple juris-dictions continue to find that about 50% of a city's serious crime is located at less than 5% of its addresses and street blocks. Hot spots policing refers to a general strategy of targeting crime concentrations with police resources.

Note: The term "hot spots policing" does not point to a specific tactic. A "hot spot" approach, can be applied to many plays, and simply means that a play is targeted to a specific place that has high levels of persistent crime problems. However, what police do at hot spots matters to both their ability to prevent crime and maintain citizen trust and confidence. General visibility at crime hot spots may have some effect on deterring crime, but problem-solving approaches at crime hot spots may have greater long-term effects. Some strategies that have been used at hot spots such as high dosages of misdemeanor arrests of stop-question-and-frisks have led to negative community reaction.

There is no agreement on what the size of hot spots should be. However, successful interventions tend to target locations that are much smaller than neighborhoods—they are often specific addresses, street blocks, intersections, alleys, floors/sections of a high-rise building, a section of a mall, certain places within a school or airport, or a section of a park.

Plays that target hot spots are more likely to be effective.

For more on Hot Spot Policing, see this handy summary: http://cebcp.org/evidence-based-policing/what-works-in-policing/research-evidence-review/hot-spots-policing/.

---

because stop-and-frisk has often been used in directed patrol in places with high levels of gun crime, and this play presents an opportunity to remind officers of when and how they can use this tactic. The refresher is shown in Box 11.7.

Similarly, in the *Gun Crime and Shootings Play* (Box 11.8), we also link to the *Refresher on Stop-and-Frisk*, given that this play directly focuses on gun crimes. In this play we also provide alternative ideas to a hot spots approach, including focused deterrence approaches as well as a U.S. Department of Justice initiative known as Project Safe Neighborhoods.[4]

In this play we also reference the refresher in the Playbook on the *SARA Problem-Oriented Policing Model* (see Eck and Spelman 1987). The SARA model itself uses a form of scientific method, and is a useful way for officers to incor-porate their own experiences and observations ("Scanning") with systematic crime analysis ("Analysis"). While the actual interventions that officers can take

---

[4] In the Playbook, we link specifically to one Project Safe Neighborhoods example (see https://www.crimesolutions.gov/ProgramDetails.aspx?ID=258). For more on Project Safe Neighborhoods, see https://www.bja.gov/programdetails.aspx?program_id=74.

Box 11.7 Refresher on Stop-and-Frisk

Stop-question-and-frisk, also known as "Terry stops," "Terry frisks," or "pedestrian stops," should only be used when legally/constitutionally justified, and with the highest levels of professionalism, respectfulness, restraint, and empathy (see the trust and confidence play *Improving Exchanges with Citizens*. Some important points to remember:

1. "Stop" and "frisk" are two separate acts with two separate legal standards. For the stop *only* (no frisk), officers must have reasonable suspicion that an individual is about to commit/has just committed a crime.
2. If the officer chooses to stop *and* frisk, the officer must have reasonable suspicion that the individual is armed and presently dangerous. Note that it is unconstitutional to conduct a stop-and-frisk to search for drugs.
3. If the officer does have reasonable suspicion that the individual is armed and proceeds with patting down a person's outer clothing, and it becomes immediately apparent that what the officer is touching is contraband, then those drugs can be seized.
4. Stop-and-frisk has increasingly led to negative citizen reactions to police behavior, likely because of its excessive use in searching for drugs. Stop-and-frisk can only be used when constitutional, within high-violence areas, and with professionalism, respectfulness, restraint, and empathy.

in the SARA model ("Response") can vary in both type and research support, and while officers may not have time to determine whether their intervention was effective ("Assessment"), the SARA model can be a helpful way for officers to take a place-based, proactive, and tailored approach. The SARA refresher is shown in Box 11.9.

Another play that reflects much of the research evidence discussed in Chapter 5 is the *Focused Deterrence Play* for high-risk offenders (Box 11.10). Because we are also interested in disseminating evidence in these plays for learning opportunities, we provide links within the Playbook to other plays which may be relevant, as well as more information on Operation Ceasefire from our one-pagers resource.

For many agencies, persistent open-air drug markets continue to be both a nuisance and safety concern. Mazerolle, Soole, and Rombouts (2007) have conducted a systematic review of research on street-level drug enforcement for the Campbell Collaboration, which we reduce into the *Open-Air Drug Markets Play* (Box 11.11). Again, rather than provide the extensive research information found in that review, we provide three guiding points.

The most common approach used by patrol officers to address street robberies is to respond to them after the fact, to look out for suspects, or to keep an eye on places with lots of robberies. Of these three, the most common response is

---

Box 11.8 Gun Crimes and Shootings Play

CONDITION: Gun crimes and shootings at specific locations, for example, around a club, bar, or establishment, or on specific streets, parks, alleys, etc.

1. Conduct directed patrols in gun crime hot spots focused on the detection of gun carrying on a person. For gun crimes, traffic and pedestrian stops have been shown to be effective. See *Refresher on Stop-and-Frisk* and also *Improving Exchanges with Citizens Play* for advice on conducting these lawfully and respectfully.
2. The *Focused Deterrence Play* has been effective when used for gun offenders and those at risk for gun violence. More generally, officers should be aware of high-risk people linked to gun crime hot spots, including known gun offenders, probationers, parolees, and gang members. See your crime analysis or intelligence units for assistance with such information. Monitoring these people and making contact with them may be an effective way to deter their involvement in future gun violence.
3. Examine underlying causes at gun-crime locations, which may be connected to other problems such as open-air drug markets, problem night clubs, retaliation shootings, or gang disputes. Consider applying the *Case of Places Play* or using the *Refresher on the SARA Model and Problem-Oriented Policing.*
4. If there has been a recent shooting, consider the possibility of retaliation, and help detectives who may not be as familiar with the area identify possible future offenders or victims. Some communities have critical incident teams or other groups that try to reduce the possibility of retaliation. These may already be operational, such as those under Project Safe Neighborhoods Interventions.
5. In domestic violence cases, try to determine whether a gun is in the home and whether local and/or state laws allow you to remove guns from the home.
6. More information[5] on directed patrols to reduce gun violence.

---

rapid response to a robbery via the computer-aided dispatch system. The officer gets to the scene, canvasses the area, and may drive the victim around the location to search for the suspect. The officer will most likely write a report given the serious nature of the event, and perhaps provide the information to robbery detectives, who may follow up with the victim in the future. This approach to dealing with robberies is the most likely strategy that new officers will pick up during field training and when deployed into patrol. But street robberies can also be prevented by actions an officer takes during the time in between calls for service. Some of these strategies may be less known or obvious to officers, which are provided in the *Street Robberies Play*, in Box 11.12.

---

[5] The Playbook is interactive. This word is linked in the Playbook to http://cebcp.org/evidence-based-policing/what-works-in-policing/research-evidence-review/directed-patrol-for-gun-violence/.

Box 11.9 Refresher on the SARA Model and Problem-Oriented Policing

The SARA model builds on Herman Goldstein's *Problem-Oriented Policing* and was developed and coined by John Eck and William Spelman (1987) in *Problem Solving: Problem-Oriented Policing in Newport News*. Washington, DC: Police Executive Research Forum.

The SARA model is a decision-making model that incorporates analysis and research, tailoring solutions to specific problems, and most importantly, evaluating the effectiveness of those responses. The acronym SARA stands for:

SCANNING: Identifying, prioritizing, and selecting problems that need addressing using both data from police and other sources and from community and citizen input.

ANALYSIS: Deeply analyzing the causes of the problem, including the underlying causes of repeated calls for service and crime incidents.

RESPONSE: Determining and implementing a response to a particular problem. Ideas for responses should be "evidence based" when possible (see, e.g., the Matrix), or at least tailored to the specific problem at hand using general principles of good crime prevention.

ASSESSMENT: Often the most ignored part of the SARA model, this requires assessing and evaluating the impact of a particular response, and the willingness to try something different if the response was not effective.

For more information, see this Matrix resource as well as the POP Center (http://www.popcenter.org/).

Plays can also be developed to prevent other issues that are not necessarily crime. Police officers handle a wide variety of concerns that have also been researched. Persistent traffic problems and accidents, for example, can benefit from evidence-based approaches because they happen so frequently. We developed a play on traffic accidents that incorporates the use of crime analysts to help officers deal with these problems (see Box 11.13). In this play, we linked to a resource from the National Highway Traffic Safety Administration known as DDACTS, or Data-Driven Approaches to Crime and Traffic Safety.[6]

Also included in the Playbook is a *Refresher on Responding to Domestic Violence*. As we discussed in Chapter 5, research on domestic violence is complicated. However, improving domestic violence response and finding ways to reduce harm by understanding risk in domestic violence is information that would be useful to officers responding to domestic violence. In this refresher, we talk about that research, but also show items from a checklist developed by the Fairfax County (Virginia) Police Department domestic violence unit to improve response to domestic violence. This checklist includes the following items:

---

[6] See http://www.nhtsa.gov/Driving+Safety/Enforcement+&+Justice+Services/Data-Driven+Approaches+to+Crime+and+Traffic+Safety%28DDACTS%29.

Box 11.10 Focused Deterrence Play

CONDITION: This is a general play that can be used in conjunction with other plays, and focuses on targeting high-risk repeat offenders of serious crimes.

1. Establish a working group partnership (see *Seeking Partners for Prevention Play*) consisting of crime analysts, probation, parole, prosecution, and social service providers to assist with below tasks.
2. Identify high-risk repeat offenders with the help of crime analysis. Be targeted and specific; for example, if you are working on reducing an armed robbery problem in your area of responsibility, those with repeat misdemeanor offenses or low-level disorders may not be appropriate to target.
3. Make contact personally and by notifications with these individuals to communicate to them that the agency is partnering with probation, parole, and the state's attorney to focus on violent crimes in this area, discussing specific consequences of their future offending to them.
4. When possible, try to connect high-risk offenders with social services.

   The above reflects a "pulling levers" approach. For more information on this approach and also "Operation Ceasefire" visit this resource: http://cebcp.org/evidence-based-policing/what-works-in-policing/research-evidence-review/focused-deterrence/.

---

1. Take photos of the victim, suspect, and scene if possible.
2. Speak to all parties, including the suspect, and try to lock in their version of the events.
3. Obtain from the victim a clear background and history of abuse, rather than only what happened in the particular incident to which you have responded. Add to the report any call or incident history you can obtain from the agency's information systems that provide more information about this victim or suspect.
4. Obtain a working phone number(s) from the victim and update it in the agency's information systems if necessary so the detective can follow up with the victim.
5. Obtain the names and ages of children present so the information can be forwarded to child protective services.
6. Forensics nurses may be available at the hospital to fully document the victim's injuries and account of what happened.
7. Ask if any of the assaults took place while the victim was calling 911 and include that information on the report so that detectives can pull the 911 call for court.
8. Leave a copy of any emergency protective order with the agency's domestic violence unit.

Box 11.11 Open-Air Drug Markets Play

CONDITION: Persistent open-air drug markets.

1. Geographically targeted problem-oriented policing interventions, involving partnerships between police and municipal departments, community groups, and/or place managers (businesses, residential managers), tend to be more effective at disrupting street-level drug markets than policing efforts that involve partnerships but are spread across a community. (Note: We also suggest coordinating efforts to the timing of drug markets.)

2. Increasing police presence or intervention (e.g., arrests) is more effective when targeted on micro hot spots rather than spread across neighborhoods. However, increasing presence or intervention at hot spots alone is less effective than: (i) forging productive partnerships with government and community partners; and (ii) making efforts to alter the underlying conditions that exist in places that may contribute to street-level drug market problems.

3. Some recent research indicates that patrol cars with license plate cameras on them seem to reduce drug calls in crime hot spots.

Note: Problem solving approaches in this review also included nuisance abatement and closing down problem locations as well as contacting appropriate municipal agencies regarding code violations. Also, see the Focused Deterrence Play, variations of which have also been used with some success to target actors in drug markets.

Officers might find many of these crime prevention plays and tips obvious. This may certainly be the case for officers who have been on the street for some time, and may have used these approaches, regardless of their knowledge of the research underpinning them. However, new officers may not know about such strategies and tactics. Depending on their interactions with others, the quality of their squads, or their training, they may or may not have been exposed to these ideas. The objective of the Playbook is to provide an expanded toolkit to officers as well as a visual reminder about the many options that police have. Similarly, the Playbook is meant to give officers ideas on how to use their non-committed time in ways that optimize their crime prevention impact. Officers may generally know about these tactics, but whether they use them strategically may vary from officer to officer. Finally, the Playbook provides a tangible reference to which they can link and record specific activities of which they engage on their daily reports or weekly performance reviews.

Box 11.12 Street Robberies Play

CONDITION: Persistent street robberies at specific locations.

1. Intermittent, unpredictable directed patrols at high-crime locations (see *Directed Koper Patrols Play*).
2. Understand why some places bring together potential victims with valuables and suspects who wish to rob them (e.g., convenience stores, check-cashing locations, drug markets, banks and ATMs).
3. Using CPTED unit or CPTED processes (see the *Refresher on CPTED*) as well as the *Case of Places Play*, identify opportunities connected to street robberies (ATMs, lack of lighting, alleys, unattended parking lots, intoxicated patrons, open-air drug dealing), addressing opportunities specifically (e.g., through CCTV, improved lighting, working with municipality to fence off cuts in between buildings, signage, etc.).
4. Consider pedestrian and traffic stops when dealing with armed street robberies. See the *Refresher on Stop-and-Frisk* and also the *Improving Exchanges with Citizens Play*.
5. For cell phone snatch-and-grabs, consider placing signage and providing pedestrians with information about cell phone robberies in an area to increase awareness and reduce victimization.
6. Carry out focused deterrence efforts on repeat and other known offenders (like probationers and parolees) and/or gang members (see *Focused Deterrence Play*).

Trust and Confidence Plays

Our draft Playbook also offers plays to improve trust and confidence with citizens. The research here is not as strongly developed as the crime prevention area (see our discussion in Chapter 6; see also discussions of this issue by Gill, Weisburd, Telep et al. 2014; Nagin and Telep, forthcoming). However, including such plays in law enforcement patrol playbooks is absolutely essential, as maintaining high levels of confidence and trust with citizens is an important bedrock of policing in modern democracies. Often, some of these philosophies and ideas are taught in general community policing classes in the academy. But clear directives and ideas for patrol officers can also be useful.

For example, take our *Improving Exchanges with Citizens Play* (Box 11.14). Here, we provide general guidance for high-quality exchanges with citizens, based on what we know so far from systematic reviews of research knowledge on community policing (see Gill et al. 2014) and procedural justice (Mazerolle, Bennett, Manning et al. 2013; Nagin and Telep, forthcoming). As with our football example above, some football playbooks have basic information that may seem so obvious (e.g., how to stand in ready position), but serve as important reminders to players who are inundated with so much information that they

---

Box 11.13 Traffic Problems and Accidents Play

CONDITION: Persistent traffic problems, accidents, speeding, or other motor vehicle violations.

1. Identify the specific nature and location of the problem and the possible causes of that problem. Use crime analysis information if available, information from traffic units, or past call history information at that area. Talk to pedestrians or residents in the area to obtain a better picture of the problem.
2. Work with the traffic unit and municipality to implement solutions, which may include traffic cameras, speed bumps, signage, speed cameras, and/or license plate recognition technology.
3. Increase patrol visibility at peak problem times, combined with citations and use of license plate readers connected to motor vehicle violations for that specific problem.
4. For traffic problems around specific situations, such as bar closing times, work with traffic enforcement to consider barriers, redirecting traffic or pedestrian movement.
5. Consider employing an approach called "DDACTS," or Data-Driven Approaches to Crime and Traffic Safety.
6. The traffic unit may have an analytic approach to determine the "top ten (or fifteen, twenty, etc.)" intersections/streets with traffic problems. Consider conducting traffic stops and visible patrol at those locations during peak hours of accidents and moving violations in between calls for service.

---

may forget or slack on a particular part of the basic ready position, causing them to be easily overrun or blocked. Similarly with policing, the *Improving Exchanges with Citizens Play* may seem obvious, but systematic social observations of officers on the street has shown a great deal of variation in these behaviors.

Some trust and confidence plays are much more specific, and might be carried out during an officer's non-committed time. For example, with the help of officers at the NYPD, we developed the *3-1-1 Play*, shown in Box 11.15. This play has yet to be tested for effectiveness in improving trust and confidence, but at least reflects the knowledge gained from the community policing literature more generally. Additionally, this play can be used during short periods of time in between calls for service.

Another trust and confidence play—*Seeking Partners for Prevention*—provides guidance to officers on how to establish partnerships with groups who can facilitate effective crime prevention activities (see Box 11.16). Again, within this play, we reference a number of free resources available at the Center for Evidence-Based Crime Policy.

Box. 11.14 Improving Exchanges with Citizens Play

Here we provide general guidance for high-quality exchanges with citizens, including those who report crime, suspects, victims, witnesses, bystanders, and others. Research shows that when officers act in these ways, they can not only increase citizen satisfaction with their services, but potentially increase a citizen's cooperation and compliance, even when outcomes may not be favorable to that individual (e.g., the person is being arrested or a case cannot be resolved).

1. Treat parties professionally, respectfully, fairly, and with restraint and empathy. This includes avoiding foul language, judgment, and ridicule.
2. Respect an individual's privacy.
3. Be neutral to all parties involved.
4. Explain to individuals the reason why you stopped them and the actions you will or have taken.
5. Explain to individuals your broader crime prevention goals and the reasons for your actions.
6. Ask victims and witnesses what they would like to see happen, or ask community members for input on how to address a problem.
7. Be empathetic by imagining yourself in the individual's shoes.
8. Thank people for their time, statements, and cooperation.

Box 11.15 The 311 Play

CONDITION: This play is designed to improve positive exchanges and customer service with citizens. This play—like the Directed Koper Patrol Play*—is especially amenable to shorter periods when an officer is not committed to answering a call for service but may not have enough time to carry out problem-solving interventions. SUPERVISORS: Be a resource to your officers by knowing how to access "open" 311 calls that have yet to receive a follow-up.*

1. Find out how to access 311 calls (see supervisory note above) and determine which calls have not received a response.
2. Follow up on specific calls for service in your area of responsibility, preferably by visiting individuals in person if the issue is not sensitive, or by calling the individual.
3. Even if a complaint cannot be remedied, a follow-up visit to ask for more information or to express empathy can foster trust, confidence, and citizen satisfaction with police service.
4. Use the information provided by 311 calls to assist with other problem-solving activities you are conducting.
5. If possible, develop tangible approaches to dealing with a particular problem, and when tasks are completed, report back to the complainant as to what was done.

Box 11.16 Seeking Partners for Prevention Play

Research indicates that police can improve their effectiveness and legitimacy by partnering with others to solve problems. Partners you may consider in your problem-solving efforts can include:

1. Place managers can help increase your ability to strengthen guardianship at a location: Place managers include apartment/high rise owners and property managers, supervisors, valets, door/front desk attendants, parking garage attendants, private security guards, school principals, church leaders, neighborhood block captains, and even non-person managers such as surveillance technologies. Ways to partner: Know who they are and where they are located; make contact and have regular meetings or follow-ups; ask them for input on how to deal with problems; keep them informed through an email or social media system.

2. Your local crime analyst: Many of the proactive strategies in this Playbook require information that can be generated by crime analysts. Learn what they do, how they can help, the types of information they collect, and their thoughts on how you might be more proactive. The CEBCP has free resources on using crime analysis for operations, command, and first-line supervision. Leaders should advocate for increasing personnel and resources for crime analysis units.

3. Social and community services: In the area you patrol, there may be social and community services that are available for high-risk families and youth that provide addiction services or re-entry and employment resources, or community groups who specialize in tackling retaliation after critical incidents. You can provide this information to citizens, but also consider partnering with these groups to help facilitate certain plays.

4. Municipal services that can help with physical disorder (clean-up and repair); agencies that enforce various health and safety codes; and civil attorneys for the jurisdiction that can assist with nuisance abatement.

5. Probation and parole: Understanding who the high-risk individuals are may require accessing updated information on repeat offenders through probation and parole offices. This may be useful for plays such as the *Burglary Prevention Play*, the *Focused Deterrence Play*, or the *Gun Crimes and Shootings Play.*

6. State's Attorneys: Partnering with the state's attorneys is needed for the *Focused Deterrence Play*, but might also be useful for gang-related interventions related to gun crimes.

7. Researchers: There are many researchers who are interested in partnering with local police agencies to develop strategies to prevent crime and improve citizen trust and confidence. A bank of nearby university-affiliated researchers who work on crime projects and evaluation can be found at the eConsortium, a free resource from the CEBCP that links university researchers with criminal justice practitioners.

Conclusion

Patrol deployment in evidence-based policing agencies would look funda-mentally different from deployment within the standard model of policing. In particular, patrol deployments in an evidence-based policing agency tend to emphasize the importance of what police officers are doing during their non-committed time, with the goal of preventing crime and calls for service rather than simply responding to them after the fact. Because of this, patrol officer activity and attitudes are a critical litmus test for whether evidence-based policing has been institutionalized into an organization. In agencies that use evidence-based policing, patrol officers are proactive; focus on specific places, times, and people that are at high risk for crime and offending; and use problem-solving strategies that are tailored to specific problems at hand. Officers in such agencies would have a broader toolkit of enforcement and/or non-enforcement prevention measures to use, and engage community partners when possible. Patrol officers within an evidence-based model also have access to feedback about crime *and* citizen reactions to their efforts (see Lum and Nagin 2017). The use of playbooks like the one described above can help to distill lessons from policing research into operational ideas so that evidence-based policing can be achieved.

It is important to note that the Playbook is not a standalone translation sys-tem. To be effective, officers have to be trained on its content and be held accountable for carrying out plays, as described in Chapter 10. Supervisors also have to reinforce this material, and performance metrics need to be developed around plays so that officers can record and get credit for their efforts. We explore these issues more in Chapter 14.

12

THE CASE OF PLACE
INVESTIGATIVE STRATEGY

In Chapter 11, we suggested the use of playbooks to institutionalize evidence-based practices into patrol. In this chapter, we provide another translation tool from the Matrix Demonstration Project focused on institutionalizing evidence-based practices into various types of investigative operations—the Case of Place approach.[1] As we discussed in Chapter 4, numerous studies show that crime is highly concentrated at a very small percentage of identifiable places (i.e., specific addresses, intersections, street blocks, and clusters of blocks) and that police interventions focused on these locations can prevent crime without displacing it elsewhere. Applying problem-oriented policing (POP) approaches to hot spots can be particularly effective for developing enforcement and prevention-oriented interventions that address the underlying causes of crime and disorder at these locations.

Although many police agencies report using hot spot policing, there is arguably much more that needs to be done to develop, translate, and institutionalize place-based approaches into law enforcement operations. Place-based prevention is still *not* a central focus of police operations (Weisburd 2008). In many agencies, problem-solving approaches at hot spots are likely to be ad hoc or limited to specialized units—and thus not a feature of regular patrol or investigative operations. Further, many officers and detectives may not see the value in these approaches (e.g., Koper, Lum, Willis et al. 2015c; Lum, Telep, Koper et al. 2012). While there likely have been many attempts to incorporate problem solving at places using specialized units, overtime assignments, and other incentives, the mainstays of the standard model of policing—reactive beat patrol, case-by-case investigations, and answering 911 calls—continue to dominate policing. A place-based approach will require police to place more

---

[1] Portions of this chapter are adapted from Koper, Egge, and Lum (2015a).

emphasis on regularly investigating, tracking, and managing problem places, consistent with Sherman's (2013) "Triple-T" strategy of targeting, tracking, and testing in police operations. In part, this will require police to collect more systematic data on crime trends, problems, actors, social and physical features, and interventions at hot spots (Weisburd 2008).

The advent of POP and its subsequent operationalization through the SARA process (scanning for problems, analysis of problems, development and implementation of responses, and follow-up assessment of results—see Eck and Spelman 1987) were significant developments toward this goal. Nonetheless, police have continued to treat problem solving as tangential to the core policing function. The reasons for this are many, but one may be that SARA, while providing a very logical framework for problem solving, needs to be better institutionalized into existing policing systems. By the same token, finding ways to centralize places as an essential focus of police efforts and resources, and expanding the knowledge base and toolkit of police officers to address high-crime places continue to be a major challenge to evidence-based policing. Here, we discuss how this might be done within a system of policing that often receives a great deal of attention, status, and resources—investigations.

Investigating Places, Not Just People

To institutionalize place-based practices using an existing system of policing, we developed the "Case of Place" investigative strategy (first introduced in Lum and Koper 2012). The Case of Place strategy involves applying a very familiar policing method—criminal investigation—to a different unit of investigation— a problem place. In other words, the Case of Place approach encourages officers, investigators, and their commanders to consider investigating not only individuals suspected of having committed crimes, but also places which may be connected to numerous crimes. The idea is that "arresting" a problem place with evidence-based, proactive, problem-oriented crime prevention strategies may have a much greater effect on crime than solving any one case or arresting an individual offender. From a translation perspective, the idea is to use a familiar policing system, but with just a different unit of investigation, to institutionalize place-based approaches.

The Case of Place strategy rests on three principles:

1. Law enforcement agencies should devote as many resources to investigating problem places as they do to investigating crime suspects, given the known crime control benefits of focusing on places.
2. Using existing cultural and organizational structures and status surrounding detective work may be a better approach to institutionalizing place-based policing than using an ad hoc, special projects approach.
3. Place-based policing is a crime prevention concept strongly supported by research. The Case of Place approach is designed to support place-based

policing by facilitating efforts to track the history of crime problems, actors, and police actions at hot spots.

Following the Case of Place strategy, police are encouraged to open investigative case files on problem places but with the standard elements of a detective's case folder translated into place-based equivalents. For example, a "suspect" in a Case of Place might be a person or group, a building, a business, or something in the location's physical environment that causes crime. Similarly, "victims" might be people, businesses, or properties, while "witnesses" or "informants" might be residents, business people, or even technologies (such as CCTV cameras) that can serve as guardians and witnesses of what happens at a location. The detective team, which could consist of detectives, officers, and crime analysts, would seek out clues and evidence about suspects, victims, and witnesses, building a case on the place for the "arrest" (i.e., the intervention or problem-solving strategy). Case building would entail quantitative and qualitative information gathering and analysis of all aspects of a location that might contribute to the crime problem there.[2] Just like investigative cases, the placed-based case file would also document the "arrest," which would be the intervention(s) implemented at the location. The case folder might also document follow-up assessment of results through a post-case review.

In summary, treating places as units of investigation conveys the message that the control of problem places should receive similar resources and priority as those afforded to individual crimes and people. The Case of Place method tries to institutionalize and incentivize crime prevention research into police practice by using existing systems and cultures related to investigations and investigative case work. As with investigations more generally, the Case of Place strategy also provides a means by which police can systematically create an institutional record (i.e., an investigative case file) documenting the dynamics of a crime hot spot and efforts to address problems at the location over time. This documentation can be tied into unit performance measures and achievement, including investigator promotions and rewards (see Chapter 14). Indeed, assigning detectives to investigate problem places, or even establishing a special detectives' unit for this purpose, could be one way of integrating them more formally into hot spot policing and expanding their role in proactive crime prevention efforts.

The Case of Place Tool

The Case of Place forms, guides, and checklist can be downloaded freely.[3] We also provide the template in its entirety at the end of this chapter for easy

---

[2] The "Case of Place" concept draws from theoretical perspectives on criminal opportunities and routine activities, as well as practice-based innovations in situational crime prevention, problem solving, intelligence-led policing, and crime prevention through environmental design.

[3] At: http://cebcp.org/evidence-based-policing/the-matrix/matrix-demonstration-project/case-of-places/.

reference as we discuss each section below. As the reader can see, there is nothing fancy about the Case of Place tool. In its raw form, the tool mirrors the elements of a common case folder that detectives use but with a slight twist on the unit of investigation. In fact, in creating the Case of Place tool, we worked with detectives and the detective commander of the Richmond (Virginia) Police Department to mimic one of their case folder formats, though we note that this could also be adapted to agencies that use electronic records management for their investigative case folders.

The Case of Place case folder is divided into five investigative sections: crime history of a place; place-based suspects; place-based victims and witnesses; identified guardians and potential for crime prevention; and documentation of the intervention. We now discuss each in turn.

Section A: Crime history of the place

The crime history of a place might be viewed as equivalent to the "crime incident" in a traditional investigation, although with important differences. It is a fuller description of what brings community and police attention to a particular location. We include the location's history because we want to recognize that no one single event caused this place to need intervention, but rather a stable series of events over the course of time. Further, attention to the location may or may not have been initiated by an analysis of places that revealed this hot spot. For example, community members might prompt officers to initiate a Case of Place on a street corner based on their understanding and concerns about that location. Or, a beat officer who constantly deals with problems in an area of a local park might initiate a Case of Place on that location. An investigation of a place might result from the scanning process in a problem-solving exercise or be initiated in managerial meetings such as Compstat. However the case came to the attention of the investigator, Section A1 (see the template below) asks detectives to document this process of discovery of the location for case development.

Section A2 documents the crime history of this location. In most investigations, investigators are asked to research the suspect's history, which is often the criminal (or victim) history of a single person, or perhaps a group of people. In that background check, the suspect's arrest record and incident/supplemental reports are often included. For the investigation of places, building the "rap sheet" of a place is essential, which includes the collection of information on past calls for service, past crime reports, prior arrests, and other information that can help establish the problem(s) at that location. Investigators can also determine whether this is a location that officers, residents, and police commanders view as a regular problem and how long the problem has persisted. For generating this and many other sections, crime analytic members of the detective's unit would play a central role. Sources of information may include the records management system, computer-aided dispatch, crime analysis, intelligence information, and other data sources. In keeping with the research about crime hot spots we discussed in Chapter 4, collected information might include long-term (between one and five years) trends of incidents, arrests, and calls for service; recent (past thirty days) trends of incidents, arrests, and calls for service; and other known problems at this place (e.g., gangs, unsupervised juveniles, probationers, and other disorders).

Section A3 asks detectives to document existing community information about the investigated place. This is important, as it provides a qualitative context to the problems at this place that cannot normally be discerned from crime analytic or quantitative data. Here, detectives might speak informally to community members about their understanding of a place or have their own understanding based on working at the location. Community groups might collect information about their communities on a regular basis, and even survey residents, providing a valuable historical perspective. Community members may also have insight into what types of law enforcement practices have worked or not worked in the area, providing a much-needed feedback mechanism. Beat officers or community liaisons working in an area may possess knowledge about the context and history of the location. As with Section A2 above, detectives are asked not only to fill out the section, but also, as with other detective work, to provide supplemental information to add to the case folder.

Section A4 continues by asking about known city records or complaints about this place. In traditional investigations, detectives may reach out to other agencies, like the postal service, electric companies, regional or federal agencies, or the school system to gather more information about an individual. Here, Section A4 is similar in that detectives of places are accessing additional information about the problems of the place from the city government. For example, there may be histories of liquor license violations for clubs and bars at the location or problems with how outside promoters are booking the location for parties (see e.g., Royan and Eck 2015). These are non-police, non-community sources that may provide valuable information, including code or ordinance violations, for example. Municipal or county sources may include a wealth of information about the social characteristics of a place.

This section of the case folder closes with Section A5, which provides initial surveillance details about the place. In the Jacksonville example we provide later in this chapter, problem-solving units were asked to initially surveil a place, rather than go in and make immediate arrests or initiate a crackdown. Again, this is similar to the "scanning" step of the POP model. However, members of the Case of Place team might document routines and activities that may not be gleaned from any of the information collected in Sections A1–A4. This could be a short narrative about, as Hawley (1950) describes, the "rhythm," "tempo," and "timing" of a location. Detectives might also describe the opportunity structure of a location, or the physical, environmental, and social characteristics of a location that contribute to potential crime opportunities. More of this information will be captured in later sections, but a preliminary scan of the area can be helpful.

Section B: Place-based suspects

Section B focuses on the situations, persons, or physical structures that might be attracting, generating, or facilitating crime opportunities at this place. In traditional investigations of persons, information is collected on a specific individual or individuals suspected of committing the crime under investigation. But in a Case of Place, multiple individuals might be the cause of this hot spot of crime. Moreover, suspects may not be persons at all. Rather, the place-based suspect could be a business or abandoned property that provides opportunities for criminal activity. The suspect may not even be crime related, as the Case of Place investigation could also be used for other types of events, such as traffic problems, for example. In this instance, a case might be opened on a high-accident intersection, and the "suspect" might be the lack of a crosswalk or a bunch of bushes that blocks the visibility of on-coming cars in the cross street.

Section B1 documents the suspicious people at this place that might be contributing to the problem at hand. These individuals could include active and known offenders such as probationers, parolees, or pretrial supervisees. They might also include individuals previously arrested or stopped at the location, gangs, co-offending groups, or other juvenile delinquents. Remember that a Case of Place revolves around problem solving, not simply using arrest as a solution. Thus, these individuals may not necessarily be involved in wrongdoing in a Case of Place, but may contribute to the physical or social disorder at the location. Examples might include vagrants, the homeless or mentally ill, individuals frequenting bars and being drunk in the area, or truants and unsupervised teens. These can be potential suspects or victims, as we will discuss in Section C.

Because this is a case on a *place*, suspects can also be addresses, buildings, and other locations. Section B2 focuses on documenting specific problem locations. These can include a bar or club that facilitates robberies, drunk driving, and fights late at night, or a bathroom in a park in which prostitution or predatory acts occur. Other types of problem locations at a place could include transit locations such as a bus stop, subway station entrance, or bus terminal. Or, suspect locations might be a particular alleyway, a vacant house, or the corner of an apartment complex not visible from the street. Each of these is an even more specific location than the identified hot spot of interest and helps detectives pinpoint the specific locations within the overall problem place that might be contributing to that place's problems. These types of locations are often referred to as crime attractors or crime generators; they are physical elements in the environment that attract or generate crime, or places that provide opportunities for crime to thrive. Similarly, Section B3 documents the environmental "suspects" of a place, which might consist of poor lighting, graffiti, trash, abandonment, overgrown lots, abandoned cars, and other social and physical disorders. Research in the field of environmental criminology has long documented aspects of social and physical disorder as well as environmental cues and conditions that signal crime opportunities.

Section C: Victims and place-based targets of crime

As in a traditional investigative case folder, victim information is also included in the Case of Place. In a traditional investigation, a victim can be an individual person, a piece of property or society more generally, with no specific victim (as with drug crimes, for example). Similarly, in a case of a place, the victim can be particular individuals or properties, identifiable groups or the community more generally. The victim assessment might also reflect some of the more intangible ways that crime affects the general community with respect to the quality of life of an area, an area's social cohesion and collective efficacy, or a community's fear of crime. The police or the city could also be part of this victimization, especially in the case of violent crime, if the police or city government agencies are losing their legitimacy or the community's faith that they can provide for citizen safety.

Again, each section in this part of the Case of Place case folder presses detectives to collect information as they would in a traditional case folder. Sections C1 and C2 ask for profiles of the people, groups, or properties that may have been victimized, perhaps repeatedly, at this location. Victimized individuals (and their cases) may provide helpful insights into what might be leading to their repeat victimization, and detectives—as they would in a regular investigation—interview these individuals. There may be a general typology of victims at this specific place—for example, school children, the elderly, homeless individuals, people coming to buy drugs, individuals who use this space to park their cars, or even properties with particular types of characteristics (if crimes of graffiti and burglary are occurring at this location). Section C3 prompts detectives to summarize the broader harm or impact of the problem on the community in that place or encompassing that location. For this item, the place-detective may assess fear levels from community members he or she has spoken to, or perhaps gauge the deterioration of the community's quality of life. There may be a story not captured in the above data—for example, information that an investor decided not to establish a business at a location because of the problems that the place poses.

Section D: Guardians and potential for deterrence

Although traditional investigations do not necessarily investigate guardians of a location or the potential for reducing recidivism of a suspected individual, this section of the Case of Place philosophy is key to building adequate interventions for the problem place. In the terminology of place-based policing, "guardians" refer to individuals, groups, or physical features that have the potential to deter, handle, or manage the problem(s) at a hot spot (Cohen and Felson 1979; Eck 1994; Felson 1995). Consideration of guardians also helps to identify people that could be involved in the intervention for the problem at the place.

Guardians can include non-police and informal guardians, which are identified in Section D1 of the case folder. In traditional case investigations, detectives often rely on informants, police contacts, and witnesses to help with the investigation. This action is a modified version of that approach for the Case of Place investigation. One way to identify non-police guardians is by identifying repeat callers (keeping information sensitive) about problems at the place. Another way to identify guardians is to determine who might be around during peak crime hours or days of the week. Guardians may also include people who can exercise informal control over problem people at the location. To facilitate the eventual intervention, detectives might focus on identifying who the guardians are (e.g., neighbors, community watch members, parents, clergy, business owners, property managers, etc.), when guardians are present (and their amount of presence), and when they are not present (and thus, when crime opportunities might increase due to lack of guardianship).

Section D2 documents formal police and government guardians and asks detectives to also seek out their counsel and advice on guardianship in the area. Examples may include the police, but can also include private security officers, city managers and council members responsible for that location, code enforcers, probation officers, principals and teachers, social workers, or housing managers. Finally, Section D3 asks detectives to identify non-person guardians such as CCTV cameras, fences, locks, signage, gates, and security systems. These items, or the lack thereof, may be important clues in developing effective interventions at these places.

Section E: The intervention

Finally, Section E of the Case of Place tool asks the detective team to document the intervention itself. Because problem places are more complex and involve more stakeholders than traditional investigations, interventions could be developed by a team of individuals with working knowledge of the information collected in the case folder. This includes the team of individuals investigating this case, but may also include key guardians discovered in Section D.

One important part of the case folder is Section E1, which asks the team to document previously significant police or community efforts in this place. Because of the reactive, case-by-case approach of the standard model of policing, police agencies often do not document past interventions in a systematic way. However, if such information is available, understanding what types of interventions have been used in this place may give the team insight into what has worked or not worked in the past. Evaluation information from past interventions should also be collected if available. Documenting both the intervention for the current Case of Place and past interventions also creates a record of ideas for the police agency to use in future Case of Place investigations that address similar problems.

Section E2 reflects a component of evidence-based policing often not used in police interventions—requiring detectives to seek out research evidence that may point to effective interventions for similar types of places and problems. In the Case of Place tool, we provide a simple checklist for detectives to prompt them about these resources, as shown in Section E2 below. As of this writing, several such guides are readily available. In the future, more such guides may also be available (e.g., the *Global Policing Database* in Australia is being developed at the time of writing of this book).[4]

Section E3 then asks detectives to describe the plan for the intervention itself, using data collected in the case folder. This template is shown in the appendix to this chapter. Just as investigators often plan out the arrest of a serious violent offender (especially if the arrest involves obtaining a warrant, a raid, or a dangerous situation), a proper plan of action for a place can also ensure smoother implementation. A well-written plan can also help future Case of Place investigators to replicate effective interventions. Detectives should identify what might be considered a successful "arrest" of the problem of the place. They should also document what types of outcomes are sought from the intervention. Note that the template in the appendix does not only emphasize police actions as part of the intervention, but also the use of guardians and actions related to the physical environment.

Finally, in Section E4, just as it would document an arrest or a search and seizure through a report, the detective team would also do the same here. But in this case, the detectives describe how the intervention went, its implementation challenges, and also the results of the intervention based on post-intervention follow-up, debriefing, surveys, after action reports, and the like. Detectives might also document follow-up and maintenance of this Case of Place, and may choose to leave this case open if the problem persists.

Case of Places in practice

As we said before, this Case of Place template is just that—a template for agencies to use. We provide it in a very simple document format so that agencies can modify the template to their own needs, requirements and systems. But the Case of Place template is evidence based. It follows the evidence on place-based and environmental criminology, reflects what we know about effective policing, and also attempts to incorporate research knowledge into the development and implementation of interventions. It is translational in that it tries to use an existing system—detective case folders—to implement and institutionalize these ideas. The Case of Place strategy also attempts to improve the receptivity of police to focusing on places by using an existing system that is

---

[4] See http://www.gpd.uq.edu.au/.

well understood and used by police officers, detectives and their command. Investigation is a normal, everyday activity in policing, which is couched in existing rules, resources, procedures, and status.

Elsewhere, we have written with crime analyst Renee Tate and Officer Thomas Neale about a pilot effort in which the Richmond Police Department used the Case of Place strategy to conduct an in-depth assessment of one particular hot spot in Richmond's downtown (Tate, Neal, Lum et al. 2013).[5] To stimulate further thinking about how police might apply the Case of Place concept, we now describe more extensive efforts to investigate places by police in Minneapolis (Minnesota) and Jacksonville (Florida). In Minneapolis, the Minneapolis Police Department used the Case of Place idea as a basis for profiling the city's most chronic shooting hot spots. The Jacksonville (Florida) Sheriff's Office went further with the idea of place-based investigations by implementing an investigative problem-solving unit to address hot spots of violent crime. Jacksonville had its own system of investigating places, and is an example of how the Case of Place philosophy can be used within other templates.

Investigating Gun Crime Hot Spots in Minneapolis

One example of the Case of Place approach was implemented by Sgt. Jeffery Egge, supervisor of the Minneapolis Police Department (MPD) crime analysis unit. In collaboration with the authors, he opened a Case of Place on hot spots of gun crime in Minneapolis (Koper et al. 2015a). MPD has been looking for innovative ways to target its hot spot policing efforts and to develop more holistic responses to these locations that combine enforcement and prevention measures in collaboration with other government and community partners. To this end, MPD's crime analysis unit has taken the initiative to better understand the city's hot spots as a preliminary step toward developing a Case of Place approach.

MPD opened its initial Case of Place investigation on hot spots of gun violence, which has been a priority issue for the agency in recent years (the city has been experiencing roughly between 1,300 and 1,450 murders, assaults and robberies committed with guns annually). The investigation focused on shootings, which MPD analysts define as including fatal and non-fatal criminal gunshot victimizations, assaults in which assailants fired at victims, and other serious gun discharge incidents. The objectives of this initial investigation

---

[5] A presentation on the Richmond project by Captain Emmett Williams (RPD's detective supervisor) and Officer Thomas Neale is available from the video library of the Center for Evidence-Based Crime Policy (CEBCP). See the 2012 CEBCP Policing Workshop session on "Case of Place" held at George Mason University in August 2012: https://www.youtube.com/watch?v=24De6vvZFrU&list=PL4E509820FD3010E9&index=3. Also see Tate, Neal, and Lum et al. (2013).

were to identify long-term shooting hot spots and to begin building profiles of the physical and social features of these locations that may help to explain the nature of their crime problems and lay the foundations for Case of Place investigations.

Identifying the suspects of investigation

For many agencies, adopting a Case of Place approach will require adjustments to their methods of crime analysis, and this was true for MPD as well. To start with, the identification of chronic problem locations requires attention to long-term patterns at hot spots (just as one might focus on a "repeat" or "serious" offender). Although MPD analysts often examine crime patterns over one-to-five-year periods (which is a longer time frame than that used by most agencies for hot spot identification—see Koper 2014), they used a more extensive historical analysis to search for chronic shooting hot spots, analyzing data from the twenty-five-year period of 1990 through 2014 (during which time there were 16,144 shooting incidents in the city).

The Case of Place approach is also meant to focus attention on micro hot spots, where crime is most concentrated and where specific criminogenic conditions can be most readily identified and addressed through problem solving. This may require police to shift their analyses and operational emphasis to smaller geographic units than that to which they are accustomed (e.g., see Koper 2014). As also described in Chapter 4, for some years, MPD's primary method of identifying hot spots has been to identify clusters of high-risk blocks using kernel density analysis. MPD crime analysts draw boundaries around these clusters, creating "focus zones" that commanders use to guide operations. Although the size of these places varies, a typical zone might be roughly 0.25 square miles. However, to more specifically identify "suspects" for a Case of Place strategy, they further narrowed their geographic analyses to the street block level, which allowed for a more precise identification of the convergence of offenders, targets, and opportunities that lead to crime (see Chapter 4 for further discussion of the importance of street blocks in analyses of hot spots). Indeed, MPD's analysis of the distribution of shootings at street segments revealed that the city's shootings had been highly concentrated by street segment over time. Just 8% of the city's street blocks accounted for about two-thirds of the city's shootings during the twenty-five-year analysis period, and the top 3% accounted for more than one-third. This type of analysis can thus facilitate the development of more targeted problem-solving efforts even within MPD's original hot spot zones.

Based on this analysis, the primary "suspects" selected for this preliminary investigation included the city's top thirty-one blocks for shootings. These blocks had an average of thirty-one shootings (and a median of thirty) from 1990 through 2014, and in total produced 973 shootings. About half of them had also continued to produce one or more shootings annually during the last three to five years. Considering these numbers, it would seem that targeting these locations for investigation and intervention offers a potentially much greater return on investment than the resources that a police agency would typically apply to the investigation of any one shooting or shooting suspect—indeed, consider the likelihood of identifying thirty-one people responsible for 973 shootings!

Building cases on problem places

In a traditional incident or offender-focused investigation, an investigator's early steps involve collecting information on a criminal incident and examining the criminal histories of potential suspects. In a similar manner, a Case of Place investigation involves gathering further information on the criminal histories of hot spots in order to understand their full range of crime problems. This can involve analyzing a variety of data sources from within a police agency (e.g., calls for service, incident reports, arrests, intelligence, and observations of officers working the area) as well as information from community sources (e.g., views of community members or data from other government agencies). As a first step in building such histories on the selected shooting hot spots, MPD conducted an assessment of other recent crime and disorder problems at these places as measured by calls for service and gang contacts recorded by MPD officers.

Approximately three-quarters of the top shooting blocks were located within larger MPD focus zones for violent crime, making them high-risk places for violence in general. But more specifically, MPD found that domestic disturbances were among the top call categories at many of the blocks, with domestic abuse in particular being a common source of domestic calls across these locations. Police contacts with gang members were also quite common across the locations. In contrast, drug problems did not appear to be a primary cause of violence and shooting at most of these places.

These patterns point toward potentially important actors—both suspects and victims—that police might investigate further at these places. For example, interventions targeting gang members may be needed in many of the hot spots. Officers might also explore possible connections between domestic violence and shootings. For example, how many shootings at the hot spots occur in the course of domestic violence or stem directly from prior domestic incidents? Are persons involved in domestic violence as offenders or victims likely to be involved in non-domestic shootings at these places? Might strengthening police responses and partnerships to address domestic violence prove to be an important aspect of prevention efforts at these hot spots?

In the context of a Case of Place investigation, suspects, victims, and potential guardians may be specific individuals or groups tied to the location, or even more general categories of people (e.g., people robbed near check-cashing businesses on paydays). At the same time, they may also include particular addresses, establishments, or features of a hot spot that affect its risk for crime. Drawing on public and other government data that were readily available, MPD therefore looked for the presence of several types of establishments, facilities, and features that might contribute to or facilitate crime in the shooting hot spots. These characteristics included the type of street at the location as well as the presence of the following on or nearby the street segment: commercial businesses, particularly grocery or convenience stores and places that sell or serve alcohol; multi-family dwellings, particularly apartment complexes; group facilities (i.e., halfway houses); schools of different sorts; problem properties; and vacant land parcels. These characteristics and features may serve as possible "suspects" or "victims" in the Case of Place vernacular or lead to the identification of potential "guardians" (e.g., place managers) who can assist police. As with the analyses of the locations' criminal histories, this was not intended to be a comprehensive list of potentially important characteristics but, rather, a first pass assessment to begin longer-term efforts to investigate these places.

As expected, the shooting hot spots commonly had environmental characteristics or establishments that might serve as crime attractors or facilitators. About half of the segments were on or very near major roadways, and nearly three-quarters had at least one bus stop. This makes them more accessible, potentially increasing the convergence of potential offenders and victims. Other common establishments that may serve as activity magnets for offenders and targets include grocery or convenience stores, which were present on more than three-quarters of the blocks, as well as apartment buildings and schools, which were each present on roughly one-third of the blocks. Most of the blocks also had other features that might contribute to crime problems. More than three-quarters had vacant lots, and more than half had problem properties (i.e., locations identified by city authorities for nuisance problems) located within one block. Finally, a smaller number had group residences (i.e., halfway houses) (6%) or establishments serving alcohol (13%) on the block or very nearby. On average, the highlighted blocks had four of the aforementioned risk factors, and all had at least one.

Additional site-specific investigation would be necessary to understand the opportunity structures that contribute to violence at these places. However, this examination of features and establishments provides obvious starting points for problem-solving assessments. For instance, we can reasonably speculate that convenience stores, bus stops, and vacant lots, which were all very common at these locations, are important in drawing potential victims to the hot spots (especially stores and bus stops). They may also serve as locations for loitering by high-risk people. Developing interventions to prevent crime at these types of problem places (e.g., installing video cameras at locations that draw victims and troublesome groups) might thus be important initial steps in reducing their risk of shootings.

Finally, MPD extended its preliminary investigation to the environment surrounding these street segments. The occurrence of crime at hot spots can often be linked to social features and happenings of nearby places, and crime problems may extend across multiple street segments (Weisburd, Groff, and Yang 2012). Studies of offenders' travel patterns also suggest that many crimes committed at high-risk blocks are likely to have been committed by offenders who currently live or previously lived nearby, if not on the blocks (e.g., Bernasco 2010; Eck and Weisburd 1995; Gabor and Gottheil 1984). Understanding these patterns may prove valuable in understanding the dynamics of a hot spot and developing interventions to reduce crime at the location.

As noted, many of the top shooting blocks were located within larger hot spot clusters for violent crime. As an example, Figure 12.1 illustrates several dozen high-risk blocks within one of MPD's larger focus zones. In total, the street blocks in this area experienced 658 shootings from 1990 through 2014. Three of these segments (highlighted in bold) were among the top thirty-one shooting blocks discussed above and together accounted for 121 shootings. The leading block had sixty-six shootings and was the top street segment for shootings in the entire city. This block, which is the site of large public housing complex, generates high levels of domestic disturbance calls and has a heavy gang presence that includes several rival gangs. The next two most dangerous segments in this cluster, which experienced between twenty-five and thirty shootings each during the study period, are located just a few blocks from the aforementioned housing complex and appear to be key activity nodes for people in the vicinity. One is a major avenue with a grocery/convenience store, bus stops, and rental apartments; the other has rental apartments, multiple schools, and close proximity to two parks. Both segments also have an active gang presence as well as other risk factors discussed above. These three blocks would appear to be the most important segments, or certainly among them, for understanding and addressing violence problems in the larger zone. A more in-depth Case of Place analysis might thus investigate possible interconnections between actors (i.e., offenders, targets, and guardians), routine activities and crime problems across these top segments and others in the zone (note that there are several other blocks in this vicinity that also experienced more than ten shootings during the study period). Hence, the identification and cross-referencing of known offenders, victims, and associates in both the hot spot and wider zone might be one valuable avenue of investigation.

In summary, MPD's effort illustrates the first steps in opening Case of Place investigations to address hot spots of gun violence in Minneapolis. This preliminary analysis identified candidate locations for investigation, examined potential "suspects" or "victims" associated with these places, and considered the

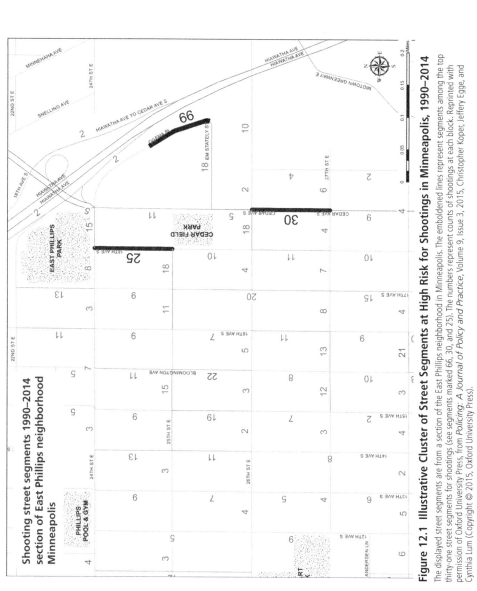

Figure 12.1 Illustrative Cluster of Street Segments at High Risk for Shootings in Minneapolis, 1990–2014

The displayed street segments are from a section of the East Phillips neighborhood in Minneapolis. The emboldened lines represent segments among the top thirty-one street segments for shootings (see segments marked 66, 30, and 25). The numbers represent counts of shootings at each block. Reprinted with permission of Oxford University Press, from *Policing: A Journal of Policy and Practice*, Volume 9, Issue 3, 2015, Christopher Koper, Jeffery Egge, and Cynthia Lum (Copyright © 2015, Oxford University Press).

types of "evidence" that might be gathered to facilitate "arrests" of these places through problem-solving efforts. Much more in-depth investigation, based on analysis of police and non-police records as well as on-site observations and interviews, would be necessary to more fully understand the social context and crime problems at the profiled hot spots and to develop enforcement and pre-vention strategies tailored to each of these places. Nonetheless, MPD has taken a significant step—and one that is likely rare among police—in identifying chronic micro-place hot spots and compiling systematic data on their characteristics.

A Place-Based Investigative Strategy in Jacksonville

The illustration of the Case of Place idea in Minneapolis focused on data collec-tion and the initial investigation of problem locations. Such efforts begin the process of creating institutional records on hot spots and can lay the ground-work for a later reorientation of investigative operations to target hot spots. As an additional example, we highlight the experience of the Jacksonville, Florida Sheriff's Office (JSO), which adopted a more advanced placed-based policing strategy by establishing a special unit to investigate hot spots of violent crime.

The JSO initiative grew out of a hot spots policing experiment that the agency conducted in 2009 with a team of researchers that included the sec-ond author. This experiment, which was discussed in Chapter 4, tested the effects of problem-solving and directed patrol strategies at hot spots of violent crime in Jacksonville (Taylor, Koper, and Woods 2011a). Effects were strongest in the problem-solving locations, where serious violence decreased by 33%. The problem-solving activities were conducted by teams of supervisors, offi-cers, and crime analysts who were trained in POP and assigned to cover the initial twenty-two problem-solving hot spots on a full-time basis. The teams attempted to identify and address the underlying factors driving crime in these locations, working closely with community partners when possible. Their anal-yses of problems and implemented responses were recorded in presentations for command staff. Officers implemented a wide array of measures, including situational crime prevention, code enforcement and nuisance abatement, part-nerships with business owners and rental property managers, community orga-nizing, improvement of social services, aesthetic improvements, and targeted investigation or enforcement. In addition to the positive outcome evaluation results, many officers who took part in the POP effort, including some who were initially skeptical or reluctant about the approach, also expressed positive views about the project in after-action debriefings.

Based on these results, JSO leadership was committed to building on the study and institutionalizing this approach to hot spots. Therefore, the agency created the Operation Safe Streets (OSS) unit in June 2009 to continue the problem-solving work that began during the experiment. The OSS consisted of twenty officers, selected largely from the experimental problem-solving group, who were dedicated to full-time problem solving focused on violent crime hot spots. Below, we describe the investigative process used by the OSS team and some of the challenges the agency faced in implementing this approach as described by JSO staff in presentations, articles, and interviews with the authors.[6]

The place-based investigative process

Hot spot "suspects" targeted for investigation were initially chosen by JSO's crime analysis unit (CAU) based on their histories and levels of street violence. Selected locations were typically around six to ten blocks in size, and multiple officers (at least two and often between three and five) were assigned to each location. Over time, officers investigating the locations would identify more specific micro places that were causing problems within these small areas. During the initial experiment, investigations and responses were conducted within a ninety-day period, but this time limit was later removed to facilitate more thorough investigations and problem-solving assessments.

The investigations would begin with an observation phase during which OSS officers conducted both covert and overt surveillance of the locations to observe places, people, and routines. Based on early experience with the initiative, JSO's command staff and CAU decided not to provide officers with detailed crime analysis about the locations at the outset of the investigations. As described by Jamie Roush, JSO's former crime analysis manager and a key architect of the OSS initiative, withholding detailed CAU data in the early stage of each investigation encouraged the officers to follow their investigative instincts and to more intensively engage individuals with knowledge of the area (e.g., beat officers, business owners, citizens, city officials, and even offenders) to develop an unbiased understanding of the location's characteristics and problems and to also see if their observations aligned with crime analytic data. During this phase, OSS officers observed the locations at different times of day and on different days of the week (taking notes, pictures, and videos) and developed contacts and information sources. Through their investigations, the OSS officers sought to understand key players, activities, and routines in the area; key activity spots; environmental factors that contributed to crime; and other social features of the hot spot (as identified through sources such as Census data or city data on problem properties).

After the initial observation phase, the OSS officers engaged in further analysis of the locations based on examination of CAU data (e.g., maps, trends, and patterns), incident reports, case narratives, and calls for service. Officers also consulted various other sources to gather additional information on suspects, victims, businesses, and other people in the location. These sources included

---

[6] More on JSO's activities can be seen from a video presentation by the JSO officers at a 2012 Policing Workshop of the Matrix Demonstration Project held at George Mason University in August 2012. The video is entitled "Jacksonville Operation Safe Streets" and can be accessed at:https://www.youtube.com/watch?v=24De6vvZFrU&list=PL4E509820FD3010E9&index=3. More information can also be found in Roush and Koper (2012).

JSO and other criminal justice databases (e.g., gang databases, regional polic-ing databases, and corrections data on probationers and parolees), other gov-ernment databases (e.g., driving records, business licensing, and other city websites), and public sources (e.g., Facebook). The OSS officers sometimes con-ducted community surveys and interviewed both community members and offenders (including incarcerated offenders) in order to better understand sus-pects, victims, and potential guardians associated with the hot spots.

The CAU also played a critical role in OSS, assisting the officers in several ways. In addition to providing training on problem-solving approaches like SARA and crime analysis for the hot spots, they developed tools (similar to our Case of Place guide above) to help officers in their assessments of the hot spots. These tools included a problem-solving checklist outlining different types of data to gather (and sources to consult) on locations, suspects, victims, social ser-vices/facilities, and temporal patterns of the hot spots; an observation checklist guide; and a problem-solving template that OSS officers used to identify very specific problems in each hot spot (e.g., poor lighting and visibility in a particu-lar alley or nuisance problems at a particular address) and the types of informa-tion that had been gathered on these problems. The CAU also worked with OSS officers on the development of responses to identified problems. OSS officers were encouraged to consider and implement a wide variety of prevention and enforcement responses tailored to each hot spot and to involve outside agencies (e.g., zoning, code enforcement, public works, and transit authorities) and com-munity members to the extent possible. CAU also provided ongoing feedback on how the implemented responses were affecting crime in the hot spots.

Challenges to implementing place-based investigations

Implementing this place-based investigative program posed a number of chal-lenges for JSO. One of these involved garnering support and resources for the project, especially as it had been implemented at a time when the agency was experiencing resource cutbacks and layoffs. As described by Jamie Roush, "JSO command staff and OSS managers had to vigorously market the success of the previous project [the initial 90-day pilot project] and the concept of problem-solving—in staff meetings, agency roll calls, informal training sessions, and an agency-wide computerized training session" (Roush and Koper 2012, 10). OSS unit officers also tried to serve as "ambassadors for problem-solving to their peers" by connecting with other officers working in the hot spot areas, incorpo-rating their knowledge into the process, and informally educating them on the process and its benefits. All of this helped other commanders and officers in the agency to understand how OSS complemented and enhanced their own efforts. Leadership support in the agency was also critical, as the project was cham-pioned by JSO's sheriff and by its director of patrol and enforcement, under whom it operated.

Picking the right officers for the initiative was another central consideration. JSO did not put detectives into the OSS unit, but it picked patrol officers that could be developed into good investigators. The program needed officers who were willing to be patient, open-minded, and not simply focused on making quick arrests. OSS commanders also tried to pick officers who had good analytic abilities as well as the social skills to communicate and work with a variety of other officers and community members, including known offenders. Changing the mindset of many officers from that of react and arrest to that of analytic problem solving and prevention was a key focus. Of course, the initiative also required supervisors who understood and supported the strategy and could give officers the coaching and reinforcement they needed to carry out this new approach.

Finally, continual assessment of training needs and strategy refinement was essential to the project's success, especially since JSO had little experience with POP prior to the project. As documented by Roush and Koper (2012, 11):

> ... OSS managers continually try to identify and provide training on specialized skills that officers need for problem-solving. For example, some officers were conducting surveys and interviewing ex-offenders to obtain information about their hot spots. However, many of the officers had little preparation for such efforts. Therefore, OSS managers arranged for officers to receive training on how to develop, analyze, and use surveys to understand crime problems. Officers were also trained on how to interview ex-offenders, not for prosecution but to obtain information about hot spots where they live or have committed crimes.

OSS commanders and the CAU provided formal and informal training of various sorts to OSS officers on an ongoing basis. Further, OSS supervisors and the CAU sought to refine the process over time as the unit gained more experience with the initiative. Lifting the ninety-day limit on each investigation and instituting an observation phase to each case (as discussed above) represented some of JSO's efforts to enhance the process. OSS officers also met regularly to discuss their progress. This allowed officers working in different locations to discuss problem-solving efforts in an open and dynamic forum where they could learn from one another. Maintaining case files on their efforts also provided institutional records to facilitate ongoing assessment and strategy development.

In short, the JSO OSS initiative represented an advanced form of place-based policing that made hot spots a central focus of investigative and problem-solving efforts. OSS continued the program for several years after its initial pilot phase, but it was eventually discontinued in response to changes in leadership, resource availability, and strategic direction. This again underscores the challenges of institutionalizing evidence-based practices in policing. Nonetheless, initiatives like OSS provide valuable lessons that others can build on in promoting innovative and effective approaches to policing.

Conclusion

In order promote further development and institutionalization of place-based strategies in everyday police operations, we have advocated in this chapter for a "Case of Place" strategy that broadens the focus of investigative work to include places as well as people. In a manner akin to developing investigative case files on people or incidents, the Case of Place approach entails systematic investigation and tracking of hot spots to develop problem-solving interventions tailored to specific places.

More generally, this idea highlights the potential for institutionalizing innovation in a high-status policing activity—investigations. This will require the commitment of detectives, patrol officers, and crime analysts to collaboratively investigate hot spots, develop tailored interventions for them, and follow through on assessment of results and continued monitoring. Allocating as many resources to place-based investigations as police do to individual investigations of people seems justified given what research shows about the benefits of focusing on crime hot spots. This strategy may also raise the status of crime analysis, which is an essential component of crime prevention and proactive policing. By providing analytic support to a Case of Place strategy (i.e., identifying hot spots for investigation, assessing their common features and problems, and helping to track and evaluate interventions), crime analysts can help to facilitate the development, testing, and dissemination of common strategies that officers can use to address different types of hot spots.

Implementing and sustaining place-based investigations will likely be challenging in many agencies, as it requires a substantial shift in organizational thinking and resources. The early Case of Place efforts documented in Minneapolis, as well as those we have documented elsewhere in Richmond (Tate et al. 2013), have not yet been institutionalized into those agencies' field operations. The initiative in Jacksonville, though extensive and successful, did not involve detectives and was eventually scaled back. Nonetheless, the experiences and knowledge gained through these efforts can lay the groundwork for future progress; anecdotally, we are aware of yet other agencies that are teaming with researchers to experiment with place-based investigative efforts inspired by the ones described here. Moving forward, the adoption of a Case of Place approach may be one notable way to help police to institutionalize a stronger and more precise emphasis on problem places in daily operations, promote the development of more tailored and effective strategies to address these locations, and facilitate more optimal uses of investigative and prevention resources.

The Case of Places Template
Case of Place Cover Report

1. Case number	
2. Specific geographic location (please include printed map)	
3. Describe location (i.e., school, residential, business, mixed, etc.: be specific)	
4. Date case is opened	
5. Date case is closed	
6. Detective(s) assigned	
7. Supervisor assigned	
8. Problem(s) at this place	

Section A: Crime History of the Place

SECTION A1: How did this place come to the attention of the police? *Be specific, noting whether the source was the community, the police, management meetings, or another source.*

SECTION A2: Criminal history trends for this place. *Crime analysis units may be useful in providing this information. Please attach documents as supplements to this form.*

1. Reported crime incidents at this place one to five years[7]	Describe briefly here and attach crime analysis information as supplements.
2. Arrest history for one to five years (amount and type)	Describe briefly here and attach crime analysis information as supplements.

---

[7] "One to five years" is only a suggestion. The goal is for agencies to consider examining the historic trends of crime at this place.

3. Calls for service for one to five years (amount and type)	Describe briefly here and attach crime analysis information as supplements.
4. Immediate crime incident history of this place (past thirty days)	Describe briefly here and attach crime analysis information as supplements.
5. Immediate arrest history of this place (past thirty days)	Describe briefly here and attach crime analysis information as supplements.
6. Immediate calls for service history of this place (past thirty days)	Describe briefly here and attach crime analysis information as supplements.
7. Other crime history of this place (gangs, juveniles, probationers, etc.)	Describe briefly here and attach crime analysis information as supplements.

SECTION A3: Existing community information about this place. *Please attach any documents as supplements to this form. Proactive information gathering from officers, community members and other sources is conducted in sections B–D. This is just existing historical information about this place.*

From officers	
From community members	
From other sources (census, city data, etc.)	

SECTION A4: Known city records or complaints about this place. *Please attach any documents as supplements to this form.*

SECTION A5: Initial surveillance about this place.

1. Date of preliminary surveillance	
2. Surveillance conducted by	
3. Is surveillance consistent with historical trends described above?	
4. Write a general narrative describing the nature of this location given the surveillance and analysis collected.	

Section B: Place-Based Suspects

SECTION B1: Suspicious people at this place

1. Active/known offenders or arrestees	List names and attach supplemental information about individuals, arrest records and types of crimes, whereabouts.
2. Probationers/parolees	List names and attach supplemental information about individuals, arrest records and types of crimes, whereabouts.
3. Field interviews (past and present)	List here and attach forms as supplements.
4. Gangs and groups	List here and attach forms as supplements.
5. Vagrants, homeless, mentally ill, drunk in public	List here and attach forms as supplements.
6. Truants, juvenile delinquents	List here and attach forms as supplements.

SECTION B2: Specific problem locations at this place

1. Problem residential or business addresses	List here, and provide information as supplements.
2. Other problem locations (such as a bus stop, park, corner, alley, or lot)	List here, and provide information as supplements.

SECTION B3: Environmental "suspects"—problem conditions at this place. *List environmental suspects such as poor lighting, graffiti, trash, abandonment, overgrown lots, abandoned cars, other social and physical disorders, and vulnerable spots. Attach information and photographs as supplements.*

Section C: Victims and Place-Based Targets of Crime

SECTION C1: Victims (people)

1. General profile of types of people who are victimized	
2. Repeat victims	List names and locations and attach supplemental information.

223

SECTION C2: Victims (property)

1. General profile of types of property being victimized	
2. Properties repeatedly victimized	List locations and attach supplemental information

SECTION C3. Summarize the broader harm or impact of the problem on the community. *Describe additional ways crime has impacted this community. Be specific: Fear? Quality of life? Abandonment? Lack of investment or involvement? More crime?*

Section D: Guardians and Potential for Prevention and Deterrences

SECTION D1: Non-police, informal guardians. *Identify and describe the nature of these guardians and the types and levels of guardianship they provide. Examples include business and civic leaders, apartment and business managers, citizens, neighborhood watch groups, etc.*

SECTION D2: Formal police/government guardians. *Identify and describe the nature of these guardians and the types and levels of guardianship they provide. Examples include the police, probation officers, school teachers, social services, private security, and/ or code enforcers.*

SECTION D3: Technology and physical features to prevent crime. *List other technology and physical features, including CCTV, fences, locks, signage, gates, etc. used to prevent crime.*

Section E: The Intervention

SECTION E1. Past significant police and community efforts/interventions at this place. *Identify past interventions at the place and their impacts if known.*

| 1. Police operations | Describe operation and impacts, as well as who led operation. |
| 2. Community efforts | Describe operation and impacts, as well as who led operation. |

SECTION E2: Review/find information or research about what may work for this problem

Checked?	SOURCE
Y/N	Evidence-Based Policing Matrix: http://www.policingmatrix.org
Y/N	POP CENTER guides: http://www.popcenter.org/guides/
Y/N	COPS OFFICE: http://www.cops.usdoj.gov
Y/N	Campbell Collaboration Crime and Justice Coordinating Group:https://www. campbellcollaboration.org/library.html?filter=crimeandjustice
Y/N	Office of Justice Programs CRIMESOLUTIONS.GOV: http://crimesolutions.gov
Y/N	Subject matter experts on the eConsortium of University Centers and Researchers by area of expertise: http://gmuconsortium.org/
Y/N	Smart Policing Initiative: http://www.smartpolicinginitiative.com/

Which sources apply and what information is useful?

225

SECTION E3: Describe the plan for the intervention(s). *Utilizing information collected on problems and victims, as well as potentially effective interventions, describe in detail the plan for intervention here.*

1. Police actions	List the step-by-step plan of action the police will take based on the information collected in Sections A–E.
2. Non-police guardians	Role for non-police guardians (as described in Section D) if applicable. Describe here.
3. Community members	Role for community members (as described in Section D) if applicable. Describe here.
4. Other formal guardians	Role for other formal guardians (as described in Section D) if applicable. Describe here.
5. Other actions related to physical environment	Describe in detail.

SECTION E4. Document intervention and results post-intervention, and plans for follow-up and maintenance. *Describe the actual intervention, its implementation and results based on post-intervention follow-up and de-briefing. Attach crime analysis before–after information if available, or after-action reports. Document plans for follow-up and maintenance.*

13

THE ROLE OF CRIME ANALYSIS IN EVIDENCE-BASED POLICING

In addition to training and the tools we have discussed thus far, agencies also need resources to accomplish evidence-based policing. These resources include personnel who can generate, translate, and disseminate knowledge, and technologies that manage and record information so that agencies can better track crime, community trust and reactions, and the activities that the agency takes to affect these outcomes. Over the years, one important technological resource that has proved vital in building capacity for evidence-based policing is crime analysis (and the crime analyst). As discussed in Chapter 1, a major pillar of evidence-based policing involves using research and analysis to guide both internal and external operations, and crime analysts are central to providing this information. Crime analysts can also support the development, application, and evaluation of evidence-based strategies and can translate research knowledge into practical applications. In this chapter, we discuss the development of crime analysis in policing and the extent to which this has moved police agencies in the direction of evidence-based practice. After considering the benefits and limitations of current crime analysis practices, we also provide suggestions and illustrations of ways that crime analysis can be expanded and used more strategically to facilitate evidence-based policing.

Crime Analysis and Policing

Many agencies today have some crime analytic capacity, the development of which has been a significant advancement in modern policing. As described by Taylor and Boba (Santos) (2011, 6), "crime analysis involves the use of large amounts of data and modern technology—along with a set of systematic methods and techniques that identify patterns and relationships between crime data and other relevant information sources—to assist police in criminal apprehension, crime and disorder reduction, crime prevention, and evaluation." In their national survey of U.S. police agencies, Taylor and Boba (2011) found that 57% of police agencies have staff whose primary responsibility is conducting crime analysis, and 89% of agencies have personnel whose primary or secondary responsibility is conducting crime analysis.

Early efforts by crime analysts focused on the tabulation of Uniform Crime Reports (UCR) statistics, hand mapping of crime events, or the creation of crime prevention bulletins. Today, analysts are engaged in a variety of activities, which have been facilitated by the improvement of police data systems and the development of computer software for specialized applications such as geographical and intelligence analyses. Indeed, Weisburd and Lum (2005) found that computerized crime mapping and the use of geographic information systems (GIS) spread rapidly in policing in the late 1990s, and was a significant impetus in facilitating one evidence-based policing practice—hot spots policing.

Besides crime mapping and hot spot analysis, crime analysis can also involve finding crime patterns and trends using various data analysis techniques. These techniques can include analyzing offender methods to identify related offenses, searching various types of data sources to identify and locate criminal suspects, analyzing temporal patterns in offending, tracking crime trends over time in particular places, using social network analysis to understand co-offending, using "nearest neighbor" analysis to identify victimization risk, and/or employing predictive policing techniques to make very specific predictions about crime at particular places or among particular individuals (see more examples in Ratcliffe 2008; Taylor and Boba 2011).

Although they are often assigned to generate crime trend statistics and crime maps for command-level meetings like Compstat, crime analysts may also be assigned to investigative units to help solve cases, or to crime prevention and community policing units to proactively deal with crime patterns. Sometimes crime analysts are assigned to specific patrol precincts or districts to assist with local concerns. The sophistication of crime analysis capabilities and work assignments can vary considerably across agencies. Important predictors of the range and sophistication of crime analysis across agencies include the availability of hardware and software, data collection capabilities, training, and structural characteristics such as whether an agency has a specialized crime analysis unit (O'Shea and Nicholls 2003).

The question for evidence-based policing is not whether agencies should have crime analysis units, as they are a "must have" in any agency. But the more important question is *how* analysts are used. Like the technologies we discussed in Chapter 7, crime analysis can be used to facilitate evidence-based approaches such as proactivity or problem solving, or it can easily be used to strengthen police practices that are not evidence based, or that reinforce reactive approaches to policing. Analysts can be used to help generate new knowledge through research and evaluation, or they may serve largely for reporting purposes (such as generating crime statistics for UCR reporting).

How analysts are deployed reflects how an agency views its function and purpose. The earliest forms of crime analysis, for instance, likely focused on the collection of crime statistics and data for the UCR system; in some agencies, crime analysis units are still used largely for this purpose. This is consistent with the goals of the standard model of policing to deliver a professional, procedures-oriented, and standardized response to a call for service, thus prioritizing the recording of those calls and clearances of reported crimes. At the same time, crime analysis can also be leveraged to implement evidence-based alternatives to the standard model, including hot spots policing, problem solving, intelligence-led, and even community policing. In these models, crime analysis is central to analyzing seemingly disparate crime and community data to find underlying problems and trends, and to develop and assess the effectiveness of tactical and strategic options. Some agencies actively integrate analysts into operations, while other agencies treat them as outsiders who primarily work for command staff. Observing how analysts are treated, used, and incorporated into the police function is one litmus test of an agency's policing approach.

The most common applications of crime analysis today both support and expand the standard model and are driven primarily by command staff, not the analysts themselves (Koper, Lum, Willis et al. 2015c; Taylor and Boba 2011). For instance, one very common use of crime analysis is to track police activity and crime numbers for discussion in management meetings (i.e., Compstat-type meetings). This tracking is typically done for administratively defined areas such as police beats, districts, zones, and the like. This use of crime analysis has the benefit of providing at least basic forms of outcome monitoring (see Rossi, Lipsey, and Freeman 2004), highlighting crime types that are rising and places where crime is increasing, and relating these outcomes to variations in police activities and outputs. This, in turn, enhances the accountability of commanders for responding to local crime patterns and pushes an agency towards data-driven approaches that should produce more refined and targeted responses to crime problems (see descriptions by Bratton and Knobler 1998; McDonald, Greenberg, and Bratton 2001; Weisburd, Mastrofski, and McNally et al. 2003b).

At the same time, there are limitations to some of the common ways that crime analysis is practiced. For one, analyses are not necessarily focused on precise areas or micro hot spots where crime is most concentrated. Although many agencies report using crime analysis for hot spot identification, as we discussed in Chapter 4, the term "hot spot" is used broadly in practice, often referring to larger areas like neighborhoods, police beats, or even larger areas. And as noted, crime reporting at police management meetings such as Compstat often focuses on administratively defined areas and their short-term fluctuations, as well as the use of analysis to solve specific crimes. There is much less emphasis on systematic tracking and discussion of high-risk groups and individuals, or micro crime hot spots and their environmental, geographic, situational, and routine activities correlates. In addition, counted police activities tend to emphasize measures like field interviews, traffic stops, and arrests rather than things like patrol dosage in hot spots or problem-solving activities conducted by officers. Further, changes in crime are typically reported without any sense of whether they represent meaningfully large changes (i.e., "statistically significant" changes in the language of science) or simply normal weekly or monthly fluctuations. The potential benefits of the analyses that are produced are also muted to some degree as supervisors and officers in many agencies do not seem to consistently access this information and use it to guide their proactive patrol or problem-solving efforts (e.g., Koper et al. 2015c; also see Koper, Lum, and Hibdon 2015b; Lum, Koper, and Willis 2016b; and Chapter 7).

Crime analysts also work in support of detectives in many agencies, helping to identify and locate suspects utilizing various data sources and tools. This may improve case clearance rates and reduce the time it takes to close investigations (though we have not seen any specific evidence of this), but it seems rarer for detectives to use crime analysis information to try to prevent crime. Even in the most innovative agencies, crime analysts are valued the most for their ability to strengthen the reaction of the police through this investigative support (Koper et al. 2015c; also see Lum et al. 2016b).

Hence, while crime analysis has likely brought significant improvements in police performance, it seems that there is much room for improvement. However, there are many obstacles to implementing crime analysis in the context of evidence-based policing. These can include a police culture that doesn't value analytical work, the reactive nature of policing, and a disregard for crime analysis that is done largely by civilians (Lum 2013; Santos 2014; Taylor and Boba 2011). In practice, officers may not use products like maps and may find them of little value in their work (Cope 2004; Cordner and Biebel 2005; Paulson 2004). Indeed, crime analysis is mostly produced for police managers. While managers tend to be the heaviest users of analysis, they often focus largely on criminal apprehension and short-term tactical planning rather than long-term strategic planning (Harris 2007; O'Shea and Nicholls 2003; Taylor and Boba 2011). Realizing the full potential of crime analysis in an evidence-based policing framework thus requires more emphasis on long-term strategic planning, more attention to developing analytical products of value to officers, and proper training, coaching, support, and reinforcement at all levels in the agency. O'Shea and Nicholls (2003) have also shown that stronger management support and appreciation by target audiences have a positive impact on crime analysis functions and sophistication.

The Roles of Crime Analysts in Evidence-Based Policing

Despite the obstacles noted above, crime analysts have nonetheless played central roles in evidence-based policing. Below, we discuss several key ways in which crime analysts have contributed to this movement.

(1) Crime analysts contribute to the supply of research evidence

Analysts have been central to generating the underlying evidence for evidence-based policing. A significant share of the evaluation studies in the Evidence-Based Policing Matrix, as well as much of the empirical evidence about crime more generally, has been developed with some help from crime analysts. In many research studies, crime analysts work directly with research partners to develop and evaluate interventions. They might also help to generate new data that is not readily available that researchers need for their evaluations. For example, they can facilitate surveys of officers and analyze unique sources of information such as automated vehicle locator data, license plate reader scans, or body-worn camera video footage. One major evidence-based policing initiative supporting this type of role for analysts is the Bureau of Justice Assistance's (U.S. Department of Justice) Smart Policing Initiative.[1] Although more broadly focused on developing stronger partnerships between researchers and police agencies to carry out evidence-based policing, one by-product of these initiatives has been crime analysts contributing to the evaluation of policing programs that in turn become part of the evidence base for policing.

Two excellent examples from our own experiences include working with Jamie Roush, the former crime analysis manager of the Jacksonville (Florida) Sheriff's Office, and Renee Mitchell, a sergeant of the Sacramento (California) Police Department. Both were directly involved in two studies in the Matrix—the Jacksonville study comparing directed patrol and problem solving at hot spots (Taylor, Koper, and Woods 2011a; also see Koper, Taylor, and Roush 2013a) and the Sacramento Hot Spots study using the Koper Curve principle (Telep, Mitchell, and Weisburd 2014).

Jamie Roush during her tenure at the Jacksonville Sheriff's Office (JSO) was instrumental in advancing the use of crime analysis, problem solving, and evidence-based policing in her agency. This was also facilitated by a progressive and supportive sheriff, undersheriff, and commanding officer who were all committed to using research and crime analysis in innovative ways. In 2008, JSO committed to undertake a ground-breaking randomized experiment with

---

[1] See http://www.smartpolicinginitiative.com/.

the second author and his colleagues, the first to test the comparative effectiveness of directed patrol and problem-oriented policing (POP) approaches at hot spots of violent crime (see our discussion of this study in Chapters 4 and 12).

Roush and former Jacksonville analyst Matt White were crucial to advocating for the experiment with the agency's command staff, designing the experiment in collaboration with researchers, and helping to train and coach officers on concepts behind POP, routine activities theory, and crime prevention. During the experiment, Roush and her analysts worked directly with officers to help diagnose problems at hot spots and to develop problem-solving responses for the locations.

As another example, we highlight Sgt. Renee Mitchell, who is the founder of the American Chapter of the Society of Evidence-Based Policing and the former director of crime analysis for the Sacramento Police Department. The first author met Mitchell in a training session at the Redlands (CA) Police Department. Mitchell took it upon herself to work with the first author to learn about evidence-based policing, hot spots patrol, and the Koper Curve principle. She and the first author eventually designed a hot spots intervention based on Lum, Willis (Hibdon), Cave et al.'s (2011c) license plate reader patrol experiment that used the Koper Curve principal. Rather than wait for a grant to fund the experiment, Mitchell led a within-agency randomized controlled experiment to test the impact of patrol deployment with the Koper Curve principle using existing officers during their regular shifts. Along with her colleagues in the Sacramento Police Department's crime analysis unit, she identified appropriate hot spots for the intervention, designed treatment protocols, and oversaw the implementation of the ninety-day trial. With the help of Cody Telep, at the time a research assistant at George Mason University, Mitchell analyzed the results of this experiment, which showed statistically significant decreases in major crimes in experimental hots spots versus their controls. This study was an example of a crime analyst creating and carrying out an evaluation of a policing tactic completely within the constraints of her role as a police officer and analyst, while contributing important new knowledge to the field about patrol at hot spots.

However, the challenge to this type of work by analysts is in sustaining such efforts. Crime analysts are often pulled in many different directions, making it hard to dedicate the time and resources to generate high-quality evaluations on a regular basis. Federal funding support such as the Smart Policing Initiative as well as strong partnerships with researchers can certainly help. However, agencies who are interested in evaluating their various efforts (whether they are crime related, community-centric, or related to internal organization and management) likely have to increase the amount of analysts they employ to strengthen these efforts.

(2) Crime analysts contribute to implementing evidence-based practices

Analysts have played a pivotal role in not only generating research knowledge but also implementing evidence-based practices. For example, as described in Chapter 2, the Matrix reveals three crime prevention generalizations or principles that police agencies can focus on to increase their odds of effectively preventing crime. Recall, these include (i) targeting high-crime places (and also repeat and serious offenders within those places) rather than only focusing on individuals and a case-by-case approach; (ii) tailoring approaches to specific problems at hand rather than only applying general prevention measures across the board; and (iii) acting proactively. To implement evidence-based policing, therefore, police agencies need to locate crime concentrations, identify serious and repeat offenders, determine underlying problems that contribute to crime patterns, and anticipate crime and other concerns in order to prevent them before they happen. Analysts facilitate these activities.

One very common type of crime analysis is computerized mapping and hot spots determination. Mapping is a core function in crime analysis and one that is historically central to the diffusion of crime analysis in policing (see Weisburd and Lum 2005). Aside from the counting of crime statistics, hand and computerized mapping are likely the oldest forms of crime analysis. Some of the pioneers of crime analysis were also pioneers of crime mapping. Today, crime mapping is central to agencies taking a place-based approach to policing. Further, researchers working with police agencies have been at the forefront of developing sophisticated forms of crime mapping, as well as understanding the environmental and social conditions at places that contribute to spatial crime patterns (e.g., see work by Martin Andresen, Kate Bowers, Patricia, Paul and Jeff Brantingham, Joel Caplan, John Eck, Elizabeth Groff, Shane Johnson, Jerry Ratcliffe, and George Rengert, to name only a few).

In addition to pinpointing problem places, crime analysts can also play a role in evidence-based policing when they identify, track, and develop information on high-rate offenders and other dangerous groups to facilitate intelligence-led approaches (Ratcliffe 2008). This might be done in combination with hot spots analysis (e.g., Egge 2011) and sometimes involves efforts to rate offenders and groups for dangerousness based on risk assessments. Such information can be valuable in guiding agency deployments and informing the efforts of patrol officers, investigators, and special units in the field (e.g., see our discussion in Chapter 5). Of course, standard crime analysis also involves efforts to discern patterns in criminal activity that illuminate related events and improve the ability of officers to identify and apprehend suspects.

Crime analysts can also play a critical role in evidence-based policing through their problem solving. Through their analyses of crime patterns and trends (and in some cases their specialized knowledge of criminology), analysts illuminate underlying problems to facilitate more tailored and proactive policing approaches. Indeed, while it has perhaps been linked most prominently to hot spots policing and Compstat, crime analysis can also be a valuable component of POP, in particular for executing the "As" in the SARA process—analysis and assessment. The "Case of Place" examples described in Chapter 12 provide good illustrations of this. Crime analysts like Jeff Egge in Minneapolis and Renee Tate in Richmond, VA were central in collecting, analyzing, and interpreting data on crime hot spots for use in those problem-solving assessments that helped to illuminate conditions, routines, and actors that gave rise to crime at those locations. The Jacksonville hot spots experiment noted above provides another good example, as it involved crime analysts working with officers in conducting POP at hot spots.

Analysts might also generate more systematic information on other phenomena that can help their agencies build strategies in an evidence-based way. For example, perhaps a police chief wants to conduct a survey of the community to gauge overall satisfaction with police services. There is a variety of ways such a survey can be carried out, from the very unscientific to the more rigorous. Crime analysts may also be those who are knowledgeable about what makes for good and bad research, and can help implement such surveys in ways that are representative of populations of interest and collected with scientific integrity. Similarly, crime analysts in some agencies may have the scientific knowledge and skills needed to conduct more refined assessments of crime trends (i.e., determining when changes in crime represent statistically meaningful changes as opposed to random fluctuations) and design scientifically rigorous evaluations of new programs (see Chapter 2). In these examples, applying good scientific processes to carry out surveys, trend analyses, or evaluations would be yet another way that analysts might play a role in evidence-based policing.

Further, within the evidence-based policing framework, such analytic work need not be constrained to only crime and other community problems. Statistical modeling, for example, might be used to determine specific factors that put individual officers at higher risk for citizen complaints, uses of force, or even suicide. Analysts can also play an important role examining use of force data, complaints, and internal information related to officer job satisfaction or health to support evidence-based practices in these areas. Police agencies are also concerned about employee health and wellness, internal corruption and fraud, and the impact of training on behavior and outcomes. Research evidence on these organizational factors also points to effective strategies and practices. Agency analysts can also help in understanding these issues so that agencies can be more proactive in identifying and mitigating problems proactively.

Finally, crime analysts can also play key roles in institutionalizing evidence-based practices as illustrated by our discussion of Jamie Roush's role in developing Jacksonville's special unit focused on violent crime hot spots (see Chapter 12). However, by being central to the implementation of evidence-based policing, analysts have also borne the brunt of the challenges associated with implementing evidence-based practices. Unlike police chiefs, their longer tenures have given them a long-term view of implementation that may not be shared by their ever-changing command staff. In the case of Mitchell's Sacramento experiment, implementing the deployment style she found to be effective was a hard sell to both patrol officers and to new and changing commanders, and the agency did not continue the hot spots patrols. Our many conversations with analysts indicate that they are less supported in an evidence-based policing mode than they are in the Compstat or number-crunching mode. As we said in Chapter 1, evidence-based policing requires a commitment to ideas and values that may fly in the face of the status quo or existing policing traditions.

Betsy Stanko's efforts for the City of London and the London Metropolitan Police Service provide insights into implementing and sustaining evidence-based practices (as well as generating research evidence). Stanko began in the "Corporate Development" unit in the Metropolitan Police Service in London and helped develop and transform the use of research and crime analysis for the Met. Later, she led the "Evidence and Insight" department of the Mayor's Office for Policing and Crime in London. In her and Dawson's (2016) recent monograph for our *Translational Criminology* series, they provide the example of the "Pathways Initiative" to showcase the challenges of implementing evidence-based practices in policing. The London Pathways Initiative was a community-based multiagency program to reduce gang violence, built off the research evidence from the Boston Ceasefire approach (see Braga and Weisburd 2012). Stanko and Dawson discuss how local interests wished to modify the strategy to fit local needs and constraints, to the point of changing the core rationale and theory of the effective Ceasefire approach. At the same time, they argue that implementing evidence-based practices is not simply "advocating a 'cookie cutter' approach" and that "[p]olice officers not only need to know which tactic works best, but they also need to know how to supervise and monitor the delivery of success that is compatible with the theory of change.... there needs to be an awareness as to the limits or flex to an evidence based model, and how much dilution to a model is acceptable before it breaks. This is a fundamental change to the craft of policing and an even more nuanced and pragmatic approach to working with programme integrity.... this requires additional training around programme management and integrity so to establish a policing culture that is more conducive to routinely achieving desirable outcomes." (Stanko and Dawson 2016, 30–1).

(3) Analysts as "translators" of research

Crime analysts have become "translators" of research knowledge and directly help to fulfill our more holistic definition of evidence-based policing. They may be more likely than patrol officers or commanders to be exposed to a wide variety of research knowledge as well as research methods. At the same time, their daily interactions, experiences, and efforts with police officers make them uniquely positioned to translate the meaning of research findings into practice. Some analysts have taken on the direct role of training and educating officers about problem solving, crime analysis, and findings from evaluations. Others might focus on knowledge from environmental criminology or routine activities to convey through their analysis this area of research. Crime analysts also work as translators in their choices of what analyses to carry out and how to convey them to the operational units with which they work.

Crime analysts who are familiar with research evidence in the field can also help supervisors and command staff to assess whether an agency's practices are aligned with what research indicates is effective. In Chapter 14, we refer to a methodology for doing such assessments using the Matrix. We promote this idea as a form of strategic management that provides a way for police commanders to evaluate their agency's practices in lieu of conducting formal scientific evaluations (which may not be feasible or necessary in all contexts). Crime analysts are well positioned to assist in this task and contribute to discussions about how an agency might strengthen its crime prevention and control measures.

Optimizing Crime Analysis

In summary, to optimize the use of crime analysis and analysts in agencies pursuing a more evidence-based approach, agencies might consider the following ideas:

1. Crime analysis units can only be evidence based to the extent that a police agency makes a strong and tangible commitment to institutionalizing proactive strategies that are focused, targeted, place based (when appropriate), and problem oriented. This requires a major adjustment to traditional patrol deployment *and* investigative strategies. Agencies can start by unchaining themselves from reactive beat patrol. This requires developing deployment strategies based on geographic crime patterns rather than political boundaries. Further, this also calls for first-line supervisors and officers to focus their attention not simply on calls for service but the time in between calls for service that can be reaped for crime prevention.

2. Agencies might also consider not only using detectives to pursue traditional units of investigation (individuals and individual cases), but to combine analysts and investigators to focus on other units of investigation that may be more fruitful in reducing the opportunity for victimization in the first place. These other investigative units could be places, as we described in Chapter 12. However, they could also include criminal networks, or high-risk situations and routine activities that contribute to crime.

3. Law enforcement agencies need to rethink the way analysts are utilized and incorporated into management meetings. Lead analysts should be treated as

professional equals with others at the table, engaging in conversations with them about the nature of crime in the jurisdiction, relationships between environment and crime, relationships between deployment and crime, and discussions of how different types of analysis might support the development, implementation, and evaluation of tactics and strategies. We have also seen some police use crime analysis to guide management meetings; in such cases, the meetings focus largely on new crime patterns and trends as determined by crime analysts. Using analysts only to generate and report on crime statistics for administrative areas simply is a waste of this resource and disconnected from an evidence-based approach.

4. Police agencies have to invest in crime analysis as a major unit within the agency in order to accomplish the ideas above. This means increasing the size of analysis units at the possible expense of reducing the number of sworn officers or purchasing new technologies. Agencies have to treat these units as seriously as they do investigative or patrol units, and stop using crime analysis units as places to rotate employees who do not have analytic skills or as the first units to cut in times of austerity.

5. Agencies also have to think more broadly about the way crime analysis can be used. Besides mapping crime and tracking trends in police activity and crime (all of which could be further refined in ways discussed above), analysts should also be actively involved in developing crime prevention and community engagement strategies, working on problem-solving efforts with line-level staff, investigating and tracking problem places and persons, conducting evaluations and other research projects, and analyzing community and organizational issues that go beyond crime prevention. As one example, analysts could support community policing efforts by developing and implementing methodologically rigorous community surveys that include scientific sampling strategies, longitudinal survey plans, and questions that are informed by what we know from survey research to be most appropriate in gauging the issues of interest.

6. Training about the use and importance of crime analysis should be incorporated into academy and in-service training, just as officers and commanders are trained about the importance and use of weapons, cars, mobile computers, and radios. We have developed two freely available training modules with Jamie Roush that can be used for this purpose (see http://cebcp. org/evidence-based-policing/the-matrix/matrix-demonstration-project/ academy-curriculum/).

Like all technologies, innovations, or deployments, agencies have to determine the most cost-effective way to use crime analysis to reduce crime, increase legitimacy, and improve internal management. This is especially important, given that so many evidence-based practices rely on its proper use. From an evidence-based perspective, crime analysis can be the most cost-effective when it is used to develop geographic and person-based crime patterns, conduct network analysis, identify problems, evaluate interventions and performance measures on a regular basis, assess the pulse of the community and its relationships with officers and the department, and identify internal organizational concerns to help commanders proactively address them. This also requires, like other deployments, that crime analysis is regularly assessed and evaluated for its use and effectiveness.

14

SUPERVISION, MANAGEMENT, STRATEGIC PLANNING, AND LEADERSHIP FOR EVIDENCE-BASED POLICING

Institutionalizing evidence-based policing requires adjusting accountability, supervisory, managerial, and leadership systems. These systems can reinforce and solidify certain types of behaviors and attitudes of personnel because they are closely tied to systems of reward, promotion, punishment, and status. These systems are also complex, contradicting, and not always aligned. They are entangled in organizational culture, the public's expectations, and the daily activities of police personnel. Because of this, adjusting supervisory, managerial, strategic planning, and leadership systems toward being more amenable to evidence-based policing is no small or simple task. Indeed, many of these same organizational issues have often been discussed as key challenges to implementing other reforms like community- and problem-oriented policing (e.g., Skogan, Hartnett, DuBois et al. 2000; Trojanowicz and Bucqueroux 1997).

In this chapter, we provide examples of how evidence-based policing might be infused into systems of supervision, management, strategic planning, public engagement, and leadership. Specifically, we focus on: adjusting performance metrics, rewards, and promotions; elevating and activating the role of first-line supervisors; using evidence to influence strategic planning as well as managerial infrastructure; and, finally, showing examples of leadership in an evidence-based policing paradigm.

Performance Metrics

Performance metrics can be powerful motivators in policing, although the use of such metrics has not always been a major part of policing. Officers are most often judged on their knowledge of, and competence with, criminal procedures and organizational rules rather than outcomes related to crime prevention or community trust. They may also be judged on more general employment matters such as their ability to work with others, their initiative, or their ability to follow orders. This judgment begins early in the police academy and field training using various tests and assessments of these procedures and rules. Officer performance continues to be assessed in various stages throughout their careers. In many agencies, all sworn personnel might be assessed in semi-annual or annual performance reviews, which judge them primarily on metrics directly or indirectly connected to organizational procedures and rules. Police agencies may or may not have systems of accountability and discipline with regard to when procedures and rules are violated. Certainly, when laws are broken by officers, they might be criminally charged. When officers violate organizational procedures and rules, agencies may have disciplinary matrices that they apply. When officers are not making enough arrests, citations, or community contacts, or not getting to calls for service quickly, they may also be informally reprimanded or encouraged by supervisors, or these concerns may be noted in monthly, quarterly, or annual reviews of officers by their supervisors. Or, there may be no note of this performance at all.

Modern police agencies vary as to how they formally measure performance. Some agencies may use quantitative metrics, such as the number of arrests, citations, or community contacts that a patrol officer makes, or how many cases a detective clears in a given time frame. Similarly, organizations might be judged by their case clearance rates or levels of crime in their jurisdiction. At the agency level, these metrics have manifested most famously in Compstat meetings, and we have seen some organizations show performance statistics at the officer level in various district stations. The performance of individual officers and the agency can also be measured qualitatively, including how citizens, the media, and community groups judge or talk about the police, or the informal feedback that an officer receives from his or her supervisor after he or she handles an incident. Qualitative metrics might manifest as an officer receiving a medal for bravery, a citizen filing a complaint, or a journalist writing about the goings-on of an agency.

The important question for implementing evidence-based policing is not whether performance metrics should exist, but rather what performance metrics are used and do some of them reflect values and knowledge from an evidence-based policing approach? The choice of performance metrics matters and is both a reflection and reinforcement of an agency's philosophical approach to policing and its sought-after outcomes. For example, if the number of arrests and citations that an officer makes are used to judge her performance, then this will reinforce her using arrest and citation as her primary crime-fighting strategy. However, if that same officer is judged by the amount of proactive problem-solving activities she engages in, then her crime-fighting strategy will be different.

To develop or recreate performance metrics requires an agency to engage in a philosophical discussion about its role and function. Lum and Nagin (2017) argue that two principles that are heavily supported by research provide guidance to this process. The first principle is that preventing crime, not making arrests, should be the primary metric for judging police success. The second principle is that citizen reactions matter. That is, in a democratic society, performance metrics of the police should also include citizen reaction and response to police activity. Policing is certainly not an easy profession in this regard; officers and the agency are judged on not only their ability to prevent crime and thus maintain safety, but on their ability to do so in a way that is legal, respectful of human rights, and that does not degrade citizens' trust and confidence in the police.

But if members of a police agency do not have a consensus about policing's function and role in society, then they also cannot agree upon what might be considered "good" performance. Despite what leaders and officers might think, we now have evidence that there may be a large amount of incongruence about expectations and beliefs about the role of police in society across ranks, units, and divisions in a police agency. This incongruence can lead to conflict and suspicion about new paradigms—like evidence-based policing—that are brought into an organization by a specific group or individual within the organization. As we show in the "Leadership" section below, successful evidence-based policing leaders are those who have these discussions with members of their agencies and communities and try to build congruence across different units, ranks, and individuals about what are the functions and goals of the police in a democratic society.

Once this foundation has been laid, one place to begin adjusting performance metrics towards an evidence-based policing approach would be in patrol officer performance evaluations. These are monthly, quarterly, or annual evaluations usually filled out by first-line supervisors assessing the performance of officers under their supervision. The content and frequency of assessments can vary across agencies and include assessments of many issues, including an officer's appearance, demeanor, and performance in the field and adherence to agency rules and procedures. Some information collected may be personnel-related data points, such as an officer's absenteeism, complaints that s/he has sustained, disciplinary actions, and the like. Others might be assessments of an officer's ability to respond to particular types of situations. In some agencies, generic municipal government forms that apply to all county or city workers are used.

To adjust these evaluations to accommodate evidence-based policing, patrol commanders might consider the objectives of performance evaluations for both the officer and the supervisor completing them, and find ways to infuse aspects of evidence-based policing into them. For example, one goal of rethinking performance evaluations in an evidence-based policing mode is adjusting metrics toward specific and meaningful values, and not necessarily "targets." Agencies might consider performance metrics that characterize and document how officers are spending their time in between calls for service—for example, whether they are proactively patrolling hot spots, monitoring high-risk people in their patrol area, or carrying out problem-solving activities. Performance evaluations could also be used to test officer knowledge on some of these issues (e.g., whether they know where hot spots are and understand why those locations are hot), and provide for learning opportunities. Performance evaluations could also be adjusted to record if officers carried out evidence-based activities, such as a "Case of Place" investigation, a CPTED evaluation, or a situational crime prevention assessment of a building or area. Or, assessments might document ways that officers engaged with community members and whether their actions align with what we know about effective citizen–police relations.

One tangible way to achieve infusing evidence-based policing into performance evaluations is to align portions of the evaluation with Playbook plays (or another similar evidence-based guide). For example, for those agencies in which officers document their daily activity on logs or "run sheets," the officer can simply denote the name of the play carried out at any given time and the result of implementing the play. Run sheets and daily logs, however, are becoming antiquated; computer-aided dispatch generally records an officer's daily activity. Thus, officers can report to the dispatcher or CAD system when they are implementing a play, where they are implementing it, and when they are done. This, in turn, can provide empirical information for quarterly performance evaluations that attempt to gauge if officers are carrying out proactive, problem-oriented, place-based, or tailored strategies.

Here, we pause to make a crucial point. In order for this to work—that is, in order for an officer to be able to tell the dispatcher (and thus account for) when he or she is carrying out a specific evidence-based play—the dispatcher (or the computer system) has to have a way to absorb this information and ideally link it to a particular location (like a designated micro hot spot), date, time, and officer. Many CAD systems have the ability to do this in theory. In practice, however, CAD systems often have set codes that describe a great deal of officer activity that unfortunately does not include evidence-based activities. We have worked with a large amount of calls for service data, analyzing the categories of activities that are recorded. These often reflect specific categories of calls for service (i.e., robbery, disorderly contact, drugs, traffic accident), or even administrative duties (i.e., getting gas for the car, submitting evidence, taking a lunch break, transporting a witness to the police station). Because CAD categories were created to support and anchor many of the practices of the standard model, CAD codes rarely, if ever, have categories for evidence-based practices such as "proactive policing," "hot spots policing," "proactively reaching out to citizens," or "opening a case on a place." These activities often get lumped into nondescript categories such as "other" or "administration." If we want an officer to be able to tell the dispatcher that he is conducting hot spots policing at Fifth and Main Streets just as easily as he can tell the dispatcher that he is filling his car with gas at 123 Smith Street, and if we want those two activities *not* to both be categorized as "other" in the CAD system so that the evidence-based activity can be appropriately counted (and rewarded), then the way that police record and account for using evidence-based plays has to change.

An additional goal of revamping a performance metric or evaluation system might be to adjust officer mentality so that that they are more critical, problem oriented, and tailored in carrying out their daily activities. This is a deeper training goal that isn't so much focused on the actual evidence, but more on adjusting mindsets so that in the future officers will be more amenable to innovations and new reforms that come from the evidence (see discussion by Grieco 2016). Here, performance metrics and evaluations might serve as a training or mentoring opportunity. As already mentioned, officers could be quizzed on their knowledge of evidence-based policing they learned in the academy or during in-service training. They might be asked to carry out a problem-solving exercise while being observed by a supervisor. This type of performance evaluation might also be used to evaluate the officer's ability and knowledge in accessing and interpreting relevant analytic information that can help them with their daily efforts. Officers might be asked to discuss a recurring crime problem and what s/he has done to understand that problem more deeply (so as to effectively deal with it). Recall, evidence-based policing is not just about crime prevention. One might imagine that learning opportunities might incorporate ideas such as procedural justice, implicit bias, or officer wellness, as well as knowledge about mental illness or addiction.

Adjusting performance metrics in these ways could also present an opportunity to change the way supervisors and officers interact and modify the role of supervisors more generally. New performance metrics and evaluation exercises like the examples above may increase the mentorship role of the supervisor, or provide opportunities where supervisors can act as translators of evidence to officers. This would also be aligned with evidence on leadership—such an approach could provide a more transformational as opposed to transactional interaction between supervisors and officers which might also facilitate an evidence-based approach (McCardle 2011).

Rewards, Incentives, and Promotions

Having systems to assess performance in meaningful ways is a major part of achieving evidence-based policing. However, as seen from our performance metric discussion above, strengthening accountability to evidence-based practices requires more than just redoing an evaluation sheet. Fundamental changes to the CAD system, for example, or the way supervisors interact with officers, are just two of the many systemic changes that will be prompted by adjustments to performance evaluations and metrics. Organizational incentives also need to be revamped in ways that reflect these metrics. If performance metrics are adjusted to be more aligned with what we know is effective in terms of crime prevention or improving community trust and confidence, but if officers are promoted or paid primarily based on seniority, time in service, or an exam which tests their knowledge of organizational policies and procedures, then many officers will see little incentive to care about new performance metrics. Additionally, if performance metrics are seen as rigid, having little to do with substance and more to do with just numbers and statistics, officers will find less incentive in using them.

Rewards, promotions, incentives, and informal "pats on the back," are important managerial and accountability systems that shape the expectations and tendencies of both leaders and the rank and file. Officers are often looking to advance themselves, whether by transferring to a detective or specialized unit or by applying for promotion to a higher rank. Even if officers do not have lofty leadership goals, getting rewarded in different ways is important in policing (and any other profession, for that matter). Rewards and positive reinforcement are important because satisfied officers with excellent critical thinking skills may be less likely to resist new innovations and may thus have a greater capacity to carry out deployments that are more proactive or complex. Rewards can include receiving medals, preferences for days off, or eligibility for special training or assignments. Even informal acknowledgments and pats on the back in roll calls can be incentives in a profession that is often filled with more negative than positive aspects.

Behaviors that an agency and its leaders choose to reward and how agencies promote officers reveal what the agency values, what it sees as its role and function in society, and the activities and outcomes it prioritizes. If officers or groups of officers are either formally or informally rewarded for making arrests and citations, then those things become valued in policing and also work their way into definitions of "good policing." Similarly, if performance indicators at the precinct level focus on counts of traditional policing activities (e.g., traffic stops, arrests, and citations), clearing of specific cases, or short-term crime trends, then commanders will concentrate on activities that satisfy those concerns. On the other hand, if officers are rewarded for innovative crime prevention activities, improving police–citizen interactions, innovating in patrol during non-committed times (even if the activity did not produce any outcome), and producing long-term, sustained reductions in crime and calls for service, then they will be incentivized to carry out those activities.

Adjusting both formal and informal rewards and incentive structures are therefore an important part of institutionalizing evidence-based practices. For example, tests and interview questions for promotion to detective units or supervisory positions may need to be re-designed. Presently, officers testing for promotion to supervisory positions such as sergeant or lieutenant are likely asked about their knowledge of the proper handling of common supervisory problems, standard operating procedures, or how they might command a homicide scene or critical incident. But in an agency with an evidence-based policing philosophy, officers vying for a sergeant's position could be tested on not only procedures, but also on knowledge about effective crime prevention measures, ways community trust can be improved, and/or their understanding of the importance of crime analysis or surveys that gauge community reaction to policing. First-line supervisors applying for promotion might be asked to produce documentation of their capacity to lead squads in conducting evidence-based practices such as patrolling crime hot spots during non-committed time or engaging in problem-solving activities. This is important, since a mark of good leadership in an evidence-based approach is the ability to inspire officers and subordinates to carry out strategies and tactics that are unfamiliar, new, and different from those to which officers are accustomed.

One idea is to use tools like the Matrix to assess a promotional candidate's tendencies from an evidence-based perspective. Take, for example, Figure 14.1. This shows the Matrix, populated with studies. As we discussed in Chapter 3, statistically significant positive findings (black dots) tend to cluster around

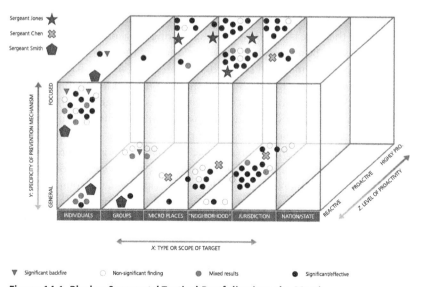

Figure 14.1 Placing Sergeants' Tactical Portfolios into the Matrix

the areas of the Matrix characterized by three intersecting dimensions—micro place-based, proactive, and tailored or focused. In this figure we also show a hypothetical mapping of three sergeants' activities into the Matrix during a promotions process. Sergeants Jones, Chen, and Smith might have numerous initiatives and activities that they implemented with their patrol squads, each represented by their respective shapes in Figure 14.1: stars, crosses, or pentagons. Only four shapes per sergeant are shown here, but one could imagine many data points per sergeant based on the various activities they undertake with their squads that they record on their performance evaluations over time. Mapping their efforts into the intersecting dimensions that describe each activity can help illuminate the overall tendencies of that supervisor.

For example, Sergeant Jones primarily engages in initiatives that are place based, focused and mostly proactive. Perhaps she asks her squad to participate in problem-solving team activities at places. Sergeant Chen, while carrying out one focused activity, tends to favor activities that are more general in nature, but that also are placed based. These might include general hot-spotting activity that he asks his squad to carry out during their non-committed time. Sergeant Smith, on the other hand, tends to use strategies and tactics focused on arresting or targeting individuals, mostly in reactive ways, and with a mix of general and tailored strategies. Although the evidence indicates that Sergeant Jones and Chen tend to be most aligned with what we know prevents crime, this does not necessarily rule out Sergeant Smith for promotion. A closer inspection of his interventions might show that they are closely aligned to activities within that area of the Matrix that has been shown to be effective. However, Smith also shows a tendency to carry out reactive activity, which may not be the direction in which the command staff wants the police agency to go. Mapping promotional applicants' tactical and strategic portfolios against a standard like the Matrix can help present more empirical information about an individual's capabilities.

Of course, there are challenges to re-engineering these promotional systems. Sergeants have to be aware that this will be one way they are judged and they have to be given the tools and knowledge to carry out evidence-based practices in the first place. There may also be substantial pushback from police unions about changing promotional practices. Promotions are highly politicized and unionized in policing for various reasons, which ultimately has led to very rigid promotions structures that rely on tests of procedures rather than more qualitative assessments. Providing a standard like the Matrix and giving promotional applicants adequate opportunities to adjust to the new system is one way to readjust this system in policing towards a more evidence-based approach.

We also note that rewards and incentives come in many other forms. For example, agencies give medals and citations for a variety of achievements such as for bravery or for special service. Imagine if a medal was given for the use of research knowledge in practice or for problem solving to reduce crime! What about a medal for increasing citizen trust and confidence in the police? While some might not consider these to be equivalent to an act that leads to receiving a medal of bravery, those who have engaged in evidence-based policing can attest to the difficulty and high risk of engaging in innovation amongst skeptical colleagues or superiors. The crime prevention work of crime analysts, for example, has contributed a great deal to public safety, but as our research and that of others has shown, they continue to be viewed with some suspicion or indifference by officers.

Ultimately, the culture of policing has to change so that the definition of a "good officer" also changes. Supervisors and command staff also have to praise efforts that reflect effectiveness in not only apprehending criminals, but also in preventing crime, reducing calls for service, and improving community trust and confidence. We don't have a quick solution here; changing these informal incentives can be part of the broader discussion that agencies undertake when they decide to commit to a more evidence-based approach.

First-Line Supervision

Since we focused on sergeants and first-line supervisors in our illustration and discussion of Figure 14.1, we would like to take a short diversion to discuss first-line supervisors in more detail. Interestingly, while U.S. first-line supervisors tend to be given very passive and reactive leadership roles, they are likely the most critical component for agencies to achieve reforms like evidence-based policing. Ultimately, they and their squads are responsible for implementing reforms. Thus, how first-line supervisors portray, support, reject, or block reform and change can matter a great deal. First-line supervision is, therefore, a critical system that needs attention when attempting to institutionalize evidence-based policing into practice.

At the same time, first-line supervisors can be the hardest group to convince about the merits of change. Over time, they have received numerous commands and ideas from the higher-ups, and they are expected to carry out those ideas with little guidance, knowledge, or justification about why they need to do what they are asked to do. This may lead them to tell their officers to "just do it because the chief wants it", which does not help to win the hearts and minds of officers or detectives. The high turnover of chief executives and command staff also makes reform and change unstable and hardly long-lasting, and supervisors know this. Any move towards evidence-based policing has to include this group directly in learning about and deciding on how such changes will occur, as well as activating and incentivizing them to carry out new approaches to policing.

This is, of course, much easier said than done. Traditional approaches to policing have created first-line supervisors in U.S. agencies that tend to focus on ensuring regulations and procedures are followed and reacting to problems after they occur. They are not often given the leadership, power, or resources to successfully accomplish many of the ideas we described in this book. Additionally, many are promoted directly from patrol, where they know and are friendly with officers that they now have to supervise and possibly discipline. First-line supervision is a challenging position, as sergeants have to not only command their subordinates' respect, but also convince officers to implement both basic commands and new ideas.

For supervisors who are interested in becoming more evidence based, we present a few suggestions based on our experiences working with first-line supervisors. Many will be obvious to the supervisors who are reading this, but these simple activities can help supervisors and their squads institutionalize a more evidence-based approach:

1. Be the point of knowledge acquisition, training, and mentorship on these ideas. This can be as simple as providing and explaining the Playbook, or even just providing officers with the three principles of good crime prevention from the Matrix. Supervisors can explain to officers what procedural justice or implicit bias means, and what it means for them. Use the "refreshers" in the Playbook (see Chapter 11) for learning modules, or read a quick summary or one-pager on a study and discuss it. We also caution first-line supervisors to be careful about *how* they talk about all of these topics. Your officers watch you carefully to see if you buy into and support new ideas.

2. Keep up with new knowledge and keep your officers regularly informed. Consider a working-group approach with your units, meeting regularly to determine conditions and problems, work on existing and new tactics, and develop ideas for implementing proactive activities in between calls for service. In these working groups, consider developing more plays for the Playbook tailored to the problems and conditions of your specific area. Try out new plays and discuss how they went or how they might be improved.

3. Analyze the amount of non-committed time in your squad on an average day (see our discussion of this as a training exercise in Chapter 10). Refocus your officers on the time in between calls for service and strategize about how to address that time systematically. Determine the style of each officer in your unit in terms of how they use their downtime and encourage them to adapt their own styles and interests to various evidence-based activities. Try out different types of evidence-based deployment for different officers or sets of officers. Some might be more amenable to in-depth problem-solving approaches, while others are better at patrolling hot spots, making contacts with high-risk people, or using prevention techniques like CPTED. This allows officers to exercise their discretion and various skill sets while still engaging in a wide range of effective policing practices.

4. Consider evaluating or at least carrying out the last "A" in the SARA process (assessment). Consider partnering with a researcher or analyst to assess different tactics and strategies your squad is doing. This doesn't just apply to patrol supervisors; detective sergeants and lieutenants can also carry out

evaluations and do evidence-based approaches (like Case of Places, or pulling levers/Ceasefire operations).

5. Acknowledge and recognize officers who practice evidence-based approaches and help them record their efforts on their performance sheets. Develop regular exchanges with officers, providing them with feedback and suggestions. Encourage officers to be proactive, place based, aware of high-risk actors, and problem oriented. Engage in regular dialogue with officers to discuss possible unintended consequences of their choices and actions with citizens and the community.

6. Help connect officers with crime analytic resources and show them how to use those resources in their daily deployment. If crime analysis is not readily available, help officers develop alternatives in which to identify problem places, people, or conditions. This might entail identifying specific addresses that generate high levels of calls for service, collecting and examining past incident reports, or asking community leaders about specific problem places or people. For example, officers who can access CAD information might be able to identify the top ten locations that get the most crime in their beat each shift. In some agencies, this type of information may also be available from automated "dashboards" created by the crime analysis unit.

7. Conduct plays from the Playbook with officers and conduct after-action debriefings after implementing those plays, discussing officers' perspectives on the success or failure of implementing certain plays. For exchanges with citizens, newer officers may not know how to engage with community groups; being a part of those exchanges may put the officer at ease and help informally mentor him or her on developing much-needed partnerships for problem solving.

Strategic Planning and Management

Another avenue for institutionalizing evidence-based policing includes strategic planning, management, and rethinking how managerial meetings (like Compstat) are run and used. These types of activities tend to take place at second-line supervisory levels or higher and involve long-term planning for the agency, broader deployment goals for patrol or investigations, and decisions on how resources might be allocated to achieve particular goals in the agency. While many decisions at this level involve activities outside of the realm of evidence-based policing, the goal is to infuse research into some decision-making systems of policing in various ways, either to plan strategies or to use management and planning systems as a conduit for training and knowledge exchange.

For example, one idea for institutionalizing the use of research for strategic planning involves using the Matrix in a manner similar to that described above in our discussion of promotions in Figure 14.1. This was demonstrated by Howard Veigas of the Derbyshire Police Service in the United Kingdom (see Veigas and Lum 2013). At that time, Veigas, a superintendent in the Derbyshire Police Service, was working with his command to re-evaluate their use of resources during a time of fiscal austerity in the United Kingdom. Veigas and his team were given the task of recommending which deployment programs might be worth keeping in Derbyshire and which might be ended due to fiscal constraints. Working with the first author as part of his educational program at the University of Cambridge, Veigas used the evidence in the Matrix to guide this decision making.

To carry out this task, Veigas used an approach known as "evidence assessment." Evidence assessment is a translational criminology method (see Chapter 15) first described for policing and security by Lum and Koper (2011). Evidence assessments use visualizations and organizations of research evidence (such as the Evidence-Based Policing Matrix) to make a rough estimate of the evidence base of a portfolio of tactics or strategies that have not been—and may not be for various reasons—evaluated through a scientific study. By comparing actual tactics used by an agency against existing evidence on effective practices, evidence assessments preliminarily help to (i) examine whether interventions are grounded in theories supported by research; (ii) determine the nature of interventions in their basic form (their "mechanisms of prevention"); and (iii) assess whether those mechanisms have similarities to interventions already evaluated. In turn, these steps allow the assessor to critically appraise whether an agency's deployment approach or tendencies are aligned with what is known to be effective. Evidence assessments can also identify misalignments between strategies and the totality of relevant evaluation research, stimulating discussion between an agency and its research partners about how the agency might strengthen its crime prevention and control measures. The goal of an evidence assessment is not to provide definitive answers as to whether an agency's practices are effective; only rigorous evaluation using sound scientific methods can attempt that. However, results from an evidence assessment can help an agency judge whether its practices are more or less likely to be effective. [1]

---

[1] Evidence-assessments also help to suggest where more information, data, evaluation, and analysis are needed to design a more effective portfolio of interventions. Lum and Koper (2007, 2011) first used evidence assessments to answer the question of whether criminologists might contribute to thinking about the effectiveness of counterterrorism measures. Since little to no publicly available evaluation evidence exists on many counterterrorism measures, the idea of evidence assessments is to use existing policing and crime prevention research, distil effective strategies down to their prevention mechanisms, and then examine whether counterterrorism interventions that share similar prevention mechanisms might have a higher potential of being effective. Since then, Lum, Gill, Cave et al. (2011a) have applied this approach to assess the potential effectiveness of Transportation Security Administration activities at airports; Gill, Lum, Cave et al. (2012) used the method to examine a number of crime prevention programs for the City of Seattle; and Lum, Cave, and Nichols (2013) conducted an evidence assessment on the Federal Protective Service's building security tactics.

The example of mapping sergeants' activities shown in Figure 14.1 above is one example of an evidence assessment of a patrol sergeant's deployment portfolio. Veigas wished to do this with an entire police agency's patrol activities. In the case the Derbyshire Police Service, Veigas first identified twenty-two deployment strategies used by the police service that needed to be prioritized. This exercise itself was a valuable activity, as police agencies often use a wide variety of strategies and tactics that may or may not be officially documented. These included a range of community-oriented policing tactics (e.g., knock-and-talks, newsletters, community briefings); special operations for specific problems (e.g., drunk driving, gangs); patrol operations (e.g., hot spots policing, foot patrols, reacting to 999 calls), and the like. Previously, decisions about which programs to keep were made by commanders based on a broad range of factors, including popularity with officers or citizens, commander preferences, politics, or even best guesses about intervention effectiveness. As one might imagine, such an approach to strategic decision making could put some interventions at risk if they were viewed as unpopular, difficult to accomplish, or unexciting.

Instead, Veigas determined the specific mechanism of prevention for each of these interventions, along the three axes of the Matrix described in Chapter 3. Veigas then mapped Derbyshire's patrol tactics into the Matrix along these dimensions, comparing them against the Matrix. This comparison is shown in Figure 14.2 and is described in Veigas and Lum (2013).

From this evidence assessment and mapping of Derbyshire's activities, a number of observations become apparent. First, patrol strategies in Derbyshire tended to be concentrated on targeting individuals and also carrying out neighborhood strategies. Strategies also were evenly split among interventions that were both general and more focused. Half of the patrol activities were reactive in nature, and less than one-third were proactive. Further, while nine tactics were hypothesized to have a greater chance of being effective given what we know about effective interventions, thirteen were assessed as not likely to be effective given what was known from evaluations of similar interventions. For those tactics that were person based, only one-third were assessed as likely to be promising. Thus, while there was some alignment of Derbyshire's patrol activities with the evidence, there was also misalignment, with many tactics having a greater risk of not being effective in preventing or reducing crime.[2]

Beyond providing Derbyshire with the evidence assessment itself, this exercise may also prove to be an effective institutionalization tool for other reasons. Such an assessment exposes the police to the evidence and requires agency commanders to carefully examine the types of activities on which they spend their time. Prior to this assessment, the police service had no distinct method of examining their entire portfolio of patrol activities in a systematic or objective

---

[2] In a related analysis, for example, Veigas also looked at the time spent on each activity. See Veigas (2010).

(a) The Matrix (at the time of this assessment)

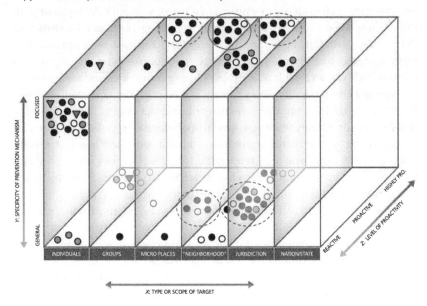

(b) Derbyshire's patrol strategies

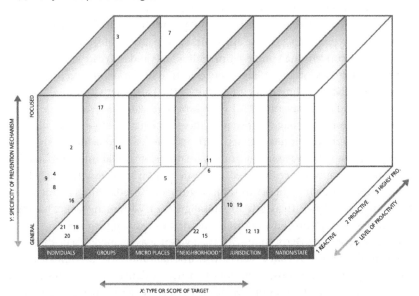

Figure 14.2 Evidence-Assessment of Derbyshire Police Service's Patrol Deployment Portfolio

The image in 14.2(b) is reprinted with permission of Oxford University Press, from *Policing: A Journal of Policy and Practice*, Volume 7, Issue 3, 2013, Howard Veigas and Cynthia Lum (Copyright © 2013, Oxford University Press).

way. This assessment thus afforded an opportunity for command staff to take a careful look at what they were doing to prevent crime and how resources were being used on potentially ineffective activities. Derbyshire's effort not only reflects the first time the Matrix was used in this way, but also provides a useful example of how research evidence might be institutionalized into strategic planning activities.[3]

Yet another way evidence-based policing might be institutionalized in strategic planning and management can be through meetings like Compstat. Having attended countless Compstat-like meetings in large, medium, and small agencies, we think it may be time for police to reconsider the format, substance, and objectives of these meetings. The philosophy behind Compstat of accountability, responsiveness, and transparency are all valuable to evidence-based policing. But at the same time, the obsessiveness with short-term crime trends, the continued focus on individuals and their apprehension, and the lack of dynamic learning, critical analysis, problem-solving, and active interaction and knowledge exchange in many of the meetings we have attended for the past twenty years is discouraging. However, Compstat meetings provide unique opportunities for introducing and using research and analytic evidence at the command level.

For example, departments can conduct evidence assessments like the ones shown in Figure 14.2 in real time in Compstat meetings as a way to stimulate dynamic discussions about the types of tactics the agency uses and the justification for their use. Compstat might also be used as a forum to discuss and debate new research about contemporary issues or tactical ideas and innovations. Organizations like our Center for Evidence-Based Crime Policy often disseminate information about new research in various forms, including straightforward and police-friendly "one-pagers," short videos, or through symposia and workshops. Meetings could shift from recitations of statistics or one-way question-and-answers by high command to greater use of Compstat meetings as learning environments that use these free resources to prompt these discussions. Such meetings could also involve both internal and external analysts and researchers.

Additionally, Compstat meetings might be used to build new interventions around knowledge from evidence and research. For example, crime analysts could contribute not only by identifying crime hot spots, but by carrying out Case of Place investigations to share in management meetings so that commanders can better tailor strategies for specific problems. These activities can help to target, track, and test activities as suggested by Sherman (2013). Such meetings might also be forums in which assessments of community reaction and receptivity towards an agency's activities might be presented and discussed, so as to strategize about improving community relationships.

---

[3] See https://www.youtube.com/watch?v=R11zFPYP7fg for a video presentation by Howard Veigas of his efforts.

Finally, an essential part of strategic planning and management within an evidence-based paradigm is establishing strong partnerships with outside researchers. These efforts are well underway by many in the field. In the United States, these partnerships are currently supported by funding from the federal National Institute of Justice and Bureau of Justice Assistance, or informally by police agencies themselves. In Scotland, these partnerships are more formalized between the national police service and the Scottish Institute for Policing Research.[4] Such partnerships help agencies become more familiar with the evidence base in policing and can also provide agencies with access to specialized expertise on program evaluation, evidence assessments, and research that may not be readily available within the law enforcement agency. Research partnerships are also essential for maintaining and growing the evidence-base for policing for subjects of direct concern to the police, such as officer wellness and safety. Agencies successful at implementing evidence-based policing are open to these partnerships, as shown in our discussion of leadership below. And, in a time of austerity and tight budgets for both police and universities, leveraging one another to improve practices, shake up traditions and cultures, and provide meaningful experiences to advance each other can be a win–win for all involved.

Engaging the Public

An additional organizational adjustment that starts with an agency's top leadership but should extend throughout the organization is the establishment of systems and processes for regularly engaging the public as a means of enhancing both performance and accountability. An evidence-based policing agency engages the public in various ways that go beyond traditional community policing approaches. For one, its personnel will care about citizens' views on community problems and police activity, and they will collect systematic data to gauge these views on a regular basis. Data might be collected through general community surveys and/or surveys of people who have had recorded contacts with police. Police might also assess community views through analysis of complaints data or by soliciting regular and systematic input from community groups. Such approaches are in keeping with the community policing philosophy discussed in Chapter 6. Evidence-based agencies also share and actively discuss those findings with academy trainees, officers receiving in-service training, and during managerial meetings. As they plan crime prevention strategies, they also strategize about how to target, test, and track their efforts in improving their interactions and legitimacy with the public.

Also, as discussed in Chapters 4 through 6, successful crime prevention approaches often involve engagement with the community in the analysis of

---

[4] See http://www.sipr.ac.uk/.

problems and the development of problem-solving strategies that apply prevention as well as enforcement. Community partners in these endeavors include other criminal justice and government agencies, community groups, businesses, and other residents. An evidence-based agency will also try to inform the public on the merits of evidence-based policing approaches through solid communication channels with the public. Consistent with the community policing philosophy, this serves important purposes of public accountability and transparency. Moreover, developing an outside constituency for evidence-based policing, particularly among elected officials, may also help police leaders to institutionalize the evidence-based policing philosophy for the longer term.

Leading with Evidence

As we have emphasized throughout this book, evidence-based policing is no small nor easy task. It requires a great deal of both individual officer commitment and systemic changes, as we have described. One important and often amorphous quality of police agencies who are successful in implementing evidence-based policing is good leadership. But leadership in an evidence-based policing paradigm looks different than leadership in a traditional or standard policing model. Institutionalizing research into law enforcement organizations therefore requires rethinking what "good leadership" entails (just like it requires rethinking the definition of "good policing").

We are not police leaders and are certainly not experts at running police agencies. Further, there is no doubt that being a leader in policing is a difficult and sometimes thankless task, and one in which high turnover is common. Thus, rather than theorize about what might make a good leader in an evidence-based paradigm, we instead share real examples of individuals who have succeeded and excelled in evidence-based policing. These individuals can be found in the *Evidence-Based Policing Hall of Fame*,[5] an award we established in 2010 to recognize leaders working to advance evidence-based policing. Our goal in creating the Hall of Fame was to recognize excellent examples of leadership in evidence-based policing, and to use the Hall as a translation tool for others to view examples of what such leadership might look like in practice. We describe some of the members here to show the high level of commitment needed by police leaders to advance evidence-based policing and to illustrate common themes that contribute to these leaders' success.

For example, some leaders have been instrumental in supporting and seeing the completion of groundbreaking research studies that have impacted policing and the evidence base for policing. Anthony Bouza, as the police chief in Minneapolis, helped to facilitate the famous Minneapolis hots spots study (see Sherman and Weisburd 1995), the Minneapolis domestic violence experiment

---

[5] See http://cebcp.org/hall-of-fame/.

(see Sherman and Berk 1984), and the Minneapolis RECAP experiment (see Sherman, Buerger, Gartin et al. 1989b). Another example is Hubert Williams, who as police director in Newark, New Jersey, made possible the famous Newark Foot Patrol Experiment, as well as the National Institute of Justice-funded fear reduction experiments (see Police Foundation 1981 and Pate, Wycoff, Skogan et al. 1986, respectively). Frank Gajewski initiated a series of partnerships with researchers at Rutgers University and the Police Foundation to advance policing in Jersey City, New Jersey, leading to the Jersey City Drug Market Analysis Experiment and then later the Jersey City Problem-Oriented Policing Experiment (see Braga, Weisburd, Waring et al. 1999). Weisburd's major study on displacement and diffusion was also facilitated by Gajewski (see Weisburd et al. 2006).

More examples of those advancing major studies of policing include Ian Stewart of the Queensland Police Service. Stewart and his command were responsible for implementing the Queensland Community Engagement Trial (QCET), the world's first randomized field trial investigating the effects of police–citizen encounters on citizen perceptions of police (see Mazerolle, Bennett, Manning et al. 2013). More recently, Tony Farrar was instrumental in initiating the first experimental evaluation of body-worn cameras (Ariel, Farrar, and Sutherland 2015), which paved the way for numerous other body-worn camera studies. Additionally, Theron Bowman facilitated the now famous shift length study by Amendola, Weisburd, Hamilton et al. (2011).

Some hall-of-famers have advanced evidence-based policing in ways that reflect fundamental shifts in policing deployment paradigms. Darrel Stephens, for example, is widely recognized as being one of the most innovative police chiefs in modern U.S. policing, and served as Chief of Police for two well-known progressive departments (Charlotte-Mecklenburg, North Carolina, and Newport News, Virginia). He is best known for advancing problem-oriented policing in the United States during his tenure in the Newport News Police Department and at the Police Executive Research Forum (where he served as Executive Director for several years). In particular, his leadership in advancing problem-oriented policing in the United States contributed to advancing evidence-based policing, and he also developed the problem-oriented policing conferences, which were the first to recognize empirical, analytic work in policing. During his tenure as police chief in different agencies, he was well known for regularly welcoming researchers into his agencies. His openness to researchers, inclusion of lower ranks in advanced problem solving, and push for infrastructure that could facilitate crime analysis, evidence-based policing, and problem solving were key to his leadership style and success in evidence-based policing.

Another example is Charles Ramsey. Ramsey served as police commissioner of the Philadelphia Police Department, and previously as chief of police in Washington, D.C. He is well-known for his expertise in community policing, and for co-chairing President Obama's Task Force on Twenty-First Century

Policing with former Assistant Attorney General Laurie O. Robinson.[6] His leadership in evidence-based policing comes from supporting evaluations and research partnerships throughout his career and then implementing those findings as police chief in Chicago, Washington, D.C., and Philadelphia (see, e.g., Ratcliffe, Tamiguchi, Groff et al. 2011). In Chicago, for example, he was instrumental in designing and implementing with Wesley Skogan the Chicago Alternative Policing Strategies (CAPS), which became one of the most well-known models of community policing in practice (see Skogan 2006a; Skogan and Hartnett 1997).

Some individuals have pressed for evidence-based policing reforms from major leadership positions in the United States and the United Kingdom. Peter Neyroud, who served as the Chief Constable of the Thames Valley Police Service, continued to advance evidence-based policing as the Chief Executive of the National Policing Improvement Agency (NPIA) in the United Kingdom, where he became a champion of changing policing culture and standards using research, tackling the more difficult systems-based approach to evidence-based policing described above. This style of leadership in carrying out internal assessments of police activity on a regular basis and also taking a leadership role in pushing for evidence-based policing, is also a trait of Alex Murray of the West Midlands Police Service in England, who leads the society for evidence-based policing in the United Kingdom. Similarly, Denis O'Connor worked as the Vice President of the Association of Chief Police Officers (ACPO) in the United Kingdom, leading the piloting of the U.K.'s National Reassurance Policing Programme, the pre-cursor to the Neighbourhood Policing Programme (see Tuffin, Morris, and Poole 2006), while also advocating for more evidence-based approaches from higher leadership positions.

James Bueermann, currently the President of the Police Foundation in Washington, D.C., served as the Chief of Police in the Redlands, CA Police Department, where his efforts are an example of a leader engaging in fundamental philosophical discussions about the roles and functions of policing with his officers. His push to make research a regular part of the strategic planning and assessment of his agency led to a number of key studies of crime and policing (some which are in the Matrix). Bueermann tried to "flip" patrol as we described in Chapter 4 by transitioning his entire police department from a beat patrol system to a crime concentration or hot spots policing approach. He also focused on training officers in evidence-based practices and making knowledge of research a part of officer incentives and promotions.

Another national leader for evidence-based policing in the United States has been James Burch. While serving as the director of the federal Bureau of Justice Assistance, Burch advanced efforts to promote evidence-based practices through federal funding to states and localities, and he was an advocate for programs

---

[6] See http://www.cops.usdoj.gov/policingtaskforce.

like the Matrix and Matrix Demonstration Projects. At the Bureau of Alcohol, Tobacco, Firearms and Explosives, he also tried to incorporate evidence-based policing ideas into the Bureau's practices. He continues these efforts now as a vice-president of the Police Foundation, where he has worked with the authors to create a web-based evidence-based policing "app" that officers can use to access the Matrix, the Playbook, and other research resources from the field.

Others have shown high levels of commitment to evidence-based policing through sustained partnerships with researchers, helping to not only generate research but use research in practice. Edward Davis, for example, as the commissioner of the City of Boston, and previously the Superintendent of Police in Lowell, Massachusetts, established a strong relationship with researcher Anthony Braga, and many of their research efforts appear in the Matrix. Thus, in Davis's case, his leadership focused on generating evidence for his agencies through the use of an embedded researcher so as to reduce violence in Lowell and Boston using Ceasefire and pulling levers approaches (see Braga 2013).

Peter Martin, currently the Deputy Commissioner of the Queensland Police Service in Queensland, Australia, has actively supported research being conducted in his police service (and played a role in doing this research) and is also is known for strengthening long-term research partnerships with local universities and researchers. Martin's work on developing evidence-based guidance to help officers engage citizens, deal with major events, and control use of force are examples of institutionalizing evidence into strategic policy making.

A similar example of this systemic approach can be found in Hassan Aden, who served as chief of the Greenville Police Department in North Carolina and previously as deputy chief of the Alexandria Police Department in Virginia. Aden was instrumental in helping to implement and support one of the earliest randomized controlled studies of license plate readers discussed in Chapter 7 (see Lum, Willis (Hibdon), Cave et al. 2011c) and also supported the first random-sample community survey gauging community perceptions and concerns about license plate readers. In addition to helping to generate research in Alexandria, he transformed his patrol sector from a reactive beat patrol approach to a hot spots approach, and was one of the earliest individuals to use the Koper Curve principle in practice (see Aden and Koper 2011). He also led the development of a performance measurement system that tracked officers' time and activities in designated hot spots for use in performance appraisals.

Yet another example is Edward Flynn of the Milwaukee Police Department. Most recently, Chief Flynn helped facilitate the first long-term (twenty-three-year) follow-up of Sherman and Berk's (1984) Milwaukee Domestic Violence Experiment, which tested the effects of arrest and other approaches for handling misdemeanor domestic violence incidents (see Sherman and Harris 2013, 2015). But prior to this, Flynn focused on reorienting his police agency toward more evidence-based approaches, bringing in researchers to expose all of his officers to the evidence, and then implementing initiatives to reduce fear of crime, establish place-based and hot spots policing strategies, and reduce firearms crime using Koper Curve strategies, homicide incident reviews (see Azrael, Braga, and O'Brien 2013), and investigation of the sources of guns used in crime. He is known for his strong and public stance supporting science and research, even when it may not be popular. Similarly, Tim Hegarty also tried to infuse evidence-based approaches into patrol operations, sometimes in spite of pushbacks (another common theme among all of the Hall-of-Famers). For example, he supported a hot spots Koper Curve patrol study in Manhattan, Kansas that was discussed in Chapter 4. His efforts advanced our understanding of how evidence-based policing might work in smaller agencies, which presents different types of challenges from big agencies like Milwaukee.

Some members of the Hall of Fame are not police chiefs but have played significant roles in advancing evidence-based policing among their peers. Many of these individuals are crime analysts or planners, such as Jamie Roush, Renee Mitchell, John Kapinos (formerly of the Fairfax County, Virginia Police Department), and Sean Malinowski (Los Angeles Police Department), and some are commanders with analytic skills, such as Roberto Santos (Port St. Lucie, Florida Police Department). These leaders have worked to implement evidence-based policing from an analytic or planning perspective, developing deployment or training programs, new research, partnerships, and strategies to bring more knowledge into their agencies. One important trait that ties the leaders in the Hall of Fame together is not only their support of research partnerships, but their support of analysts and strengthening crime analysis capabilities in their own departments. Micheal Edwards' efforts to implement evidence-based and data-driven approaches with Jamie Roush in the Jacksonville, Florida Police Department were particularly notable.

What all of the evidence-based policing Hall-of-Famers have in common is their commitment to the multiple aspects of evidence-based policing we have discussed throughout this book. These innovators know the evidence, how it is generated, why it is important, and when to be cautious about research, as we described in Chapters 1, 2, and 3. Many are actively engaged in generating new evidence for the field as well. As we emphasized in Chapter 2, good evidence-based policing leaders need not be methodologists, but they value what science can bring to the policing profession and are actively involved in generating new knowledge. They also are able to take complex ideas from research, such as that discussed in Chapters 4–7, and turn them into meaningful and digestible forms for their commanders and officers. These leaders of evidence-based policing also focus on institutionalizing research into practice, in various ways, including normalizing ideas and values of evidence-based policing into their agencies. These elements of leadership are different from leadership requirements of the standard model of policing, not only because of the different knowledge and skill sets required, but also because it requires a special type of leadership to challenge the core values and status quo of policing. Because of this, leaders in evidence-based policing also have to have—unselfishly—longer-term horizons. The leaders developing research and infrastructure for evidence-based policing today are doing it to strengthen policing more generally for tomorrow, and may not see significant changes during their tenures.

Conclusion

Evidence-based policing holds that research, evaluation, analysis, and scientific processes should have a place at the table in law enforcement decision making about tactics, strategies, and policies. But science cannot stand on its own in policing. Thus, we hope we made our point clear: Evidence-based policing is not just about evaluating police practices or doing analysis. It is also the process of translating that knowledge into digestible and usable forms, as well as institutionalizing research processes and findings into everyday policing systems. As we said at the beginning, evidence-based policing is a challenging path. But it is also rewarding. Using good information to make decisions can better connect policing actions and resource allocation to outcomes that police and their communities seek.

Part Three of our book shows that achieving evidence-based policing cannot be done with ad hoc, temporary, or short-term goals, but requires fundamental adjustments to core values and systems in policing long entrenched in history, tradition, and policies. Evidence-based policing thus requires agencies and their leaders to reimagine and rebuild policing in a different way, and then strategize, plan, and recreate infrastructure to support these adjustments. The systems and infrastructure that need to be reimagined are the ones most entrenched in the daily lives of personnel, including training, deployment, supervision, performance metrics and accountability, rewards, promotions, management, strategic planning, and leadership.

Changing systems also manifests itself in adjustments to organizational culture and officer attitudes. The culture and attitudes of an agency are hard to measure, but there are many litmus tests an agency can use. Such tests are especially useful at the unranked patrol officer or detective level. For example, litmus tests in patrol for evidence-based policing could include how officers use their non-committed time (see Chapter 4, 5, 6, and 11); their units of investigations (Chapter 12); what officers consider to be effective policing practices for reducing crime and maintaining citizen trust (see Chapter 8); the balance of proactive and reactive deployment in patrol (see Wu and Lum 2016); or how technologies are used (see Chapter 7 and 13). Another litmus test to gauge how aligned an agency is with evidence-based policing is how crime analysts are treated and utilized, or whether researchers have regular interactions with the agency (see Chapter 13). Yet another litmus test is to ask officers and first-line supervisors what they think they need to do to be rewarded, or promoted, and to examine the substance of training. Such litmus tests and others can also help determine whether evidence-based policing is institutionalized into common systems of policing we have discussed in these chapters.

Policing is a complicated, intricate institution that has to fulfill a number of goals in a democratic society. On the one hand, the police must enforce the law, prevent crime, and ensure safety, potentially putting their lives at risk in the process. On the other hand, they have to do all of these things lawfully, in ways that are fair and respectful and don't undermine their legitimacy (and authority). To add to this, we are also asking the police to be accountable to science. But as we write this, policing is also in crisis. In the United States, police are confronted by challenges to their authority in the wake of what seems to be a wave of shootings of and by police, accusations of bias and incompetence, and federal investigations. Across the world, police departments were hit hard by the recession of the late 2000s as well as the rapid development and adoption of new and untested technologies. It is fair to say that in this environment, we suspect police might not be as motivated or open to the ideas of evidence-based policing described in this book.

At the same time, we think this is an opportune and fruitful time for policing. At no other time in the history of policing have officers and agencies been as open as they are now to research, analysis, and new ways of thinking about law enforcement. We see this optimism and interest in every agency we visit and with the many officers and analysts with whom we work. Officers don't always agree with us, and we've spent many hours debating and defending research and evidence-based policing. But agencies have been willing to listen, and many have been willing to try out and test new ideas on how to translate and institutionalize research into practice. Equally important, researchers including ourselves have adjusted our perspectives about the role and nature of science because of these interactions. These exchanges also have started to reshape our academic disciplines and what types of scholarly activity is considered valuable.

We hope we have convinced the reader of the merits to evidence-based policing while also illustrating tangible ways to achieve it.

PART FOUR

Researchers and
the Advancement
of Evidence-Based Policing

15

TRANSLATIONAL CRIMINOLOGY
Ideas for Researchers

Much of our book has been geared to law enforcement officers who are in various stages of implementing evidence-based policing. But researchers are equally important in this venture. Not only have they been central to the generation of the evidence base for policing, but they have also been instrumental in institutionalizing research into practice, developing crime analysis and research and planning units, providing opportunities for police personnel to learn about and do research, informally educating agencies about research findings, and finding creative ways to increase the receptivity of officers to research.

Thus, we close our volume by presenting ideas for researchers on how they might continue to advance evidence-based policing from their vantage point. Specifically, we focus on two themes that can be broadly subsumed under a concept called "translational criminology," which we will define below. The first is that researchers can contribute to the study of the use of research and the effectiveness of strategies and interventions designed to increase research use in practice—i.e., the evidence for implementing evidence-based policing. The second perhaps presupposes the first—that researchers can develop strategies and interventions to increase research use in the first place.

What is Translational Criminology?

Criminologists, sociologists, and others studying criminal justice have long devoted their study to two fundamental and arguably inseparable questions: (i) Why do people commit crime (or, why does crime occur); and (ii) what should be done about it? However, as Francis Cullen (2011), a former president of the American Society of Criminology has pointed out, the second question has incurred much more disciplinary skepticism. For example, Travis Hirschi, a leading theorist in juvenile delinquency and the field, offered a decidedly negative opinion of this area of study, which he disdainfully labeled "administrative criminology" or "practical criminology." He characterized it as atheoretical, lacking historical grounding or academic memory, and contributing to government repression of citizens (Hirschi 1993). Although Hirschi's position is likely not dominant today, it would be fair to say that the status of practice-focused research, publications, and journals is not as high as that of scholarly work engaged in tests of theories of crime.

One might argue, however, that criminology would have been half-baked had it only focused on etiology; a natural extension of explaining why a phenomenon occurs—especially one that is viewed as a social negative—is determining what should be done about it. Indeed, the study of how these two areas of inquiry are connected and what that connection means to the practice of criminal justice has a long history in our discipline. When Shaw, McKay, and their colleagues first mapped out residences of juvenile delinquents in Chicago, they did so not only to explain what they believed was the cause of delinquency, but also to develop the Chicago Area Projects to do something about crime problems (Shaw and McKay 1942; see also Bernard, Snipes, and Gerould 2010; Sampson 2011). Those studying developmental criminology not only worked to understand why juveniles commit crime but also were motivated to develop more tailored approaches to combating delinquency and antisocial behavior at different stages of the life course (Loeber and Stouthamer-Loeber 1996; Sampson and Laub 1993). And, those studying crime concentrations and hot spots (see, e.g., Sherman and Weisburd 1995; Sherman, Gartin, and Buerger 1989a; Weisburd 2002) not only increased our knowledge of deterrence theory and place-based criminology, but also facilitated the development of a police deployment model to reduce crime. These are only three of many examples that abound in our field.

This tradition of linking theoretical and practice-oriented research in criminology and then using that research to inform policy is the foundation for translational criminology (see Laub 2011). Translational criminology is the theory and study of how the products of criminological and criminal justice research turn into outputs, tools, programs, interventions, and actions in criminal justice practice. While evidence-based policing and translational criminology are related, they are different. Recall, our vision of evidence-based policing includes not only the generation of research knowledge about policing (interventions, organization, behavior, etc.), but also the translation, use, implementation, and institutionalization of those findings into practice. Translational criminology is both the study of those latter processes and the creation of strategies for research use that in turn can be implemented and studied.

What follows is a discussion about these two themes of translational criminology with ideas for researchers on advancing evidence-based policing. Researchers have already done a great deal to advance evidence-based policing, especially in the area of evaluating policing interventions and understanding police behavior and organizations. However, we advocate for more research in an area where there is little research knowledge: the evidence for implementing and institutionalizing evidence-based policing as we have described it. Second, we conclude with activities that researchers might consider exploring, in a translational criminology mode, to advance evidence-based policing.

Building the Evidence for Evidence-Based Policing

Police researchers and their practitioner partners have done a great deal to build the knowledge base about police functions, organizations, activities, behaviors, and relationships and interactions with citizens. And advocates for evidence-based practices in policing have tried many ways to institutionalize research use and increase its receptivity that run the gamut of ideas in this book. But what is the evidence for the effectiveness of these activities? Do some translation efforts work better than others? If so, why? If research is not being used, why is this the case, and what can be done to increase the receptivity of research in practice?

Without a reliable knowledge base about *how* we can translate research into practice effectively and what leads to successful evidence-based practice, much of the effort to increase the use of research outputs in the evidence-based crime policy arena may be viewed as best guesses or best practices based on anecdotal experience. Perhaps more appropriately phrased, they may not be evidence based. Specifically, we need to develop and test theories about how research turns into policing outputs, and we need to test interventions that attempt to achieve translation or increase receptivity to research. We also need to understand what the protective and risk factors are that facilitate or hinder translating and implementing science in policing. Questions about how research impacts practice and how long it takes (and whether such processes might be sped up) continue to be unclear and underdeveloped.

More specifically, translational research for evidence-based policing can include a wide variety of topic areas and specific questions. For example, what factors lead law enforcement agencies and their personnel to be receptive to—or demand—research knowledge? Building research evidence for receptivity requires research knowledge on how practitioners receive knowledge from research and what influences their receptivity and use of that information. It also requires understanding what types of institutional infrastructure and systems are needed for agencies and their officers to be receptive to research. For instance, perhaps adjusting rewards and incentives structures is much more effective and cost-efficient in getting police to act in ways that are evidence based than is investing in expensive training modules developed by specialists. Or, perhaps both are needed in conjunction.

We also would need to know more about the best mechanisms by which to translate or disseminate research ideas into practice. For example, does our Matrix work to translate research to practice? How about Crimesolutions.gov[1] or the Global Policing Database?[2] Is training the way to go? What types of partnerships seem to work best to increase research receptivity? Finally, can we measure the "gap" between research and practice in an empirical way, and can we document this gap over time? What influences the size of the gap across agencies or knowledge areas? What reduces this gap over time?

Translational criminology questions might also focus on the supply or generation of research. For example, what motivates the development of certain types of research in policing? Is it the needs and pressures of practitioners, or the needs and interests of researchers? What academic infrastructures inhibit or encourage scholars to engage with practitioners? What forms can research take that make it more digestible and useable? Can funding programs that support researcher–practitioner collaboration (like Smart Policing and Project Safe Neighborhoods in the United States) significantly influence the generation of usable research?

Translational criminology also includes the evaluation of tools and ideas that are created to implement evidence-based policing or institutionalize research into practice. All of the tools and ideas in this book are subject to testing, including the Matrix, the Playbook, Case of Places, ideas for academy and field training, and activities for supervisors, leaders, and strategic planning. Just as we evaluate interventions used to reduce crime or improve police–citizen relations, so too can these activities be assessed for their ability to achieve evidence-based policing.

Policing scholars may take some cues from other fields about how some of these questions might be studied. Weiss and Bucuvalas (1980) empirically examined receptivity to mental health research by decision makers through interviews about their views and use of research, and by examining whether factors such as attitudes, education, experience, and personal characteristics influence personal receptivity to research. Nutley, Walter, and Davies (2007) lay out different taxonomies of research use as well as different models of translation. These can also be examined and tested empirically in a criminal justice setting.

In policing, we already have some examples to build upon. A logical place to start might be examining the numerous research–practitioner partnerships in policing that have occurred over decades, as done by Alpert, Rojek, and Hansen

---

[1] See https://www.crimesolutions.gov/.

[2] See http://www.gpd.uq.edu.au/search.php.

(2013), Grieco, Vovak, and Lum (2014), or Rojek, Alpert, and Smith (2012a, see also Rojek, Smith, and Alpert 2012b). Some partnerships focus specifically on developing knowledge about the nature of crime or police processes with little expectation that research outputs will turn into actual police tactics once the research projects are complete. Other partnerships ground themselves in a training and technical assistance approach. Still others are ad hoc or are created by accident, with like-minded individuals from research and practice stumbling upon each other by happenstance. Understanding why partnerships develop, how they work, which types work best, what types of research come from which partnerships, and to what extent those partnerships turn into actual police practice are fruitful areas of translational research.

Another type of translational research we covered in Chapter 8, and which is also influenced by Weiss, Nutley, and colleagues, is the study of receptivity. What makes police personnel and organizations receptive to or dismissive of research? Here, both within-agency and across-agency research are important. For example, Lum, Telep, Koper et al. (2012) and Telep and Lum (2014) report on multiple agency-wide surveys asking questions related to officer interest, use, understanding, and knowledge about research and research processes. Receptivity studies like these can help us better understand how much practitioners know about research, how open they are to ideas from research, and whether they value scientific knowledge.

Case studies may also prove useful, especially across agencies that have consistently used or rejected a particular type of scientific evidence. For example, Birkeland, Murphy-Graham, and Weiss (2005) examined why evaluation findings of DARE (Drug Abuse Resistance Education) are often ignored by schools (see also Weiss, Murphy-Graham, and Birkeland 2005). They studied eight schools, six of which had continued to implement DARE despite negative evaluation results. As part of their study, they examined the reasons given for not abandoning DARE (and therefore, in a sense, rejecting the research findings). Some schools and police officials felt that the evaluations were measuring unrealistic program goals. Others felt that the evaluations overlooked the program's ability to build relationships between police, students, and their families.

Implementation research, an area of study in which scholars often use ethnographies and case studies, focuses on knowledge that arises from the implementation of evidence-based practices or other interventions that are being tested in the field. Many evaluation studies have already examined the factors that may contribute to successful or not-so-successful implementation and maintenance of evidence-based interventions. Some of these studies provide extensive documentation of either the implementation of a research design or the implementation of a practice based on scientific research. Implementation research is often better than other types of research at raising specific questions of interest in translational criminology.

Finally, police researchers are very familiar with program and outcome evaluation research, which are briefly described in Chapter 2. Those tools can also be used to study the questions above to build the evidence base for implementing evidence-based policing.

Creating Strategies and Mechanisms for the Use of Research

Much of our book is focused on this second area of translational criminology—creating the strategies, mechanisms, and tools that facilitate the use of research. As we emphasize above, these tools also have to be evaluated and studied for their outcome effectiveness and implementation feasibility. But here we give police researchers some ideas, based on the activities we engage in, about creating mechanisms for research use. We return to Nutley et al. (2007), whose research review in the areas of public health, education, social work, and criminal justice has found five mechanisms that seem to emerge across the knowledge use literature. These are *dissemination, interaction, social influence, facilitation,* and *incentives and reinforcement.* As examples of these strategies, we highlight specific efforts that we have engaged in as researchers, many as part of our broader efforts for the Center for Evidence-Based Crime Policy (CEBCP).[3] To their ideas, we also add some additional thoughts about the need for researchers to focus on *developing operational guidance* for practitioners in the spirit of what some refer to as the "engineering tradition" (Rossi, Lipsey, and Freeman 2004, 391).

Dissemination

Dissemination focuses on efforts to distribute research to practitioners, and to turn their eyes toward this outside source of knowledge. Because evidence-based policing is not simply about generating research knowledge, but also using that research, a translational approach to dissemination means that evidence-based policing researchers have to find other ways to disseminate research that extend beyond what Rossi et al. (2004) call "primary" dissemination (381) to more "secondary" dissemination options. Primary dissemination includes disseminating our work in scholarly journal articles and technical reports. Secondary dissemination includes distributing information through avenues created for wider audiences of stakeholders such as *The Police Chief* (International Association of Chiefs of Police), or *Translational Criminology Magazine* (the magazine of CEBCP, founded and edited by the first author).

Secondary written dissemination can also take the form of easy-to-digest summaries of research that are freely accessible to police practitioners. Many officers

---

[3] See http://www.cebcp.org. The first author is the Director of the Center for Evidence-Based Crime Policy at George Mason University and created many of these ideas as part of the translational criminology core of that center.

do not have library access to journal articles, nor have the time or specialized knowledge to read them. One idea we developed in the CEBCP is to distribute "one-pagers,"[4] which reduce complex and lengthy research reports and journal articles into easy-to-read one-pagers. For example, take the Koper Curve article (Koper 1995). This article uses statistical jargon and a research design that may be hard for practitioners to understand. Thus, we created a much-shortened one-pager that summarizes the main points of the Koper Curve.[5] These one-pagers are also similar to the individual summaries of research we set up for each study in the Matrix. For example, Rosenfeld, Deckard, and Blackburn's (2014) study on the effects of directed patrol and self-initiated enforcement activities in our field's top journal, *Criminology*, is described in an operational way for law enforcement in our Matrix, as is every other study in the Matrix.[6]

Dissemination can also be achieved by creating panels, briefings, symposia, and conferences for practitioners. These forums provide a place to learn about the most up-to-date and cutting-edge research, as well as to network with others. For example, in the CEBCP we have developed "congressional briefings" in which research experts present short, eight-minute briefs of research at the U.S. Capitol on a variety of policy topics of interest to practitioners and policymakers.[7] Similarly, we developed the CEBCP annual symposium because no national conference existed that was freely available, that focused specifically on evidence-based crime policy, and that brought together researchers and practitioners to discuss practice-based research and translation. Researchers should also consider presenting at practitioner conferences to disseminate their work, such as the annual conferences held by the International Association of Chiefs of Police or the International Association of Crime Analysts.

Another form of dissemination we have developed are workshops in evidence-based policing, some which are supported by our funding from the Bureau of Justice Assistance for the Matrix Demonstration Projects, and some of which have been supported by law enforcement agencies and other organizations. Unlike conferences, symposia, or congressional briefings, workshops provide the opportunity to dig deeply into explaining the definition of evidence-based policing, the evidence base of policing, and translation and institutionalization efforts. Indeed, a great deal of this book began with ideas for workshops!

Many of the free congressional briefings, workshops, symposia, and special lectures we have created through the Matrix projects or in the CEBCP have been filmed. Videos are also an inexpensive way for agencies to bring specialized

---

[4] See http://cebcp.org/one-pagers/.

[5] See http://cebcp.org/wp-content/onepagers/KoperHotSpots.pdf/.

[6] See http://cebcp.org/evidence-based-policing/the-matrix/micro-places/micro-places-rosenfeld-et-al-2014-directed-patrol-plus-enforcement/.

[7] Examples of these briefings can be found here: http://cebcp.org/outreach-symposia-and-briefings/#cb.

outsider knowledge into academies and in-service training. For example, in the CEBCP we have a freely available "video library" which anyone can access to learn about research.[8] As we discussed in Chapter 14, we created some of these videos under the Matrix Demonstration Projects with the goal that they are used as points of discussion for more dynamic Compstat meetings, or for mini-training sessions at roll calls and within relevant units. Some of these videos are specifically designed for training, such as the training on the use of crime analysis for operations or commanders.[9] Other videos are simply short, practitioner-oriented summaries of significant research evidence.[10] These short videos, like the one-pagers, can be watched or read quickly in an officer's non-committed time or at the beginning of roll calls or management meetings. Researchers might consider partnering with agencies to create more videos to help disseminate knowledge to the field.

Whether by one-pager, panel discussion, video, or magazine article, disseminating research using digestible, practitioner-friendly forms can be challenging. As academics, we are often unaccustomed to writing short, punchy, and interesting summaries of our work. A few important aspects of these summaries that researchers—including ourselves—often overlook are detailed descriptions of the interventions themselves, including how interventions were implemented. Short, bulleted conclusions and thoughts about what the research means to practitioners are also important. Researchers might consider partnering with practitioners to help with these tasks. Academics may find this challenging, as we also feel the need to cite to others, and discuss important nuances, exceptions, and limitations to our work. Maintaining integrity to our discipline and academic practices but at the same time effectively communicating our work to practitioners is therefore the main challenge for dissemination.

Interaction

The second mechanism that Nutley et al. (2007) describe as prevalent in effective research use strategies is interaction between researchers and practitioners. Researchers and practitioners can advance evidence-based policing by sharing the experience of building evidence together. We often take this idea for granted, given that almost all of the research in the Matrix was derived by researchers and practitioners partnering to carry out research projects in the field (as opposed to researchers obtaining data and analyzing it in a lab or office). But the interaction that occurs in field research is necessary for learning about evidence-based policing by both researchers and practitioners, and it is something that newer researchers may need help with. For researchers,

---

[8] See http://cebcp.org/cebcp-video-library/ or our YouTube site at https://www.youtube.com/user/clsMason.

[9] See, e.g., https://www.youtube.com/playlist?list=PLoaqclcHgvIi4zkWDi0ZJ829bQL4fbTvP).

[10] E.g., the Amendola, Weisburd, Hamiilton et al. (2011) shift length study video can be found here: https://www.youtube.com/watch?v=QGxKUYBANOA.

including practitioners in every stage of program evaluation is an essential way to increase this interaction. This may mean including them in key decisions about the research process and design, and finding ways to increase the trust and confidence of practitioners toward researchers and research. Action research projects are also good examples of this, where researchers may work with police personnel to do background research on an issue, design and implement a project, evaluate and test interventions, and then adjust and re-evaluate those interventions based on ongoing findings. Doing so also increases the odds that researchers will carry out research that police agencies need. Weisburd and Neyroud (2011) go so far as to suggest that police take ownership of their own research agenda. And, as our receptivity research indicates, officers who have more exposure to doing research may be more receptive to evidence-based policing in the long run.

Fruitful interactions for evidence-based policing can occur in many other settings besides field research to achieve evidence-based policing. The workshops, symposia, conferences, and briefings that we mentioned above (and especially including practitioners on panels and as speakers) can increase regular interaction between researchers and practitioners (and also those who fund those partnerships). These settings also provide the opportunity for practitioners to tell researchers about their needs. Such interactions do not have to take place outside of the agency; police agencies can invite researchers into Compstat and other brainstorming meetings to provide expertise in developing crime prevention or community-oriented strategies that are evidence informed. Some Project Safe Neighborhood programs are designed to do this.[11] Researchers and practitioners can also interact in writing; one of the goals of the *Translational Criminology Magazine* is to encourage researcher–practitioner co-authors to write about examples of using research in practice.

Federal, state, and local governments, as well as private foundations can support this interaction. Examples include the federal Bureau of Justice Assistance's Smart Policing Initiative or a state's use of federal Justice Assistance Grant (JAG) funds to partner police agencies with researchers. The National Institute of Justice has also provided grant funding to encourage research–practitioner partnerships. Private foundations have supported advancing translational criminology through these partnerships as well. Perhaps the most well-known of such efforts is that of the William T. Grant Foundation.

An important translational question for evidence-based policing is whether these interactions can be maintained over an extended period of time and institutionalized into both the academe and police organizations. In some places, police agencies have tried to institutionalize more interaction with the research world by hiring criminologists. In other cases, criminologists have embedded themselves into agencies (Braga 2013). But interactions are primarily ad hoc or rely on centers like the CEBCP to facilitate them. Many interactions are also dependent on personal relationships, the personality of researchers and

---

[11] See http://www.psnmsu.com/.

practitioners, or other informal or intangible aspects. Formalizing interactions through memorandums of understanding, opportunities for each to participate on advisory boards of the other (e.g., like the research advisory board of the International Association of Chiefs of Police), or police leadership appointing academics to agency review boards or promotional committees (and vice versa) can help solidify such interaction over time.

Leveraging social influence

Nutley et al. (2007) also describe the use of social influence as a mechanism that seems to characterize successful uses of research in practice. As we discussed in Chapter 8, practitioners often receive their information from other practitioners, and agencies can be strongly influenced by what nearby agencies and their leaders are doing. Here, researchers might rely on thought leaders, influential individuals, and others to act as translators of research and proponents of the merits of evidence-based policing more generally. Part of the motivation for the Evidence-Based Policing Hall of Fame, as described in Chapter 14, is to identify leaders who are champions of evidence-based policing for others to emulate. Many are influential leaders and trendsetters in their own right, and their advocacy of evidence-based policing can be meaningful to other police officials. Other champions within police agencies can be crime analysts, planners, and officers and supervisors who have engaged in evidence-based policing and have benefited from its value. Researchers play a role in backing these individuals with recognition, new knowledge, and emotional support.

Researchers should also consider working with more challenging individuals in police agencies that may not buy into the ideas of evidence-based policing initially but who officers respect and follow. Our discussion of police sergeants and first-line supervisors in Chapter 14 is key here. They are often left out of discussions of change and reform in agencies, but they are highly influential individuals for effective implementation of reform efforts. First-line supervisors know their craft and know what is expected of them, and they can challenge many ideas in evidence-based policing. But because of their importance, working with them and engaging in discourse and debate with them may be critical in effectively increasing research use in policing.

Police constituent organizations can also be helpful in disseminating information and bringing practitioner eyes to research. National organizations like the Police Foundation, the International Association of Chiefs of Police (IACP), the Major City Chiefs Association (MCCA), the Police Executive Research Forum (PERF), the International Association of Crime Analysts (IACA), the International Association of Law Enforcement Planners (IALEP), the International Association of Directors of Law Enforcement Standards and Training (IADLEST), and many other organizations are well connected to their constituents and regularly provide information to them on a variety of topics. These organizations have played an increasing role in distilling and disseminating research to law enforcement practitioners. Researchers might also consider regional groups as well, such as regional crime analyst associations,[12] councils of governments,[13] and the like.

Facilitation

Nutley et al. (2007, 132) describe facilitation as "enabling the use of research, through technical, financial, organizational and emotional support." Much of this links back to dissemination and interaction, discussed above, and focuses on making it easier for the police to access and understand research so as to increase the chance of its use. But facilitation takes dissemination and interaction one step further. For example, researchers sometimes create guidebooks of different sorts (particularly when their research is supported by government grant funding) to help practitioners understand how the findings of studies can be applied to practice and policy. Our Evidence-Based Policing Matrix provides another type of tool to facilitate research use, in addition to its role as a dissemination mechanism. It also can be used for evidence assessments or evaluations of the tactical portfolios of supervisors, units, or agencies. Recently, we have partnered with the Police Foundation to create the Evidence-Based Policing App, which makes the Matrix content smartphone-friendly.[14]

Many of the tools we present in this book are also facilitators. For example, the Playbook is a tool that tries to facilitate the use of multiple research findings in daily patrol. It takes a large body of research and converts it into operational directives in an easy to access format. Officers can print out the playbook and put it in their patrol cars, or access it on their phones or mobile computer terminals to get ideas about what evidence-based approaches they can engage in during their non-committed time. Of course, the Playbook is a type of facilitator that needs to be complemented by other facilitators to be successful. These include active supervision, adjusted performance metrics, and rewards and incentives that encourage officers to use the Playbook.

Yet another facilitator of research is the Case of Place tool. The Case of Place tool creates an investigative case folder structure that can be used by a detective unit to investigate a problem-place. Rather than hope officers and investigators know and learn the research and carry out steps to investigate a problem place, we created this tool to facilitate the use of this research in an investigative mode. Similarly, risk assessment tools are also facilitators. In Chapter 5, we discussed such tools used for domestic violence, which are built from research about risk. Crime analysts are also developing risk assessments when determining high-risk

---

[12] For example, the Massachusetts Association of Crime Analysists (http://macrimeanalysts.org/).
[13] For example, the Metropolitan Washington Council of Government (https://www.mwcog.org/).
[14] To access the free app, go to https://www.microsoft.com/en-us/store/p/evidence-based-policing/9nblggh6cftl.

locations for crime or high-risk victims. The question for translational criminology is what types of facilitation are most effective in getting practitioners to look at and use research, as well as for institutionalizing research into practice.

Incentives and reinforcement

In Chapter 14, we described in detail the ways that agencies can create incentive structures to facilitate evidence-based policing. But what can researchers do? First, researchers and their organizations can find ways to reward practitioners for engaging in research. This might be recognition for participating in research projects through commendation letters to chief executives, or it could be awards like the Evidence-Based Policing Hall of Fame or the Distinguished Achievement Award in Evidence-Based Crime Policy that we give from the CEBCP. All of these might provide incentives for practitioners to engage in evidence-based policing, even if others in their agency do not support them.

Federal grants provide monetary incentives for researchers and practitioners to work together. The Bureau of Justice Assistance's Smart Policing Initiative has now funded countless research partnerships, many which have resulted in studies that appear in the Matrix. Federal sources of funding to local agencies can also provide incentives to carry out evidence-based policing, although researchers have little to do with these decisions.

An important consideration for researchers is to determine up front how they might contribute to the needs of police agencies with which they work. This might be in providing expertise on particular topics. But more specific to their research partnership, it also means considering how a research project can benefit an agency partner and sharing the results of the research with the agency staff in a manner that is helpful to them. This could mean preparing clear, concise summaries and policy recommendations for the agency, offering to brief the agency's command staff on the study in person, allowing agency staff to view and comment on draft versions of the research, offering constructive suggestions for change when a particular strategy or policy is found to be ineffective, and being sensitive to the political and social context that may surround a particular evaluation study. An agency that feels it has gained something useful from a research collaboration will likely be more open to engaging in further research with outsiders.

Developing operational guidance

Finally, we add one additional mechanism to Nutley et al.'s list—that researchers might also increase practitioners' receptivity to research by giving further attention to developing studies that provide operationally useful guidance for police agencies (e.g., Koper 2013). This idea is similar to Nutley et al.'s (2007) concept of facilitation, but it perhaps requires a more subtle shift in how police scholars view their work. To use an example from Chapter 4, it is easy enough to tell police that they should patrol more at crime hot spots, but police commanders will have numerous questions about how to operationalize this recommendation. How often should officers patrol hot spots? How long should they stay for each visit? How should officers time these visits? What should they do during these visits? And what should be the target dosage of patrol per day or per week? These sorts of operationally detailed questions are typically left unanswered in studies about hot spots policing as well as studies about many other types of police interventions; indeed, discussions of police interventions are often quite vague in police evaluations.

One likely reason that the Koper Curve (discussed in Chapter 4) has been embraced by many police agencies in the United States, the United Kingdom, and elsewhere is that it provides clear operational guidance for agencies to follow in doing hot spots policing (i.e., making periodic fifteen-minute patrol visits to micro hot spots). In this regard, police scholars may need to think more like engineers who use scientific principles (such as deterrence theory or environmental criminology) to create processes or technologies that will achieve desired ends for users (in this case, police). Evaluation experts Rossi and colleagues (2004) refer to this as an "engineering tradition" that must be further developed for applied researchers. As they state, "Engineers are distinguished from their 'pure science' counterparts by their concern with working out the details of how scientific knowledge can be used to grapple with real-life problems. It is one thing to know that gases expand when heated and that each gas has its own expansion coefficient; it is quite another to be able to use that principle to mass produce economical, high-quality gas turbine engines" (391). Additional attention to the operational details of police strategies in research studies—and thinking at the outset about how science can be used to develop interventions that also meet the practical needs and constraints faced by police—would almost certainly help agencies in adapting research to practice.

Future Prospects

Translational criminology is one way that researchers can contribute to advancing evidence-based policing. This area provides fertile ground for new ideas and research, as we have little empirical and systematic knowledge on how research gets translated into practice, and on the barriers, challenges, opportunities, and contexts related to how it happens. But perhaps an important preliminary question is whether scholars within our discipline of criminology and its subdisciplines (like policing scholarship) are motivated to explore such questions.

Ultimately, the development of translational criminology for evidence-based policing relies on existing infrastructures of research supply and demand. Scholars (especially those pre-tenure) will seek research outlets that are most likely to publish their work. It is unclear whether the journals in our field would welcome translational research. In this way, criminology is different from the medical, public health, or psychology fields that have journals devoted to translational science. Neither our *Translational Criminology* brief series by Springer nor our *Translational Criminology Magazine* are peer-reviewed outlets. Of the academic journals devoted to policing research, the closest journal to the translation concept is *Policing: A Journal of Research and Practice* (Oxford), which at the time of writing, remains unranked. Research published in practitioner journals may increase receptivity to research, but may not lead to any benefit for the academic researcher. On the demand side, it is also unclear whether law enforcement organizations might be interested in doing this type of primary research on translation. Receptivity to research may need to be established first in order for agencies to pursue related studies on translation.

One thing is certain: Pursuing translational criminology as study or as action will require a great deal of help (and interest) from our colleagues in practice as well as a cultural change in what young scholars value as "research" and how they are rewarded. This goes not only for the study of evidence-based policing, but also for its practice.

References

Aarons, Gregory A. 2004. "Mental Health Provider Attitudes toward Adoption of Evidence-Based Practice: The Evidence-Based Practice Attitude Scale (EBPAS)." *Mental Health Services Research* 6: 61–74.

Abrahamse, Allan F., Patricia A. Ebener, Peter W. Greenwood, Nora Fitzgerald, and Thomas E. Kosin. 1991. "An Experimental Evaluation of the Phoenix Repeat Offender Program." *Justice Quarterly* 8(2): 141–68.

Ackerman, Jeffrey M., and D. Kim Rossmo. 2015. "How Far to Travel? A Multilevel Analysis of the Residence-to-Crime Distance." *Journal of Quantitative Criminology* 31(2): 237–62.

Aden, Hassan, and Christopher S. Koper. 2011. "The Challenge of Hot Spots Policing." *Translational Criminology* (Summer, 2011): 6–7.

Agrawal, Manish, Raghav H. Rao, and Lawrence G. Sanders. 2003. "Impact of Mobile Computing Terminals in Police Work." *Journal of Organizational Computing and Electronic Commerce* 13(2): 73–89.

Alpert, Geoffrey P., Jeff Rojek, and Andrew Hansen. 2013. *Building Bridges between Police Researchers and Practitioners: Agents of Change in a Complex World.* Washington, DC: National Institute of Justice.

Amendola, Karen L., David Weisburd, Edwin Hamilton, Greg Jones, Meghan Slipka, Anneke Heitmann, Jon Shane, Christopher Ortiz, and Eliab Tarkghen. 2011. The *Impact of Shift Length in Policing on Performance, Health, Quality of Life, Sleep, Fatigue, and Extra-Duty Employment.* Washington, DC: Police Foundation.

Ariel, Barak, and Lawrence W. Sherman. 2012. "Mass Transit Policing: The London Underground Hot Spots Experiment." Presentation at the Annual Meeting of the American Society of Criminology, Chicago.

Ariel, Barak, William A. Farrar, and Alex Sutherland. 2015. "The Effect of Police Body-Worn Cameras on Use of Force and Citizens' Complaints against the Police: A Randomized Controlled Trial." *Journal of Quantitative Criminology* 31(3): 509–35.

Ariel, Barak, Alex Sutherland, Darren Henstock, Josh Young, Paul Drover, Jayne Sykes, Simon Megicks, and Ryan Henderson. 2016. "Report: Increases in Police Use of Force in the Presence of Body-Worn Cameras Are Driven by Officer Discretion: A Protocol-Based Subgroup Analysis of Ten Randomized Experiments." *Journal of Experimental Criminology* 12(3): 453–63.

Audit Commission. 1993. *Helping with Enquiries: Tackling Crime Effectively.* London: HMSO.

Azrael, Deborah, Anthony A. Braga, and Mallory O'Brien. 2013. *Developing the Capacity to Understand and Prevent Homicide: An Evaluation of the Milwaukee Homicide Review Commission.* Washington, DC: National Institute of Justice.

Bass, Bernard M. 1985. *Leadership and Performance beyond Expectation.* New York, NY: Free Press.

Bayley, David H. 1994. *Police for the Future.* New York, NY: Oxford University Press.

———— 1998. "Policing in America: Assessment and Prospects." *Ideas in American Policing*. Washington, DC: Police Foundation.

Bennett, Trevor. 1990. *Evaluating Neighborhood Watch*. Basingstoke, UK: Gower.

Bennett, Trevor, Katy Holloway, and David Farrington. 2008. "The Effectiveness of Neighborhood Watch: A Systematic Review." *Campbell Systematic Reviews*. https://campbellcollaboration.org/library/download/266_391a9c42e7b168611adb7afc-c492fa2d.html.

Berk, Richard A., Alec Campbell, Ruth Klap, and Bruce Western. 1992. "A Bayesian Analysis of the Colorado Springs Spouse Abuse Experiment." *Journal of Criminal Law and Criminology* 83(1): 170–200.

Berk, Richard, Lawrence Sherman, Geoffrey Barnes, Ellen Kurtz, and Lindsay Ahlman. 2009. "Forecasting Murder within a Population of Probationers and Parolees: A High Stakes Application of Statistical Learning." *Journal of the Royal Statistical Society: Series A (Statistics in Society)* 172(1): 191–211.

Bernard, Thomas J., Jeffrey B. Snipes, and Alexander L. Gerould. 2010. "Neighborhoods and Crime." In *Theoretical Criminology*, 6th edn, ed. George B. Vold, 133–53. Oxford: Oxford University Press.

Bernasco, Wim. 2010. "A Sentimental Journey to Crime: Effects of Residential History on Crime Location Choice." *Criminology* 48(2): 389–416.

Best, Allan, Robert A. Hiatt, and Cameron D. Norman. 2008. "Knowledge Integration: Conceptualizing Communications in Cancer Control Systems." *Patient Education and Counseling* 71(3): 319–27.

Birkeland, Sarah, Erin Murphy-Graham, and Carol Weiss. 2005. "Good Reasons for Ignoring Good Evaluation: The Case of the Drug Abuse Resistance Education (D.A.R.E.) Program." *Evaluation and Program Planning* 28: 247–56.

Bishop, Norman. 1970. "Regional Co-Operation in Criminological Research." *International Review of Criminal Policy* 28: 49–54.

Bittner, Egon. 1970. *The Functions of the Police in Modern Society*. Chevy Chase, MD: National Institute of Mental Health, Center for Studies of Crime and Delinquency.

Bjerregaard, Beth, and Alan J. Lizotte. 1995. "Gun Ownership and Gang Membership." *Journal of Criminal Law and Criminology* 86(1): 37–58.

Block, Richard L., and Carolyn R. Block. 1995. "Space, Place, and Crime: Hot Spot Areas and Hot Places of Liquor-Related Crime." In *Crime and Place (Crime Prevention Studies, Volume 4)*, eds John Eck and David Weisburd, 145–85. Monsey, NY: Criminal Justice Press and Police Executive Research Forum.

Blumstein, Alfred, Jacqueline Cohen, J. A. Roth, and Christy Visher. 1986. "Introduction: Studying Criminal Careers." In *Criminal Careers and "Career Criminals," Volume 1*, eds Alfred Blumstein, Jacqueline Cohen, Jeffrey Roth, and Christy Visher, 12–30. Washington, DC: National Academy Press.

Boudreau, Marie-Claude, and Daniel Robey. 2005. "Enacting Integrated Information Technology: A Human Agency Perspective." *Organization Science* 16(1): 3–18.

Bowers, Kate, and Shane D. Johnson. 2005. "Domestic Burglary Repeats and Space–Time Clusters: The Dimensions of Risk." *European Journal of Criminology* 2(1): 67–92.

Bowers, Kate, Shane Johnson, Rob Guerette, Lucia Summers, and Suzanne Poynton. 2011. "Spatial Displacement and Diffusion of Benefits among Geographically Focused Policing Initiatives." *Campbell Systematic Reviews*. https://campbellcollaboration.org/library/download/610_7606539c824beef405e3e45ef5441c33.html.

Braga, Anthony A. 2008. "Pulling Levers Focused Deterrence Strategies and the Prevention of Gun Homicide." *Journal of Criminal Justice* 36(4): 332–43.

——— 2013. "Embedded Criminologists in Police Departments." *Ideas in American Policing*. Washington, DC: Police Foundation.

Braga, Anthony A., and Brenda J. Bond. 2008. "Policing Crime and Disorder Hot Spots: A Randomized Controlled Trial." *Criminology* 46(3): 577–607.

Braga, Anthony A., and David L. Weisburd. 2006. *Police Innovation and Crime Prevention: Lessons Learned from Police Research Over the Past 20 Years*. Washington, DC: National Institute of Justice.

Braga, Anthony A., and David L. Weisburd. 2012. "The Effects of 'Pulling Levers' Focused Deterrence Strategies on Crime." *Campbell Systematic Reviews*. https://campbellcollaboration.org/library/download/51_ae344925cc24112a9469a00d-f723ce77.html.

Braga, Anthony A., David L. Weisburd, Elin J. Waring, Lorraine G. Mazerolle, William Spelman, and Francis Gajewski. 1999. "Problem-Oriented Policing in Violent Crime Places: A Randomized Controlled Experiment." *Criminology* 37(3): 541–80.

Braga, Anthony A., David M. Kennedy, Anne M. Piehl, and Elin J. Waring. 2001. "Measuring the Impact of Operation Ceasefire." In *Reducing Gun Violence: The Boston Gun Project's Operation Ceasefire*, 55–71. Washington, DC: National Institute of Justice.

Braga, Anthony A., David M. Kennedy, Elin J. Waring, and Anne M. Piehl. 2001. "Problem-Oriented Policing, Deterrence, and Youth Violence: An Evaluation of Boston's Operation Ceasefire." *Journal of Research in Crime and Delinquency* 38: 195–225.

Braga, Anthony A., Glen L. Pierce, Jack McDevitt, Brenda J. Bond, and Shea Cronin. 2008. "The Strategic Prevention of Gun Violence among Gang-Involved Offenders." *Justice Quarterly* 25(1): 132–62.

Braga, Anthony A., Edward A. Flynn, George L. Kelling, and Christine M. Cole. 2011. "Moving the Work of Criminal Investigators toward Crime Control." *New Perspectives in Policing*. Washington, DC: National Institute of Justice.

Braga, Anthony A., Andrew Papachristos, and David Hureau. 2012. "Hot Spots Policing Effects on Crime." *Campbell Systematic Reviews*. https://campbellcollaboration.org/library/download/539_e65f16af53f9dea195ee2615853784bd.html.

Braga, Anthony A., David M. Hureau, and Andrew V. Papachristos. 2014. "Deterring Gang-Involved Gun Violence: Measuring the Impact of Boston's Operational Ceasefire on Street Gang Behavior." *Journal of Quantitative Criminology* 30: 113–39.

Braga, Anthony A., Brandon C. Welsh, and Cory Schnell. 2015. "Can Policing Disorder Reduce Crime? A Systematic Review and Meta-Analysis." *Journal of Research in Crime and Delinquency* 52(4): 567–88.

Braithwaite, John. 1989. *Crime, Shame, and Reintegration*. Cambridge: Cambridge University Press.

——— 1999. "Restorative Justice: Assessing Optimistic and Pessimistic Accounts." *Crime and Justice* 25: 1–127.

Brantingham, Patricia L., and Paul J. Brantingham. 1991. *Environmental Criminology*, 2nd edn. Prospect Heights, IL: Waveland Press.

——— 1993. "Environment, Routine and Situation: Toward a Pattern Theory of Crime." *Advances in Criminological Theory* 5: 259–94.

Bratton, William J., and Peter Knobler. 1998. *Turnaround: How America's Top Cop Reversed the Crime Epidemic.* Random House, New York.

Bratton, William J., and Sean W. Malinowski. 2008. "Police Performance Management in Practice: Taking Compstat to the Next Level." *Policing* 2(3): 259–65.

Brown, Mary M. 2001. "The Benefits and Costs of Information Technology Innovations: An Empirical Assessment of a Local Government Agency." *Public Performance & Management Review* 24(4): 351–66.

——2015. "Revisiting the It Productivity Paradox." *American Review of Public Administration* 45(5): 565–83.

Brown, Mary M., and Jeffrey L. Brudney. 2003. "Learning Organizations in the Public Sector? A Study of Police Agencies Employing Information and Technology to Advance Knowledge." *Public Administration Review* 63(1): 30–43.

Brown, Michael L. In Progress. "A Study of Officer Perceptions and Decision-Making in Discretionary Patrol Practices within a Hot Spots Environment Applying Expectancy Motivation Theory." Ph.D. Dissertation, George Mason University.

Buerger, Michael E., and Lorraine Green Mazerolle. 1998. "Third-Party Policing: A Theoretical Analysis of an Emerging Trend." *Justice Quarterly* 15(2): 301–27.

Burch, Andrea M. 2012. *Sheriffs' Offices, 2007—Statistical Tables.* Washington, DC: Bureau of Justice Statistics.

Bynum, Timothy S., and Sean P. Varano. 2003. "The Anti-Gang Initiative in Detroit: An Aggressive Enforcement Approach to Gangs." In *Policing Gangs and Youth Violence,* ed. Scott Decker, 214–38. Belmont, CA: Wadsworth/Thomson Learning.

Bynum, Timothy S., Eric Grommon, and John D. McCluskey. 2014. *Evaluation of a Comprehensive Approach to Reducing Gun Violence in Detroit.* Washington, DC: National Institute of Justice.

Byrne, James, and Gary Marx. 2011. "Technological Innovations in Crime Prevention and Policing. A Review of the Research on Implementation and Impact." *Journal of Police Studies* 20(3): 17–40.

Caeti, Tory J. 1999. "Houston's Targeted Beat Program: A Quasi-Experimental Test of Police Patrol Strategies." Ph.D. Dissertation, Sam Houston State University.

Cahill, Meagan, Mark Coggeshall, David Hayeslip, Ashley Wolffe, Erica Lagerson, Michelle Scott, Elizabeth Davies, Kevin Roland, and Scott Decker. 2008. *Community Collaboratives Addressing Youth Gangs: Interim Findings from a Gang Reduction Program.* Washington, DC: Urban Institute.

Campbell, Jacquelyn, C., Daniel W. Webster, and Nancy Glass. 2009. "The Danger Assessment: Validation of a Lethality Risk Assessment Instrument for Intimate Partner Femicide." *Journal of Interpersonal Violence,* 24(4): 653–74.

Caplan, Nathan, Russel J. Morrison, and Andrea Stambaugh. 1975. The *Use of Social Science Knowledge in Policy Decisions at the National Level: A Report to Respondents.* Ann Arbor, MI: University of Michigan, Institute for Social Research, Center for Research on Utilization of Scientific Knowledge.

Casey, Robert, Miriam Berkman, Carla Smith Stover, Kelley Gill, Sasha Durso, and Steven Marans. 2007. "Preliminary Results of a Police-Advocate Home-Visit Intervention Project for Victims of Domestic Violence." *Journal of Psychological Trauma* 6(1): 39–49.

Chagnon, François, Louise Pouliot, Claire Malo, Marie-Joëlle Gervais, and Marie-Ève Pigeon. 2010. "Comparison of Determinants of Research Knowledge Utilization by Practitioners and Administrators in the Field of Child and Family Social Services." *Implementation Science* 5: 41–53.

Chaiken, Jan M. 1975. The *Criminal Investigation Process Volume I. i: Survey of Municipal and County Police Departments*. Santa Monica, CA: Rand Corporation.

Chaiken, Jan M., Peter W. Greenwood, and Joan R. Petersilia. 1976. *The Criminal Investigation Process: A Summary Report*. Santa Monica, CA: Rand Corporation,

Chalmers, Iain. 2003. "Trying to Do More Good Than Harm in Policy and Practice: The Role of Rigorous, Transparent, Up-to-Date Evaluations." *Annals of the American Academy of Political and Social Science* 589(1): 22–40.

Chan, Janet. 2001. "The Technological Game: How Information Technology Is Transforming Police Practice." *Criminology and Criminal Justice* 1(2): 139–59.

—— 2003. "Police and New Technologies." In *Handbook of Policing*, ed. Tim Newburn, 655–79. Portland, OR: Willan Publishing.

Chan, Janet, David Brereton, Margot Legosz, and Sally Doran. 2001. *E-Policing: The Impact of Information Technology on Police Practices*. Brisbane: Criminal Justice Commission.

Chan, Janet, Chris Devery, and Sally Doran. 2003. *Fair Cop: Learning the Art of Policing*. Toronto, On: University of Toronto.

Chermak, Steven, and Edmund McGarrell. 2004. "Problem-Solving Approaches to Homicide: An Evaluation of the Indianapolis Violence Reduction Partnership." *Criminal Justice Policy Review* 15(2): 161–92.

Cho, Hyunkag, and Dina J. Wilke. 2010. "Does Police Intervention in Intimate Partner Violence Work? Estimating the Impact of Batterer Arrest in Reducing Revictimization." *Advances in Social Work* 11(2): 283–302.

Clapp, John D., Mark Johnson, Robert B. Voas, James E. Lange, Audrey Shillington, and Cristel Russell. 2005. "Reducing Dui among Us College Students: Results of an Environmental Prevention Trial." *Addiction* 100(3): 327–34.

Clarke, Ronald V. 1980. "Situational Crime Prevention: Theory and Practice." *British Journal of Criminology* 20(2): 136–47.

—— 1983. "Situational Crime Prevention: Its Theoretical Basis and Practical Scope." *Crime and Justice* 4: 225–56.

—— 1997. *Situational Crime Prevention: Successful Case Studies*. Albany, NY: Harrow & Heston.

Clarke, Ronald V., and Derek B. Cornish. 1985. "Modeling Offenders' Decisions: A Framework for Research and Policy." *Crime and Justice* 6: 147–85.

—— 2003. "Opportunities, Precipitators and Criminal Decisions: A Reply to Wortley's Critique of Situational Crime Prevention." *Crime Prevention Studies* 16: 41–96.

Clarke, Ronald V., and Marcus Felson (eds). 1993. *Routine Activity and Rational Choice*. *Advances in Criminological Theory, Vol. 5*. New Brunswick, NJ: Transaction Books.

Clarke, Ronald V., and James M. Hough. 1980. The *Effectiveness of Policing*. Aldershot, England: Gower Press.

Clarke, Ronald V., and David Weisburd. 1994. "Diffusion of Crime Control Benefits: Observations on the Reverse of Displacement." In *Crime Prevention Studies, Vol. 2*, ed. Ronald V. Clarke, 165–82. Monsey, NY: Criminal Justice Press.

Cohen, Irwin M., Darryl Plecas, and Amanda V. McCormick. 2007. *A Report on the Utility of the Automated License Plate Recognition System in British Columbia*. Abbotsford, British Columbia: School of Criminology and Criminal Justice, University College of the Fraser Valley.

Cohen, Jacqueline, and Jens Ludwig. 2003. "Policing Crime Guns." In *Evaluating Gun Policy: Effects on Crime and Violence*, eds Jens Ludwig and Philip J. Cook, 217–39. Washington, DC: Brookings Institution Press.

Cohen, Lawrence E., and Marcus Felson. 1979. "Social Change and Crime Rates: A Routine Activity Approach." *American Sociological Review* 44: 588–608.

Colvin, Caran. 2001. "Evaluation of Innovative Technology: Implications for the Community Policing Roles of Law Enforcement Officers." San Francisco: Psychology Department, San Francisco State University.

Connell, Nadine M., Kristen Miggans, and Jean Marie McGloin. 2008. "Can a Community Policing Initiative Reduce Serious Crime? A Local Evaluation." *Police Quarterly* 11(2): 127–50.

Cook, Philip J., Jens Ludwig, and Anthony A. Braga. 2005. "Criminal Records of Homicide Offenders." *Jama* 294(5): 598–601.

Cook, Thomas D. 2003. "Why Have Educational Evaluators Chosen Not to Do Randomized Experiments?" *Annals of the American Academy of Political and Social Science* 589(1): 114–49.

Cope, Nina. 2004. "Intelligence Led Policing or Policing Led Intelligence? Integrating Volume Crime Analysis into Policing." *British Journal of Criminology* 44(2): 188–203.

Cordner, Gary, and Elizabeth Perkins Biebel. 2005. "Problem-Oriented Policing in Practice." *Criminology & Public Policy* 4(2): 155–80.

Cornish, Derek, and Ronald V. Clarke. 2003. "Opportunities, Precipitators, and Criminal Decisions: A Reply to Wortley's Critique of Situational Crime Prevention." In *Evaluation for Crime Prevention (Crime Prevention Studies, Volume Vol. 16)*, Edited byed. Nick Tilly, 41–96. Monsey, NY: Criminal Justice Press.

Corsaro, Nicholas, Eleazer D. Hunt, Natalie K. Hipple, and Edmund F. McGarrell. 2012. "The Impact of Drug Market Pulling Levers Policing on Neighborhood Violence." *Criminology & Public Policy* 11: 167–99.

Cullen, Francis T. 2011. "Beyond Adolescence-Limited Criminology: Choosing Our Future." *Criminology* 49: 287–330.

Cullen, Francis T., Andrew J. Myer, and Edward J. Latessa. 2009. "Eight Lessons from Moneyball: The High Cost of Ignoring Evidence-Based Corrections." *Victims and Offenders* 4: 97–213.

Danziger, James N., and Kenneth L. Kraemer. 1985. "Computerized Data-Based Systems and Productivity among Professional Workers: The Case of Detectives." *Public Administration Review* (January/February, 1985): 196–209.

Davis, Robert, David Weisburd, and Bruce Taylor. 2008. "Effects of Second Responder Programs on Repeat Incidents of Family Abuse." *Campbell Systematic Reviews*, 15(November). https://campbellcollaboration.org/library/download/160_7b6109f9183e77971917b312321de2b9.html.

Decker, Scott H. (ed.). 2003. *Policing Gangs and Youth Violence*. Belmont, CA: Wadsworth/Thomson Learning.

——— 2008. *Strategies to Address Gang Crime: A Guidebook for Local Law Enforcement*. Washington, DC: Office of Community Oriented Policing Services.

Decker, Scott, and David Curry. 2003. "Suppression Without Prevention, Prevention Without Suppression." In *Policing Gangs and Youth Violence*, ed. Scott Decker, 191–213. Belmont, Ca: Wadsworth/Thomson Learning.

Decker, Scott H., Edmund F. McGarrell, Heather Perez, Natalie K. Hipple, and Timothy S. Bynum. 2007. *Strategic Problem-Solving Responses to Gang Crime and Gang Problems: Case Study 8*. Washington, DC: Office of Justice Programs, U.S. Department of Justice.

Dermody, Jim. 2013. "Changing the Culture of Uncommitted Patrol Time: A Work in Progress." *Translational Criminology* (Spring, 2013): 8–9.

Dewey, John. 1954. The *Public and Its Problems*. Athens, OH: Swallow Press.

Ditella, Rafael, and Ernesto Schargrodsky. 2004. "Do Police Reduce Crime? Estimates Using the Allocation of Police Forces after a Terrorist Attack." *American Economic Review* 94(1): 115–33.

Dunford, Franklyn W. 1990. "System-Initiated Warrants for Suspects of Misdemeanor Domestic Assault: A Pilot Study." *Justice Quarterly* 7: 631–53.

Durlauf, Steven N., and Daniel S. Nagin. 2011. "Imprisonment and Crime: Can Both Be Reduced?" *Criminology & Public Policy* 10(1): 9–54.

Eck, John E. 1979. *Managing Case Assignments: The Burglary Investigation Decision Model Replication*. Washington, DC: Police Executive Research Forum.

—— 1983. *Solving Crimes: The Investigation of Burglary and Robbery*. Washington, DC: Police Executive Research Forum.

—— 1994. "Drug Markets and Drug Places: A Case Control Study of the Spatial Structure of Illicit Drug Dealing." Ph.D. Dissertation, University of Maryland.

—— 2002. "Preventing Crime at Places." In *Evidence-Based Crime Prevention*, eds Lawrence W. Sherman, David Farrington, Brandon Welsh, and Doris Layton MacKenzie, 241–94. New York, NY: Routledge.

—— 2005. "Crime Hot Spots: What they Are, Why We Have Them and How to Map Them." In *Mapping Crime: Understanding Hot Spots*, eds John E. Eck, Spencer Chainey, James G. Cameron, Michael Leitner, and Ronald E. Wilson, 1–14. Washington, DC: National Institute of Justice.

—— 2006. "Science, Values, and Problem-Oriented Policing: Why Problem-Oriented Policing." In *Police Innovation: Contrasting Perspectives*, eds David Weisburd and Anthony Braga, 117–32. Cambridge: Cambridge University Press.

Eck, John E., and Dennis Rosenbaum. 1994. "The New Police Order: Effectiveness, Equity, and Efficiency in Community Policing." In *The Challenge of Community Policing: Testing the Promises*, ed. Dennis Rosenbaum, 3–26. Newbury Park: Sage Publications.

Eck, John E., and William Spelman. 1987. *Problem-Solving: Problem-Oriented Policing in Newport News*. Washington, DC: National Institute of Justice.

Eck, John E., and Julie Wartell. 1998. "Improving the Management of Rental Properties with Drug Problems: A Randomized Experiment." In *Civil Remedies and Crime Prevention (Crime Prevention Studies, Vol. 9)*, eds Lorraine Mazerolle and Jan Roehl, 161–85. Monsey, NY: Criminal Justice Press.

Eck, John E., and David Weisburd (eds).. 1995. "Crime Places in Crime Theory." In *Crime and Place (Crime Prevention Studies, Vol. 4)*, eds John Eck and David Weisburd, 1–34. Monsey, NY: Criminal Justice Press.

Edmond, Tonya, Deborah Megivern, Cynthia Williams, Estelle Rochman, and Matthew Howard. 2006. "Integrating Evidence-Based Practice and Social Work Field Education." *Journal of Social Work Education* 42: 377–96.

Egge, Jeff. 2011. "Experimenting with Future-Oriented Analysis at Crime Hot Spots in Minneapolis." *Geography and Public Safety* 2(4): 6–9.

Egley Jr, Arlen, and Christina E. Ritz. 2006. *Highlights of the 2004 National Youth Gang Survey: Fact Sheet*. Washington, DC: Office of Juvenile Justice and Delinquency Prevention.

Engel, Robin S., Marie Skubak Tillyer, and Nicholas Corsaro. 2011 (Online First). "Reducing Gang Violence Using Focused Deterrence: Evaluating the Cincinnati Initiative to Reduce Violence (CIRV)." *Justice Quarterly* 30(3): 403–39.

Erickson, Maynard L., and Jack P. Gibbs. 1975. "Specific versus General Properties of Legal Punishments and Deterrence." *Social Science Quarterly* 56: 390–97.

Ericson, Richard V., and Kevin D. Haggerty. 1997. *Policing the Risk Society*. Toronto: University of Toronto Press.

Esbensen, Finn-Aage. 1987. "Foot Patrols: of What Value?" *American Journal of Police* 6: 45–65.

—— 2002. *National Evaluation of the Gang Resistance Education and Training (G.R.E.A.T.) Program. Final Report*. Washington, DC: National Institute of Justice.

Esbensen, Finn-Aage, and David Huizinga. 1993. "Gangs, Drugs, and Delinquency in a Survey of Urban Youth." *Criminology* 31(4): 565–89.

Esbensen, Finn-Aage, Dana Peterson, Terrance J. Taylor, and D. Wayne Osgood. 2012. "Results from a Multi-Site Evaluation of the Great Program." *Justice Quarterly* 29(1): 125–51.

Exum, M. Lyn, Jennifer L. Hartman, Paul C. Friday, and Vivian B. Lord. 2014. "Policing Domestic Violence in the Post-SARP Era: The Impact of a Domestic Violence Police Unit." *Crime & Delinquency* 60(7): 999–1032.

Famega, Christine N. 2005. "Variation in Officer Downtime: A Review of the Research." *Policing: An International Journal of Police Strategies & Management* 28(3): 388–414.

Famega, Christine N., James Frank, and Lorraine Mazerolle. 2005. "Managing Police Patrol Time: The Role of Supervisor Directives." *Justice Quarterly* 22(4): 540–59.

Farrar, William A., and Barak Ariel. 2013. *Self-Awareness to Being Watched and Socially-Desirable Behavior: A Field Experiment on the Effect of Body-Worn Cameras on Police Use of Force*. Washington, DC: Police Foundation.

Farrington, David P., and Anthony Petrosino. 2001. "The Campbell Collaboration Crime and Justice Group." *Annals of the American Academy of Political and Social Science* 578(1): 35–49.

Felson, Marcus. 1987. "Routine Activities and Crime Prevention in the Developing Metropolis." *Criminology* 25: 911–31.

—— 1994. *Crime and Everyday Life: Insight and Implications for Society*. Thousand Oaks, CA: Pine Forge Press.

—— 1995. "Those Who Discourage Crime." In *Crime and Place*, eds John Eck and David Weisburd, 53–66. Monsey, NY: Criminal Justice Press.

—— 2002. *Crime and Everyday Life*, 3rd edn. Thousand Oaks, CA: Sage Publications.

Florence, Curtis, Jonathan Shepherd, Iain Brennan, and Thomas Simon. 2011. "Effectiveness of Anonymised Information Sharing and Use in Health Service,

Police, and Local Government Partnership for Preventing Violence Related Injury: Experimental Study and Time Series Analysis." *British Medical Journal* 342: d3313.

Frank, James, Steven G. Brandl, and R. Cory Watkins. 1997. "The Content of Community Policing: A Comparison of the Daily Activities of Community and 'Beat' Officers." *Policing: An International Journal of Police Strategies & Management* 20(4): 716–28.

Fritsch, Eric J., Tory J. Caeti, and Robert W. Taylor. 1999. "Gang Suppression through Saturation Patrol, Aggressive Curfew, and Truancy Enforcement: A Quasi-Experimental Test of the Dallas Anti-Gang Initiative." *Crime & Delinquency* 45(1): 122–39.

Gabor, Thomas, and Ellen Gottheil. 1984. "Offender Characteristics and Spatial Mobility: An Empirical Study and Some Policy Implications." *Canadian Journal of Criminology 26*: 267–81.

Garicano, Luis, and Paul Heaton. 2010. "Information Technology, Organization, and Productivity in the Public Sector: Evidence from Police Departments." *Journal of Labor Economics* 28(1): 167–201.

Giacomazzi, Andrew. L. 1995. "Community Crime Prevention, Community Policing, and Public Housing: An Evaluation of a Multi-Level, Collaborative Drug-Crime Elimination Program in Spokane, Washington." Ph.D. Dissertation, Washington State University.

Giblin, Matthew J. 2002. "Using Police Officers to Enhance the Supervision of Juvenile Probationers: An Evaluation of the Anchorage Can Program." *Crime & Delinquency* 48(1): 116–37.

Gill, Charlotte, David Weisburd, Cody W. Telep, Zoe Vitter, and Trevor Bennett. 2014. "Community-Oriented Policing to Reduce Crime, Disorder and Fear and Increase Satisfaction and Legitimacy among Citizens: A Systematic Review." *Journal of Experimental Criminology* 10(4): 399–428.

Gill, Charlotte, Alese Wooditch, and David Weisburd. 2016. "Testing the 'Law of Crime Concentration at Place' in a Suburban Setting: Implications for Research and Practice." *Journal of Experimental Criminology*. DOI:10.1007/S10940-016-9304-Y.

Glasziou, Paul, and Brian Haynes. 2005. "The Paths from Research to Improved Health Outcomes." *Evidence Based Nursing* 8(2): 36–8.

Goldstein, Herman. 1979. "Improving Policing: A Problem-Oriented Approach." *Crime & Delinquency* 25(2): 236–58.

——— 1990. *Problem-Oriented Policing*. Philadelphia, Pa.: Temple University Press.

Goldstein, Joseph. "Street Stops Still a 'Basic Tool,' Bratton Says." *New York Times*, March 4, 2014.

Goodall, Martin. 2007. *Guidance for the Police Use of Body-Worn Video Devices*. London: Home Office. http://library.college.police.uk/docs/homeoffice/guidance-body-worn-devices.pdf.

Graham, William. 2016. "Glasgow's Community Initiative to Reduce Violence: An Example of International Criminal Justice Policy Transfer Between the US and UK." *Translational Criminology* (Fall 2016): 14–16.

Greene, Jack R. 2000. "Community Policing in America: Changing the Nature, Structure and Function of the Police." In *Policies, Processes and Decisions of the Criminal Justice System*, Criminal Justice 2000 Series, Vol. 3, eds Julie Horney, Ruth Peterson, Doris MacKenzie, John Martin, and Dennis Rosenbaum, 299–370. Washington, DC: National Institute of Justice.

Greene, Jack R., and Stephen D. Mastrofski (eds). 1988. *Community Policing: Rhetoric or Reality*. New York, NY: Praeger.

Greene, Jack R., and William V. Pelfrey Jr. 1997. "Shifting the Balance of Power between Police and Community: Responsibility for Crime Control." In *Critical Issues in Policing: Contemporary Readings*, eds Robert Dunham and Geoff Alpert, 393–423. Prospects Heights, IL: Waveland Press.

Greenwood, Peter W., and Joan Petersilia. 1975. *The Criminal Investigation Process, Vol. I: Summary and Policy Implications*. Santa Monica, CA: Rand Corporation.

Grieco, Julie. 2016. "Attitudinal Dimensions and Openness to Evidence-Based Policing: Perspectives of Academy Recruits." Ph.D. Dissertation, George Mason University.

Grieco, Julie, Heather Vovak, and Cynthia Lum. 2014. "Examining Research-Practice Partnerships in Policing Evaluations." *Policing* 8: 368–78.

Groff, Elizabeth R., and Brian Lockwood. 2014. "Criminogenic Facilities and Crime across Street Segments in Philadelphia: Uncovering Evidence about the Spatial Extent of Facility Influence." *Journal of Research in Crime and Delinquency* 51(3): 277–314.

Groff, Elizabeth R., and Tom McEwen. 2008. *Identifying and Measuring the Effects of Information Technologies on Law Enforcement Agencies*. Washington, DC: Office of Community Oriented Policing Services; Alexandria, VA: Institute for Law and Justice.

Groff, Elizabeth R., Jerry H. Ratcliffe, Cory P. Haberman, Evan T. Sorg, Nola M. Joyce, and Ralph B. Taylor. 2015. "Does What Police Do at Hot Spots Matter? The Philadelphia Policing Tactics Experiment." *Criminology* 53(1): 23–53.

Harcourt, Bernard E. 2001. *Illusion of Order: The False Promise of Broken Windows Policing*. Cambridge, Ma: Harvard University Press.

Harris, Christopher J. 2007. "The Police and Soft Technology: How Information Technology Contributes to Police Decision Making." In *The New Technology of Crime, Law and Social Control*, eds James M. Byrne and Donald J. Rebovich, 153–83. Monsey, NY: Criminal Justice Press.

Hawley, Amos. 1950. *Human Ecology: A Theory of Community Structure*. New York, NY: The Ronald Press Company.

Hegarty, Tim, L., Sue Williams, Shaun Stanton, and William Chernoff. 2014. "Evidence-Based Policing at Work in Smaller Jurisdictions." *Translational Criminology* (Spring, 2014): 14–15.

Hibdon, Julie. 2013. "Crime Hot Spots in Suburbia: A Case Study." Presented at the American Society of Criminology Annual Meeting, November, 2013, Atlanta, Ga.

Hirschi, Travis. 1993. "Administrative Criminology." *Contemporary Sociology* 22(3): 348–50.

Hirschkorn, Mark, and David Geelan. 2008. "Bridging the Research-Practice Gap: Research Translation and/or Research Transformation." *Alberta Journal of Educational Research* 54: 1–13.

HMIC. 1997. "Policing with Intelligence." London: Her Majesty's Inspectorate of the Constabulary.

Horvath, Frank, Robert T. Meesig, and Yung Hyeock Lee. 2001. *A National Survey of Police Policies and Practices Regarding the Criminal Investigation Process: Twenty-Five Years after Rand*. Report for the National Institute of Justice. Ann Arbor, MI: Michigan State University.

Howell, James C. 2000. *Youth Gang Programs and Strategies*. Washington, DC: Office of Juvenile Justice and Delinquency Prevention.

Huey, Laura, and Renée Mitchell. 2016. "Unearthing Hidden Keys: Why Pracademics Are an Invaluable (If Underutilized) Resource in Policing Research." *Policing: A Journal of Policy and Practice*. DOI:10.1093/police/paw029.

Hunt, Priscilla, Jessica Saunders, and John S. Hollywood. 2014. *Evaluation of the Shreveport Predictive Policing Experiment*. Rand Corporation.

Ioimo, Ralph E., and Jay E. Aronson. 2003. "The Benefits of Police Field Mobile Computing Realized by Non-Patrol Sections of a Police Department." *International Journal of Police Science & Management* 5(3): 195–206.

—— 2004. "Police Field Mobile Computing: Applying the Theory of Task-Technology Fit." *Police Quarterly* 7(4): 403–28.

Johnson, Shane D., and Kate J. Bowers. 2004. "The Burglary as Clue to the Future: The Beginnings of Prospective Hot-Spotting." *European Journal of Criminology* 1(2): 237–55.

——. 2014. "Near Repeats and Crime Forecasting." In *Encyclopedia of Criminology and Criminal Justice*, eds Gerben Bruinsma and David Weisburd, 3242–254. New York, NY: Springer.

Johnson, Shane D., Wim Bernasco, Kate J. Bowers, Henk Elffers, Jerry Ratcliffe, George Rengert, and Michael Townsley. 2007. "Space-Time Patterns of Risk: A Cross National Assessment of Residential Burglary Victimization." *Journal of Quantitative Criminology* 23(3): 201–19.

Jolin, Annette, William Feyerherm, Robert Fountain, and Sharon Friedman. 1998. *Beyond Arrest: The Portland, Oregon Domestic Violence Experiment, Final Report*. Washington, DC: National Institute of Justice.

Kansas City Police. 1977. *Response Time Analysis Reports*. Kansas City, Missouri.

Katz, Charles M., David E. Choate, Justin R. Ready, and Lidia Nuño. 2014. *Evaluating the Impact of Officer Worn Body Cameras in the Phoenix Police Department*. Phoenix, AZ: Center for Violence Prevention & Community Safety, Arizona State University

Kelling, George, and Catherine Coles. 1996. *Fixing Broken Windows: Restoring Order and Reducing Crime in Our Communities*. New York, NY: Simon and Schuster, Touchstone Books.

Kelling, George L., and Mark H. Moore. 1988. "The Evolution of the Current Strategy of Policing." *Perspectives on Policing*, No. 4. Washington, DC: National Institute of Justice.

Kelling, George L., Anthony M. Pate, Duane Dieckman, and Charles E. Brown. 1974. The *Kansas City Preventive Patrol Experiment: A Summary Report*. Washington, DC: Police Foundation.

Kennedy, David, Anthony Braga and Anne Piehl. 2001. "Developing and Implementing Operation Ceasefire." In *Reducing Gun Violence: The Boston Gun Project's Operation Ceasefire*, 5–54. Washington, DC: National Institute of Justice.

Kennedy, David M., Anne M. Piehl, and Anthony A. Braga. 1996. "Youth Violence in Boston: Gun Markets, Serious Youth Offenders, and a Use-Reduction Strategy." *Law and Contemporary Problems* 59(1): 147–96.

Kennedy, Leslie, Joel Caplan, and Eric Piza. 2015. *A Multi--Jurisdictional Test of Risk Terrain Modeling and a Place-Based Evaluation of Environmental Risk-Based Patrol Deployment Strategies*. Washington, DC: National Institute of Justice. http://www.rutgerscps.org/uploads/2/7/3/7/27370595/nij6city_results_inbrief_final.pdf

Klein, Malcolm W. 1986. "Labeling Theory and Delinquency Policy an Experimental Test." *Criminal Justice and Behavior* 13(1): 47–79.

Klein, Malcolm W., and Cheryl L. Maxson. 2006. *Street Gang Patterns and Policies*. New York, NY: Oxford University Press.

Klobuchar, Amy, Nancy K. Mehrkens Steblay, and Hilary Lindell Caligiuri. 2006. "Improving Eyewitness Identifications: Hennepin County's Blind Sequential Lineup Pilot Project." *Cardozo Public Law, Policy & Ethics Journal* 4: 381–414.

Knott, Jack, and Aaron Wildavsky. 1980. "If Dissemination Is the Solution, What Is the Problem?" *Knowledge: Creation, Diffusion, Utilization, Volume* 1(4): 537–78.

Knoxville Police Department 2002. "Knoxville PD Public Safety Collaborative." Herman Goldstein Award Submission.

Kochel, Tammy Rinehart, David B. Wilson, and Stephen D. Mastrofski. 2011. "Effect of Suspect Race on Officers' Arrest Decisions." *Criminology* 49(2): 473–512.

Koen, Marthinus. 2016. "Technological Frames: Making Sense of Body-Worn Cameras in a Police Organization." Ph.D. Dissertation, George Mason University.

Koper, Christopher S. 1995. "Just Enough Police Presence: Reducing Crime and Disorderly Behavior by Optimizing Patrol Time in Crime Hot Spots." *Justice Quarterly* 12: 649–72.

—— 2013. "Putting Hot Spots Research into Practice." Speech 6th International Conference on Evidence-Based Policing. Cambridge University, United Kingdom.

—— 2014. "Assessing the Practice of Hot Spots Policing: Survey Results from a National Convenience Sample of Local Police Agencies." *Journal of Contemporary Criminal Justice* 30(2): 123–46.

Koper, Christopher S., and Evan Mayo-Wilson. 2006. "Police Crackdowns on Illegal Gun Carrying: A Systematic Review of Their Impacts on Gun Crime." *Journal of Experimental Criminology* 2(2):227–61.

Koper, Christopher S., and Evan Mayo-Wilson. 2012. "Police Strategies for Reducing Illegal Possession and Carrying of Firearms: Effects on Gun Crime." *Campbell Systematic Reviews*. https://campbellcollaboration.org/library/download/44_47886645b5186aa651f548a1a501f585.html.

Koper, Christopher S. and Jeffrey A. Roth. 2000. "Putting 100,000 Officers on the Street: Progress as of 1998 and Preliminary Projections through 2003." In *National Evaluation of the Cops Program-Title I of the 1994 Crime Act*, eds Jeffery A. Roth, Joseph F. Ryan, Stephan J. Gaffigan, Christopher S. Koper, Mark H. Moore, Janice A. Roehl et al., 149–78. Washington, DC: National Institute of Justice.

Koper, Christopher S., Gretchen E. Moore, and Jeffrey A. Roth. 2002. *Putting 100,000 Officers on the Street: A Survey-Based Assessment of the Federal Cops Program*. Washington, DC: The Urban Institute.

Koper, Christopher S., Bruce G. Taylor, and Bruce E. Kubu. 2009. *Law Enforcement Technology Needs Assessment: Future Technologies to Address the Operational Needs of Law Enforcement*. Washington, DC: Police Executive Research Forum and the Lockheed Martin Corporation.

Koper, Christopher. S., Debra A. Hoffmaster, Andrea Luna, Shannon McFadden, and Daniel J. Woods. 2010. *Developing a St. Louis Model for Reducing Gun Violence: A Report from the Police Executive Research Forum to the St. Louis Metropolitan Police Department*. Washington, DC: Police Executive Research Forum.

Koper, Christopher S., Bruce Taylor, and Jamie Roush. 2013a. "What Works Best at Violent Crime Hot Spots? A Test of Directed Patrol and Problem-Solving Approaches in Jacksonville, Florida." *Research in Brief, the Police Chief* 80: 12–13.

Koper, Christopher S., Bruce G. Taylor, and Daniel J. Woods. 2013b. "A Randomized Test of Initial and Residual Deterrence from Directed Patrols and Use of License Plate Readers at Crime Hot Spots." *Journal of Experimental Criminology* 9(2): 213–44.

Koper, Christopher S., Daniel J. Woods, and Bruce E. Kubu. 2013c. "Gun Violence Prevention Practices among Local Police in the United States." *Policing: An International Journal of Police Strategies & Management* 36(3): 577–603.

Koper, Christopher S., Cynthia Lum, and James J. Willis. 2014. "Optimizing the Use of Technology in Policing: Results and Implications from a Multi-Site Study of the Social, Organizational, and Behavioral Aspects of Implementing Police Technologies." *Policing: A Journal of Policy and Practice* 8(2): 212–21.

Koper, Christopher S., Jeffery Egge, and Cynthia Lum. 2015a. "Institutionalizing Place-Based Approaches: Opening a Case on a Gun Crime Hot Spot." *Policing: A Journal of Policy and Practice* 9(3): 242–54.

Koper, Christopher S., Cynthia Lum, and Julie Hibdon. 2015b. "The Uses and Impacts of Mobile Computing Technology in Hot Spots Policing." *Evaluation Review* 39(6): 587–624.

Koper, Christopher S., Cynthia Lum, James J. Willis, Daniel J. Woods, and Julie Hibdon. 2015c. *Realizing the Potential of Technology in Policing: A Multi-Site Study of the Social, Organizational, and Behavioral Aspects of Implementing Policing Technologies*. Report to the National Institute of Justice. Fairfax, VA: Center for Evidence-Based Crime Policy, George Mason University.

Koper, Christopher S., Daniel J. Woods, and Daniel Isom. 2016. "Evaluating a Police-Led Community Initiative to Reduce Gun Violence in St. Louis." *Police Quarterly* 19(2): 115–49.

Kraemer, Kenneth L., and James N. Danziger. 1984. "Computers and Control in the Work Environment." *Public Administration Review* 44(1): 32–42.

Krimmel, John T., and Marie Mele. 1998. "Investigating Stolen Vehicle Dump Sites: An Interrupted Time Series Quasi-Experiment." *Policing: An International Journal of Police Strategies & Management* 21(3): 479–89.

Lacey, E. Anne. 1994. "Research Utilization in Nursing Practice—A Pilot Study." *Journal of Advanced Nursing* 19: 987–95.

Landry, R., N. Amara, and M. Lamari. 2001. "Utilization of Social Science Research in Canada." *Research Policy* 30(2): 333–49.

Lasley, James R. 1998. *"Designing Out" Gang Homicides and Street Assaults*. Washington, DC: National Institute of Justice.

Laub, John H. 2009. Lecture Given at the University of Pennsylvania, April 9-10, 2009.
——— 2011. "Translational Criminology." Speech Given March 1, 2011 for the National Institute of Justice. Http://Nij.Gov/About/Speeches/Pages/Translational-Criminology-3-1-2011.Aspx.

Lawton, Brian, Ralph B. Taylor, and Anthony J. Luongo. 2005. "Police Officers on Drug Corners in Philadelphia, Drug Crime, and Violent Crime: Intended, Diffusion, and Displacement Impacts." *Justice Quarterly* 22: 427–51.

Laycock, Gloria. 1991. "Operation Identification, or the Power of Publicity?" *Security Journal* 2: 67–72.

—— 2012. "In Support of Evidence-Based Approaches: A Response to Lum and Kennedy." *Policing* 6: 324–26.

Lewis, Dan A., and Michael G. Maxfield. 1980. "Fear in the Neighborhoods: An Investigation of the Impact of Crime." *Journal of Research in Crime and Delinquency* 17(2): 160–89.

Lewis, Dan A., and Greta W. Salem. 1986. *Fear of Crime*. Transaction Publishers.

Lindsay, Betsy, and Daniel McGillis. 1986. "Citywide Community Crime Prevention: An Assessment of the Seattle Program." In *Community Crime Prevention: Does It Work?*, ed. Dennis Rosenbaum, 46–67. Beverly Hills, CA: Sage.

Loeber, Rolf, and Magda Stouthamer-Loeber. 1996. "The Development of Offending." *Criminal Justice and Behavior* 23: 12–24.

Lu, Yongmei. 2003. "Getting Away with the Stolen Vehicle: An Investigation of Journey-After-Crime." *Professional Geographer* 554: 422–33.

Lum, Cynthia. 2008. "Translating Police Research into Practice." Ideas in American Policing Lecture at the Police Foundation, Washington, DC, November 17, 2008.

—— 2009. "Translating Police Research into Practice." *Ideas in American Policing*. Washington, DC: Police Foundation.

—— 2010. "Technology and the Mythology of Progress in American Law Enforcement." Science Progress (Center for American Progress). February 11. Http://Www.Scienceprogress.Org/2010/02/Police-Technology/

—— 2011. "The Influence of Places on Police Decision Pathways: From Call for Service to Arrest." *Justice Quarterly* 28(4): 631–65.

—— 2013. "Is Crime Analysis Evidence-Based?" *Translational Criminology* (Fall, 2013): 12–14.

Lum, Cynthia, and Nicholas Fyfe. 2015. "Space, Place, and Policing: Exploring Geographies of Research and Practice." *Policing* 9(3): 219–22.

Lum, Cynthia, and Christopher S. Koper. 2007. "Is Crime Prevention Relevant to Counter-Terrorism?" Presentation at the University of Maryland (College Park, MD), February 14, 2007.

—— 2011. "Is Crime Prevention Relevant to Counter-Terrorism?" In *Criminologists on Terrorism and Homeland Security*, eds. Brian Forst, Jack Greene, and James Lynch, 129–49. Cambridge: Cambridge University Press.

—— 2012. "Incorporating Research into Daily Police Practices: The Matrix Demonstration Project." *Transitional Criminology* Fall: 16–17.

Lum, Cynthia, and Lorraine Mazerolle. 2014. "History of Randomized Controlled Experiments in Criminal Justice." In *Encyclopedia of Criminology and Criminal Justice*, eds. Gerben Bruinsma and David Weisburd, 2227–239. New York, NY: Springer.

Lum, Cynthia, and Daniel Nagin. 2017. "Reinventing American Policing: A Seven-Point Blueprint for the 21st Century." *Crime and Justice* 46.

Lum, Cynthia, and Sue-Ming Yang. 2005. "Why Do Evaluation Researchers in Crime and Justice Choose Non-Experimental Methods?" *Journal of Experimental Criminology* 1(2): 191–213.

Lum, Cynthia, Linda Merola, Julie Willis (Hibdon), and Breanne Cave. 2010a. *License Plate Recognition Technology: Impact Evaluation and Community Assessment*. Final Report for the National Institute of Justice. http://cebcp.org/wp-content/evidence-based-policing/LPR_FINAL.pdf.

Lum, Cynthia, Charlotte Gill, Breanne Cave, Julie Hibdon, and David Weisburd. 2011a. "Translational Criminology: Using Existing Evidence for Assessing

TSA's Comprehensive Security Strategy at U.S. Airports." In *Evidence-Based Counterterrorism Policy*, eds Cynthia Lum and Leslie Kennedy, 209–51. New York, NY: Springer.

Lum, Cynthia, Christopher S. Koper, and Cody W. Telep. 2011b. "The Evidence-Based Policing Matrix." *Journal of Experimental Criminology* 7(1): 3–26.

Lum, Cynthia, Julie Willis (Hibdon), Breanne Cave, Christopher S. Koper, and Linda Merola. 2011c. "License Plate Reader (LPR) Police Patrols in Crime Hot Spots: An Experimental Evaluation in Two Adjacent Jurisdictions." *Journal of Experimental Criminology* 7(4): 321–45.

Lum, Cynthia, Cody W. Telep, Christopher S. Koper, and Julie Grieco. 2012. "Receptivity to Research in Policing." *Justice Research and Policy* 14: 61–96.

Lum, Cynthia, Christopher S. Koper, Linda M. Merola, Amber Scherer, and Amanda Reioux. 2015. *Existing and Ongoing Body Worn Camera Research: Knowledge Gaps and Opportunities*. Fairfax, VA: Center for Evidence-Based Crime Policy, George Mason University.

Lum, Cynthia, Christopher S. Koper, Charlotte Gill, Julie Hibdon, Cody W. Telep, and Laurie Robinson. 2016a. *An Evidence-Assessment of the Recommendations of the President's Task Force for 21st Century Policing: Implementation and Research Priorities*. Fairfax, VA: Center for Evidence-Based Crime Policy, George Mason University.

Lum, Cynthia, Christopher S. Koper, and James Willis. 2016b. "Understanding the Limits of Technology's Impact on Police Effectiveness." *Police Quarterly*. DOI:10.1177/1098611116667279.

Lum, Cynthia, Christopher S. Koper, James J. Willis, Stephen Happeny, Heather Vovak, and Jordan Nichols. 2016c. "The Rapid Diffusion of License Plate Readers in U.S. Law Enforcement Agencies: A National Survey." Report to the National Institute of Justice, U.S. Department of Justice. Fairfax, VA: Center for Evidence-Based Crime Policy, George Mason University.

Lum, Cynthia, Charles Wellford, Thomas Scott, and Heather Vovak. 2016d. "*Trajectories of U.S. Crime Clearance Rates*. Report for the Laura and John Arnold Foundation." Fairfax, VA: Center for Evidence-Based Crime Policy, George Mason University.

MacKenzie, Doris Layton. 2000. "Evidence-Based Corrections: Identifying What Works." *Crime & Delinquency* 46: 457–71.

Mahoney, Kristen. 2012. "How States Can Leverage Research and Analysis to Fight Crime." *Translational Criminology* (Winter, 2012): 6–7.

Malm, Aili E., and George E. Tita. 2006. "A Spatial Analysis of Green Teams: A Tactical Response to Marijuana Production in British Columbia." *Policy Sciences* 39(4): 361–77.

Manning, Peter K. 1992. "Technological Dramas and the Police: Statement and Counterstatement in Organizational Analysis." *Criminology* 30(3): 327–46.

——— 2008. The *Technology of Policing*. New York, NY: NYU Press.

Martin, Susan, and Lawrence W. Sherman. 1986. "Selective Apprehension: A Police Strategy for Repeat Offenders." *Criminology* 24: 155–72.

Maryland State Highway Authority. 2005. *Evaluation of the License Plate Recognition System*. American Association of State Highway and Transportation Officials. http://stsmo.transportation.org/Documents/LPR_report_part3.pdf

Mastrofski, Stephen D. 1998. "Community Policing and Police Organization Structure." In *How to Recognize Good Policing: Problems and Issues*, ed. Jean Paul Brodeur, 161–89. Thousand Oaks, CA: Sage Publications.

——— 1999. "Policing for People." *Ideas in American Policing*. Washington, DC: Police Foundation.

——— 2006. "Community Policing: A Skeptical View." In *Police Innovation: Contrasting Perspectives*, eds David Weisburd and Anthony Braga, 44–73. Cambridge: Cambridge University Press.

Mastrofski, Stephen D., and Robert Wadman. 1991. "Personnel and Agency Performance Measurement." In *Local Government Police Management*, ed. Bernard L. Garmire, 363–97. Washington, DC: International City Management Association.

Mastrofski, Stephen D., and James J. Willis. 2010. "Police Organization Continuity and Change: Into the Twenty-First Century." *Crime and Justice* 39: 55–144.

Mastrofski, Stephen D., Robert E. Worden, and Jeffrey B. Snipes. 1995. "Law Enforcement in a Time of Community Policing." *Criminology* 33(4): 539–63.

Mastrofski, Stephen D., Roger B. Parks, Albert J. Reiss, and Robert E. Worden. 1998. *Policing Neighborhoods: A Report from Indianapolis*. Research Preview. Washington, DC: National Institute of Justice.

Mastrofski, Stephen D., James J. Willis, and Tammy Rinehart Kochel. 2007. "The Challenges of Implementing Community Policing in the United States." *Policing* 1(2): 223–34.

Mazerolle, Lorraine, and Janet Ransley. 2005. *Third Party Policing*. Cambridge: Cambridge University Press.

——— 2006. "Advocate: The Case for Third Party Policing." In *Police Innovation: Contrasting Perspectives*, eds David Weisburd and Anthony Braga, 191–206. Cambridge: Cambridge University Press.

Mazerolle, Lorraine G., James F. Price, and Jan Roehl. 2000a. "Civil Remedies and Drug Control: A Randomized Field Trial in Oakland, Ca." *Evaluation Review* 24: 212–41.

Mazerolle, Loraine G., Justin Ready, William Terrill, and Elin Waring. 2000b. "Problem-Oriented Policing in Public Housing: The Jersey City Evaluation." *Justice Quarterly 17*: 129–58.

Mazerolle, Lorraine, David W. Soole, and Sacha Rombouts. 2007. "Street-Level Drug Law Enforcement: A Meta-Analytic Review." *Campbell Systematic Reviews*. https://campbellcollaboration.org/library/download/198_247729cdd60be199eeb-6510a6c28a9d6.html.

Mazerolle, Lorraine, Sarah Bennett, Jacqueline Davis, Elise Sargeant, and Matthew Manning. 2013. "Procedural Justice and Police Legitimacy: A Systematic Review of the Research Evidence." *Journal of Experimental Criminology* 9: 245–74.

Mazerolle, Lorraine, Cynthia Lum, and Anthony A. Braga. 2014. "Using Experimental Designs to Study Police Interventions." In *Oxford Handbook on Police and Policing*, eds Michael D. Reisig and Robert J. Kane, 497–517. New York, NY: Oxford University Press.

Mazerolle, Paul, Kim Adams, Dennis Budz, Chris Cockerill, and Matt Vance. 2003. *On the Beat: An Evaluation of Beat Policing in Queensland*. Brisbane: Crime and Misconduct Commission.

Mayer, Richard E. 2003. "The Promise of Multimedia Learning: Using the Same Instructional Design Methods across Different Media." *Learning and Instruction 13*: 125–39.

McCabe, James E. 2009. "The Narcotics Initiative: An Examination of the NYPD Approach to Drug Enforcement, 1995–2001." *Criminal Justice Policy Review* 20: 170–87.

McCardle, Bernard. 2011. "Activating Officers: The Relationship between Leadership Styles and Officer Engagement." Master's Thesis, Cambridge University.

McCold, Paul, and Benjamin Wachtel. 1998. *Restorative Policing Experiment: The Bethlehem Pennsylvania Police Family Group Conferencing Project.* Pipersville, PA: Community Service Foundation.

McDonald, Phyllis P., Sheldon Greenberg and William J. Bratton. 2001. *Managing Police Operations: Implementing the NYPD Crime Control Model Using Compstat.* Belmont, CA: Wadsworth Publishing.

McEwen, J. Thomas, Edward F. Connors, and Marcia I. Cohen. 1986. *Evaluation of the Differential Police Response Field Test.* Washington, DC: National Institute of Justice.

McGarrell, Edmund F., Steven Chermak, Alexander Weiss, and Jeremy Wilson. 2001. "Reducing Firearms Violence through Directed Police Patrol." *Criminology & Public Policy* 1: 119–48.

McGarrell Edmund F., Steven Chermak, Jeremy M. Wilson, and Nicholas Corsaro, 2006. "Reducing Homicide through a 'Lever-Pulling' Strategy." *Justice Quarterly* 23: 214–31.

McGarrell, Edmund F., Nicholas Corsaro, Natalie Kroovand Hipple, and Timothy S. Bynum. 2010. "Project Safe Neighborhoods and Violent Crime Trends in Us Cities: Assessing Violent Crime Impact." *Journal of Quantitative Criminology* 26(2): 165–90.

McGarrell, Edmund F., Nicholas Corsaro, Chris Melde, Natalie Hipple, Jennifer Cobbina, Timothy Bynum, and Heather Perez. 2012. *An Assessment of the Comprehensive Anti-Gang Initiative: Final Project Report.* Washington, DC: National Institute of Justice.

McGarrell, Edmund F., Nicholas Corsaro, Chris Melde, Natalie K. Hipple, Timothy Bynum, and Jennifer Cobbina. 2013. "Attempting to Reduce Firearms Violence through a Comprehensive Anti-Gang Initiative (CAGI): An Evaluation of Process and Impact." *Journal of Criminal Justice* 41(1): 33–43.

McGuire, Tarrick, and Carlin Caliman. 2016. "Evidence-Based Youth Mentoring Systems: Constructing Models to Address Systemic Issues That Communities Face." *Translational Criminology* (Fall, 2016, forthcoming).

Mears, Daniel P. 2007. "Towards Rational and Evidence-Based Crime Policy." *Journal of Criminal Justice* 35: 667–82.

Mecklenburg, Sheri H. 2006. *Report to the Legislature of the State of Illinois: The Illinois Pilot Program on Double-Blind, Sequential Lineup Procedures.* Springfield, IL: Illinois State Police.

Meissner, Christian, Allison Redlich, Sujeeta Bhatt, and Susan Brandon. 2012. "Interview and Interrogation Methods and Their Effects on Investigative Outcomes." *Campbell Systematic Reviews.* https://campbellcollaboration.org/library/download/16_253b17227ad4e2fd63824f77da5c8302.html.

Merola, Linda M., and Cynthia Lum. 2013. "Predicting Public Support for the Use of License Plate Recognition Technology by Police." *Police Practice and Research: An International Journal.* DOI:10.1080/15614263.2013.814906.

Merola, Linda M., Cynthia Lum, Breanne Cave, and Julie Hibdon. 2014. "Community Support for the Use of License Plate Recognition by Police." *Policing: An International Journal of Police Strategies and Management* 37(1): 30–51.

Messing, Jill T., Jacquelyn Campbell, Daniel W. Webster, Sheryll Brown, Beverly Patchell, and Janet Sullivan Wilson. 2015a. "The Oklahoma Lethality Assessment Study: A Quasi-Experimental Evaluation of the Lethality Assessment Program." *Social Service Review* 89(3): 499–530.

Messing, Jill T., Jacquelyn Campbell, and Janet Sullivan Wilson. 2015b. "Research Designs in the Real World: Testing the Effectiveness of an IPV Intervention." *National Institute of Justice Journal* 275 (September): 48–56.

Mitchell, Renee. 2011. "An Example of Conducting an Experiment in the Sacramento Police Department." Presentation at the Evidence Based Policing Leadership Workshop, Center for Evidence Based Crime Policy, August 15.

——— 2014, "Within-Agency Experimental Evaluation." Presentation at the Evidence-Based Policing for First Line Supervisors, January 24.

Mohler, George O., Martin B. Short, Sean Malinowski, Mark Johnson, George E. Tita, Andrea L. Bertozzi, and P. Jeffery Brantingham. 2015. "Randomized Controlled Field Trials of Predictive Policing." *Journal of the American Statistical Association* 110(512): 1399–1411.

Nachman, Corey. 2011. "This Is What the Inside of an NFL Playbook Looks Like." *Business Insider* August 4. http://www.businessinsider.com/what-the-inside-of-an-nfl-playbook-looks-like-2011-8.

Nagin, Daniel S. 1978. "General Deterrence: A Review of the Empirical Evidence." In *Deterrence and Incapacitation: Estimating the Effects of Criminal Sanction on Crime Rates*, eds Alfred Blumstein, Jacqueline Cohen, and Daniel S. Nagin. Washington, DC: National Academies Press.

——— 1998. "Criminal Deterrence Research at the Outset of the Twenty-First Century." *Crime and Justice* 23: 1–42.

——— 2013. "Deterrence in the Twenty-First Century." *Crime and Justice* 42: 199–263.

Nagin, Daniel S., and Cody W. Telep. Forthcoming. "Procedural Justice and Legal Compliance." *Annual Review of Law and Social Science* 13.

Nagin, Daniel S., Robert M. Solow, and Cynthia Lum. 2015. "Deterrence Criminal Opportunities, and Police." *Criminology* 53(1): 74–100.

National Center for the Dissemination of Disability Research. 1996. A *Review of the Literature on Dissemination and Knowledge Utilization*. Austin: Southwest Educational Development Laboratory.

National Crime Prevention Council. 1997. *Designing Safer Communities: A Crime Prevention through Environmental Design Handbook*. Washington, DC: National Crime Prevention Council.

National Research Council. 2004. *Fairness and Effectiveness in Policing: The Evidence*. Washington, DC: National Academies Press.

New York State Office of the Attorney General. 2013. *A Report on Arrests Arising from the New York City Police Department's Stop-and-Frisk Practices*. New York, NY: Office of the New York State Attorney General, Civil Rights Bureau.

Nunn, Samuel. 1994. "How Capital Technologies Affect Municipal Service Outcomes: The Case of Police Mobile Digital Terminals and Stolen Vehicle Recoveries." *Journal of Policy Analysis and Management* 13(3): 539–59.

Nunn, Samuel, and Kenna Quinet. 2002. "Evaluating the Effects of Information Technology on Problem-Oriented-Policing If It Doesn't Fit, Must We Quit?" *Evaluation Review* 26(1): 81–108.

Nunn, Samuel, Kenna Quinet, Kelley Rowe, and Donald Christ. 2006. "Interdiction Day: Covert Surveillance Operations, Drugs, and Serious Crime in an Inner-City Neighborhood." *Police Quarterly* 9(1): 73–99.

Nutley, Sandra M., Isabel Walter, and Huw Davies. 2007. *Using Evidence: How Research Can Inform Public Services*. Bristol, UK: Policy Press.

ODS Consulting. 2011. *Body Worn Video Projects in Paisley and Aberdeen, Self Evaluation*. Glasgow: ODS Consulting.

Ohio State Highway Patrol. 2005. *Automatic Plate Reader Technology*. Columbus, OH: Ohio Planning Services Section, Research and Development Unit, Ohio State Highway Patrol.

O'Neill, Megan E., Monique Marks, and Anne-Marie Singh. 2007. *Police Occupational Culture: New Debates and Directions*. Sociology of Crime, Law and Deviance, Volume 8. Oxford: Elsevier/Jai Press.

Orlikowski, Wanda J. 1992. "The Duality of Technology: Rethinking the Concept of Technology in Organizations." *Organization Science* 3(3): 398–427.

Orlikowski, Wanda J., and Debra C. Gash. 1994. "Technological Frames: Making Sense of Information Technology in Organizations." *ACM Transactions on Information Systems (TOIS)* 12(2): 174–207.

O'Shea, Timothy, and Keith Nicholls. 2003. "Police Crime Analysis: A Survey of Us Police Departments with 100 or More Sworn Personnel." *Police Practice and Research* 4(3): 233–50.

Owens, Catherine, David Mann, and Rory Mckenna. 2014. *The Essex BWV Trial: The Impact of BWV on Criminal Justice Outcomes of Domestic Abuse Incidents*. London,: College of Policing.

Pa Consulting Group. 2003. *Engaging Criminality—Denying Criminals Use of the Roads*. London: Author.

—— 2006. *Police Standards Unit: Thematic Review of the Use of Automatic Number Plate Recognition within Police Forces*. London: Author.

Palmer, Ian. 2011. "Is the United Kingdom Police Service Receptive to Evidence-Based Policing? Testing Attitudes towards Experimentation." Master's Thesis, Cambridge University.

Palys, Ted S., Ehor O. Boyanowsky, and Donald G. Dutton. 1984. "Mobile Data Access Terminals and Their Implications for Policing." *Journal of Social Issues* 40(3): 113–27.

Papachristos, Andrew V., Tracey L. Meares, and Jeffrey Fagan. 2007. "Attention Felons: Evaluating Project Safe Neighborhoods in Chicago." *Journal of Empirical Legal Studies* 4(2): 223–72.

Patch, David. 2005. *License Plate Scanners Lead to Recovery of Stolen Vehicles*. Toledoblade. Com. Http://Toledoblade.Com/Apps/Pbcs.Dll/Article?Aid=/20050105/News11/501050412

Pate, Anthony M. and Edwin E. Hamilton. 1992. "Formal and Informal Deterrents to Domestic Violence: The Dade County Spouse Assault Experiment. *American Sociological Review* 57(5): 691–7.

Pate, Tony, Amy Ferrara, Robert A. Bowers, and Jon Lorence. 1976. *Police Response Time: Its Determinants and Effects*. Washington, DC: Police Foundation.

Pate, Anthony M., Paul J. Lavrakas, Mary Ann Wycoff, Wesley G. Skogan, and Lawrence W. Sherman. 1985a. *Neighborhood Police Newsletters: Experiments in Newark and Houston, Technical Report*. Washington, DC: Police Foundation.

Pate, Anthony M., Wesley G. Skogan, Mary Ann Wycoff, and Lawrence W. Sherman. 1985b. *Reducing the "Signs of Crime": The Newark Experience.* Washington, DC: Police Foundation.

—— 1985c. *Coordinated Community Policing: The Newark Experience. Technical Report.* Washington, DC: Police Foundation.

Pate, Anthony M., Mary Ann Wycoff, Wesley G. Skogan, and Lawrence W. Sherman. 1986. *Reducing Fear of Crime in Houston and Newark: A Summary Report.* Washington, DC: Police Foundation.

Pate, Antony M., Marlys McPherson, and Glenn Silloway. 1987. *The Minneapolis Community Crime Prevention Experiment: Draft Evaluation Report.* Washington, DC: Police Foundation.

Parahoo, K., and Eilis McCaughan. 2001. "Research Utilization among Medical and Surgical Nurses: A Comparison of their Self-Reports and Perceptions of Barriers and Facilitators." *Journal of Nursing Management* 9: 21–30.

Paulsen, Derek J. 2004. "To Map or Not to Map: Assessing the Impact of Crime Maps on Police Officer Perceptions of Crime." *International Journal of Police Science & Management* 6(4): 234–46.

Perry, Cheryl L., Kelli A. Komro, Sara Veblen-Mortenson, Linda M. Bosma, Kian Farbakhsh, Karen A. Munson, Melissa H. Stigler, and Leslie A. Lytle. 2003. "A Randomized Controlled Trial of the Middle and Junior High School DARE and DARE Plus Programs." *Archives of Pediatrics & Adolescent Medicine* 157(2): 178–84.

Perry, Walter L., Brian McInnis, Carter C. Price, Susan Smith, and John S. Hollywood. 2013. *Predictive Policing: The Role of Crime Forecasting in Law Enforcement Operations.* Los Angeles, CA: Rand Corporation.

Petrosino A., C. Turpin-Petrosino, and S. Guckenburg. 2010. "Formal System Processing of Juveniles: Effects on Delinquency." *Campbell Systematic Reviews.* https://campbellcollaboration.org/library/download/146_c0259853e5ede2720ad-52c996382faac.html.

Pierce, Glen L., Susan Spaar, and Lebaron R. Briggs. 1988. The *Character of Police Work: Strategic and Tactical Implications.* Boston, Ma: Center for Applied Social Research, Northeastern University

Police Executive Research Forum. 2007. *Violent Crime in America: "A Tale of Two Cities".* Washington, DC: Police Executive Research Forum.

—— 2008. *Violent Crime in America: What We Know About Hot Spots Enforcement.* Washington, DC: Police Executive Research Forum.

Police Foundation. 1981. *The Newark Foot Patrol Experiment.* Washington, DC: Police Foundation.

President's Task Force on 21st Century Policing. 2015. *Final Report of the President's Task Force on 21st Century Policing.* Washington, DC: Office of Community Oriented Policing Services.

Ratcliffe, Jerry H. 2008. *Intelligence-Led Policing.* Cullompton: Willan Publishing.

Ratcliffe, Jerry, H., and Michael J. McCullagh. 2001. "Chasing Ghosts? Police Perception of High Crime Areas." *British Journal of Criminology* 41(2): 330–41.

Ratcliffe, Jerry, Travis Taniguchi, Elizabeth R. Groff, and Jennifer Wood. 2011. "The Philadelphia Foot Patrol Experiment: A Randomized Controlled Trial of Police Patrol Effectiveness in Violent Crime Hotspots." *Criminology* 49(3): 795–831.

Ready, Justin T., and Jacob T. Young. 2015. "The Impact of On-Officer Video Cameras on Police-Citizen Contacts: Findings from a Controlled Experiment in Mesa, Az." *Journal of Experimental Criminology* 11(3): 445–58.

Reaves, Brian A. 2010. *Local Police Departments, 2007*. Washington, DC: Bureau of Justice Statistics.

—— 2015. *Local Police Departments, 2013: Equipment and Technology*. Washington, DC: Bureau of Justice Statistics.

Reiss, Albert J. 1971. The *Police and the Public*. New Haven, CT: Yale University Press.

—— 1984. "Consequences of Compliance and Deterrence Models of Law Enforcement for the Exercise of Police Discretion." *Law and Contemporary Problems* 47(4): 83–122.

—— 1985. *Policing a City's Central District: The Oakland Story*. Research Report. Washington, DC: National Institute of Justice.

Roberts, David J., and Meghann Casanova. 2012. *Automated License Plate Recognition (ALPR) Systems: Policy and Operational Guidance for Law Enforcement*. Washington, DC: National Institute of Justice.

Robey, Daniel, Marie-Claude Boudreau, and Gregory M. Rose. 2000. "Information Technology and Organizational Learning: A Review and Assessment of Research." *Accounting, Management and Information Technologies* 10(2): 125–55.

Rocheleau, Bruce. 1993. "Evaluating Public Sector Information Systems: Satisfaction versus Impact." *Evaluation and Program Planning* 16(2): 119–29.

Roehl, Janice, Chris O'Sullivan, Daniel Webster, and Jacquilyn Campbell. 2005. "Intimate Partner Violence Risk Assessment Validation Study: The Rave Study Practitioner Summary and Recommendations: Validation of Tools for Assessing Risk from Violent Intimate Partners". Report to the National Institute of Justice. Baltimore, MD: Johns Hopkins University.

Rojek, Jeff, Geoffery Alpert, and Hayden Smith. 2012a. "The Utilization of Research by Police." *Police Practice and Research* 13(4): 329–41.

Rojek, Jeff, Peter Martin., Geoffrey Alpert. 2014. *Developing and Maintaining Police-Researcher Partnerships to Facilitate Research Use*. Springer Briefs in Translational Criminology. New York, NY: Springer.

Rojek, Jeff, Hayden P. Smith, and Geoffrey P. Albert. 2012b. "The Prevalence and Characteristics of Police Practitioner-Researcher Partnerships." *Police Quarterly* 15: 241–61.

Roman, Caterina, Meagan Cahill, Mark Coggeshall, Erica Lagerson, and Shannon Courtney. 2005. *The Weed and Seed Initiative and Crime Displacement in South Florida: An Examination of Spatial Displacement Associated with Crime Control Initiatives and the Redevelopment of Public Housing*. Washington, DC: Urban Institute, Justice Policy Center.

Roman, John K., Shannon Reid, Jay Reid, Aaron Chalfin, William Adams, and Carly Knight. 2008. *The DNA Field Experiment: Cost-Effectiveness Analysis of the Use of DNA in the Investigation of High-Volume Crimes*. Washington, DC: The Urban Institute.

Rose, Gordon, and R. A. Hamilton. 1970. "Effects of a Juvenile Liaison Scheme." *British Journal of Criminology* 10(1): 2–20.

Rosenbaum, Dennis P. (ed.). 1994. The *Challenge of Community Policing: Testing the Promises*. Newbury Park, CA: Sage Publications.

Rosenbaum, Dennis, and Gordon S. Hanson. 1998. "Assessing the Effects of School-Based Drug Education: A Six-Year Multi-Level Analysis of Project D.A.R.E." *Journal of Research in Crime and Delinquency* 35(4): 381–412.

299

Rosenbaum, Dennis P., Dan A. Lewis, and Jane Grant. 1986. "Neighborhood-Based Crime Prevention: Assessing the Efficacy of Community Organizing in Chicago." In *Community Crime Prevention: Does It Work?*, ed. Dennis P. Rosenbaum, 109–36. Beverly Hills, CA: Sage.

Rosenbaum, Dennis P., Robert L. Flewelling, Susan L. Bailey, Chris L. Ringwalt, and Deanna L. Wilkinson. 1994. "Cops in the Classroom: A Longitudinal Evaluation of Drug Abuse Resistance Education (Dare)." *Journal of Research in Crime & Delinquency* 31: 3–31.

Rosenberg, Mark, and Lyndee M. Knox. 2005. "The Matrix Comes to Youth Violence Prevention: A Strengths-Based, Ecologic and Developmental Framework." *American Journal of Preventive Medicine* 29: 185–90.

Rosenfeld, Richard and Robert Fornango. 2014. "The Impact of Police Stops on Precinct Robbery and Burglary Rates in New York City, 2003—2010." *Justice Quarterly* 31(1): 96–122.

Rosenfeld, Richard, Michael Deckard, and Emily Blackburn. 2014. "The Effects of Directed Patrol and Self-Initiated Enforcement on Firearm Violence: A Randomized Controlled Study of Hot Spot Policing." *Criminology* 52(3): 428–49.

Rossi, Peter H., Mark W. Lipsey, and Howard E. Freeman. 2004. *Evaluation: A Systematic Approach*. Seventh edn. Thousand Oaks, CA: Sage Publications.

Roth, Jeffrey A., Joseph F. Ryan, Stephen J. Gaffigan, Christopher S. Koper, Mark H. Moore, Janice A. Roehl, Calvin C. Johnson, et al. 2000. *National Evaluation of the Cops Program Title I of the 1994 Crime Act*. Washington, DC: National Institute of Justice.

Roush, Jamie, and Christopher S. Koper. 2012. "From Research to Practice: How the Jacksonville, Florida Sheriff's Office Institutionalized Results from a Problem-Oriented, Hot Spots Experiment." *Translational Criminology* (Winter, 2012): 10–11.

Royan, James, and John E. Eck. 2015. "Knowledge Transfer in Action: Crime Reduction through a Regulatory Approach." *Translational Criminology* (Spring, 2015): 14–16.

Sampson, Robert. 2011. "Chapter 8: The Community." In *Crime and Public Policy*, eds James Q. Wilson and Joan Petersilia, 210–36. Oxford: Oxford University Press.

Sampson, Robert J., and John Laub. 1993. *Crime in the Making: Pathways and Turning Points through Life*. Cambridge, Ma: Harvard University Press.

Sampson, Robert J., and Stephen W. Raudenbush. 1999. "Systematic Social Observation of Public Spaces: A New Look at Disorder in Urban Neighborhoods." *American Journal of Sociology* 105(3): 603–51.

Sanders, Carrie B., and Samantha Henderson. 2013. "Police 'Empires' and Information Technologies: Uncovering Material and Organisational Barriers to Information Sharing in Canadian Police Services." *Policing and Society* 23(2): 243–60.

Sanders, Carrie B., Crystal Weston, and Nicole Schott. 2015. "Police Innovations, 'Secret Squirrels' and Accountability: Empirically Studying Intelligence-Led Policing in Canada." *British Journal of Criminology* 55(4): 711–29.

Sanderson, Ian. 2006. "Complexity, 'Practical Rationality' and Evidence-Based Policy Making." *Policy and Politics* 34(1): 1–22.

—— 2009. "Intelligent Policy Making for a Complex World: Pragmatism, Evidence and Learning." *Political Studies* 57(4) 699–719.

Santos, Rachel Boba. 2014. "The Effectiveness of Crime Analysis for Crime Reduction Cure or Diagnosis?" *Journal of Contemporary Criminal Justice* 30(2): 147–68.

Santos, Rachel Boba, and Bruce Taylor. 2014. "The Integration of Crime Analysis into Police Patrol Work: Results from a National Survey of Law Enforcement." *Policing: An International Journal of Police Strategies and Management 37*(3): 501–20.

Santos, Roberto G., and Rachel Boba-Santos. 2015. "An Ex Post Facto Evaluation of Tactical Police Response in Residential Theft from Vehicle Micro-Time Hot Spots." *Journal of Quantitative Criminology 31*(4): 679–98.

Scocas, Evelyn, Richard Harris, Charles Huenke, and Le'verne Cecere. 1997. *Wilmington Shootings 1996: A Comparative Study of Victims and Suspects in Wilmington, Delaware.* Dover, De: Statistical Analysis Center and Criminal Justice Council, State of Delaware.

Scott, Michael S. 2000. *Problem-Oriented Policing: Reflections on the First 20 Years.* Washington, DC: Office of Community Oriented Policing Services.

Seagrave, Jayne. 1996. "Defining Community Policing." *American Journal of Police* 15(2): 1–22.

Shaw, Clifford R., and Henry D. McKay. 1942. *Juvenile Delinquency in Urban Areas.* Chicago, IL: University of Chicago Press.

Sheley, Joseph F., and James D. Wright. 1993. *Gun Acquisition and Possession in Selected Juvenile Samples.* Washington, DC: National Institute of Justice.

Sherman, Lawrence W. 1983. "Patrol Strategies for Police." In *Crime and Public Policy,* ed. James Q. Wilson, 145–63. San Francisco, CA: ICS Press/Transaction Books.

—— 1984. "Experiments in Police Discretion: Scientific Boon or Dangerous Knowledge?" *Law and Contemporary Problems* 47(4): 61–81.

—— 1986. "Policing Communities: What Works?" *Crime and Justice* 8: 343–86.

—— 1990. "Police Crackdowns: Initial and Residual Deterrence." *Crime and Justice* 12: 1–48.

—— 1992. "Attacking Crime: Police and Crime Control." *Crime and Justice* 15: 159–230.

—— 1995. "The Police." In *Crime,* eds James Q. Wilson and Joan Petersilia, 327–48. San Francisco, CA: Institute for Contemporary Studies.

—— 1997. "Policing for Crime Prevention." In *Preventing Crime: What Works, What Doesn't, What's Promising,* eds L. W. Sherman, D. Gottfredson, D., MacKenzie, J. Eck, P. Reuter, and S. Bushway. Washington, DC: National Institute of Justice. https://www.ncjrs.gov/works/chapter8.htm

—— 1998. "Evidence-Based Policing." *Ideas in American Policing.* Washington, DC: Police Foundation.

—— 2003a. "Misleading Evidence and Evidence-Led Policy: Making Social Science More Experimental." *Annals of the American Academy of Political and Social Science* 589(1): 6–19.

—— 2003b. "Reason for Emotion: Reinventing Justice with Theories, Innovations, and Research." *Criminology* 41 (1): 1–38.

—— 2013. "The Rise of Evidence-Based Policing: Targeting, Testing and Tracking." *Crime and Justice* 42: 377–451.

Sherman, Lawrence W., and Richard A. Berk. 1984. "The Specific Deterrent Effects of Arrest for Domestic Assault." *American Sociological Review* 49(2): 261–72.

Sherman, Lawrence W., and John E. Eck. 2002. "Policing for Crime Prevention." In *Evidence-Based Crime Prevention,* eds Lawrence W. Sherman, David P. Farrington, Brandon C. Welsh, and Doris Layton MacKenzie, 295–329. London: Routledge.

Sherman, Lawrence W., and Heather M. Harris. 2013. "Increased Homicide Victimization of Suspects Arrested for Domestic Assault: A 23-Year Follow-Up of the Milwaukee Domestic Violence Experiment (MILDVE)." *Journal of Experimental Criminology* 9(4): 491–514.

——— 2015. "Increased Death Rates of Domestic Violence Victims from Arresting Vs. Warning Suspects in the Milwaukee Domestic Violence Experiment (MILDVE)." *Journal of Experimental Criminology* 11(1): 1–20.

Sherman, Lawrence W., and Dennis P. Rogan. 1995. "Deterrent Effects of Police Raids on Crack Houses: A Randomized, Controlled Experiment." *Justice Quarterly* 12(4): 755–81.

Sherman, Lawrence W., and David Weisburd. 1995. "General Deterrent Effects of Police Patrol in Crime 'Hot Spots': A Randomized, Controlled Trial." *Justice Quarterly* 12(4): 625–48.

Sherman, Lawrence W., Patrick R. Gartin, and Michael E. Buerger. 1989a. "Hot Spots of Predatory Crime: Routine Activities and the Criminology of Place." *Criminology* 27(1): 27–56.

Sherman, Lawrence W., Michael Buerger, Patrick Gartin, R. Dell'erba, and D. Doi. 1989b. "Repeat Call Address Policing: The Minneapolis Recap Experiment." Report to the National Institute of Justice. Washington, DC: Crime Control Institute.

Sherman, Lawrence W., Janell D. Schmidt, Dennis P. Rogan, and Patrick R. Gartin. 1991. "From Initial Deterrence to Long-Term Escalation: Short-Custody Arrest for Poverty Ghetto Domestic Violence." *Criminology* 29: 821.

Sherman, Lawrence W., Janell D. Schmidt, Dennis P. Rogan, Douglas A. Smith, Patrick R. Gartin, Ellen G. Cohn, J. Collins, and Anthony R. Bacich. 1992. "The Variable Effects of Arrest on Criminal Careers: The Milwaukee Domestic Violence Experiment." *Journal of Criminal Law and Criminology* 83(1): 137–69.

Sherman, Lawrence W., James W. Shaw, and Dennis P. Rogan. 1995. "The Kansas City Gun Experiment." *Research in Brief*. Washington, DC: National Institute of Justice.

Sherman, Lawrence W., Denise Gottfredson, Doris MacKenzie, John Eck, Peter Reuter, and Shawn Bushway. 1997. *Preventing Crime: What Works, What Doesn't, What's Promising: A Report to the United States Congress*. Washington, DC: National Institute of Justice.

Sherman, Lawrence W., Heather Strang, and Daniel J. Woods. 2000. *Recidivism Patterns in the Canberra Reintegrative Shaming Experiments (Rise)*. Canberra: Centre for Restorative Justice, Australian National University.

Sherman, Lawrence W., David P. Farrington, Brandon C. Welsh, and Doris Layton MacKenzie. 2002. *Evidence-Based Crime Prevention*. London: Routledge.

Sherman, Lawrence W., Stephen Williams, Barak Ariel, Lucinda R. Strang, Neil Wain, Molly Slothower, and Andre Norton. 2014. "An Integrated Theory of Hot Spots Patrol Strategy Implementing Prevention by Scaling Up and Feeding Back." *Journal of Contemporary Criminal Justice* 30(2): 95–122.

Sherman, Lawrence W., Heather Strang, Geoffrey Barnes, Daniel J. Woods, Sarah Bennett, Nova Inkpen, Dorothy Newbury-Birch, et al. 2015. "Twelve Experiments in Restorative Justice: The Jerry Lee Program of Randomized Trials of Restorative Justice Conferences." *Journal of Experimental Criminology* 11(4): 501–40.

Silverman, Eli. 2006. "Compstat's Innovation." In *Police Innovation: Contrasting Perspectives*, eds D. L. Weisburd and A. A. Braga, 267–83. Cambridge, Ma: Cambridge University Press.

Skogan, Wesley G. 1986. "Fear of Crime and Neighborhood Change." *Crime and Justice* 8: 203–29.

——— 1990. *Disorder and Decline: Crime and the Spiral of Decay in American Cities.* New York, NY: Free Press.

——— 2004. *Community Policing: Can It Work?* Belmont, CA: Wadsworth/Thomson Learning.

——— 2006. *Police and Community in Chicago: A Tale of Three Cities.* New York, NY: Oxford University Press.

Skogan, Wesley G., and Susan M. Hartnett. 1997. *Community Policing, Chicago Style.* New York, NY: Oxford University Press.

Skogan, Wesley G., Susan M. Harnett, and Justine H. Lovig. 1995. *Community Policing in Chicago, Year Two.* Chicago, IL: Criminal Justice Information Authority.

Skogan, Wesley G., Susan M. Hartnett, Jill Dubois, Jennifer T. Comey, Marianne Kaiser, and Justine H. Lovig. 2000. *Problem Solving in Practice: Implementing Community Policing in Chicago.* Chicago, IL: Northwestern University.

Skolnick, Jerome H. 1999. "On Democratic Policing." *Ideas in American Policing.* Washington, DC: Police Foundation.

Sloboda, Zili, Richard C. Stephens, Peggy C. Stephens, Scott F. Grey, Brent Teasdale, Richard D. Hawthorne, Joseph Williams, and Jesse F. Marquette. 2009. "The Adolescent Substance Abuse Prevention Study: A Randomized Field Trial of a Universal Substance Abuse Prevention Program." *Drug and Alcohol Dependence* 102(1): 1–10.

Smallwood, Joanna Louise, Barak Ariel, and Neil Wain. 2014. "Using Non-Warranted Police Community Support Officers in Hot Spots of Crime and Disorder: The Birmingham South (UK) Foot Patrol Experiment." Presentation at the Annual Meeting of the American Society of Criminology, San Francisco.

Smith, Dennis C., and Robert Purtell. 2007. "An Empirical Assessment of NYPD's 'Operation Impact': A Targeted Zone Crime-Reduction Strategy." Paper presented at the annual research conference of the Association of Public Policy and Management, Washington, DC.

——— 2008. "Does Stop and Frisk Stop Crime?" Paper presented at the annual research conference of the Association of Public Policy and Management, Los Angeles.

Smith, Douglas A., and Patrick R. Gartin. 1989. "Specifying Specific Deterrence: The Influence of Arrest on Future Criminal Activity." *American Sociological Review* 54(1): 94–106.

Smith, Michael R. 2001. "Police-Led Crackdowns and Cleanups: An Evaluation of a Crime Control Initiative in Richmond, Virginia." *Crime and Delinquency* 47(1): 60–83.

Sparrow, Malcolm. 2011. "Governing Science." *New Perspectives in Policing.* Washington, DC: National Institute of Justice.

Sparrow, Malcolm K., Mark H. Moore, and David M. Kennedy. 1990. *Beyond 9-1-1: A New Era for Policing.* New York, NY: Basic Books.

Spelman, William, and Dale K. Brown. 1981. *Calling the Police: Citizen Reporting of Serious Crime.* Washington, DC: Police Executive Research Forum.

Spelman, William, and John E. Eck. 1989. "Sitting Ducks, Ravenous Wolves and Helping Hands: New Approaches to Urban Policing." *Public Affairs Comment* 35(2): 1–9.

Spergel, Irving A., and David G. Curry. 1993. "The National Youth Gang Survey: A Research and Development Process." In the *Gang Intervention Handbook*, eds Arnold Goldstein and Ronald C. Huff, 359–400. Champaign, IL: Research Press.

Spergel, Irving A., Kwai Ming Wa, and Rolando V. Sosa. 2002. "Evaluation of the Mesa Gang Intervention Program (MGIP)." Washington, DC: Report Submitted to the Office of Juvenile Justice and Delinquency Prevention.

Stafford, Mark C., and Mark Warr. 1993. "A Reconceptualization of General and Specific Deterrence." *Journal of Research in Crime and Delinquency* 30: 123–35.

Stanko, Elizabeth A., and Paul Dawson. 2016. *Police Use of Research Evidence: Recommendations for Improvement.* Springer Briefs in Translational Criminology. New York, NY: Springer.

Strang, Heather, Lawrence W. Sherman, Evan Mayo-Wilson, Daniel Woods, and Barak Ariel. 2013. "Restorative Justice Conferencing (RJC) Using Face-To-Face Meetings of Offenders and Victims: Effects on Offender Recidivism and Victim Satisfaction. A Systematic Review." *Campbell Systematic Reviews.* https://campbellcollaboration.org/library/download/309_0dc276530930eb19c3999c559a02f024.html.

Tate, Renee, Thomas Neale, Cynthia Lum, and Christopher S. Koper. 2013. "Case of Places." *Translational Criminology* (Fall, 2013): 18–21.

Taylor, Bruce, and Rachel Boba. 2011 (updated in 2013). The *Integration of Crime Analysis into Patrol Work: A Guidebook.* Washington, DC: Office of Community Oriented Policing Services.

Taylor, Bruce, and Rachel Boba-Santos. 2011. The *Integration of Crime Analysis into Patrol Work: A Guidebook.* Washington, DC: Office of Community Oriented Policing Services.

Taylor, Bruce, Christopher S. Koper, and Daniel Woods. 2011a. "A Randomized Controlled Trial of Different Policing Strategies at Hot Spots of Violent Crime." *Journal of Experimental Criminology* 7(2): 149–81.

——— 2011b. "Combating Auto Theft in Arizona: A Randomized Experiment with License Plate Recognition Technology." Final Report to the National Institute of Justice, U.S. Department of Justice. Washington, DC: Police Executive Research Forum.

——— 2012. "Combating Vehicle Theft in Arizona: A Randomized Experiment with License Plate Recognition Technology." *Criminal Justice Review* 37(1): 24–50.

Taylor, Ralph B. 1997. "Social Order and Disorder of Street Blocks and Neighborhoods: Ecology, Microecology, and the Systemic Model of Social Disorganization." *Journal of Research in Crime and Delinquency* 34(1): 113–55.

——— 1998. "Crime and Small-Scale Places: What We Know, What We Can Prevent, and What Else We Need to Know." In *Crime and Place: Plenary Papers of the 1997 Conference on Criminal Justice Research and Evaluation*, eds Ralph Taylor, Gordon Bazemore, Barbara Boland, et al., 1–22. Washington, DC: National Institute of Justice.

Telep, Cody W., and Cynthia Lum. 2014. "The Receptivity of Officers to Empirical Research and Evidence-Based Policing: An Examination of Survey Data from Three Agencies." *Police Quarterly* 17: 359–85.

Telep, Cody W., and David Weisburd. 2012. "What Is Known about the Effectiveness of Police Practices in Reducing Crime and Disorder?" *Police Quarterly* 15(4): 331–57.

——— 2015. "Hot Spots Policing." In the *Encyclopedia of Crime and Punishment*, ed. Wesley Jennings. Malden, MA: Wiley-Blackwell.

Telep, Cody W., and Steve Winegar. 2015. "Police Executive Receptivity to Research: A Survey of Chiefs and Sheriffs in Oregon." *Policing: A Journal of Policy and Practice.* DOI:10.1093/Police/Pav043.

Telep, Cody W., David Weisburd, Charlotte E. Gill, Doron Teichman, and Zoe Vitter. 2011. "Displacement of Crime and Diffusion of Crime Control Benefits in Large-Scale Geographic Areas." Presentation at the Center for Evidence-Based Crime Policy—Campbell Collaboration Joint Symposium on Evidence-Based Policy, Fairfax, VA, August 16.

Telep, Cody W., Rene J. Mitchell, and David Weisburd. 2014. "How Much Time Should the Police Spend at Crime Hot Spots? Answers from a Police Agency Directed Randomized Field Trial in Sacramento, California." *Justice Quarterly* 31: 905–33.

Thornberry, Terence P., Marvin D. Krohn, Alan J. Lizotte, and Carolyn A. Smith. 2003. *Gangs and Delinquency in Developmental Perspective.* Cambridge: Cambridge University Press.

Tierney, Joseph P., Wendy S. McClanahan, and Bill Hangley. 2001. *Murder Is No Mystery: An Analysis of Philadelphia Homicide, 1996–1999.* Philadelphia, PA: Public/Private Ventures.

Tita, George E., Jack Riley, Greg Ridgeway, Clifford Grammich, Allen F. Ambrahamse, and Peter W. Greenwood. 2003. *Reducing Gun Violence: Results from an Intervention in East Los Angeles.* Santa Monica, CA: Rand Corporation.

Tita, George E., Jack Riley, Greg Ridgeway, and Peter W. Greenwood. 2005. *Reducing Gun Violence: Operation Ceasefire in Los Angeles.* Washington, DC: National Institute of Justice.

Tolan, Patrick, David Henry, Michael Schoeny, Arin Bass, Peter Lovegrove, and Emily Nichols. 2013. "Mentoring Interventions to Affect Juvenile Delinquency and Associated Problems: A Systematic Review." *Campbell Systematic Reviews.* https://campbellcollaboration.org/library/download/297_d61ea70f176e544153d15e74f7fd0095.html.

Tonry, Michael, and Norval Morris (eds). 1992. "Modern Policing." *Crime and Justice* 15. Chicago, IL: University of Chicago Press.

Trojanowicz, Robert C. 1986. "Evaluating a Neighborhood Foot Patrol Program: The Flint, Michigan Project." In *Community Crime Prevention: Does It Work?*, ed. Dennis Rosenbaum, 157–78. Beverly Hills, CA: Sage.

———— 1994. "The Future of Community Policing." In the *Challenge of Community Policing: Testing the Promises*, ed. Dennis Rosenbaum, 258–62. Thousand Oaks, CA: Sage Publications.

Trojanowicz, Robert C., and Bonnie Bucqueroux. 1997. *Community Policing, Second Edition: How to Get Started.* Cincinnati, Oh: Anderson Publishing.

Tuffin, Rachel, Julia Morris, Alexis Poole, and Groot-Brittannië. 2006. "An Evaluation of the Impact of the National Reassurance Policing Programme." Home Office Research Study London: Research, Development and Statistics Directorate, U.K. Home Office.

Tyler, Tom. 1988. "What Is Procedural Justice? Criteria Used by Citizens to Assess the Fairness of Legal Procedures." *Law and Society Review* 22(1): 103–35.

———— 1990. *Why People Obey the Law.* New Haven, CT: Yale University Press.

Uchida, Craig D. and Marc L. Swatt. 2013. "Operation Laser and the Effectiveness of Hotspot Patrol: A Panel Analysis." *Police Quarterly* 16(3): 287–304.

Veigas, Howard. 2010. "Assessing the Evidence-, CamBase of Strategies and Tactics of Uniformed Patrol in Derbyshire Police." M.A. Thesis, University of Cambridge.

Veigas, Howard, and Cynthia Lum. 2013. "Assessing the Evidence Base of a Police Service Patrol Portfolio." *Policing: A Journal of Policy and Practice* 7(3): 248–62.

Villaveces, Andres, Peter Cummings, Victoria E. Espetia, Thomas Koepsell, Barbra McKnight, and Arthur L. Kellermann. 2000. Effect of a Ban on Carrying Firearms on Homicide Rates in 2 Columbian Cities. *Journal of the American Medical Association* 283(9): 1205–1209.

Vovak, Heather. 2016. "Examining the Relationship between Crime Rates and Clearance Rates Using Dual Trajectory Analysis." Ph.D. Dissertation, George Mason University.

Wangensteen, Sigrid, Inger S. Johansson, Monica E. Bjorkstrom, and Gun Nordstrom. 2011. "Research Utilisation and Critical Thinking among Newly Graduated Nurses: Predictors for Research Use. A Quantitative Cross-Sectional Study." *Journal of Clinical Nursing* 20: 2436–2447.

Weisburd, David. 2002. "From Criminals to Criminal Contexts: Reorienting Crime Prevention Research and Policy." In *Crime and Social Organization, Advances in Criminological Theory, Vol. 10,* eds Elin Waring and David Weisburd, 197–216. New Brunswick, NJ: Transaction Press.

—— 2003. "Ethical Practice and Evaluation of Interventions in Crime and Justice the Moral Imperative for Randomized Trials." *Evaluation Review* 27(3): 336–54.

—— 2008. "Policing Places." *Ideas in American Policing.* Washington, DC: Police Foundation.

—— 2015. "The Law of Crime Concentration and the Criminology of Place." *Criminology* 53(2): 133–57.

Weisburd, David, and Anthony A. Braga (eds). 2006. *Police Innovation: Contrasting Perspectives.* Cambridge: Cambridge University Press.

Weisburd, David, and John E. Eck. 2004. "What Can Police Do to Reduce Crime, Disorder, and Fear?" *Annals of the American Academy of Political and Social Science* 593(1): 42–65.

Weisburd, David, and Lorraine Green. 1995. "Policing Drug Hot Spots: The Jersey City Drug Market Analysis Experiment." *Justice Quarterly* 12: 711–36.

Weisburd, David, and Cynthia Lum. 2005. "The Diffusion of Computerized Crime Mapping in Policing: Linking Research and Practice." *Police Practice & Research: An International Journal* 6: 419–34.

Weisburd, David, and Peter Neyroud. 2011. "Police Science: toward a New Paradigm." *New Perspectives in Policing.* Washington, DC: National Institute of Justice.

Weisburd, David, Cynthia Lum, and Anthony Petrosino. 2001. "Does Research Design Affect Study Outcomes in Criminal Justice?" *Annals of the American Academy of Political and Social Science* 578(1): 50–70.

Weisburd, David, Cynthia Lum, and Sue-Ming Yang. 2003a. "When Can We Conclude That Treatments or Programs "Don't Work"?" *Annals of the American Academy* 587: 31–48.

Weisburd, David, Stephen D. Mastrofski, Ann McNally, Rosann Greenspan, and James J. Willis. 2003b. "Reforming to Preserve: Compstat and Strategic Problem Solving in American Policing." *Criminology & Public Policy* 2(3): 421–56.

Weisburd, David, Shawn Bushway, Cynthia Lum, and Sue-Ming Yang. 2004. "Trajectories of Crime at Places: A Longitudinal Study of Street Segments in the City of Seattle." *Criminology* 42(2): 283–322.

Weisburd, David, Wim Bernasco, and Gerben Bruinsma (eds). 2009. *Putting Crime in Its Place: Units of Analysis in Spatial Crime Research.* New York, NY: Springer.

Weisburd, David, Cody W. Telep, Joshua C. Hinkle, and John E. Eck. 2010. "Is Problem-Oriented Policing Effective in Reducing Crime and Disorder?" *Criminology & Public Policy* 9(1): 139–72.

Weisburd, David, Elizabeth R. Groff, and Sue-Ming Yang. 2012. The *Criminology of Place: Street Segments and Our Understanding of the Crime Problem.* Oxford: Oxford University Press.

Weisburd, David, Cody W. Telep, and Brian Lawton. 2014. "Could Innovations in Policing Have Contributed to the New York City Crime Drop Even in a Period of Declining Police Strength? The Case of Stop, Question, and Frisk as a Hot Spots Policing Strategy." *Justice Quarterly* 31: 129–53.

Weisburd, David, Laura Wyckoff, Justin Ready, John Eck, Josh Hinkle, and Frank Gajewski. 2006. "Does Crime Just Move Around the Corner? A Controlled Study of Spatial Displacement and Diffusion of Crime Control Benefits." *Criminology* 44: 549–92.

Weisburd, David, Alese Wooditch, Sarit Weisburd, and Sue-Ming Yang. 2016. "Do Stop, Question, and Frisk Practices Deter Crime? Evidence at Microunits of Space and Time." *Criminology & Public Policy* 14(1): 31–56.

Weiss, Carol. 1988. "Evaluation for Decisions: Is Anybody There? Does Anybody Care?" *American Journal of Evaluation* 9: 5–19.

—— 1998. "Have We Learned Anything New about the Use of Evaluation?" *American Journal of Evaluation* 19: 21–33.

Weiss, Carol H., and Michael J. Bucuvalas. 1980. *Social Science Research and Decision-Making.* New York, NY: Columbia University Press.

Weiss, Carol, Erin Murphy-Graham, and Sarah Birkeland. 2005. "An Alternative Route to Policy Influence: How Evaluations Affect Dare." *American Journal of Evaluation* 26: 12–30.

Weiss, Carol, Erin Murphy-Graham, Anthony Petrosino, and Allison G. Gandhi. 2008. "The Fairy Godmother and Her Warts: Making the Dream of Evidence-Based Policy Come True." *American Journal of Evaluation* 29: 29–47.

Wellford, Charles, and James Cronin. 1999. *An Analysis of Variables Affecting the Clearance of Homicides: A Multistate Study.* Washington, DC: Justice Research and Statistics Association.

Wellford, Charles, and Cynthia Lum (Special Issue editors). 2014. "A New Era for Hot Spots Policing." *Journal of Contemporary Criminal Justice* 30: 88–94.

Wells, Gary L., Mark Small, Steven Penrod, Roy S. Malpass, Solomon M. Fulero, and C.A.E. Brimacombe. 1998. "Eyewitness Identification Procedures: Recommendations for Lineups and Photospreads." *Law and Human Behavior* 22(6): 603.

Whitaker, Gordon P. 1982. "What Is Patrol Work?" *Police Studies* 4(4): 13–22.

White, Michael, Henry Fradella, and James "Chip" Coldren. 2015. "Why Police (and Communities) Need 'Broken Windows'." *Crime Report* (August 11, 2015). http://thecrimereport.org/2015/08/11/2015-08-why-police-and- communities-need-broken-windows/

White, Michael D., James J. Fyfe, Suzanne P. Campbell, and John S. Goldkamp. 2003. "The Police Role in Preventing Homicide: Considering the Impact of

Problem-Oriented Policing on the Prevalence of Murder." *Journal of Research in Crime and Delinquency* 40(2): 194–225.

Wicker, Allan W. 1987. "Behavior Settings Reconsidered: Temporal Stages, Resources, Internal Dynamics, Context." In *Handbook of Environmental Psychology,* eds Daniel Stokels and Irwin Altman, 613–53. New York, NY: Wiley-Interscience.

Williams-Taylor, Lisa A. 2009. "Measuring the Impact of New York City's Specially Targeted Offenders Project on Sex Offender Recidivism." Ph.D. Dissertation, City University of New York.

Willis, James J., Stephen D. Mastrofski, and David Weisburd. 2007. "Making Sense of Compstat: A Theory-Based Analysis of Change in Three Police Departments." *Law & Society Review* 42: 147–88.

Wilson, David B. 2001. "Meta-Analytic Methods for Criminology." *Annals of the American Academy of Political and Social Science* 578: 71–89.

Wilson, David B., David Weisburd, and David McClure. 2011. "Use of DNA Testing in Police Investigative Work for Increasing Offender Identification, Arrest, Conviction and Case Clearance." *Campbell Systematic Reviews.* https://www.campbellcollaboration.org/library/download/124_32dda376f87c7761c8d6cee80f537a29.html.

Wilson, James Q., and George Kelling. 1982. "Broken Windows: The Police and Neighborhood Safety." *Atlantic Monthly* 249(3): 29–38.

Wooditch, Alese, and David Weisburd. 2016. "Using Space-Time Analysis to Evaluate Criminal Justice Programs: An Application to Stop-Question-Frisk Practices." *Journal of Quantitative Criminology* 32: 191–213.

Worrall, John L., and Larry K. Gaines. 2006. "The Effect of Police-Probation Partnerships on Juvenile Arrests." *Journal of Criminal Justice* 34(6): 579–89.

Wu, Xiaoyun, and Cynthia Lum. 2016. "Measuring the Spatial and Temporal Patterns of Police Proactivity." *Journal of Quantitative Criminology.* DOI:10.1007/S10940-016-9318-5.

Wycoff, Mary Ann, Anthony M. Pate, Wesley G. Skogan, and Lawrence W. Sherman. 1985. *Citizen Contact Patrol in Houston: Executive Summary.* Washington, DC: Police Foundation.

Yang, Sue-Ming. 2010. "Assessing the Spatial-Temporal Relationship between Disorder and Violence." *Journal of Quantitative Criminology* 26(1): 139–63.

Zaworski, Martin J. 2004. "Assessing an Automated, Information Sharing Technology in the Post "9-11" Era—Do Local Law Enforcement Officers Think It Meets Their Needs?" Ph.D. Dissertation, Florida International University.

Author Index

Haberman, C. P. 64, 94
Haggerty, K. D. 116
Hamilton, E. E. 5, 82, 256
Hamilton, R. A. 90
Hangley, B. 90
Hansen, A. 268
Hanson, G. S. 37, 87
Harcourt, B. E. 85
Harris, C. J. 113, 114, 115, 116, 120, 230
Harris, H. M. 83, 258
Harris, R. 90
Hartman, J. L. 83
Hartnett, S. M. 10, 239, 257
Hawley, A. 205
Hayeslip, D. 92
Haynes, B. 134
Heaton, P. 113, 114, 116, 117
Hegarty, T. L. 71, 259
Henderson, S. 115
Henry, D. 87
Henstock, D. 125
Hiatt, R. A. 150
Hibdon, J. 61, 112n, 230, 232
Hinkle, J. 33, 39, 64, 103
Hipple, N. K. 94, 106
Hirschi, T. 266
Hirschkorn, M. 134
Hoffmaster, D. A. 104
Holloway, K. 33
Hollywood, J. S. 67
Horvath, F. 80
Howell, J. C. 92
Huenke, C. 90
Huey, L. 162
Huizinga, D. 92
Hunt, E. D. 94
Hunt, P. 67
Hureau, D. M. 93
Hyeock Lee, Y. 80

Ioimo, R. E. 113, 114, 117
Isom, D. 91, 104

Johansson, I. S. 137n
Johnson, M. (2005) 67, 107, 185
Johnson, S. D. (2007) 67, 109n, 185, 233
Jolin, A. 89

Katz, C. M. 125
Kelling, G. L. 7, 8, 9, 17, 38, 39, 48, 81, 84, 113, 161

Kennedy, D. M. 37, 90, 91, 92, 93, 114
Kennedy, L. 67, 119
Klap, R. 82
Klein, M. W. 9, 82, 92
Klobuchar, A. 80
Knobler, P. 229
Knott, J. 134
Kochel, T. R. 82, 101
Koen, M. 125
Komro, K. A. 87
Koper, C. S. 8, 9, 33, 36, 37, 43, 60, 61, 64–71, 73, 80, 91, 94n, 96, 104, 107, 109, 112–14, 117–19, 121–2, 124, 127, 134n, 148, 155, 162, 171, 175, 186–7, 189, 196, 198, 201, 202, 210, 211, 215, 216, 217n, 218, 219, 229–32, 250, 258–9, 269, 271, 276–7
Kraemer, K. L. 80, 113, 114, 117
Krimmel, J. T. 107
Kubu, B. E. 94n, 112

Lacey, E. A. 137
Lamari, M. 134
Landry, R. 134
Lasley, J. R. 106, 107
Latessa, E. J. 135
Laub, J. H. 266
Lavrakas, P. J. 104
Lawton, B. 39, 64, 66, 69, 96
Laycock, G. 19, 104
Legosz, M. 114
Lewis, D. A. 41, 84
Lindsay, B. 104
Lipsey, M. W. 23, 229, 270
Lizotte, A. J. 91
Lockwood, B. 61
Loeber, R. 266
Lovig, J. H. 38, 104
Lu, Y. 122
Ludwig, J. 90, 96, 106
Lum, C. 8, 9, 17, 28, 29, 34, 36, 37, 42n, 43, 44, 48, 52n, 53, 60–2, 76, 81–2, 85–6, 95–6, 100, 105, 109, 112n, 113–15, 117–19, 121–4, 126, 134n, 138–40, 142–6, 148, 151, 155, 180, 200–2, 210, 215, 228–30, 232–3, 241, 250–2, 258, 260, 269
Luna, A. 104
Luongo, A. J. 39, 64

MacKenzie, D. L. 12, 30
Mahoney, K. 91

Subject Index

Printed and bound by CPI Group (UK) Ltd, Croydon, CR0 4YY